THE DAWN *of* INNOVATION

ALSO BY **CHARLES R. MORRIS**

====================

THE FIRST AMERICAN
INDUSTRIAL REVOLUTION

THE DAWN *of*
INNOVATION

CHARLES R. MORRIS

Illustrations by J. E. Morris

PublicAffairs
New York

Book Design by Pauline Brown

Library of Congress Cataloging-in-Publication Data

Morris, Charles R.
   The dawn of innovation : the first American industrial revolution /
Charles R. Morris.—1st ed.
      p.   cm.
   Includes bibliographical references and index.
   ISBN 978-1-58648-828-4 (hbk.)—ISBN 978-1-61039-049-1
(electronic) 1. Industrialization—United States—History—19th
century. 2. Industrial revolution—United States. 3. United States—
Economic conditions—19th century. 4. United States—Social
conditions—19th century. I. Title.
HC105.M73 2012
338.097309'034—dc23

                                    2012016614

First Edition

10 9 8 7 6 5 4 3 2 1

To Bob Gordon and Carolyn Cooper,
scholars and gentlepersons

CONTENTS

INTRODUCTION

THREE STUPENDOUS AND STRONGLY REINFORCING INNOVATIONS IN POLITICS, in the economy, and in social relations took place in the United States in the 1820s and 1830s. Universal white male suffrage came into effect throughout the country, with voter turnouts routinely in the 80 percent range and a wide range of offices subject to the ballot. The American penchant for mechanized, large-scale production spread throughout industry, presaging the world's first mass-consumption economy. Finally, political and economic power shifted decisively away from society's traditional elites, as the world's first true middle class seized control of the political apparatus. The archetypal American was almost a new species, literate and numerate, shrewd and confident, an unvarnished striver, swimming through a delightful chaos where money and opportunity were for the grasping on every side. As the United States became the world's dominant power in the twentieth century, that model of society, albeit much adapted and trammeled, became the norm in advanced countries.

The political and cultural threads of this story have been unraveled many times, most recently in Gordon Wood's splendid *Empire of Liberty*. I will concentrate on the nitty-gritty of the economic transformation—the details of the machinery, the technologies, and the new processes and work organizations that underlay America's stunning record of growth. But the evolution of the country's politics and class relations was an essential backdrop for its economic success, so I try to keep those developments in sight at every point.

Some years ago, I wrote a book called *The Tycoons*, which told the story of how the United States, within just the three decades or so after the Civil War, blew past Great Britain and became the number one economic power in the world. I was drawn to that era because of the outsized characters, the John Rockefellers, the Andrew Carnegies, the Jay Goulds, the J. P. Morgans, who helped channel and shape the development of the new behemoth rising on the American continent.

But the tycoons were not starting from scratch. If they had never lived, the course of American industrialization would certainly have been different, but the long American boom would have happened anyway and on roughly the same scale. The country was just too productive, too entrepreneurial, too inventive, too *original* not to burst into the front rank of world powers, almost regardless of its leadership.

The Dawn of Innovation therefore takes the story back to the beginning of the century, when the country started building the economic platform that launched the astonishing industrial development in the decades after the Civil War.

I use two main thematic hooks to organize the story. First, I frame it as an implicit competition between America and Great Britain. That is the way most Americans viewed it after the old federalists like Alexander Hamilton and John Adams passed from the scene. After the Revolution, British opinion still treated the United States as a pseudo-colony, and the War of 1812 had Americans once again fighting British troops on American soil. As French and Spanish power faded, only the British stood in the way of American continental ambitions, and it was no secret that British sympathies were with the disunionists during the Civil War. Even Hamilton, a great admirer of the British system, mused that the United States might well be its equal within forty or fifty years, which wasn't far off the mark.

The second theme is to argue for a broader definition of what came to be called the American system of manufacturing. That was the name the British applied to the American machinery-intensive methods of manufacturing guns. "Armory practice" is a more appropriate designation, for while it is an important thread of American development—culminating in the great twentieth-century automobile plants—during most of the nineteenth century it applied only to a narrow range of industrial output.

There was indeed a distinctly American approach to manufacturing in the nineteenth century: it was the drive to mass production and mass distribution in every field—from foodstuffs to soap and candles, axes and locomotives, horseshoes, wooden doors, carriage wheels, bedroom furniture, and almost anything else. The nature of the machinery and the underlying technologies varied from product to product—soap making was different from steelmaking, and neither had much in common with making guns or clocks. And sometimes, American mass production was all about organization, not machinery, as in the antebellum shoe industry. It was the uniquely American penchant for scale and speed that ultimately created the mass-consumption economy. Mass consumption, the rise of a successful middle class, and a democratized government were all part of the package that was the great American experiment.

The Plan of the Book

I open with a little-known tale from the War of 1812, the shipbuilders' war on Lake Ontario. Both sides understood that controlling the lake was key to winning the war, and asymmetries in the two sides' armaments and tactics led to a classic arms race. Absurdly, by war's end the lake was home to some of the largest and most formidably armed warships in the world. Both sides' supply systems were pushed to the point of exhaustion, but the effort played a big role in jump-starting American industrialization.

The next chapter focuses on Great Britain, the nineteenth century's hyperpower. Its technical and scientific breakthroughs were the critical substrate for American progress. The British also invented mass production in their great textile industries but were amazed to discover in mid-century that the Americans were applying the same concepts across almost the whole of industry.

The story of American development can be charted as an evolution from local to regional and finally to national networks. Strong regional economies emerged in the Northeast in the first quarter of the century. By the 1820s, rural New England and the Middle Atlantic region were hotbeds of industrialization, with farms and forges working cheek by jowl and the self-subsistent farm family already an anachronism. Industries like clocks, cloth, shoes, and cast-iron stoves were achieving seaboard-wide markets. I also devote a full chapter to the development of the armory practice of the Connecticut River Valley and the great inventors who pioneered precision machine manufacturing. Important names in the immediate postwar period are Eli Terry and Chauncey Jerome, the Holleys, Oliver Evans, Francis Cabot Lowell and Paul Moody, Thomas Blanchard and John Hall.

In the 1820s and 1830s, the "West" signified the area bounded by the western slopes of the Appalachians and the eastern shores of the Mississippi. Since interior transportation was virtually nil, there evolved a pellet economy of little self-sufficient towns clustered on riverbanks. The breakthrough was the development of the western steamboat by Henry Shreve and Daniel French. It was a cunningly adapted craft that could carry massive loads on shallow, swift water, blithely steaming upstream against rapids.

Within a decade the region's great grain, lumber, and meat animal enterprises were centralizing in Cincinnati, as a tight-knit riverine economy took shape within the Ohio, Missouri, and Mississippi valleys. Cincinnati invented the meatpacking "disassembly" line later made famous by Chicago, and Cincinnati brothers-in-law Procter and Gamble were innovators in America's first chemical industry. Cincinnati and the West were also a prime subject for the finest American travel writers from this period: Alexis de Tocqueville, Frances Trollope, Harriet Martineau, Charles Dickens, and Lucy Bird.

The United States emerged as a world economic powerhouse in the 1840s and 1850s, when the railroads finally linked the Northeast and the Midwest, as it was now called, into an integrated commercial and industrial unit. The heavy industry of the Midwest flowed from its resource endowment—coal and iron, food processing, a mechanized lumber industry—as well as derivatives from steamboat building, like engines, furniture, and glass. In the Northeast, its traditional industries like clocks, textiles, and shoes grew to global scale, along with big-ticket fabrication businesses like Baldwin locomotives, Collins steamships, Hoe printing presses, and the giant Corliss engines.

The South, in the meantime, slipped into the position of an internal colony, exploiting its slaves and being exploited in turn by the Northeast and Midwest. Boston and New York controlled much of the shipping, insurance, and brokerage earnings from the cotton trade, while the earnings left over went for midwestern food, tools, and engines shipped down the Mississippi and its branches.

The British, who were habitually dismissive of "Brother Jonathan," their bumpkin transatlantic cousin, discovered American manufacturing prowess at London's Great Crystal Palace Exhibition in 1851. They particularly focused on the machine-made guns of Sam Colt and the Vermont manufacturer Robbins and Lawrence. Colt's newest factories in both London and Hartford were the most advanced precision manufacturing plants in the world at the time. The British created a new armory plant at Enfield equipped entirely with American machinery. The plant was a great success, but with no impact in the wider economy. Few Britons even noticed, as one sharp-eyed civil servant put it, that in the United States, almost all industries were "carried on in the same way as the cotton manufacture of England, viz., in large factories, with machinery applied to every process, the extreme subdivision of labour and all reduced to an almost perfect system of manufacture."

Destructive though it was, the Civil War broke the slaveocracy's power to obstruct an American development agenda. In one of the darkest years of the war, the Republican congress passed the Homestead Act, the Land Grant College Act—no other country had conceived the possibility of educating its farmers and craftsmen—and the Transcontinental Railroad Act. The rise of a new world economic hyperpower was virtually assured.

The book closes with both epilogue and prologue. Chapter 8 is a compressed account of how America caught up to and finally surpassed Great Britain in the decades after the Civil War. That story highlights the great advantages possessed by a fast-growing, emerging power moving to supplant an older incumbent. To round out the story, therefore, the book closes with an assessment of the new contest between an aging economic incumbent, now the United States, and China, the fast-surging potential usurper, and looks particularly at what is likely to be similar to and quite different from the story that began to unfold some two centuries ago.

CHAPTER ONE

The Shipbuilders' War

THE WAR OF 1812 MAY BE THE LEAST REMEMBERED OF AMERICAN WARS. And buried in the historical fog is the strange tale of a naval arms race on Lake Ontario. Ontario is the smallest of the Great Lakes and virtually landlocked. Yet in the early winter of 1815, twenty formidable warships were scheduled to take to the water at the spring thaw. Four of them would be first-raters, two of them American, two of them British, each of them ranking among the largest and most heavily armed warships in the world.

Great Britain was the world's greatest-ever naval power. Of the 600 or so war vessels in the Admiralty's active fleet, about 110 were ships of the line, all big, powerful vessels designed to overawe and overwhelm the enemy. Of the in-service ships of the line, however, only six were first-raters. They were one of the age's most complex machines, the behemoths of the ocean, two hundred feet long, displacing 2,500 tons, top masts soaring two hundred feet above waterline, carrying crews of eight hundred seamen and marines and disposing of at least 100 heavy guns in three tiers along their sides. Building a first-rater consumed 4,000 large trees; hundreds of tons of iron for fittings, cannon, and ballast; miles of rigging; an acre and a half of sail; some 1,400 ship pulley-blocks, some of them almost as tall as a man. Nelson at Trafalgar led the charge against the Napoleonic armada in his first-rater, HMS *Victory*.[1]

1

During the first year of the war, it became clear to both sides that winning control of Lake Ontario was the key to winning the war, and both poured money and resources into the effort. Both sides expected that an early naval battle would decide the issue, but inherent asymmetries in armaments and naval tactics trapped them both within the grim logic of an escalating arms race. To the surprise of both participants, the Americans doggedly matched and raised the British step by step, until both were at the point of exhaustion.

A War of Honor

The American declaration of war against Great Britain in June 1812 is a puzzlement for historians. The death struggle between the British and Napoleonic France indiscriminately inflicted damage on neutral countries. If anything, the French were the more disdainful of Americans and worked the greater destruction on American shipping. As Henry Adams pointed out, every charge in President Madison's war declaration was both factually correct and a sufficient cause for war. But the United States had patiently endured such behavior for five years, so why declare war in 1812, when the American government was close to insolvency and Great Britain was on the brink of making major trade concessions?[2]

British and Canadian historians tend to see the war as an unsuccessful American war of conquest.* Congressional war hawks, in fact, made no secret of their desire to annex parts of Canada, but they did not come close to commanding a legislative majority. Public outrage was more focused on the British impressment of American merchant seamen. In principle, the British had a right to take their own nationals, but naval captains were not overly scrupulous about trapping bona fide American citizens in their trawls. The Royal Navy was their Maginot Line against Napoleon, and years of warfare had created a terrible shortage of seamen. Even American

---

* Canadians long mistrusted American designs on their country, not without reason. As late as 1935, the American military had a "War Plan Red" for an invasion of Canada, including poison gas attacks on Halifax. There was at least one formal exercise.

officials privately acknowledged that up to a quarter of US merchant seamen were deserted British nationals, and citizenship papers for British seamen were sold openly in most American ports.[3]

Behind the headline issues, the old characterization of the war as the second war for American independence has considerable truth. The British still reflexively treated America as a component of its colonial/mercantile empire, high-handedly issuing detailed trade licenses while refusing a generalized trade treaty. Royal Navy captains felt free to sail into American ports and haughtily, and occasionally forcefully, sequester scarce provisions. The London *Times* sneered in 1807 that Americans could not "cross to Staten Island" without the Royal Navy's permission.[4]

But national pride couldn't dispel the reality that the United States was in no shape to fight a war. Years of British and French blockades had devastated customs revenues. Its navy consisted of some coastal gunboats and a handful of frigates, all built in the 1790s. The army was small and scattered through frontier outposts, so the primary ground forces were state militias, which were inconsistently trained and armed, if at all, and often prevented by law from serving outside their home states. Governors in several federalist states, moreover, announced that they would not release their militias for federal service on constitutional grounds.[5] Few senior officials had significant recent military experience.

The war proceeded on several loosely connected fronts. In the first year of the war, the most spectacular encounters were a series of frigate-to-frigate ocean battles.* The *Constitution*'s half-hour destruction of the British *Guerrière* prompted unrestrained celebration in America and shocked laments in London. The Royal Navy finally put an end to such impertinences by imposing a suffocating blockade up and down the coast

---

* Frigates, with just one gun deck, did not rank as ships of the line. Used mostly for detached duty, they were glamor commands because officers and crewmen could make large amounts of money by taking enemy prizes. American frigates were typically much heavier and better armed than their British counterparts. More importantly, overconfident British captains plunged into the early encounters as if the Americans didn't know the rudiments of fighting. In the last of the frigate-to-frigate battles, however, the two were evenly matched, and it was the American captain who was reckless. It took only minutes for the British *Shannon* to destroy the *Chesapeake*.

that kept the frigates almost entirely port-bound for the duration of the war.

With the blockade in place, sea action shifted to an intense informal war between the Royal Navy and American privateers, especially the famous Chesapeake Schooners, or Baltimore Clippers. They were the leopards of the sea: up to a hundred feet long, mounting up to 18 guns, with vast expanses of sail, deep keels for rapid maneuverability, and superb hydrodynamics. They consistently outsailed and outwitted British warships, and by the later stages of the war, even prowled in the Thames.[6] In addition, throughout the war years Andrew Jackson led a sporadic Indian war in the Southeast, an early salvo in a two-decade-long ethnic-cleansing operation. He and other local commanders raised and equipped their troops and operated more or less independently of Washington.

The most important fighting, however, whether measured by casualties, commitment of resources, or persistence, was centered on the lakes, especially Ontario and Erie, reinforcing the contention that the war was about Canada, for whoever controlled the lakes would inevitably control Canada.

The Lake Arena:
Early Stumbles

The British had only the lightest of colonial presences in Canada. There was a world-class Royal Navy port at Halifax, Nova Scotia, and just to the west the territory of Lower Canada, predominately French, included substantial commercial centers at Quebec and Montreal. Upper Canada stretched along the lakeshores: it was primitive and Anglophone, probably mostly settled by Americans who had straggled across the border. Both Upper and Lower Canada were under the direction of Governor-General George Prevost, an experienced British general officer based in Quebec.

The only practical access to Upper Canada was via the St. Lawrence. The river was navigable by ship as far as Montreal; from there, the 150-mile stretch to Lake Ontario was dominated by rapids and shallows traversed by towed bateaux and barges. The territory was barely self-sufficient in food, with few roads and little in the way of industry, so a defense force would be completely dependent on river-borne supplies. Losing control of the St. Lawrence or of Lake Ontario virtually guaranteed the loss of Upper Canada and could put much of Lower Canada at risk.

The demographics of the lakes clearly favored the Americans, whose lakeshores were more populous, with better internal transportation, highly productive farmland, and budding iron industries that could support the war effort. But the British compensated by fashioning broad alliances with Indian tribes seeking to stop American settlement. Western settlers were in terror of the Indians, especially after the success of the great Indian leader Tecumseh in cobbling together a serious Indian confederacy. The battle with Tecumseh's forces at Tippecanoe, in November 1811, was officially celebrated as an American triumph, but cognoscenti knew it was a close-run thing, with Americans taking the heavier casualties. Even militias panicked and ran from Indian detachments in the early stages of the war.

The Americans took the early military initiatives in the summer of 1812, almost all on the ground, producing pratfalling, Marx Brothers–class fiascos, too costly and bloody to be comic. General William Hull made a timorous thrust up the Detroit River and surrendered to a much smaller force at almost the first shots, giving up his army, Ft. Detroit, a warship, and the entire Michigan territory. Henry Dearborn, another aging Revolutionary War general, launched a large, lethargic, but complex nighttime attack in the Niagara peninsula. Amid indiscipline and chaos, his ill-prepared troops took very heavy casualties. Dearborn later tried a second action directed at Montreal but retired to winter quarters after a brief skirmish near Plattsburgh. A wag called it a failure "without even the heroism of a disaster."[7]

If nothing else, the early failures demonstrated that naval control of the lakes was crucial for effective movement of troops and supplies. The Americans were the first to respond, naming Isaac Chauncey to a new post of naval commander of the lakes. Chauncey was an experienced, active, officer and, fortuitously, had most recently been commander of the New York Navy Yard. It took until the following spring for London to realize that Chauncey's vigor was putting Canada at risk. They responded in

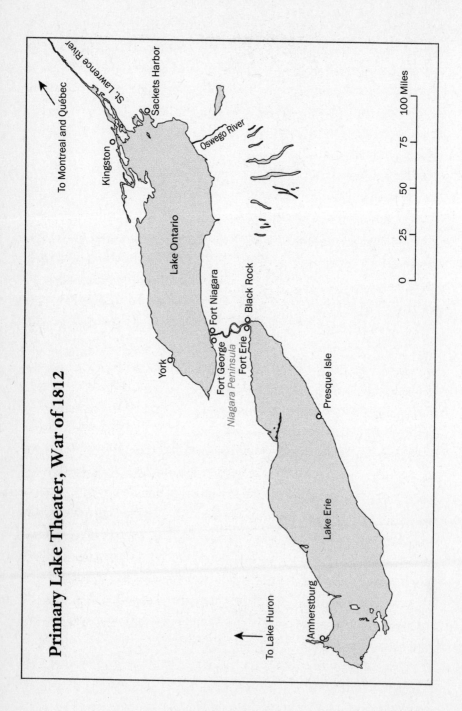

Primary Lake Theater, War of 1812

To Montreal and Québec

St. Lawrence River

Sackets Harbor

Kingston

Oswego River

Lake Ontario

York

Fort George

Fort Niagara

Niagara Peninsula

Fort Erie

Black Rock

Presque Isle

Lake Erie

Amherstburg

To Lake Huron

0   25   50   75   100 Miles

March 1813 by appointing Sir James Lucas Yeo to lead a naval expeditionary force to the lakes. Only thirty years old, Yeo was already a post-captain, with a long record as a fighting officer, and possessed by the same drive and force of personality as Chauncey. When Yeo arrived at Lake Ontario in May 1813, the shipbuilders' war was on.

Industrial War in the Wilderness

The shipbuilders' war lasted for two and a half years. Both sides constructed substantial cities at their primary bases near the mouth of the St. Lawrence. The British base at Kingston, on the north shore, was a thirty-mile sail from the American base on the opposite shore, at Sackets Harbor. By war's end, each was able to house and feed some 5,000 semipermanent residents—seamen, marines, and their officers; shipwrights, smiths, and other craftsmen—plus massive ship factories and associated shops, as well as facilities for short-term feeding and support of the thousands of infantrymen mustered from time to time for amphibious operations.

It was easy to underestimate the challenges of the lakes—on maps they looked like mere puddles. But winds were highly variable, and violent storms sprang up almost without warning. (Shallow waters often generate the most violent storms; ocean depths absorb the force of surface disturbances.) The lakes' heavy fogs and frequent squalls, and the near-constant presence of a lee shore, jangled captains' nerves. On Lake Huron, an American captain found himself "embayed in a gale of Wind on a rocky Ironbound shore . . . shipping such immense quantities of water as to give me very serious alarm for some hours." The whole coast, he said, was "a steep perpendicular Rock" and navigation "extremely dangerous . . . falling suddenly from no soundings into 3 fathoms [18 feet] & twice into ¼ less twain [10½ feet]."[8]

The challenge was to build "weatherly" fighting ships fast and cheaply—cutting corners without compromising performance. Ships built of unseasoned wood go to rot within just a few years, so many finishing details could be dispensed with. With no need to carry water or long-term supplies, they had smaller holds and shallower drafts, enabling close approaches to shore. The American ships especially carried large expanses of sail and heavy gunnery for their size. For example, to the British the American *Pike* was a difficult sailer, but in the hands of an expert crew, it was among the quickest and most maneuverable warships on the lakes.

Chauncey's orders were the kind commanders dream of. He was "to obtain control of the Lakes Ontario & Erie, with the least possible delay. . . . With respect to the means to be employed, you will consider yourself unrestrained [and] . . . at liberty to *purchase, hire* or *build*, such [vessels] . . . of such form & armament" as he chose.[9]

His prize acquisition was Henry Eckford, one of the age's great naval architects and owner of a private shipyard in New York. He turned out to be a master of improvisation—as in devising easier-to-build bracings for ships with short shelf lives. Old hands expected Eckford's ships to break in two when they were launched down the slipway, but all of them performed well. Backing up Eckford were the Brown brothers, Noah and Adam, who also operated a New York boatyard. The Browns designed and built the ships on Lakes Erie and Champlain, and worked so smoothly with Eckford on Ontario that scholars have difficulty in distinguishing their work from his.

The British building program was supervised mostly by William Bell, a Canadian who had run a boatyard on Lake Erie, and later by Thomas Kendrick, an experienced naval architect from London. A senior British officer, Capt. Richard O'Conor, was assigned full-time to manage the yards. Both sides achieved rapid construction schedules, although fully masted ships often sat at shipyard docks for weeks or months waiting for critical components, like cannon or ship's cable.

Chauncey was also something of a gadgeteer. His fleet usually had between a dozen to sixteen of its long guns on swivels, so they could be deployed on either broadside. He also experimented with rapid-fire weapons, known as Chambers guns, after their Philadelphia inventor. A British spy described them as having: "seven barrels . . . throw[ing]

250 balls at each fire . . . [with] one Lock & the fire is communicated fm. Barrel to Barrel—& they discharge successively at the Interval of one Second."[10]

Wars turn on logistics. In the shipbuilders' war both sides had endless supplies of timber for the taking but had to import virtually all tools and nonwooden materials, like rope, ordnance, iron fittings, and shot. The Americans had decent river and canal transport from New York City to the port of Oswego on Lake Ontario, although it required some portages. For Lake Erie there was inland ground transport from Philadelphia and Pittsburgh, but in that era, almost all roads were execrable most of the time. An artillery major bringing cannon from Pittsburgh in the early winter of 1813 wrote of days at a stretch when they were "with our horses to their middles in mud and water."[11] Even in the dry summer of 1812, Chauncey lost whole cannons when wagons overturned in a mire.

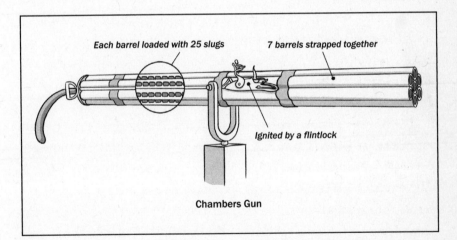

Each barrel loaded with 25 slugs

7 barrels strapped together

Ignited by a flintlock

Chambers Gun

The Chambers Gun was a fusillade weapon, firing a hail of cylindrical slugs. Ignition was by single flintlock in front, and was communicated from barrel to barrel through touch holes and a roman-candle-type fuse. The firing spark also traveled backward through the slugs by fuses that ignited powder packed throughout the column. The guns were said to be rapidly loaded. It is possible that the slugs, powder, and fuses were prepacked in copper tubes that could be loaded and extracted rather like modern ammunition clips.

For the British, it was actually an advantage to source supplies from England, since ship transport from Portsmouth to Montreal was fast and reliable, while bateaux transport to Lake Ontario took only a few days. The problem was getting from the lake entrance to the British base at Kingston. When the lake was under American control, a war schooner or two sitting at the mouth of the St. Lawrence stopped the British supply train cold. In periods when the lake was contested, the trip required military escort, and jam-ups of cargo bateaux awaiting escort could stretch for miles. Overland transport was a poor option: some supplies could get through, but not enough to sustain a burgeoning military presence. British food requirements were magnified by the Indian alliances, for the tribes quickly learned the advantages of takeout service from the British mess. One commander wrote in alarm to headquarters in 1813, "The quantity of Beef and flour consumed here is tremendous, there are such hordes of Indians with their *wives* and *children*."[12]

Chauncey Rules Ontario: October 1812 to May 1813

Within weeks of his appointment, Chauncey started a massive caravan of shipwrights, mechanics, sailors, marines, ordnance, and supplies on the road to Sackets Harbor. Eckford went with the earliest groups to start laying out construction plans. Militarily, they were starting almost from scratch (see Table 1.1).[13]

By mid-November, Chauncey and Eckford had built a naval yard and dry dock and facilities for 1,000 men and officers. The *Madison*, a graceful, new 24-gun corvette, or subfrigate, was launched on November 26, just forty-five days from starting its keel. By that time, Chauncey had also bought up a number of lakers, local transport workhorses. He netted several modest schooners, which were slow but could carry up to 10 guns, and some smaller gunboats with both sails and rowing stations. Outfitted with 1 or 2 long guns, the gunboats could pose a real threat to shoreside troops or to a becalmed warship. Also in May, a daring long boat raid on

TABLE 1.1 Naval Forces on the Lakes: September 1812			
British		**American**	
Huron & Erie[a]			
Name	Guns	Name	Guns
Queen Charlotte	16		
General Hunter	6	None	
Detroit[b]	12		
Lady Prevost	10		
Ontario			
Name	Guns	Name	Guns
Earl of Moira	14	*Oneida*	18
Duke of Gloucester	6		
Royal George	20		
Prince Regent	12		
Total Ships	**8**	**Total Ships**	**1**
Total Guns	**96**	**Total Guns**	**18**

[a] Lakes Huron and Erie had a navigable, if difficult, water connection, so ships are grouped.
[b] Formerly the USS *Adams*, captured from Hull's Detroit expedition and renamed.

Lake Erie, led by Lt. Jesse Elliott, cut out and burnt the *Detroit* and captured a gunboat, the *Caledonia*.

Even better, once Chauncey took the *Oneida* out on the lake, he discovered that the Provincial Marine, which was trained as a security service, didn't fight. He began to attack British shipping at every opportunity, taking several prizes, and at one point chased the *Royal George* all the way into Kingston. Even without the *Madison*, he could truthfully report that he had "command of the Lake" and could transport troops and stores anywhere "without any risk of an attack by the Enemy."[14]

The lakes were icebound in winter, which facilitated troop movements and led to more American disasters. An American offensive in the

Detroit area ended with a large detachment being "cut to pieces."[15] American prisoners were later massacred by a party of Indians near the River Raisin: "Remember the Raisin" became an American rallying cry. The British cemented their control of the St. Lawrence by capturing the town of Ogdensburg. The Americans fended off an attack at Ft. Meigs, on the Detroit River, but lost almost all of an American relief force, some of whom were also massacred by Indians.

In Washington, there was a shake-up in the military departments. John Armstrong, a former senator and ambassador with presidential ambitions and a reputation as a strategist, took over the war department. He proved to be an intriguer and a windbag with an unparalleled gift for sowing confusion. The new naval secretary, William Jones, was a former shipwright who had risen to head a large merchant house. His dispatches were informed, crisp, and intelligent. As the tightening British coastal blockade kept the Atlantic fleet locked in port, he started transferring their crews to the lakes—among them a fast-rising young naval captain, Oliver Hazard Perry, who joined Chauncey with 150 men and was given command of Lake Erie, with Lt. Elliott as his second.

Chauncey was back on Lake Ontario with the first thaw. In late April he coordinated an attack on York, the provincial capital (and present-day Toronto), where the British were constructing a major new warship. Chauncey took his whole fleet: the *Madison*, the *Oneida*, and eleven lakers, wallowing with the weight of 1,700 ground troops.

York was defended by British regulars, but the beach assault came off briskly, as the warships silenced York's artillery. Within a couple of hours, the British were in retreat, the new warship was burnt, the *Duke of Gloucester* taken, and large amounts of stores captured, all with light casualties. An easy victory turned to disaster when an arms magazine that had been mined by the retreating British blew up next to the main American infantry group. Gen. Zebulon Pike, the American infantry commander, and another 38 soldiers were killed, with 221 wounded. Technically, the action met its objectives, but the butcher's bill—320 casualties in all—was grossly disproportionate.

A month later, Chauncey took the fleet to Niagara for an attack on Britain's Ft. George. A 4,000-man army, with promising new second-rank commanders like Winfield Scott, was assembled and waiting for naval support. Once again, the beach assault went like clockwork, as warships poured grapeshot into the defenders and pounded their artillery emplacements. By ten AM, with the fort in flames and the *Madison* disgorging yet more fresh troops, the British commander sounded a withdrawal. The army then quickly rolled up the rest of the peninsula, including the British outpost at Ft. Erie. Both expeditions were striking demonstrations of the potential of combined-arms operations on the lakes.

Countermove

Shortly before Chauncey mounted his Niagara campaign, Commodore Yeo had arrived at Kingston, with a cadre of 465 officers and seamen. He was met by Governor-General Prevost, his local superior, and Roger Sheaffe, the military commander for Upper Canada who had marched his troops there after the bloodying at York. The three were holding war councils when a huge plume of black smoke from the west announced the siege of Ft. George. With the whole American fleet up-lake, they decided to mount a surprise attack on Sackets Harbor. On May 26, the British dispatched an 800-strong assault force, including all four of Yeo's warships and a half dozen gunboats, towing a flotilla of landing craft—thirty-three boats in all.

Tactically, the assault was a failure. A first attempt was interrupted by a sudden storm, so the Americans had an extra day to organize their defense. When the British made the beach the next day, they took heavy fire. Casualties would have been much worse if a seven-hundred-strong contingent of state militiamen, carefully positioned in ambush, had not broken and run at the first shots. Then a young American lieutenant mistakenly fired Sackets's stores and a nearly finished new warship. By that time, the assault force's casualties exceeded a quarter of its men. The British commander chose to assume that the smoke signaled destruction

TABLE 1.2 Naval Forces, Lake Ontario: August 1813

British			American[a]		
Name	Guns	Metal Weight	Name	Guns	Metal Weight
Sir Sidney Smith	18	344	Oneida	18	396
Earl of Moira	14	324	Madison	24	688
Royal George	20	748	Gen. Zebulon Pike	26	624
Beresford[b]	14	132	Sylph	18	402
Wolfe	22	804	Hamilton (L)[c]	9	168
Lord Melville	16	384	Scourge (L)	10	48
			Nine Gunboats (L)	26	368
Long guns	14	166	Long guns	66	1,142
Carronades	90	2,570	Carronades	60	1,552
Total	104	2,736	Total	126	2,694

[a] Omits *Lady of the Lake* (1) since purely a courier ship
[b] Formerly *Prince Regent*
[c] L = Converted Lakers

of the warship and sounded the withdrawal. In fact, the ship was only scorched, and the burnt stores were replaced within a few weeks. Strategically, however, the raid radically changed the calculus of power. From that point, Chauncey was almost paranoid about Sackets's defenses and sharply curtailed his participation in joint land-sea operations.

In the meantime, the construction race moved into higher gear. The British had launched the *Wolfe*, a 22-gun corvette, in April, followed by the launch of a war schooner, the *Lord Melville* (16), in July. Chauncey countered with the *General Zebulon Pike*, the ship that was scorched during the Sackets raid. It may have been Eckford's masterpiece, a beautiful 26-gun corvette, the fastest and most powerful warship on the lake. The *Pike* was followed in August by a new war schooner, the *Sylph* (18), together with a very fast single-gun courier sloop, *Lady of the Lake*. Table 1.2 shows the state of the standoff on Ontario as of about mid-August.

With such an investment, both national capitals expected a climactic early battle to settle the war. It never happened—because inherent asymmetries in the fleets and their tactics made it almost impossible for the two commanders to agree to fight.

To begin with, the favored Royal Navy ordnance were carronades: stubby, relatively inaccurate guns with heavy payloads that were easy to reload. Nelson's doctrine was "no captain can do very wrong if he places his ship alongside that of the enemy."[16] The standard British tactic—bloody but fearsome and effective—was to close rapidly, pound away hull to hull, then grapple and board. Most ships mounted just a few long-range guns, and few captains even practiced long gunnery.

The Americans had a much higher ratio of long guns—Chauncey insisted on it. He drilled in gunnery, and his crews were decent artillerists. As Table 1.2 shows, the throw weight of metal[*] for the two fleets was the same—about 2,700 pounds—but more than 40 percent of the American throw weight was in long guns, compared to a peashooter's worth for the British. In a fight, the American long-range advantage was even higher, since 15 of their long guns were on swivels and could fight on either side, while the British had only 1 small swivel gun. The advantage shifted to the British in hull-to-hull battles: nominal throw weights were the same, but carronades used smaller crews and had faster firing cycles.

Sailing characteristics reinforced the asymmetry. Eckford's ships the *Madison*, the *Pike*, and the *Sylph* were superb, but the *Oneida* was "a perfect slug,"[17] and the rest, all converted lakers, were notoriously clumsy sailers, so Chauncey had serious problems keeping his squadron together. The Royal Navy, by contrast, placed a high premium on convoy sailing, and it was a constant focus of their drills. Chauncey and his officers marveled at

---

[*] The throw-weight calculation assumes a single shot from all the guns, each using a ball of the rated weight. In battle, gun crews often stuffed their cannon with multiple cannon balls, bags of scrap metal, grape shot (a half dozen small iron balls on a rod or a chain), and almost whatever else came to hand. Overweighting the payload reduced a gun's punching power, but at close range it could increase its shattering impact on a wooden hull, and if you were attacking a ship's crew, a deck-top blast of flying shards of metal was viciously effective.

Yeo's tight-formation fleet maneuvers: "all sailing alike and able to support each other in any weather."[18]

Yeo would therefore naturally choose to engage the Americans on a day of tricky winds and choppy waters. The weather would scatter the American fleet and degrade its long-range gunnery, while superior British convoy sailing would allow them to swarm their targets. Chauncey's preferred scenario was precisely the opposite. With calm waters, he could stand off beyond carronade range, pound away at British rigging and gunports, and then close against wounded targets. In other words, with roughly equal forces, the two commanders would almost never choose to fight at the same time.

The obvious way to break the impasse was to acquire such overwhelming force that the asymmetries ceased to matter. But that would provoke the weaker opponent to avoid a fight at all costs, while redoubling his building efforts. In short, the Ontario shipbuilders' war was a classic arms race, like the Soviet-American missile race, that would continue until one side or the other was exhausted. All the professionals on the lake understood this and frequently commented on it, even as Chauncey and Yeo, in their dispatches to headquarters, lamented in almost identical tones the unwillingness of the other to engage in a climactic battle.

Some Not-So-Close Encounters: Ontario, Summer–Fall 1813

Yeo's temporary dominance of the lake ended on July 22, when Chauncey, leading his fleet in the *Pike*, mounted another raid on York, then dropped down to Niagara and sent off one hundred experienced seamen to man Perry's Erie squadron. A week later, with the *Melville* entering service, Yeo felt strong enough to go out and hunt for Chauncey. On the morning of August 7, the two fleets sighted each near the mouth of the Niagara River, and both announced their intent to fight by firing cannons.

The two fleets proceeded on a tack to meet just west of the river. Yeo was in the *Wolfe*, with all five of his other warships. Chauncey was in the *Pike*, with the *Madison* and the *Oneida* and nine of his lakers. The British stayed in tight formation, but the American fleet quickly broke into three clusters. Chauncey reversed his course to gather up the fleet. Yeo turned as well but headed in the opposite direction. Watchers on the shore expecting to see the long-awaited showdown could not believe their eyes.

Yeo was just being sensible. By reversing course to await his lakers, Chauncey signaled his intent to open the battle at long range—the lakers had a third of his long guns. The water was calm, ideal for American gunnery, and Yeo had no interest in playing target-practice dummy.[19]

That night, the British lay near York, while Chauncey was still far across the lake. A sudden, and violent, electrical storm capsized the two largest lakers, the *Hamilton* and *Scourge*, with the loss between them of some eighty men and 19 guns. After a service for the drowned men, Chauncey brought his fleet to within firing range of Yeo. As they were on the point of engaging, a nasty squall sprang up, and both sides broke off. Chauncey decided that from then on his newer warships would tow the lakers to the point of an engagement.

Finally, the fourth day of the encounter, August 10, appeared to offer a real fight. Yeo's fleet, caught in a calm, was spotted by the Americans, who were about twenty miles away with a good breeze. Chauncey poured on the sail, dragging the lakers with him, but as they neared the British, the wind suddenly kicked up and shifted in Yeo's favor. Yeo quickly formed a line and started for the Americans. Two of the lakers, off their tow, missed a signal and sailed toward the British. They were quickly captured, and the two sides broke off the engagement.

Although there had been no real action, Yeo had clearly won on points. Including the capsized schooners, Chauncey had lost four lakers with upward of two hundred men and 26 guns. A string of anonymous complaints about Chauncey's timidity, apparently from crewmen, found their way into public press.

The two fleets spotted each other several times over the next couple of weeks, but without an engagement. Toward the end of August, Chauncey more than made up for the loss of his lakers by the launch of the *Sylph*, a fast sailer with 18 guns, including 4 long 32-pounders on swivels.

On September 11, returning from Niagara, Chauncey spotted the British fleet becalmed near the mouth of the Genesee River on the American side of the lake. The *Pike* and the *Sylph* closed within three-quarters of a mile and began to pound away with their long guns. The lakers, dragged along for just such an engagement, once again did not get into the action. A land breeze kicked up in time for the British to escape with only modest casualties and damage. The Americans gave chase across the lake, breaking off when Yeo tried to set an ambush behind some islands on the Canadian side. Theodore Roosevelt, who wrote a small masterpiece on the naval war, was no fan of Chauncey, but he mocked Yeo's battle report for failing to admit that his fleet "ran away."[20] Prevost complained to London of his "disappointment" at Yeo's "having been so many days in sight of the enemy's squadron without having obtained a significant advantage."[21]

On September 28, the fleets met again while both were on transport duty in the lake's western end—Yeo on the northern side sailing eastward and Chauncey to the south but moving northwest. There was a strong easterly wind, so Chauncey had the weather gage.* Yeo turned southward, while Chauncey ran north and then turned, with the *Pike* in the lead, to approach Yeo at an angle with the wind. Both sides cleared their decks for battle. This time Chauncey did not attempt to stay at long range but sailed right into the *Wolfe's* broadside, taking fire from the *Beresford* and *Royal George* at the same time. At a distance of several hundred yards, the *Pike* veered to unleash a full powerful broadside. The *Wolfe* reeled, and the *Pike* lost part of its topmast. A second exchange of broadsides took down the *Wolfe's* whole topmast. The *Wolfe* "staggered and lost its heading . . . its deck a scene of chaos,"[22] as the *Pike* closed in for the kill.

At that moment, the *Wolfe* was all but lost. A major mast in the water effectively anchored the ship. Until its frantic crew could chop away the dense tangle of thick ropes that held the mast, it was utterly exposed to the *Pike's* heavy guns. With the *Wolfe* out of action, the rest of the British

* Captains usually preferred to go into battle with the wind, since they could maneuver more easily than a ship beating windward.

fleet could not stand against the *Pike*, the *Madison*, and the *Sylph*. Chauncey, as hungry for glory as any captain, suddenly had the lake, and possibly the war, in his grasp.

Yeo was saved when his number two, William Mulcaster, arguably the best sailor on the lake, darted the *Royal George* between Chauncey and Yeo and fired his broadside on the *Pike*, giving Yeo a respite to regroup. There was a disorganized melee on the *Wolfe* for some fifteen minutes, while the crew got free of its shattered masts and cleared away its dead and wounded. By then the *Madison* and the *Oneida* were in the fray, and the easterly wind a gale. Yeo signaled the fleet to make an all-out run to Burlington, a harbor on the far western shore. Off they went, with the Americans in chase, covering fifteen miles in ninety minutes, an extraordinary pace for square-rigs. Spectators on shore dubbed the episode "the Burlington Races."

The Americans were hampered by Chauncey's insistence on towing the lakers, which seems clearly wrong. Neither the *Sylph* nor the *Madison* could stay abreast during the chase, so it was only the *Pike*, which had absorbed most of the British gunnery during the battle, that was in truly hot pursuit, although leaking badly, with cut-up rigging and topmasts. Chauncey's hope of a glorious victory disappeared when one of his big guns exploded, killing or wounding twenty-two men. With several others showing cracks, Chauncey finally gave up the chase. His fleet then faced a long struggle into the teeth of the gale to get back to the safety of the natural harbor at Niagara.

"The battle, if such it may be called," Roosevelt wrote, "completely established Chauncey's supremacy, Yeo spending most of the remainder of the season blockaded in Kingston." By Roosevelt's count, the Americans enjoyed unrestricted movement on Ontario for 107 days in the 1813 sailing season, while the British had only 48 days, and another 69 days were contested.[23] And despite the complaints about Chauncey's caution, his attack on the *Wolfe* was arguably the single most aggressive naval action during the entire Lake Ontario face-off.

Chauncey finally enjoyed a crowning bit of luck. On his return to Sackets a week later, his squadron ran into a large British transport caravan, guarded only by gunboats. The *Sylph* quickly rounded them up, costing the British a substantial shipment of military stores and 252 prisoners. The loss put Yeo in a rage, for as a British historian writes, he "had suffered a series of setbacks quite unlike anything in his career to date."[24]

The truly momentous news of that fall, however, came from Lake Erie, for just before Chauncey and Yeo engaged in their September quasi-combat, news filtered in that Perry had cleared the British from the lake.

The Battle of Lake Erie

The opposing commanders on Erie, Oliver Hazard Perry and Robert Heriot Barclay, were both in their late twenties and both rising stars. Perry had been with Stephen Decatur, then a captain, at Tripoli during the Barbary War, and Barclay had lost an arm at Trafalgar. Both developed testy relationships with their respective superiors, Chauncey and Yeo, because they felt shortchanged on men and materials.

When Perry took command, he had the captured gunboat *Caledonia* (3), and a handful of other gunboats that Eckford and Elliott built at the village of Black Rock, on the Niagara River near the entrance to the lake. The British had three warships on the lake, with 38 guns between them. The American victory at Niagara in May, however, had chased the British from Ft. Erie, an artillery outpost that covered the lake entrance. With the fort in friendly hands, Perry could tow his little Black Rock armada onto Lake Erie. (The current flowing out from the lake, on its way to the falls, is very strong. The tow took several weeks with oxen and two hundred men pulling from the shoreline.) From there, it was a hundred-mile sail to a new American base at Presque Isle, near the present Erie, Pennsylvania. Barclay was prowling the lake to prevent just such a move, but dense fogs helped the Americans slip through.

Presque Isle was far from an ideal base. It was protected by a sandbar that allowed only five to eight feet of clearance: enough for a gunboat but not a warship. Perry chose it because it was the only protected harbor on the American side of the lake, but it meant that new warships would have to be lifted over the bar before they could get into action.

Barclay's position, despite his advantage in warships, was becoming untenable. He was dependent on uncertain supply lines that had been badly disrupted by Chauncey's raids on York. His supply problems were made much worse by Yeo's high state of nervousness, for he regularly preempted men and weapons that the Admiralty intended for Barclay.

Barclay maintained a watchful blockade much of the summer, while scrounging materials for a new 19-gun corvette, the *Detroit*. Perry stayed stuck behind his sandbar, building twin 20-gun corvettes, the *Lawrence* and the *Niagara*, armed almost entirely with carronades. For some reason, Barclay raised the blockade on July 29 and returned to his base at Amherstburg on the western end of the lake till August 4—just time enough for Perry to get his ships out. Crossing the bar was accomplished with "camels," fifty-foot-long waterproof casks on each side of a ship's hull. The camels were filled with water and sunk; when they were pumped full of air, they raised the whole ship.

With Perry's fleet on the lake, Barclay was doomed. As shown in Table 1.3, even though the British had more guns, the Americans had twice the firepower, although concentrated in carronades.

TABLE 1.3 Naval Forces, Lake Erie: September 1813

British			American		
Name	Guns	Throw Weight	Name	Guns	Throw Weight
Detroit	19	252	*Lawrence*	20	600
Queen Charlotte	17	366	*Niagara*	20	600
Lady Prevost	13	141	*Caledonia*	3	80
Hunter	10	60	*Ariel*	4	48
Little Belt	3	24	*Somers*	2	56
Chippeway	1	9	*Scorpion*	2	64
			Porcupine	1	32
			Tigress	1	32
			Trippe	1	24
Long guns	**35**	**330**	**Long guns**	**15**	**288**
Carronades	**26**	**522**	**Carronades**	**39**	**1,248**
Total	**63**	**852**	**Total**	**54**	**1,536**

Barclay retired to Amherstburg to finish the *Detroit*, while railing at Prevost and Yeo over his lack of men and supplies. The *Detroit* was armed mostly by cannibalizing guns from the Amherstburg fort; they were missing locks and had to be fired by flashing pistols next to their touch holes.[*] Although Barclay also complained bitterly of the quality of his men, both forces acquitted themselves well. It was a close-run fight, one that Perry nearly lost and probably deserved to.

Perry maintained a loose blockade on Barclay's base at Amherstburg while the *Detroit* was being finished. Barclay finally brought his ships out for battle on September 9. Ready or not, Amherstburg was running out of food. The fleets spotted each other mid-morning the next day and cleared for battle. Barclay kept his ships in a tight line, while Perry, in the *Lawrence*, attacked with the weather gage, in a light wind, closing on a parallel line to get close enough to use his carronades.

Perry's line started with two gunboats with 3 heavy long guns between them, followed by the *Lawrence*, the *Caledonia*, the *Niagara* under Elliott, and then the rest of the gunboats. Perry's original line had the *Niagara* in second position, but he changed it at the last minute. The *Caledonia*, however, was a notoriously slow sailer: with Elliott keeping his third position, the *Lawrence* quickly pulled far ahead of the rest of the squadron.

Perry took a number of hits as he closed to carronade range. Then he stood broadside to broadside against the *Detroit*, the *Queen Charlotte*, and the *Hunter* for some two and a half hours. The long guns on the gunboats worked severe damage on the British warships—Roosevelt argues that they were decisive—but the British fire was concentrated solely on the *Lawrence*. Between the gunboats and the *Lawrence*'s heavy carronades, the *Hunter* was put out of the battle and the *Detroit* and *Queen Charlotte* severely battered. But the *Lawrence* was a complete wreck—its sailing master called it "a confused heap of horrid ruins." All of its guns were out of action and 80 percent of the crew killed or wounded, although Perry himself was unharmed.

---

[*] The scavenging of army forts explains Barclay's high proportion of long guns. Perry was likely stuck with carronades because Chauncey was picking off new long guns for himself. Perry also bought cannon in Pittsburgh, where there were two new cannon foundries, but newer foundries naturally focused on carronades, since they were easier to make.

At the point when the *Lawrence* was clearly lost, Perry spotted Elliott finally coming up, his ship still virtually unscathed. He promptly had himself rowed to the *Niagara*, sending Elliott back to organize the rest of the gunboats. Perry turned the *Niagara* directly into the British line, unleashing broadsides from both sides. It was over in another half hour. The *Detroit* and the *Queen Charlotte*, with nearly all their masts already down, became tangled with each other. Wallowing helplessly, with the *Niagara* coming about for yet another murderous broadside, both struck their colors. Barclay's remaining arm was shattered in a wound the surgeons thought was mortal, but he stayed on deck almost to the end. His official report read in part: "The American Commander seeing that the day was against him (. . . [the *Lawrence*] having struck as soon as he left her) and all the British boats badly shot up . . . made a noble, and alas, too successful an effort to regain it, for he [changed ships and] bore up and supported by his small Vessels passed within Pistol Shot and took a raking position* on our Bow, nor could I prevent it, as the unfortunate situation of the *Queen Charlotte* prevented us from wearing, in attempting it we fell outboard her." A junior lieutenant, George Inglis, the only officer still standing, completed the report: "Every brace cut away, the Mizen Topmast and Gaff down, all the other Masts badly wounded, not a Stay left forward. . . . I was under the painful necessity of answering the Enemy to say we had struck, the *Queen Charlotte* having previously done so."[25]

With the warships gone, it was a simple matter for the Americans to round up the rest of the British squadron. From that point, Erie was an American lake.

The victory on Lake Erie effectively cut off supplies to the interior of Canada. The British infantry commander on the spot, Col. Henry Proctor, correctly called it "calamitous."[26] Low on supplies and cold weather gear, and unable to defend Amherstburg, he burnt the base and began a retreat northeastward, to the fury of Tecumseh. William Henry Harrison took a

---

* In a "raking position" the attacking ship was positioned perpendicularly to the target, so fire was directed lengthwise along the deck, wreaking havoc on the crew.

large force of Ohio and Kentucky volunteers in pursuit. Proctor fought an orderly retreat, but Tecumseh attempted to make a stand at the Thames River, where he was shot in the heart and reportedly skinned by Harrison's frontiersmen. With him died the idea of a northwestern Indian alliance.

Perry's courage was widely celebrated. He embarked on a national tour of parades and speaking engagements, and his victory became a fabled episode in elementary school textbooks. But the fact remains that the *Lawrence* and the *Niagara*, fighting together, greatly outgunned the British and should have scored an easy win. A vast literature sprang up on the questions of why Elliott hung back, for his record had been one of great boldness. Whispers of cowardice dogged Elliott throughout a long career, and Roosevelt assailed him for "misconduct." (Elliott's explanation was that he had initially held to his position as instructed and then lost his wind, which is plausible. Perry never criticized him but omitted the usual praise in his report.)

But Perry mismanaged the fleet. In the age of sail, light-wind battles were stately, slow-motion affairs, and Perry had ample opportunity to regroup his line. Barclay wasn't going anywhere. As it was, Elliott's diffidence and Perry's solo heroics almost lost the battle and may have needlessly sacrificed the *Lawrence*'s crew and officers.[27]

The 1813 sailing season on Ontario ended with Yeo blockaded in Kingston. Chauncey ferried troops for yet another misconceived infantry action, putatively against Montreal, and with much the same near-disastrous outcomes as in the previous summer.

The Arms Race Escalates

The most ominous developments for Americans, however, took place in Europe. After Napoleon's disaster in Russia, the European wars had turned decisively in favor of the British and their continental allies. As 1814 opened with Napoleon all but defeated, the British turned with some pleasure to the task of inflicting punishment on the jackal former colony whose conduct had been "so black, so loathsome, so hateful," as the London *Times* put it.[28] There were large transfers of veteran ground troops and ships and seamen from the European theater. Naval forces up and down the American coast mounted punitive search-and-destroy missions up rivers and inlets, culminating in the burning of Washington in the late summer.

On the lakes, British war policy expressly shifted to the offensive, with the objective of moving the Canadian border southward and eastward. Much of the current state of Maine was already under British occupation. Yeo radically scaled up his building program, starting on two outsized frigates with 58 and 44 guns, four large new gunboats, and a massive ship of the line. During the winter of 1813–1814, in a rapid-strike campaign, the British army under Gen. George Drummond retook virtually the whole of the Niagara peninsula.

The Americans were determined to hold fast. In January, Chauncey got another carte-blanche general order from naval secretary Jones: "You are directed by the President of the United States . . . to make such requisitions, take such order and employ such means as shall appear to you best."[29] The near-totally blockaded coastal fleet was stripped of crews, guns, and other supplies for the lakes, and substantial raises were granted to lake seamen and officers.

Both Chauncey and Yeo maintained a steady flow of alarms to their political masters, although Yeo—perhaps smarting from the naval failures of 1813—was much the more strident, to the point where Prevost felt constrained to correct his exaggerations. In truth, since Yeo did not wait for permission to start his winter build, he was months ahead of Chauncey (see Table 1.4).*[30]

Yeo's two new warships, the *Princess Charlotte* and the *Prince Regent*, decisively shifted the advantage. Bulked up by 68-pound carronades and

---

* He subsequently got the required clearances and more. The Admiralty even came up with the idea of prebuilding hulls in England and shipping them to Kingston. Yeo and Prevost agreed it was a terrible idea. Building hulls wasn't a bottleneck, and transporting them would require completely new St. Lawrence barges and severely disrupt already-strained logistics. Wary of rejecting an Admiralty gift, they convened an advisory committee that, after an appropriate deliberation, recommended against it. By that time, the Admiralty had already started on one, which was delivered in late fall and launched at Kingston in December 1814 as the *Psyche*, a big sixty-gun frigate, although it never sailed on the lake.

TABLE 1.4 Naval Forces, Lake Ontario: May 1814

British			American		
Name	Guns	Metal Weight	Name	Guns	Metal Weight
Magnet[a]	18	344	Oneida	18	396
Charwell[b]	14	324	Madison	24	688
Niagara[c]	20	748	Gen. Zebulon Pike	26	624
Netley[d]	14	132	Sylph	18	402
Wolfe	22	804	Jefferson	20	768
Star[e]	16	384	Jones	20	768
Princess Charlotte	40	1,088			
Prince Regent	58	1,904			
Long guns	**68**	**1,462**	**Long guns[f]**	**50**	**1,272**
Carronades	**134**	**4,266**	**Carronades**	**76**	**2,374**
Total	**202**	**5,728**	**Total**	**126**	**3,646**

[a] formerly *Sir Sidney Smith* (Yeo frequently renamed his vessels.)
[b] formerly *Earl of Moira*
[c] formerly *Royal George*
[d] formerly *Beresford*
[e] formerly *Lord Melville*
[f] Gunboats are omitted from the table, since both commanders now used them primarily in shore actions or as armed transports.

32-pound long guns, total British throw weight was now about 1.6 times that of the Americans, and they even had an edge in long-range firepower as well. At the same time, large transfers of Royal Navy veterans doubled Yeo's manning complement and ratcheted up their skill level. The big force increment intensified pressures for success. The semiofficial *Naval Chronicle* pointedly hoped that Britons would "not again be distressed at the recital of misfortune or failure from want of long guns" but would rather "soon be gratified with the glad tidings that his [Yeo's] efforts have been crowned with success."[31]

Chauncey, of course, had no intention of fighting. Snugly ensconced at Sackets, the base ringing with shipwrights' hammers, his own oversized frigates rising in the boatyard, he could wait for better odds. Drummond and Yeo plumped hard for an attack on Sackets itself, which would require large reinforcements from Montreal. Prevost refused it as too risky. The two pressed their case through the summer and finally decided to attack the American depot at Oswego to help make their case.

The Oswego river empties into Lake Ontario about fifty miles west of Sackets Harbor and was the drop-off point for much of the ordnance and other supplies shipping through western New York. Losing it would have seriously disrupted American logistics. The American presence comprised a modest fort, storehouses, and a garrison of some three hundred marines and soldiers. The attack got underway on May 6 and involved Yeo's entire fleet, some thirty vessels, including gunboats and troop transports. Chauncey was quickly made aware of the assault but decided he had to sit it out. Yeo had good intelligence on the defenses and went in with more than a two-to-one manpower advantage.

The postbattle reports from Yeo and Drummond border on the ecstatic: the attack was "a compleat success," "nothing could exceed the coolness and gallantry in action, or the unwearied exertions," and much else in that vein. In fact, it clinched Prevost's case against an attempt on Sackets, which had been strongly reinforced over the winter. Oswego cost the British ninety casualties, a relatively high number. (The Americans had several of the rapid-firing Chambers guns.) For that, they sunk some transports, which were quickly raised, and captured seven heavy guns, some rope and other naval supplies, and several weeks' supply of food, which the British badly needed. The loss of the guns delayed Chauncey's big new ships by several weeks, but all the rest of the supplies were readily replaced.[32]

The British success at Oswego was offset three weeks later by a sharp reverse on the same shore. The American commander at Oswego, Lt. Melancthon Woolsey, had hidden substantial amounts of ordnance and other supplies before the attack, and more was arriving by the day. At the end of May, he decided to make a night run through the British blockade, taking nineteen boats escorted by a substantial force of riflemen and friendly Oneidas; Chauncey also sent a detachment of mounted dragoons to meet him. Woolsey was spotted en route and chased by a force of some 250 marines and seamen in two groups of small craft. He made it to Sandys

Creek, a winding inlet with road connections to Sackets. The British fool-ishly followed and got trapped in an ambush. Their entire force, equivalent to the crew for a sizeable brig, was captured with very heavy casualties.

For all practical purposes, Sandys Creek marked the end of Yeo's con-trol of the lakes. Chauncey now had all his ordnance, and final preparation of two powerful new frigates, the Superior and the Mohawk, was proceed-ing apace. Chauncey had promised to be on the lake early in July but was taken seriously ill, with one of the fevers that regularly decimated Sack-ets.[*][33] Fears for Chauncey's recovery were such that Jones asked Stephen Decatur to transfer to the lake and take temporary command. In the event, on July 25, Chauncey was carried to his cabin on the Superior and sailed forth once more as ruler of the lake, while Yeo retreated to Kingston.

The total American throw weight of metal (see Table 1.5) was about 20 percent greater than that of the British, and they had more than double the long-range firepower. The long-range power of just the Superior and the Mohawk was greater than that of the entire British squadron, while the rest of the American fleet, no longer burdened with lakers, outgunned and could mostly outsail their opposite numbers. Yeo had no interest in taking on such a force; instead, he concentrated feverishly, almost fanatically, on building the ultimate naval weapon: a true first-rater.

The summer of 1814, especially from July through September, was a decisive period in the war. There were bitter, brutal land battles up and down the Niagara peninsula. Large forces were involved from both sides; Lundys Lane was one of the largest troop engagements of the war. Battles were fought to a standstill, and casualties were very high, especially among the Indians, who basically withdrew from the fighting.[**][34]

---

* Sackets Harbor was a cul-de-sac, unlike Kingston, which was on a free-flowing channel. The substantial permanent population created "excrementious" conditions in the harbor, plaguing the force with gastroenteral disease.
** Different Iroquois tribal groups fought on both sides, and tribal elders were appalled at how fearfully they were being ground up. Indians and whites had very different ideas on the value of a soldier's life. Whites were horrified at the Indian penchant for killing prisoners and roasting and eating their hearts and livers. But the Indians were shocked at the whites' habit of lining up at close range in full view and firing away until one side or the other crumpled. Indians, one chief said, fought "to kill the enemy and save our own men." A white could never "lead a war party with us."

TABLE 1.5 Naval Forces, Lake Ontario: August 1814

British			American		
Name[a]	Guns	Metal Weight	Name	Guns	Metal Weight
Charwell	14	324	*Oneida*	18	396
Niagara	20	748	*Madison*	24	688
Netley	12	132	*Gen. Zebulon Pike*	26	624
Wolfe	22	804	*Sylph*	18	402
Star	14	384	*Jefferson*	20	768
Princess Charlotte	40	1,088	*Jones*	20	768
Prince Regent	58	1,904	*Superior*	58	2,100
			Mohawk	42	1,136
Long guns	**68**	**1,438**	**Long guns**	**90**	**2,904**
Carronades	**134**	**3,946**	**Carronades**	**136**	**3,978**
Total	**202**	**5,384**	**Total**	**226**	**6,882**

[a] *Magnet* was run aground by the Americans and destroyed early in August. It was an old ship and had been transferred to Drummond as a transport escort prior to that event.

The British had a modest numerical advantage most of the time but were taken aback by a new gritty, dug-in steadiness on the part of the Americans, even among militia units. American commanders made serious tactical errors throughout, but the British served their troops as badly, mounting one high-risk operation after another on the conviction that Americans always crumbled at the first exchange of fire.

The contribution of the massive Lake Ontario navies to these momentous engagements was effectively zero, since both commanders feared that supporting ground troops would dissipate their strength and put their fleets at risk. Jacob Brown, the American commander on Niagara, was so incensed by Chauncey's refusal to support him that he took the argument to the press. Drummond and Prevost made the same complaints about Yeo, if more quietly.[35]

As it happened, there was one decisive naval battle in 1814, but it took place on Lake Champlain, with minimal assistance from either of the great establishments on Ontario.

The Battle of Lake Champlain

The Battle of Lake Champlain halted a major British invasion of the American northeast and ended parliamentary hopes of "rectifying" the Canadian border. The attack had two prongs: a naval assault on the American squadron at Plattsburgh on northwest Champlain and a ground invasion down the west side of the lake by some 10,000 regulars, many of them Wellington's "best troops from Bordeaux."[36] The war secretary, John Armstrong, acted with his usual destructiveness by transferring the bulk of the American ground forces away from Plattsburgh just before the invasion.

The British naval squadron, under Captain George Downie, was spearheaded by a new frigate, *Confiance*; its 37 guns, 31 of them long-range 24-pounders, made it nearly as powerful as Chauncey's *Mohawk*. To offset *Confiance*, Thomas Macdonough, commander of the Champlain squadron, ordered the construction of the *Eagle*; it was built by the Browns, from first keel-laying to launch, in just nineteen days. (See Table 1.6.)

TABLE 1.6 Naval Forces, Lake Champlain: September 1814					
British			**American**		
Name	Guns	Metal Weight	Name	Guns	Metal Weight
Confiance	37	960	*Saratoga*	26	828
Linnet	16	192	*Eagle*	20	528
Chubb	11	192	*Ticonderoga*	17	328
Finch	11	168	*Preble*	7	63
Gunboats	17	436	Gunboats	16	300
Long guns	**45**	**986**	**Long guns**	**45**	**759**
Carronades	**47**	**962**	**Carronades**	**41**	**1,288**
Total	**92**	**1,948**	**Total**	**86**	**2,047**

At first, the campaign unfolded as planned. The infantry veterans brushed aside sporadic opposition as they moved down the western side of the lake, arriving at Plattsburgh within a few days of the naval squadron. Plattsburgh had a formidable arrangement of forts and redoubts, and the British assumed it would take about three weeks to carry them. But sieges in hostile territory are logistics-intensive; without control of the upper lake, Prevost could not secure his supply lines. From the outset, he had insisted that the campaign depended on taking out the American squadron at Plattsburgh.

The ensuing battle may be the only naval engagement of the war that turned almost entirely on a commander's thoughtful battle preparation. The Plattsburgh harbor was on a bay sheltered from northerly winds. Macdonough anchored his vessels in a line broadsides out, in a narrow portion of the bay. The details of his positioning gave him two crucial advantages. The first is that he set kedges, or auxiliary anchors, with undersea cabling so crews could winch their ships around to change broadsides without losing anchorage. The second is that the narrowness of his anchorage site helped to neutralize the *Confiance*'s great advantage in heavy long guns. (Macdonough implicitly counted on the British penchant for attacking without regard to tactical details.)

The British ground forces were mostly in position, but the siege had not commenced, when Downie's squadron appeared up the lake in the early morning of September 11, running before a brisk wind. The American masts were visible over the promontory that protected the bay, so the squadron sailed past the promontory, turned to the starboard, and proceeded directly into the bay. They lost their wind and set anchors in a line facing Macdonough's at a distance of three hundred to four hundred yards. Both sides cheered and opened fire.

After some two hours of pounding, both squadrons were near-wreckages, and casualties were high—Downie was killed in one of the first salvos. The weight of the *Confiance* was taking its toll. Although badly cut up itself, it had silenced the guns of Macdonough's flagship, the *Saratoga*. But instead of striking colors, Macdonough set his crew to the winches, and the *Saratoga* swung around to present a completely fresh broadside. Pounded anew, and increasingly defenseless itself, the *Confiance* tried a similar maneuver but got hopelessly stuck and was forced to strike. (An officer of the *Confiance* reported that its men "declared that they would stand no longer to their Quarters"—a remarkable defiance for British seamen.[37]) The Americans quickly finished off the *Linnet* and rounded up the smaller vessels. Only a few gunboats escaped.

Prevost had not yet signaled the assault on the forts when he saw his navy surrender. He immediately broke off the action and ordered a retreat, infuriating the veterans and most of his officers, although he had been quite clear on his conditions for a siege. Even Wellington later conceded that it was a correct decision.

With the failed invasion, the apparently permanent loss of both Erie and Champlain, and the standoffs on Ontario and the Niagara peninsula, Parliament's avowed objective of punishing America began to look like a very expensive self-indulgence.

Denouement

The last act of the 1814 sailing season, as imposing as it was inconsequential, came in October, when Yeo finally sailed out from Kingston in his new first-rater, the HMS *St. Lawrence*, "a behemoth of oceanic proportions, more powerful than Nelson's flagship at Trafalgar."[38] It bristled with 112 guns, almost all of them very heavy, arranged in three gun decks. At a stroke, the fleet's throw weight of metal increased by 55 percent, and its long-range firepower was more than doubled. Chauncey duly took his own armada back to the shelter of Sackets, and for a few weeks before the ice set in, the lake was Yeo's to sail in unopposed majesty.

The Americans were determined to stay in the game. By late fall, Sackets was a beehive, laying down two first-raters and two large frigates, building a rope works, and constructing a second shipyard, including housing, shops, and other facilities. A British spy, "our friend Jones," who also reported on his tête-à-tête dinners with top American generals, carefully paced off the measurements of the Sackets first-raters. (He also noted that

The *St. Lawrence*, a true British "first-rater," bristling with 112 gunports, was one of the largest ships in the world when it was launched down a Lake Ontario slipway in the fall of 1814. It was bigger and better-armed than Nelson's flagship at Trafalgar, but never fired a shot in anger. When the peace treaty was signed a few months after its launch, it was left to rot on the beach until it was disposed of in 1832.

"the great mass of the seamen appear to be coloured people."[39]) Yeo's shipyard master, Capt. Richard O'Conor, in the meantime went off to London to warn the admirals of the "very considerable . . . exertions of the Enemy."[40]

But second thoughts abounded. Prevost complained in October that outfitting the *St. Lawrence* had "absorbed almost the whole of the Summer Transport Service from Montreal,"[41] superseding far more pressing supply issues. And even Jones pleaded to Madison for a rethink of what had "become a warfare of Dockyards." "We are at War with the most potent Naval power in the world," whose global network of supplies and ordnance meant it could easily meet any demand "in less time and at one fourth the expense" as the Americans. Jones estimated that the next summer's lake fleet would require 7,000 seamen, which he saw no possibility of supplying.[42]

More practically, the American government was broke. Lake seamen and troops had not been paid for six months or more, and the militias,

Chauncey wrote, "desert by companies."[43] Eckford and the Browns had signed personal notes for $110,000 to cover payments to critical suppliers. In early February, the three of them wrote that they were bearing a weekly expense of $8,000 and would "certainly be oblig'd to stop the whole business in ten or twelve days if we are not Supply'd with money."[44]

The British were making their own calculations. The cabinet guessed that winning the war would cost another £10 million. The commercial community was strongly opposed to further taxes. They were moaning over the loss of their American markets and beginning to grasp how the war and years of blockades had been force-feeding American manufacturing.

American and British negotiators had been meeting desultorily at Ghent since August. Each side had come to the meetings with lists of non-negotiable items, with the British especially obdurate and supercilious. After months of whittling away at each other's demands, they finally agreed on Christmas Eve to drop all preconditions, cease hostilities, and refer any outstanding issues to commissions—in effect, to forget the whole thing.

The climactic battles of New Orleans were fought in mid-January, and news of the great victory spread throughout the country within weeks. When news of the peace finally arrived on February 14, the public naturally assumed that New Orleans forced the British to quit, so the war ended on a high note. Across the Atlantic, the new disaster just reinforced the wisdom of getting out. Great Britain had spent two decades more or less continuously at war. The fulminations of the *Times* notwithstanding, a war of attrition against a major trading partner on a point of honor made no sense.

By the time of the peace announcement, Chauncey had launched the *New Orleans*, even bigger than the *St. Lawrence*, although it was still being masted. A yet-unnamed companion first-rater was also being readied for the spring thaw, and the keel was laid down for another big frigate. Across the lake, Yeo was determinedly keeping pace, building another first-rater and apparently a third-rater (74).

News of the peace also brought notice of Yeo's recall. Since American roads were in decent shape, he decided to cross the lake and embark from

New York. Chauncey invited him to stop over at Sackets, and they spent more than a week together. One imagines they had much in common, including shared grievances on interservice rivalries.

The dismantling of the lake's naval establishments was underway by the end of February. The Americans sold off most of their gunboats and transport craft to commercial shippers, and both the *Oneida* and the *Sylph* had long careers as merchant vessels. Most of the rest of the warships were sold as scrap, and some were just left to rot. The hulk of the *St. Lawrence* was sold in 1832 for £25, on condition that it be removed from the lake. The *New Orleans* was planked over to preserve it and it sat on the beach until 1880, when it collapsed and was carted away.

The controversies over the performance of the two lake commanders melted away with the war. With Europe at peace, British commands were scarce, but Yeo was given an independent command interdicting slavers; he died of yellow fever in 1818. Chauncey was appointed commodore of America's second saltwater ship of the line, the USS *Washington* (74), and assumed command of the squadron in the Mediterranean. He spent another twenty-five years in the naval service.

———

THE SHIPBUILDERS' WAR IS A MOSTLY FORGOTTEN SUBPLOT OF A NEARLY forgotten war. But it cast a long shadow. The apparent victory, as Americans saw it, was a huge boost for national morale. More substantively, the war effort and the associated British trade embargo were robust stimuli to the still-fledgling native textile and iron industries. Military uniforms, tents, and the like created a New England textile boom, while foundries turning out cannon and cannon balls, shot, ship ballast, and wagon and ship fittings proliferated in a ring from Pittsburgh through upper New York State and western Connecticut. Military procurement accelerated the commercialization of agriculture, and the war broke the British-Indian alliances in the old Northwest territories, hastening the pace of settlement.

The war resolved a long-standing division over the importance of industry to the country's safety and success. Even Thomas Jefferson repudiated his former distaste for industrial-scale manufacturing, forthrightly conceding that he was wrong to hope that sheer distance was sufficient defense against outsiders. The debacles in military procurement throughout the war spurred some serious rethinking among the professional military and were a factor in the determination to increase the use of machinery in military procurement.

Most important, the war and its outcome helped banish the remnants of a colonial mind-set among Americans. Theirs was a free and independent nation with a glorious future. British power was still overwhelming, especially after the victories over Napoleon. But Americans contemplating the continent lying open before them, and the energy and prosperity in so much of the country, might foresee a day when the two countries would measure themselves against each other.

⸻

BEFORE TRACING THE PATH OF AMERICAN DEVELOPMENT, WE WILL FIRST examine industrialized Great Britain, the day's "hyperpower" and the only nation that had reached the heights America aspired to. The British development story differed in important ways from the one that evolved in America, and those differences highlight certain British dispositions that would serve them poorly in the inevitable economic contest with the United States.

CHAPTER TWO

The
Hyperpower

═══════════

TWO FULL DAYS ELAPSED AFTER NAPOLEON'S SURRENDER AT WATERLOO
before Major Henry Percy, one of Wellington's attachés, careened
through a wildly cheering crowd in a post-chaise and four, dashed into a
London ball, and knelt before the Prince Regent, announcing "Victory!
Sir! Victory!" Legend has it that Nathan Rothschild made a fortune by trading on the advance notice brought by his carrier pigeon networks from
Europe. It's almost true. Rothschild's couriers—they weren't pigeons—
did get him early word of the victory. But Rothschild didn't quite make a
killing; instead, he prevented a total family disaster by unloading part of
the bullion mountain he'd amassed in expectation of a prolonged war.[1]

The victory at Waterloo, and the American treaty ratified just months
before, left England finally at peace and in surprisingly good financial shape.
British growth in the period 1800–1830, if slow by late-nineteenth-century
standards, was markedly faster than in any previous period. Despite the immense financial drains of the late wars, Great Britain still had a surplus of
capital and was exporting capital to the world. The Rothschilds and the Barings rode that wave to new pinnacles of finance. As Byron put it in *Don Juan*:

> *Who keep the world, both old and new, in pain*
> *Or pleasure? Who makes politics run glibber all?*
> *The shade of Buonaparte's noble daring?—*
> *Jew Rothschild, and his fellow Christian Baring.*[2]

The sources of the growth are not readily explicable by changes in standard inputs like labor and capital, which suggests that much of it was driven by new technology. In other words, "Ingenuity, not accumulation, drove economic growth in this period."[3]

A Very British Industrial Revolution

In his famous account of the pin factory in the *Wealth of Nations*, Adam Smith explained how the division of labor so greatly increased labor output: "One man draws out the wire, another straights it, a third cuts it, a fourth points it, [etc. through eighteen steps]. . . . Each person, therefore, making a tenth part of forty-eight thousand pins, might be considered as making four thousand eight hundred pins in a day. But if they had all wrought separately and independently, and without any of them have been educated to this peculiar business, they certainly could not each of them have made twenty, perhaps not one pin in a day."[4] Smith gives the impression that this is a firsthand account, but sharp-eyed scholars noticed that it matched, process for process, the description of a French pin factory in Diderot's *Encyclopédie*. The dead giveaway is that in Smith's factory the workers were still making pins by hand, while contemporary English factories were water-powered. British plants used far fewer workers than their French counterparts, and the work was laid out to accommodate the mechanization. Although the French plant cited by Diderot was next to a river, it did not even have a waterwheel.

The French preference for manual over mechanized processes was not irrational. Labor was very cheap in France, and capital was scarce, so pins were best made by people. In Great Britain, it was labor that was expensive, while capital was readily available and energy, in the form of coal, was very cheap. That's the reason a profit-driven British pin maker chose to use a big, and quite inefficient, Newcomen steam engine to recirculate his water to steady its flow rate, and by extension, that's why the Industrial Revolution happened in Great Britain and not in France.[5] But that just shifts the question: Why was British labor expensive?

In 1500, about three-quarters of the populations of most European countries, including Great Britain, worked in agriculture. The most advanced trading countries, Netherlands and Belgium, were more urbanized than most, as to a lesser extent were Italy and Spain. By 1800, however, Great Britain had only about a third of its population in agriculture, far less than any other state, with the remainder either urbanized or working in rural industries.

Large-scale social changes were obviously afoot. Here is one plausible narrative: The Black Death (mid to late 1300s) depopulated England's countryside, freeing much high quality land for pasture. With better forage, the quality of English wool improved markedly, and England's wool trade expanded, displacing Flemish and Italian cloth. Cottage-based weaving grew apace, along with related manufacturing—spinning wheels, containers, wagons, and ships. Port cities invested heavily in harbors and dockyards, while trade deepened banking, insurance, and other services, which increased the returns from literacy and numeracy. Crucially, as their forests shrank, Britons learned how to use coal as their primary energy source, a process that took a full century.

As talented people were drawn to the cities and into business, agricultural markets expanded, pressuring agricultural productivity. Town records show common-field smallholders actively experimenting with plant varieties and crop rotation schemes to improve output. A British empirical, scientific style of thinking became a norm. And wages rose. By 1800, British wages, measured by both exchange rates and purchasing power, were the highest in Europe by a wide margin. Processes that moved at a glacial creep in the sixteenth century, coalesced and accreted in the seventeenth, and finally exploded in the eighteenth.[*6]

Cotton textile manufacture was the quintessential industry of the British Industrial Revolution. From a small cottage enterprise in the early

---

* Most historians would accept that list, or one much like it. Scholars differ on whether one particular factor, like the early spread of a scientific outlook, the rise in British wages, or an underlying culture, was the ultimate trigger. While there is much to learn from examining each strand separately, in the real world they were tightly intertwined.

1700s, it had grown by 1830 to employ 425,000 workers, accounting for one out of every six manufacturing jobs and about 8 percent of GDP. But the burst of mechanical development that created the world's first mass-production factories was preceded by seventy-five years of diligent tinkering.[7]

Yarn spinning is a quintessentially hand-labor task. Cotton fibers are delicate. To use in cloth, they first must be cleaned and straightened; then a "spinster," using the traditional spinning wheel, would repeatedly draw the fibers out under finger pressure while twisting them for strength. Drawing up machinery to replicate hand-spinning was relatively straightforward, but actually building machines that could manipulate the threads more or less as humans did, and without breaking them, took years of trial-and-error experiment. The first successful spinning machine was the jenny, built in 1767 and driven by a hand crank. James Hargreaves, a weaver, worked out a method of holding the rough cotton, or roving, with pins, while a bar stretched out and twisted the fibers. It worked well enough that an early demonstration provoked a riot by the local hand-spinners. But by the 1780s, many cottage hand-spinners were using twelve- and twenty-four-spindle jennies. A twelve-spindle jenny cost about seventy times as much as a spinning wheel, so the productivity pickup must have been very high.

Richard Arkwright was right behind with the water frame, a spinning machine designed to be water-powered. Arkwright was more entrepreneur than inventor, and he was determined to create a cotton mill industry. He bought patents and hired craftsmen to come up with the machinery. His water frame applied rolling technology similar to that used in glass and metal working. The rovings were fed into three successive rollers: the first compressed them, while the second two, each running at progressively higher speeds, both compressed and stretched the fibers as another device twisted them. Arkwright was far from the first inventor to try rollers: the challenge was getting the speeds, the pressures, and the spacing between the rollers right. Arkwright also had the insight to hire clockmakers to build his machines, for they had the most contemporary experience with precision gearing.

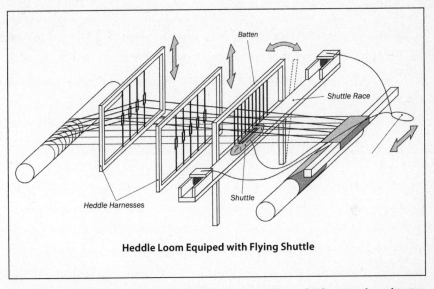

Heddle Loom Equiped with Flying Shuttle

The foot-treadle, flying shuttle, heddle loom achieved very high manual production rates. At each push of the treadle, the heddles raised and lowered alternate warp (long) threads, creating a shed to pass the weft (cross) thread through, and the batten pushed the new weft thread firmly into place. The flying shuttle allowed the operator to remain seated and very rapidly pull the weft threads back and forth through the alternating sheds. Mechanized looms worked exactly the same way, but at much higher rates of speed.

By roughly the same methods, Arkwright produced the first successful "carding" machine—for combing out the raw cotton—and then spent most of a decade trying to build a cotton mill. Cotton mill management was a new discipline: it required learning how to run banks of the new machines efficiently, how to lay out the work flow, and how to manage machined cotton. The stages from machined rovings to finished yarns were subtly different from those of hand-spun cotton. Knowing what machine speeds to apply with different fibers and spotting when a yarn was about to break, knowing how to intervene and how to restart equipment after a disaster—in effect, the basic textbook of mill management—had to be invented from scratch. Arkwright's second major mill got most of it right and was the prototype for a new British industry.

Mechanization in the textile industry was an alternating race between spinning and weaving. The fly-shuttle foot-pedal heddle loom was a highly rationalized machine that quickly pressured the capacity of the hand-spinning industry, forcing the pace of mechanization. Mechanized spinning shifted the pressure back to weaving. The fly-shuttle loom almost cried out for mechanization; the challenge lay in tuning the pressures on the threads to produce acceptable cloth while minimizing breakage, the way a skilled human did by feel.

It was much the same with the steam engine. Galileo's pupil Evangelista Torricelli did much of the early basic science, and a Frenchman, Denis Papin, constructed early working models. The first useful industrial-scale steam engine was built by Thomas Newcomen in 1712 to lift water out of a tin mine—flooding of underground mines was a chronic problem. It used a vacuum to produce work. Steam entered a cylinder and raised a piston; a jet of water cooled the cylinder, and the steam condensed, causing the piston to fall, and thereby lift water.

Very little is known about Newcomen, except that it took him at least ten years to work out his concepts, and he was forced to share his patent with businessmen who bought a master patent on all "fire-engines" from the estate of Thomas Savery, who had failed to develop a working engine. But Newcomen's invention is a marvel. Instead of trying to lift water directly by the piston, he used it to drive an oscillating pump handle—the walking beam engine. All prior engine models required an attendant to change valve settings at each stroke, but Newcomen operated his valves from the beam motions, possibly the first self-acting engine. His method of piston sealing was standard for many years. Newcomen-type engines spread rapidly through the British and European mining industry, although their inventor may have earned little from them.

Newcomen-type engines reigned for a half century, until James Watt engineered another design leap. Watt was an instrument maker who was asked to build a model engine for teaching purposes at the University of Edinburgh. As he worked on it, it occurred to him that the engine's use of fuel was prodigious relative to its output, and he calculated that three-quarters of the fuel was spent reheating the cylinder after it had been cooled to create a vacuum. That was not a problem at coal

NEWCOMEN'S PUMPING ENGINE, 1712.

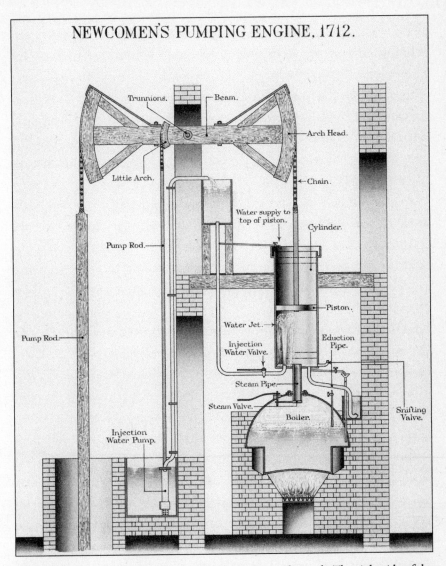

The Newcomen engine used atmospheric pressure to do work. The right side of the walking beam (large wooden horizontal piece at top) acted as a pump handle that raised water as it was pushed down. In the starting position for a new stroke, the "pump handle" was tilted up by the weight of the pump rod on left. (The beam in the picture is shown in mid-stroke.) The work sequence was: 1) Steam fills piston cylinder. 2) Jet of cold water sprays outside of cylinder, condensing the steam and creating a vacuum. 3) The weight of the atmosphere pushes pump handle down and lifts water. 4) Weight of the pump rod returns handle to initial position. Stroke rates were about twelve per minute; boiler technology limited pressures to only one or two pounds per square inch.

mines, where fuel was almost a free good, but it limited the engine's potential usefulness elsewhere. Watt's solution was to create a separate
condenser with an air pump: when the steam entered the cylinder, the
air pump created a vacuum in the condenser; the steam then rushed to
the condenser, and the piston fell, with only minimal change in the piston-
cylinder temperature. The resulting engine was more complicated but
far more efficient, and it would operate at low steam pressures, simplifying boiler construction.

Watt did little with his engine until he partnered with Matthew Boulton in 1774. Boulton was a small metal product manufacturer and an honest man who convinced Watts that he had a global business opportunity.
With Boulton in charge of the business side, and Watt steadily improving
his designs, the partnership sold hundreds of engines throughout Great
Britain and abroad. Boulton and Watt both retired when their patents expired in 1800, turning over the business to their capable sons. Over the rest
of the nineteenth century, Boulton & Watt–type engines were gradually
supplanted by lighter and less expensive high-pressure engines, developed
independently by Richard Trevithick in Great Britain and Oliver Evans in
the United States. Boulton & Watt–style engines kept a foothold well into
the nineteenth century, wherever safety and fuel efficiency were dominant
concerns, as in transatlantic steam ships.[8]

By much the same processes, the British also came to dominate in iron
and steel, although the critical innovations were powered by dire necessity. Iron and steel were among the most ancient of products, and in the
first part of the eighteenth century, the Germans, Swiss, and French all
vied for leadership. The British pulled ahead by the century's end, even
though they started from a huge disadvantage. Iron processing requires
vast amounts of fuel, traditionally charcoal, almost always used in direct
contact with the ore or metal. By the eighteenth century, however, the
British industry was close to exhausting its wood supplies and was forced
to fall back on coal, which is high in impurities that can be fatal to iron
quality. The process of overcoming that obstacle made the British industry by far the most technically sophisticated in the world. Key develop-

ments were the use of coke, a purified form of coal,[*] as a charcoal substitute; the development of the reverberatory furnace, which melted iron without direct contact with the fuel; and the puddling process, a deeply skilled craft using long poles to stir melted iron from a reverberatory furnace to create quality wrought iron. Very little of this qualified as new invention; it was instead accomplished by focused and sustained development of older technologies.

British iron prowess allowed the great machinist John Wilkinson to cast solid naval cannons and bore their holes—a formidable challenge. Other countries cast their cannon in molds, but they tended to explode. (Recall Isaac Chauncey's cannon debacle during the Burlington Races on Ontario.) A French expert reported to his government in 1775 that it had been twenty years since a British naval cannon had exploded, while French sailors "fear the guns they are serving more than those of the enemy."[9]

The crown jewel of British metallurgy was "crucible steel," which was brought to a high state of perfection by Benjamin Huntsman in the 1740s near Sheffield, traditionally the British center for high-end steelmaking. Huntsman was trying to make very durable, very hard, very thin steel for clock and watch springs. The method he finally hit on entailed remelting quality conventional steel in clay "crucibles" or pots. The resulting product was a steel that was easily poured and cast and took a superb edge. Foreign competitors found the best Sheffield steel almost impossible to replicate. (The secret of the process, deduced only much later, was the local clay used in the pots.) A Swiss reported in 1778 that "the cast steel of England is, without contradiction, the most beautiful steel in commerce; it is the hardest, the most compact, and the most homogeneous; one can recognize it at a glance."[10]

---

[*] Coke is the almost-pure carbon residue from slow burning of coal. Iron ore is smelted in direct contact with the fuel to facilitate carbon binding with the mostly oxide impurities in the ore. Subsequent processing steps, like creating wrought iron or steel, also involve manipulating the carbon content of the product and are most easily accomplished by direct-contact heating. Great Britain made the shift to coke roughly a century before the rest of Europe and the United States. In part because of its greater heat potential, coke is the superior fuel for large-scale processing, so all serious competitor countries were eventually forced to follow the British lead.

The advances fed off each other. Lighter, more efficient steam engines were the perfect power source for textile factories, blast-furnace blowers, and the lathes, forges, trip-hammers, and other essential apparatus of big-ticket manufacturing. Bigger factories meant bigger machines running at higher speeds and tighter tolerances. High-speed engines impelled deeper inquiries into the physics and chemistries of metals and fuels, which fed into the knowledge base for soap production, bleaches, etching acids, and gas lighting for 24/7 factories. Sometime in the late eighteenth century, the British achieved a point of critical mass at which understanding expanded exponentially, and inventions, technologies, and accumulating lore cohered into an irresistible surge.

The long evolution brought forth a new culture. Or perhaps it was the other way round. The great-grandfather of the British empiricist tradition, after all, was a Briton: William of Ockham, a medieval monk. Whatever the reason, the British were different from other Europeans. The eager emigrants fleeing to the American colonies may have viewed their mother country as stifling and class-ridden, but no other established nation was as free and democratic or gave as much scope to the individual. Great Britain was nominally ruled by a languid upper class, but unlike a country like France or Italy, it allowed room for energetic climbers in the middle; indeed, the top strata admitted the most successful strivers to their own ranks. Joseph Whitworth came from a middle-class family but was made a baronet in recognition of his great contributions to British technology.

England was commercial to its toes. Money talked—even dominated the conversation. Contracts were honored, patents generally respected. The country was empirical, swayed by what worked, disposed to clinch an argument with numbers. Its banking and monetary practices were the best in the world, its currency reliable. Honor was paid to the new and the better. The powers that be were more willing than elsewhere to disrupt old rhythms and break old patterns. Turnpikes, canals, and then railroads proliferated sooner than anywhere else. In short, Great Britain was the perfect petri dish for the viruses of industrial revolution, the benign and the noxious alike.[11]

All complex developments are in some degree path-dependent. Early choices and random cornerings may dominate outcomes far down the road. Because of the importance of the navy to national survival, a powerful stream of British technology was driven by naval priorities, which imparted a particular twist toward the ultraprecise. A century later, that bias, perhaps interacting with a certain upper-class intellectual style, may have disadvantaged Great Britain in its inevitable industrial confrontation with the United States.

The Longitude Problem

Eighteenth-century British admirals grumbled about keeping their ships out past August. The navigational apparatus for taking latitude readings—the north/south position—was quite accurate. The noon sighting—to fix the latitude, recalibrate the ship's clock, and turn the calendar—was inviolable ritual on British warships. A captain could readily find a line on the same latitude as the mouth of the English Channel and ride it home. Without obvious landmarks, however, it was much harder to divine how far east or west you were. That was the longitude problem, and to a seafaring nation it was of first importance. Without accurate longitude readings, ships could lose all sense of location in open oceans. Even when familiar trade routes were known to harbor pirates, merchants dared not vary from them for fear of getting lost. Muddled positioning extended voyages far beyond expectations: men got scurvy; missing a small island with fresh water could be a death sentence.

Almost all voyages home were by way of the Channel, so making the entrance was a routine but dangerous part of any sea captain's job. The Channel entrance is wide: the distance from the Isles of Scilly off the south coast of Cornwall to Ushant in Brittany is about 120 miles. It is an area of swirling currents and treacherous, relatively featureless rocky coasts, and the setting for Alfred Hitchcock's *Jamaica Inn*, in which locals live off the pickings from shipwrecks and sometimes engineer the wrecks. In fog or other difficult weather, any captain could lose his bearings.

A military convoy returning home in 1704 mistook the looming Cornwall coast for Guernsey, which is off Brittany. Believing they were in the
channel, they turned north and sailed some sixty miles up the Atlantic
coast before realizing their mistake. More tragically, in 1707, a returning
war fleet, under the impression they were well into the channel mouth,
made the turn north and ran directly on the rocks of the Scillies, losing four
warships, a popular admiral, and 2,000 crewmen. The shock led to the passage of the Longitude Act, which offered a series of prizes for full or partial
solutions to the challenge of accurately positioning a ship at sea on the
east-west axis.[12]

There were two potential solutions. One involved time. If you set a
clock at Greenwich time before leaving England, you could accurately calculate longitude simply by taking the difference between Greenwich time
and sun time at your location. But the clock had to be *extremely* accurate,
off by less than three seconds a day. If the Greenwich time readings drifted
by even very modest amounts, they would add up to disablingly large variations over the weeks or months of a typical sea voyage. Just as challenging, the clock would need to be utterly impervious to the extremities of a
sailing-era sea voyage: the sharp temperature changes, the storm batter-
ings, the salt everywhere. In 1721, no less an authority than Isaac Newton
declared that it would be all but impossible for a solution to the longitude
problem to come from the "Watchmakers."

The "Astronomical" solution, which Newton preferred, was at least as
difficult. Sailors long ago learned to fix latitudes because the apparent path
of the sun was so readily observed and easily measured. The so-called fixed
stars also had a regular apparent path around the earth, but it was far too
slow to be useful. Then there was the moon, which does have a regular
pattern but an extremely complicated one that varies with the seasons,
local variations in the earth's magnetic fields, and much else. In principle,
however, it was possible to precisely chart the moon's position with reference to the fixed stars. If you looked up the moon's position in a moon
chart, it would tell you the exact time that pattern occurred over Greenwich. If you also knew your local time, you could calculate, again in principle, your east-west position.[13]

In principle. But observational instruments were not nearly accurate enough to track anything but the grossest positional changes of the moon with reference to the fixed stars. Even if they had the requisite accuracy, it would be very difficult to take such readings from the deck of a rolling ship. There were also some nasty mathematical complications to correct both your position and the reading from Greenwich to that of an observer at the center of the earth.

Newton, for once, was wrong, and the watchmakers won. A self-taught genius named John Harrison built four candidate clocks over thirty years. They were highly innovative but extremely complex, and there were serious questions about their reproducibility. Nevertheless, all of them met the requirements for the prize, although it took the intervention of the king to secure Harrison his award, in part because of opposition from the astronomers who dominated the awards committee.[*]

In the event, roughly a quarter century after Harrison's death in 1777, watchmakers in both France and England were turning out affordable and reliable pocket-sized marine chronometers that enabled longitudinal calculations satisfactory for most purposes. Only a few of Harrison's innovations were retained. Most chronometer makers chose to stick with traditional forms and mechanisms but learned how to execute them at new orders of precision.

The astronomers got there too, by dint of an informal fifty-year international collaboration to build the necessary tables of lunar motion, along with the development of the sextant, the first instrument with the precision required for useful positional readings on the stars. The great Swiss mathematician Leonard Euler contributed practical methods for correcting the data, but they still took an expert some four hours of calculation.

---

[*] Dava Sobel's best-selling *Longitude* may be too hard on the astronomers. They certainly rallied against Harrison's solutions, and several may have been motivated by personal animus toward Harrison (who was easy to dislike). But one could fairly argue that his clocks were not a true solution, despite their clear qualification under the rules. They were resounding proof that clock-based solutions were *possible*. But each took years to build, and at least through their first three versions, the designs were secret and not obviously reproducible. In short, they were not of much use to the navy, which was the whole point of the exercise.

Their practicality, that is, was hardly better than that of Harrison's strange instruments. But the lunar charts were maintained and promulgated, and the correction math simplified, so by the first decades of the nineteenth century the two approaches were coexisting comfortably, with practical navigators frequently checking one against the other.

It is a remarkable episode. A century elapsed between the 1707 Scilly Isles tragedy and achievement of a stable solution, but it was pursued consistently and diligently over that entire span. Although there was an international flavor to the longitude project throughout, it was driven primarily by the British.

Its lasting stamp on British technology was something of an obsession for absolute mechanical precision, or what British machinists came to call "the truth."

The Quest for Truth

Until well into the nineteenth century, machinists' tools typically lacked graduated measurement markings. In fact it was hard to do. All draftsmen knew how to make accurate divisions by geometric methods, using a compass and square edge, but beyond fairly crude resolutions, any method of marking by hand was apt to be greatly inaccurate. The solution was leverage. Releasing a pin could drop a trip-hammer: a small motion was converted into a much larger one. But leverage could be reversed, and a gross movement converted into a much finer one. And that was the path of truth.[14]

The illustrations on pages 52–53 show various methods of achieving greater precision from imprecise measuring tools, most commonly by exploiting the leverage gained from screws and gears. Assume a tool or workpiece held by a chuck that is moved by a screw with twenty threads to the inch. Rotate the screw one full rotation, and the chuck advances by a twentieth of an inch. A gear train with a net twenty-to-one gear-tooth ratio would accomplish the same result. Such solutions are easy to envision, but they just relocate the problem—from making accurate measurements to making accurate screw threads and gear teeth. Clockmakers had small machines for cutting gear teeth early in the eighteenth century, but they weren't especially precise. Individual prodigies like John Harrison could work marvels of precision by hand, but that was not a solution either. The challenge was to embed the required level of precision in machinery that could make other machines, so those machines could pass on their precision to generations of new tools and instruments. That took the better part of a hundred years.

Why did it take so long? Because as a practical matter, it is not possible to make an accurate screw thread without an accurate screw-cutting lathe, which is impossible to make without tools with accurate screw threads. In other words, accuracy could be achieved only by a process of successive approximation. And that is a tedious path, with many byways, involving better metals, better bearings, even better magnifying lenses. The work took place primarily in England because naval and other high-end engineering applications had created a market for high-precision scientific instruments for astronomy, surveying, and a host of industrial uses. Brilliant scientists in other countries were not as successful. For example, a French nobleman, the Duc de Chaulnes, made several important advances in gear-cutting machinery, but he was working with his own money and lacked the thick network of machine users, designers, and craftsmen that existed in England.

Jesse Ramsden usually gets credit for inventing the first industrial-scale dividing engine. It didn't cut the gear teeth but marked their placement, which was the essential task. "Inventing," in this context, is not quite the right word, for all such machines were developments of others' work. Several important features of the Ramsden dividing engine, like screw-based motion controls, were inspired by predecessors like de Chaulnes, as Ramsden freely acknowledged. One of his best-known instruments representing "the best design of the time"[15] (from the late 1780s) was a large theodolite, or surveying telescope, which fixes locations by taking the intersection of horizontal and vertical circles. Measurements were read from verniers (see illustration) and viewed through microscopes. Ramsden built two of the

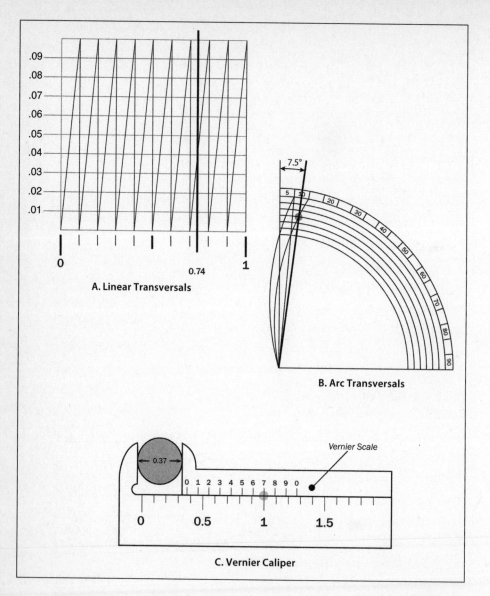

A. Linear Transversals

B. Arc Transversals

C. Vernier Caliper

A. Astronomer Tycho Brahe (1546–1601) popularized the use of linear transversals to achieve greater precision. If the marks on the two axes are at the limits of the day's technology for accurate gradation, simply making the grid and drawing the transversals as shown improves the accuracy by a factor of ten. The heavy vertical line intersects at the .04 horizontal mark. **B.** By the eighteenth century astronomers learned to improve astral measurements with arc transversals. The numbered ring is marked in 5-degree intervals. The six inner concentrics subdivide to an accuracy of 50 minutes. The right-hand heavy line from the origin intersects at the 150-minute mark, so the angle measures 5 degrees plus 150 minutes = 7.5 degrees. **C.** The Vernier Caliper uses a second sliding rule to mark out very small distances. In the example, the caliper marking is beyond the .30 position on the fixed scale. The additional distance is read from the vernier scale at the point where it lines up *most closely* with a marking on the fixed scale, as shown. (Humans are very good at recognizing when two moving lines line up—"vernier acuity.")

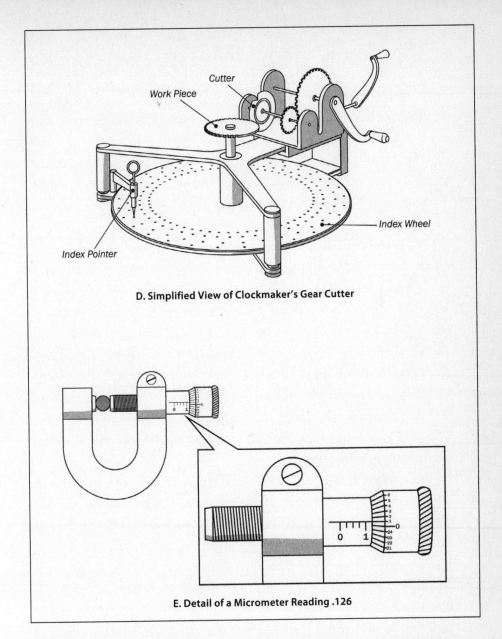

D. Simplified View of Clockmaker's Gear Cutter

Cutter

Work Piece

Index Wheel

Index Pointer

E. Detail of a Micrometer Reading .126

D. Using geometric methods, an artisan could mark reasonably-accurate divisions on a large disc, and then capture those same proportions on a much smaller workpiece, as shown. Note that the index wheel includes several choices of tooth arrangement and that the index pointer fixes the index wheel and the workpiece in position for each cut. **E.** A pocket-sized thousandth of an inch micrometer first appeared in the catalog of the Providence firm of Brown and Sharpe in 1877, and marked a high point of convenient precision in the nineteenth century. The micrometers are still in wide use. The numbered divisions on the barrel signify tenths (0.1) of an inch. Each smaller division is a fortieth (0.025) of an inch, while each small numbered marking on the handle is a thousandth (0.001) of inch. In the illustration the readout on the barrel is 0.125 inches, plus an additional .001 on the handle = 0.126 inches.

instruments, which were used for a complete survey of Great Britain. At a distance of ten miles, the instrument was accurate to one arc second, or about three inches.

The great figure in screw threads was Henry Maudslay, one of the greatest machinists of all time. Although he ran a large establishment in his later years, he was at heart a shop-floor machinist. He also appears to be have been a man of immense calm and good humor, certainly comfortably fat in his later years. His workers adored him, almost as much as they admired his technical skills. One recounted fondly, "It was a pleasure to see him handle a tool of any kind, but he was quite splendid with an eighteen-inch file."[16] Maudslay's permanent contribution was to stabilize machining at very high levels of precision, hardly surpassed to the present day.

When Maudslay began his career, screw threads were in a state of disarray with respect to pitch (thread count), shape, angle, and uniformity, and they became his pet project. While he did not invent the modern screw-cutting lathe—Ramsden anticipated much of his work—his first versions achieved such a high pitch of perfection that they became the standard for all such instruments.

In a traditional lathe, the worker held the cutting tool against the rotating workpiece. In the Maudslay screw-cutting lathe, first produced between 1797 and 1800, before he was thirty, the workpiece was positioned on a slide by a long lead screw, the cutting depth of the tool was set by a screw-driven micrometer, and a gear-set controlled the thread count of the new screw by varying the speed of the workpiece rotation relative to its lateral motion on the slide. Different gear settings allowed reliable production of a variety of thread pitches. The gearing on one early machine accommodated twenty-eight different thread pitches. One Maudslay-produced screw, created for a dividing engine to be used in the production of large astronomical instruments, was five feet long and two inches in diameter, with 50 threads per inch, or 3,000 threads in all; it came with a foot-long nut with 600 threads. No one before Maudslay could have produced such an instrument.

Maudslay's obsession with accuracy pervaded every aspect of his machinery, since vibrations, misalignments, or slightly loose fittings make a mockery of ultraprecise tool settings. Maudslay's constructions set new standards for solidity, stability, and perfection with respect to planes, angles, and uniformity of motion. He built a bench micrometer to measure deviances of a workpiece from a pattern to a ten-thousandth of an inch. He called it the "Lord Chancellor," the final arbiter of any dispute.

Maudslay also insisted on absolutely flat, smooth planes on every surface, and every machinist in his shop was equipped with a plate that met that standard. His famous protégé, James Nasmyth, wrote that they were used to test "the surfaces of slide valves, or wherever absolute true plane surfaces were essential to the attainment of the best results." When absolutely true surfaces were placed on each other, Nasmyth went on, they "would float upon the thin stratum of air between them until dislodged. . . . When they adhered closely to each other they could only be separated by sliding each off each."[17]

The method of creating perfect planes was to start with three plates machined as perfectly flat as they could be. One plate, Plate A, was then coated with a colored powder, and Plate B placed precisely on it. When the two plates were separated, the color marks on B would mark its high spots relative to A. B was then scraped by a very hard hand scraper (both machine and hand grinding were far too coarse) to remove the anomalies. The process was then reversed—coloring B and scraping the discrepancies from A—and repeated as often as necessary until each plate color-matched across its entire surface. But a perfect match between two plates did not yet prove a perfect plane, because they might embody complementary deviances. Therefore the whole process was repeated twice more, first matching A to C and then C to B, at which point, one could be confident that the three approached "absolute truth."

With some ingenuity, the method may be extended to produce perfect right angles and perfectly parallel rectangular bars with perfectly aligned plane ends. (Hint: each of those processes requires *four* plates and *two* bars.) A nineteenth-century textbook warns merely that "the only thing to be dreaded is the discovery of a hollow portion, which may compel a repetition of the procedure from the commencement."[18]

Maudslay protégés dominated the British tool industry for decades. Nasmyth invented the steam hammer in 1838. It operated on the same principle as a drop hammer: a giant hammerhead fell on a forging target. The difference was that the steam hammer's blow was piston-driven for an even more powerful impact. Nasmyth's hammer weighed two and a half tons but was under such precise control that it could rattle a whole factory or break an egg in a wine glass without disturbing the glass.[19]

Of all the Maudslay disciples, the greatest may have been Sir Joseph Whitworth, who unified British screw designs under the "Whitworth standard," specifying radii, pitches, angles, and depths that for many years served as nearly a world standard. He also carried the quest for absolute mechanical precision about as far as it could go before the age of electronics.

The Millionth-of-an-Inch Measuring Machine

Sir Joseph's portrait shows him long-faced, heavy-lidded, and skeptical. His father was a minister and schoolmaster, so he was better educated than most craftsmen and did not easily tolerate fools. Pompously ignorant officialdom was among his particular bêtes noires. As a leading machinery and metals fabricator, Whitworth was necessarily a force in armament procurement. A rigorous experimenter and prolific inventor, he produced a great flood of weapons designs and experimental new weapons, which were routinely rejected by the military authorities, although a number were later quietly adopted. Those misadventures are documented in a coldly sarcastic little book he published in 1873, when he was seventy.[20]

Whitworth was prompted to develop his measuring machine by the mid-century bumblings of a parliamentary Committee on Standards, which labored for eleven years to create a bar equal in length to a standard yard. The stumbling blocks lay in the physics of ordinary materials at microscopic dimensions. Tiny increases in ambient temperatures changed the length of a bar, the minutest forces caused nearly undetectable sags or flexes, and so forth.

But the committee painstakingly worked its way through all such obstacles to the point where the stage was set for the climactic measurements. Ambient temperature was controlled by a thermometer accurate to within $1/100°F$. The bar itself was suspended in a tub of mercury to equalize ambient pressures, while the tub was shielded within a tank of water to muffle the slightest external disturbances. The readings were taken by microscopes on platforms at each end of the suspended bar.[21]

There was no difficulty in producing an initial standard bar—a yard, after all, was whatever the bar said it was. The challenge was to produce *additional* bars of exactly the same length—enough to be distributed among the universities and science establishments to serve as the reference point for high-precision undertakings of all kinds. The Royal Astronomical Society, an unofficial kibitzer in chief, expected that standard bars should be executed in the primary metal types—"copper, brass, cast-iron, Low-Moor iron, Swedish iron and cast steel."[22]

With the elaborate arrangements all in place, the great day finally came. The committee duly selected one bar, "bronze 28," as the standard, and proceeded to measure six other bars against it. That there were differences was no surprise: everyone agreed that "bronze 19" was not exactly the same length as bronze 28. The surprise was that committee members differed on whether it was longer or shorter, although the observations had been made sequentially under completely identical conditions. Disconcerted, the committee recruited volunteer observers, all men with professional backgrounds in related fields. Some 200,000 measurements later, the committee reluctantly concluded that no consensus could be reached on any of the bars. The differences, moreover, were not random: some individuals were consistently on the short side, others consistently on the long.

Whitworth's reaction was a jeering *of course!* The measurements were taken by comparing the position of a cross-hair in the microscope with a tiny etched gradation on the bar. But the crosshair, a mere spider-silk to the naked eye, was magnified to a thick, fuzzy, line that, in the blurring vision of a committeeman, danced from one side to the other of an equally gross and irregular gradation line. The Astronomical Society put the best face on it, remarking that the uncertainties were "not likely to affect any useful observation" and that "a limit seems to be shown which, in any *optical measures*, no amount of observation in our current state of knowledge can overpass."[23]

Whitworth thought it all surpassing idiocy. The committee's measurements seemed to randomize at resolutions of about 1/30,000 of an inch. His own workshops frequently worked at tolerances of 1/50,000 of an inch, and most experienced machinists could accurately distinguish differences of 1/10,000 of an inch by feel.* Where the committee had gone astray, he argued in multiple venues, was in attempting visual assessments of length as opposed to merely determining the *difference* between two bars, which could be done mechanically with great precision. Given any standard bar with perfect plane ends, Whitworth claimed, he could determine the difference between it and any other like it at resolutions of a millionth of an inch, which he then proceeded to demonstrate. (Maudslay's micrometer measured to the ten-thousandth of an inch, a hundred times larger.)

The measuring machine Whitworth constructed to fulfill his boast comprised two parallel steel bars resting on a heavy cast-iron stand—the bars, the stand, and their respective borings all corrected to near-absolute truth. The working portion of the machine was a grip made by two opposed, perfectly trued small circular plugs. One of the plugs was driven by a leadscrew with a pitch of 20 threads to the inch; that screw was driven by a wheel with 200 teeth; that wheel in turn was driven by a "division wheel" with 250 marked divisions: $250 \times 200 \times 20 = 1,000,000$. Turning the division wheel by one notch advanced or withdrew the plug by 1/1,000,000 of an inch. Equivalently, a 1/1,000,000 of an inch movement in the lead screw generated a visible movement of about .04 inches in the division wheel, a 40,000:1 magnification.

The measuring procedure was straightforward. You fixed the standard bar in the grip with a precisely crafted "feeling piece," an extremely thin

---

* That same value is reported in American and British machining texts from both the nineteenth and twentieth centuries.

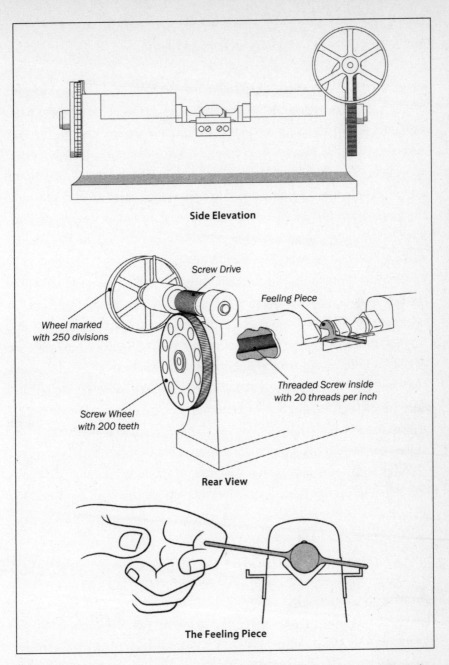

Side Elevation

Screw Drive

Feeling Piece

Wheel marked
with 250 divisions

Threaded Screw inside
with 20 threads per inch

Screw Wheel
with 200 teeth

Rear View

The Feeling Piece

Whitworth's famous measuring machine was designed to measure the *difference* between two apparently identical objects to the millionth of an inch. It takes 200 turns of the 250-division "division wheel" to turn both the 200-tooth rear wheel and the interior lead screw one full turn. Twenty full turns of the lead screw will advance the plug by a full inch—250 × 200 × 20 = 1,000,000. The bottom drawing shows the placement of the "feeling piece," a very thin sliver of metal with the shape as shown. The experimenter placed the first piece in the machine with the feeling piece, then gently relaxed the pressure until the feeling piece moved, and noted that place on the division wheel. He repeated the procedure for the second piece and compared the two markings.

sliver of steel. Whitworth stipulated a detailed protocol for inserting the feeling piece. You then slowly turned the division wheel, relaxing the pressure until the feeling piece moved, and you noted the mark on the division wheel. Repeat the process with a second bar, and the same feeling piece would expose any differences in length to a resolution of 1/1,000,000 of an inch. There was no ambiguity: when the feeling piece moved, you took the measurement and compared it to the same measurement for the standard bar. Whitworth's measuring machine was awarded the gold medal at the Great Crystal Palace Exhibition of 1851.*

The Whitworth measuring machine was a pinnacle of nineteenth-century British precision engineering: a line of development rooted in the urgent search for precision in chronometers and astronomical apparatus, one that ran through the nearly perfect machine tools turned out by Henry Maudslay and the exquisite precision of the Nasmyth steam hammer. But the somewhat defensive comment by the Royal Astronomical Society that such precision was "not likely to affect any useful observation" was true, at least in a machine setting. Even today, ultraprecision computerized machine tools work at precisions of a few hundred thousandths of an inch.

Whitworth's measuring machine still pales beside the most audacious grasp at ultraprecise complexity. The ne plus ultra of regal overreaching was Charles Babbage's calculating engines.

Charles Babbage

If there were a hall of fame of intelligent people, Charles Babbage (1791–1871) would surely have his own plaque. Born into a well-to-do family, he spent most of his career in academia and for a dozen years held the Lucasian Chair of Mathematics at Cambridge University, a post graced by luminaries from Isaac Newton through Stephen Hawking.[24]

---

* The machine is of a class of instruments called "comparators," meaning that they measure only the differences between objects rather than the dimensions of the objects. Maudslay's micrometer was of the same type. The British were quite late to shift to dimensional measuring, leaving that development primarily to the Americans. The Providence firm of Brown & Sharpe was the world leader in dimensional measuring in the second half of the century.

In Babbage's day, all calculation-intensive sciences like astronomy were dependent on thick volumes of standard tables—logarithms, sines, and other functions—each incorporating decades of laborious construction. As a newly minted mathematician, Babbage realized that even the best tables were riddled with errors. By comparing entries in different editions, it was clear that the primary problem lay in transcription and typesetting, not the original calculations. He therefore conceived of a machine, the Difference Engine,* to infallibly compute and print such tables.

By 1822, Babbage had constructed a mechanical calculator that very rapidly executed standard arithmetic operations up to eight figures. He demonstrated it at the Treasury, and proposed that the government finance a much larger machine that would calculate and print any regularly sequenced table. With the Royal Society's backing, the following year, the Treasury provided a grant of £1,500. By his own account, Babbage undertook to complete the project "in two, or at most three, years," with a commitment of his own funds of £1,500–£2,500.[25]

To execute the new machine, Babbage contracted with Joseph Clement, another former protégé of Maudslay. Clement is best-known for his large-scale metal planing machine, built sometime before 1832. The machine, with a planing bed that could hold work up to six feet square, moved on rollers so precise that "if you put a piece of paper under one of the rollers, it would stop all the rest." For more than a decade, there was no other planer of its size in the world, so Clement, who charged by the square foot, made an excellent living keeping it operating almost around the clock. His partially completed Difference Engine has been called "the most refined and intricate piece of mechanism constructed up to that time."[26] Whitworth was one of the journeyman machinists employed by Clement on the engine.

---

* The name came from Babbage's adoption of a subtraction algorithm for computing tables. For example the sequence of squares 1, 4, 9, 16, 25 shows first-order differences of 3, 5, 7, 9, which in turn have a constant second-order difference of 2. To compute the square of 6, the engine would take the previous first-order difference (25−16 = 9) and add the constant: 25 + 9 + 2 = 36; 7^2 then is 36 + 11 + 2 = 49. Higher order exponents required finding higher-order differences before arriving at the constant.

Babbage had seriously underestimated the work involved and by 1827 had expended not only the grant amount, but beyond the estimated limit of his own funds. His version of what ensued shows him as a brilliant but almost comically contentious man. He duly applied for further assistance, but as a matter of right, on the grounds that the government had committed to see the project through, which seems a strained interpretation of the record.* But he was backed by powerful friends and the Royal Society. Even the Duke of Wellington, then prime minister, became personally involved. Another £1,500 was awarded in early 1829, and yet another £3,000 later that same year, which Babbage at first refused to accept absent a firm open-ended financial commitment.[27]

Babbage had Clement construct a working segment of the Difference Engine in 1832 that, impressively, could produce a portion of the promised tables, and the government had already financed the construction of a small fireproof building to house it. By then, however, Babbage and Clement were constantly clashing over finances, and in 1833, Clement finally resigned, taking his machinery.

Amid the confusion, Babbage shifted his focus to an entirely new idea, which he called the "Analytical Engine." It was nothing less than a prototype of the modern computer executed with purely mechanical parts. Delighted and inspired by the concept, Babbage worked on it alone for several years before admitting to the government that he was making a completely new start. Not surprisingly, ministers threw up their hands. Stubbornly, Babbage worked on the Analytical Engine for the next decade, using his own dwindling resources. To stretch his finances, he retired to a modest house with his own workshop and forge and a few assistants.

In about 1843, apparently realizing that the government was never going to finance his Analytical Engine, Babbage decided on a different

---

* The original award notice from the Exchequer said that the grant was "to enable Mr. Babbage to bring his invention to perfection, in the manner recommended." By "the manner recommended," the Exchequer presumably meant Babbage's own estimate of time and cost, while Babbage insisted the phrase was an open-ended commitment to fund development until the engine reached his recommended level of perfection.

strategy: redesigning his original Difference Engine to take advantage of the new streamlined architecture of the Analytical Engine. He began to work on a "Difference Engine No. 2," in 1846, producing a completely executed set of plans by 1849. This was by far the most practicable of his inventions: a limited-purpose Analytical Engine optimized to execute the mathematical tables proposed for the first Difference Engine. The proposed apparatus would have been much more efficient than the original, with only a third as many parts. Still, since the final product would have consisted of a wall of some 8,000 whirling parts, it would have been a substantial challenge.

To Babbage's shock and disappointment, the new government, which had come to office on an austerity platform, would not even entertain the idea of another prolonged engagement with Babbage: "Mr. Babbage's projects appear to be so indefinitely expensive, the ultimate success so problematical, and the ultimate expenditure so large and so utterly incapable of being calculated, that the government would not be justified in taking upon itself any further liability."[28] For Babbage, the cold rejection of his new plan was a serious blow that embittered much of his later life. He continued to produce books and articles on an array of subjects, wistfully tinkering with the design of the analytical engine until his death in 1871.

But the design is still an intellectual monument. Babbage's inspiration was from the Jacquard loom, which used punch cards to signify any pattern of threads whatsoever. Experts rendered patterns in sequences of punch cards. The textile mill then created additional sequences of cards to specify the thread colors for the pattern.

The Analytical Engine similarly had two main components, the mill and the store. A set of operation cards, similar to IBM punch cards, defined the sequence of operations to be performed by the mill, while a second set of variable cards summoned the sequence of data to be manipulated. Other sets of cards loaded the variables and constants into the store and defined where the results of an operation were to be stored. Output could either be printed or used to impress casts for printer's type.

The machine's registers—a small brass wheel for each digit—would accommodate fifty-digit numbers, which Babbage thought sufficient for science, along with 1,000 stored constants. Sequences of cards were placed in a card reader and called on in the proper order, and all standard operations would be maintained in libraries of cards. (Babbage also worked out a provision for an unlimited number of if-then, "looped" instructions.) Gear layouts and speeds were such that the engine should have been able to perform about sixty operations a minute.[29]

Babbage topped it off with another invention, his "Mechanical Notation"—a language for specifying rigorously any machine whatsoever (or, in Babbage's mind, almost anything at all, including physiology, factory organization, or war planning).[30] It is a detailed coding system for machine parts, actions, and motions that, as he explained to the Royal Society in 1826, reflected the actual machine with such precision "that at any moment of time in the course of the cycle of operations of any machine, we may know the state of motion or rest of any particular part."[31]

Babbage told the Society that he had been compelled to develop the notation as he grappled with the complex gear sequences of the Difference Engine. Once a machine was completely rendered in notation, one could readily see whether the design would work or not, and how to simplify and improve it, without the expense of building a model. Once he had described the Difference Engine in notation, Babbage claimed, he could spot design issues much faster than the artisans. The Society presentation was illustrated by a notational description of an eight-day clock. Comprising four oversized pages of dense columns of cryptic markings, it is a beautiful and astonishing production, rather like a Japanese archival scroll. The drawings, notebooks, and other documentation for the nearly completed design of the Analytical Engine comprise nearly 7,000 pages, of which 2,200 are purely notation.[32]

Babbage thought the notation was "one of the most important contributions I have made to human knowledge. It has placed the construction of machinery in the ranks of demonstrative science. The day will arrive when no school of mechanical drawing will be thought complete without teaching it."[33] Once again, however, Babbage was pointing directly to developments still far in the future. It was only with the onset of the postwar Computer Age that technologists began to execute their chip and other hardware designs in software so they could be tested and exercised without the expense of building physical components.

And It Worked

The tantalizing historical question for Babbage admirers was always whether his machines would actually have worked. That was finally answered by an extraordinary project at the London Science Museum that built a working model of the Difference Engine No. 2 (DE2 hereafter). And yes, it actually worked.

The DE2 was the redesigned Difference Engine No. 1 using the new architecture Babbage had created for his Analytical Engine. It was the smallest of Babbage's engines and the only one with a completed design, which happened to be stored, along with its Mechanical Notation, in the museum's archives. Alan Bromley, a computer scientist at the University of Sydney, made a study of the plans over a number of years and convinced himself, and then the museum staff and directors, that it was feasible to build and would probably work as Babbage claimed.[34]

The project got underway in 1985, under the direction of Doron Swade, then the Science Museum's head of collections and an expert on Babbage and the history of computing, working on a tight six-year schedule, timed to the Babbage bicentennial in 1991. The final construct was seven feet high, eleven feet across, and eighteen inches deep. It had eight tall columns, each with thirty-one figure wheels, all of it operated by a hand crank. A few drawings had to be reconstructed, and Babbage's designs also included a small number of mistakes—this was, after all, a purely paper design, with no testing of individual modules—but they were usually obvious and readily fixed without violating the integrity of the design.

Much more impressive are the mistakes Babbage didn't make. For example, one of Swade's engineers looked at the design and said it would be impossible to run from a hand crank—the combined resistance from 4,000 gears meshing was just too great. The team went ahead anyway, and of

A modern realization of Charles Babbage's Difference Engine No. 2, a distant prototype for the modern computer. It was constructed at the London Science Museum over a six-year period, and completed in time for the Babbage centennial in 1991. The vertical columns mostly contain brass wheels—some 4,000 in total—each of which represents a digit or part of an action. The construction proved that Babbage's paper designs worked the way he said they would. The modern reconstruction used current machine-tool and dimensioning technology. Whether the machine could have been built with 1830s technology is still an open question.

course the engineer was proved right. Then they noticed a mysterious spring mechanism that Babbage had enclosed within the engine frame. Since no one knew its function, it had not yet been installed. And, yes, the purpose of the spring arrangement was to ease the frictional pressures so the hand crank worked as envisaged—an altogether astonishing degree of foresight for a paper design.

Some other difficulties, especially in the assembly of the machine, are instructive. Swade's words:

When parts were first offered up to the machine they were rarely in the correct orientation, and had to be adjusted by trial and error so that their motions harmonised with those of the rest of the mechanism. This is a tentative and exploratory process, and Babbage gives no clues to how the parts are to be oriented correctly. He blithely shows gears and levers fitted in their correct positions and fixed permanently on their shafts by pins driven through both parts locking them to each other immovably. There is no indication of how the correct rotational position of the gear is to be found before it is finally fixed. So the timing of hundreds of parts had to be determined by meticulous trial and error.[35]

The team did not quite make their schedule. They had preannounced a test case, computing a table of the digits 1 through 80 raised to the seventh power. The machine readily made the calculations but repeatedly failed to get through the entire list before something jammed. Since the test case had been preannounced, they feared that their miss would make the whole project look like a failure. After shamefacedly explaining their shortfall at a crowded press conference, they started the engine and discovered, happily, that no one cared about their test. Swade writes that the crank handle was turned, and "the rhythmic clanking and the shifting array of bronze wheels begins. The helical carry mechanisms perform their rippling dance. There are murmurs as the motions enthral and seduce. The visual spectacle of the engine works its magic. As a static exhibit, the engine is a superb piece of engineering sculpture. As a working machine, even partially working, it is arresting. . . . The Engine has cast its spell, and later that day the coverage is ungrudgingly triumphalist."[36] Within some weeks, the DE2 was flawlessly executing the test exercise over and over again. All in all, the exercise was a stupendous success and a classic example of the contributions to history and science of the best science museums.

The experience may also suggest that the various authorities who declined to provide Babbage the open-ended support he had demanded made the right decision. In ten years of off-and-on work on the DE1, Clement completed some 12,000 gears, about half the required total. Swade and his subcontractors produced 4,000 such parts in just six months using a large number of subcontractors in pattern making, gear cutting, case hardening, and many other subtrades. Gears were cut and parts were shaped with CNC (computerized numerical control) machines that can machine hundreds or thousands of parts to precise specifications with great consistency. At the level of precision that Clement was working to—2/1,000 of an inch, according to Swade's sample—it would have been very difficult for him to replicate the museum team's accomplishment. In 1830s the technology of precise working drawings and reliable dimensioning tools was still in its infancy. Identical parts were made so by laboriously fitting them to other parts. Drift away from uniformity would have been hard to avoid. And recall the problems Swade's team had in placing and orienting all the different parts, despite the high precision of CNC machining. It would have been much harder in Babbage's day. Even with the best of will and resources, it is easy to imagine the project collapsing in ignominious failure with finger-pointing and rancor on all sides.*

An intellectual achievement as monumental as the Analytical Engine is its own justification, and Babbage deserves a high place in history for it. But like Whitworth's millionth-of-an-inch measuring machine, it was another beautiful British dead end. Swade notes that Babbage never considered the cost-benefit aspect of his great projects, assuming that government officials would be as drawn as he was to "ingenuity, intricacy, mastery of mechanism, and the seductive appeal of control over number."[37]

Babbage was undoubtedly at the extreme end of other-worldliness, but he had a large and responsive audience. A book he published in 1833, *On the Economy of Machinery and Manufacturing*,[38] has an arid, academic tone; the first third is an exhaustive classification of machines as those for "Accumulating Power," "Regulating Power," "Extending the Time of Action

---

* Twenty years later, Swade is heading another team to attempt to build the Analytical Engine (AE), a much more complex challenge. Since the working drawings are not complete, they will have to reconstruct them from Babbage's "Mechanical Notation," which team members can read fluently. Tentatively, the project will be completed in distinct stages—completing the drawings, creating a virtual AE entirely in software, and finally constructing the engine itself. Indeed, if they actually succeed in building just the virtual AE, it would answer all of the remaining questions of whether Babbage actually created a workable computer design.

of Forces," and much else in that vein. Yet the first printing of 3,000 copies was sold out within a few weeks, and there were two more editions the next year. (The first printing of Charles Dickens's *A Christmas Carol*, deemed "an immediate success with the public," sold 6,000 copies.)

Babbage opens his book with a paean that played directly into the growing British self-satisfaction with their industrial triumphs:

> There exists, perhaps, no single circumstance that distinguishes our country more remarkably from all others, than the vast extent and perfection to which we have carried the contrivance of tools and machines for forming those conveniences of which so large a quantity is consumed by almost every class of the community. . . . If we look around at the rooms we inhabit, or through those storehouses of every convenience, of every luxury that man can desire, which deck the crowded streets of our larger cities, we shall find . . . in the art of making even the most insignificant of them, processes calculated to excite our imagination by their simplicity, or to rivet our attention by their unlooked-for results.

The book positioned him as a thought leader in achieving a new synthesis of traditional culture and manufacturing. Instead of merely lamenting Blake's "dark Satanic mills," thinkers like Carlyle extolled the coming of an "organic society" that integrated the "Dynamical" and "Mechanical" aspects of human nature.[39] Babbage plays directly to that sentiment, emphasizing the utilitarian beauty of machines and the elegant objects of art—the machined rosettes, lithographs, and engravings—that they can produce, or reproduce, for the masses.

Great Britain's mid-century Crystal Palace Exhibition (see Chapter 7) was organized on much the same principle: it celebrated not only the nation's technical preeminence but also the new intellectual order it signified. The exhibition's royal patron, Prince Albert, organized a yearlong lecture series to explore precisely that theme: that industrial capitalism was allowing "man to approach a more complete fulfillment of that great and sacred mission which he has to perform in this world." (There can be no doubt that by "man" he meant Anglo-Saxons.) The inaugural lecture was delivered by the master of Trinity College, William Whewell, who eulogized "the Machinery mighty as the thunderbolt to rend the oak, or light as the breath of air that carries the flower-dust to its appointed place."[40]

Self-satisfaction is a dangerous sentiment for any competitor but may be understandable in the British case, since with Napoleon vanquished, there were no obvious threats on the horizon. Yet the country's industrial revolution was advanced enough that both proprietors and workers were deeply invested in established methods. Scar tissue still remained from the fierce Luddite attacks against textile mills in the first years of the century, and the severely repressive response of the government. With the production machinery seemingly working well enough, it was seductively easy to ignore British industrial rigidities and concentrate instead on attractive challenges, like pushing out the boundaries of precision or defining a new aesthetic for an industrial age.

The Americans had no such inclinations, and since they were starting over, they faced almost no entrenched interests. Ironically, what became an American specialty, the extension of the textile-mill model of mechanized mass production to almost every major industry, was also pioneered in Great Britain, but the innovation was stillborn. The story requires winding the camera back to a critical juncture in the Napoleonic wars.

The Portsmouth Block-Making Factory

The prototype for all plants engaged in mass production of heavy industrial goods by self-acting machinery is the famous British ship-block factory at Portsmouth. It was the creation of the young Henry Maudslay and two other extraordinary men, Samuel Bentham and Marc Isambard Brunel, and was in full operation the first years of the century.[41]

Bentham, the younger brother of the utilitarian philosopher Jeremy, was a naval architect, an inventor, and something of an adventurer. He traveled to Russia as a young man to examine mining and engineering works, was a social hit at the Russian court, fell in love with a young noblewoman, and became the close friend of the Most Serene Prince Grigory

Alexandrovich Potemkin, himself a special favorite of Catherine the Great. Bentham created Western-style factories on Potemkin's estate, built a fleet of warships, distinguished himself in Russia's sea battles against the Turks, and may have been the first to use shells in naval artillery. On his return to England, his top-drawer connections helped secure him an appointment as inspector general of the navy. Among his many talents, he was an inventor with strong ideas about mechanizing the shipyards.

Brunel, a native of France, was a royalist naval officer forced to flee the avenging angels of the French Revolution. Landing in America, he worked for a half-dozen years designing canals and harbor fortifications, building a cannon foundry, and serving as chief engineer of New York City. Brunel was also a machinery inventor who filed many patents over his lifetime. At dinner at Alexander Hamilton's home, a guest held forth on Great Britain's struggle to produce ship blocks—a problem that Brunel was convinced he knew how to solve. Not yet thirty, he embarked for London, the home of his fiancée, a well-connected young Englishwoman, whom he had courted during his flight from France. He duly married on his return and became one of London's leading engineers, most famous for his pedestrian tunnel under the Thames at Rotherhite. (It took more than twenty years to complete and nearly brought him to ruin.)

Ship blocks—the enclosed pulleys that managed the miles of rope on a warship—were made of solid blocks of wood, with slots, or mortises, for one to four sheaves, or rotating pulleys. The shells were cut from logs of elm, while the sheaves were made of imported lignum vitae, a very hard and durable wood. The sheaves turned on pins made of either lignum vitae or iron, encased in friction-reducing brass bushings, or coaks. Major warships needed somewhere between 1,000 and 1,400 ship blocks, ranging in size from single-sheaved blocks a few inches long to four-sheaved blocks standing nearly four feet high. Badly made blocks could snag rigging, slow maneuvers, and endanger a ship. A single family had enjoyed an effective monopoly over naval ship-block making for nearly fifty years. Their factories were partially mechanized, but Bentham thought them excessively expensive; he had himself developed designs for more efficient machine production.

Brunel arrived in England with fairly complete drawings for four block-making machines and with a working model of at least one of them. He first met with the contractors, who had little interest in his plans, and then secured an appointment with Bentham. Before the meeting, he contracted for two more working models, fortuitously with Maudslay, who was only recently set up in his own shop. (A French acquaintance in London regularly strolled by Maudslay's shop and told Brunel of the beauty of the display pieces in the window.) Brunel was worried about premature disclosure and at their first meeting refused to tell Maudslay the purpose of his designs. But at the second meeting, Maudslay said, "Ah! Now I see what you are thinking of; you want machinery for making blocks!"[42]

The Bentham-Brunel meeting, when it took place sometime in mid-1801, was a vendor's dream. Bentham examined the drawings and the models, generously pronounced them superior to his own, and arranged an early demonstration before the naval board. A contract was awarded in 1802, and Brunel was appointed manager of a new works to be erected at Portsmouth. Maudslay began delivering machines before the end of the year. The new plant was in full production and the old contractors were out of business before the end of 1805. There were two production streams, one for the blocks and one for the sheaves. The metal pins and coaks continued to be produced by traditional methods.

The block production line started with a phalanx of saws of different sizes to cut elm logs into square blocks, followed by a succession of boring, chiseling, sawing, and shaping machines to place and cut the mortises and pin channels, trim and shape the blocks, and cut the channels for the straps that secured them in the rigging.

The sheave line began with specialty crown saws, which looked like a king's crown lying on its side, with a saw size for each type of sheave. A succession of three machines centered and cut the coak holes in the rough-sawn sheaves, placed and riveted the coaks, and reamed the coak holes into true cylinders. Finally, the sheaves were turned in a lathe that trimmed the face and edges to flat surfaces, and cut the pulley grooves for ropes.

There were just two manual processes in the woodworking: sand-finishing the blocks and the final assembly of the shells and sheavings. The total of all machines, including the saws, was about forty-five.

The machines themselves were classic Maudslay: precision slide rests, screw drives, and gear changers resting in a heavy cast-iron base. Cutting tools were of the best tool steel, and almost all of the machines were self-acting. When a mortise was cut through, for instance, an automatic stop triggered a new sequence to reposition the tool and move the block to the next cut. Only the facing machine required the presence of a skilled turner.

The factory was in full operation for more than fifty years, and no machine was ever replaced. A brochure from 1854 reports that "the only noise arises from the instruments actually in contact with work under execution, and none from the working of the machinery," but that's the way all Maudslay machines worked.[43] The plant phased down as the age of iron and steel warships dawned, and the machines were gradually moved to museums, although some of the original machines ran for up to 145 years.

The industrial historian Carolyn Cooper has matched machine descriptions to the still-extant belting shafts and pulleys and still-visible floor markings in the factory, and mined old documents and Brunel's notes and records to reconstruct the factory's output, layout, and processing flows.

The flow process was clearly thought through with care—which was unusual in that period, even in the much-touted American armories. Work in process was moved from station to station in wheeled bins. Output was high: the large mortise chisels ran at a hundred strokes per minute, and the blocks were advanced ¼ of an inch at each stroke. One man could bore and mortise 500 6-inch or 120 16-inch single-sheaved blocks in eleven and a half hours—that's two operations in about a minute and a half for the smaller blocks, and in less than six minutes for the larger ones. A figure widely quoted from Brunel's biographer, however, that 110 men had been replaced with only 10, should probably be taken with a grain of salt.[*]

---

[*] The biography is an admiring memoir published in 1862, almost sixty years after the plant opened, so it is unlikely that the author had accurate information on previous contractor manning levels. At the plant's volumes, the sheer physical work of loading logs and moving parts from station to station probably required more than ten men, not even including machine tenders.

The best estimate for the cost savings comes from the payment to Brunel, which by contract was to be equal to the savings realized in the first year after the plant achieved full operations—a very Benthamite arrangement, for brother Jeremy had long advocated for government performance contracting. The actual payment award was £17,000, based on 1808 production of 130,000 blocks at a cost of £50,000, which suggests a 25 percent savings (17,000/[17,000 + 50,000]). That tracks well with a "generally accepted," mid-nineteenth-century estimate reported by Cooper that the plant paid for itself within four years.[44] All in all, the venture must be considered a superb success, especially since the savings kept rolling in for many years after the investment was fully recovered.

Bentham and Brunel, of course, were extremely proud of their plant, and the government was delighted for once to crow about its rigorous cost management. But as a torchlight pointing toward new directions in manufacturing, the Portsmouth plant utterly fizzled. The British trumpeted its virtues, tourists oohed and aahed their way through, but it made no impact on the style and methods of British industry. Cooper has unearthed possible half-hearted imitations here and there, but nothing important or lasting.

So we see the British intellectualizing their industrial accomplishments, complacent with their methods and processes, and through most of the nineteenth century oblivious to the empirical and often original approaches of the Americans.

That may be the fate of winners, for Americans made the same mistakes a century later. In the 1950s and 1960s, executive self-celebration was assiduously watered by business school professors, who had begun churning out students with master's degrees in business administration, trained mostly in blackboard-compatible topics like finance and organization. A complacent American corporate elite, ignorant of the shop floors in their own plants, were utterly oblivious to the storm that was about to be unleashed by the new plants, the new tools, and striking new approaches taken by waves of hungry new competitors, first from Germany and Japan, and then from nearly the whole of east and south Asia.[45]

CHAPTER THREE

The Giant
as Adolescent

HEZEKIEL NILES, THE PROPRIETOR OF *NILES WEEKLY REGISTER*, AMERICA'S
first national newspaper, reported in October 1825:

> Wednesday last [October 26, 1825] was a great day in New York, the Erie
> Canal being completed. . . . The first gun, to announce the complete open-
> ing of the New York canal, was to be fired at Buffalo, on Wednesday last,
> at 10 o'clock precisely. . . . It was repeated, by heavy cannon stationed long
> the whole canal and river . . . and the gladsome sound reached the city of
> New York at 20 minutes past 11—when a grand salute was fired at fort
> Lafayette, and was reiterated back up to Buffalo. . . . The cannon . . . were
> some of those *Perry* had before used on Lake Erie, on the memorable 11th
> of September 1814.

The serious partying got under way when a flotilla of dignitaries actually arrived in the city ten days after embarking upon the canal at Buffalo.
They were received "with thunders of artillery, and the acclamations of
rejoicing scores of thousands." Niles guessed that there were "some 30 to
50,000 strangers in New York" to watch deWitt Clinton pour a barrel of
Lake Erie water into the Hudson.

> The whole population of the city exerted itself to give brilliancy to the oc-
> casion. The various banners of different bodies, highly ornamented states,
> &c. presented a whole the like of which never has before been witnessed

in America. In the evening, some of the public buildings were illuminated, and there were balls and private parties, not to be counted. . . . The whole appears to have passed off without disturbance, except at Castle Garden, in which 4 or 5,000 people were assembled to witness the second ascension by Mad. Johnson, in a balloon—but it would not rise with her; the people outside became very clamorous; and those within, at last, got impatient, and proceeded to tear the balloon into pieces and destroy the furniture within the walls, by way of satisfaction.[1]

The high spirits were fully justified, for it was hard to overestimate the importance of the Erie Canal. It welded the whole Northeast into a single economic unit, vaulting it, even in its still-primitive state, into the ranks of the world's largest economies.

Britons paid little attention to such developments. Rev. Sidney Smith, a canon of St. Paul and well-known man of letters, was speaking for the elite when he commented on an 1820 statistical review of the United States:

We are friends and admirers of Jonathan ["Brother Jonathan" was British slang for their bumptious transatlantic cousin]; But he must not grow vain and ambitious; or allow himself to grow dazzled . . . [by claims] that they are the greatest, the most refined, the most enlightened, and the most moral people upon earth. . . . The Americans are a brave, industrious, and acute people; but they have hitherto given no indication of genius, and have made no approach to the heroic. . . . Where are their Foxes, their Burkes, their Sheridans? . . .—Where their Arkwrights, their Watts, their Davys. . . . Who drinks from American glasses? Or eats from their plates?[2]

Through a European lens, in fact, America looked very backward, if only because of its overwhelmingly rural demography. In the 1820s, more than 90 percent of Americans still lived in the countryside, a pattern that had changed very little by mid-century.[3] In nineteenth-century Europe, rural areas were mostly peasant-ridden backwaters, but America's agrarian patina concealed a beehive of commercial and industrial activity. By the

Erie Canal, 1830. This bucolic scene would have been typical of virtually the entire route when the canal first opened. By connecting the port of New York City with the New York interior and all the territories bordering on the Great Lakes, it jump-started the commercialization of the entire region. Note the horse-drawn motive power.

end of the War of 1812, Gordon Wood suggests, the northern states were possibly "the most thoroughly commercialized society in the world." A Rhode Island industrialist made the same point in 1829: "The manufacturing activities of the United States are carried on in little hamlets . . . around the water fall which serves to turn the mill wheel."[4]

American historians have suffered their own bafflements. It is only in recent decades that a consensus of sorts has emerged on the nation's early growth spurt. Winifred Rothenberg did much of the groundbreaking work—twenty-five years of patient excavation of the account books, diaries, estates, mortgages, and other records of Massachusetts farmers.[5] What she finds is an organic, bottom-up form of modernization, originating in the increasing prosperity of ordinary farmers. The British experience was starkly different. The underbelly of Victorian society mapped by Charles Dickens was a rural proletariat brutally expelled from the countryside and herded into urban factories.

Many of Rothenberg's farmers were among their local elites, but outside of the South, American rural elites were decidedly middle-class, with modestly sized farms. During the immediate post-Revolutionary years, New England and Middle Atlantic farmers became strikingly more entrepreneurial. Farmers started making more frequent, and longer, marketing trips, evidencing a search for best-price markets. Those trips ceased abruptly in the 1820s, as thickening networks of local merchants made them unnecessary. Price disparities for crops or tools virtually disappeared over wide regions. That same market-driven behavior can be seen in farmers' own operations. Wage labor became a favored form of farm employment, with consistent skill-based wage rates. Farm surpluses were often invested in mercantile and industrial undertakings instead of land, and farmer's estates showed a clear trend toward financial instruments: mortgages, canal and bridge bonds, even company stock.

As the Erie Canal exposed Rothenberg's farmers to new competitive threats from larger-scale New York grain farms, they quickly shifted into labor-intensive, high-productivity lines like dairying and hay production. The timing of hog slaughtering suggests that farmers made sophisticated profit calculations: stretching out fattening periods when feed was cheap and meat was dear, and vice versa. All in all, it was a sharp departure from pre-Revolutionary behavior, when the forebears of these same farmers were far less experimental than the English in adopting new farming methods or searching for higher-return crops.[6]

Local merchants often provided the impetus toward new enterprises. The Holleys of Salisbury, in the northwest corner of Connecticut, are a good example. The family was old farming stock who had been in western Connecticut for generations. Holley males were mostly farmers and ministers until Luther Holley opened a store and trading operation in the mid-eighteenth century. Salisbury also had good-quality iron deposits, and Luther traded iron from local smelters from the start.

A group that included Ethan Allen of Revolutionary War fame opened a blast furnace in 1762. Although the Allen group failed, subsequent owners prospered during the war, even casting cannons for the American forces.[7] After the war, as the iron business went into decline, Luther started buying ironworking properties to lock up supply for his iron trading and by 1799 had the largest local holdings. He took in his son John as a partner, and when Luther retired in 1810, John formed a new partnership with another merchant and iron trader, John Coffing.[8]

Neither Coffing nor John Holley considered themselves "iron men." They were merchants who happened to trade their own iron and iron kettles, along with grains, liquors, cloth, and whatever else they could readily sell. But they had a good eye for talent and knew the top local artisans. During the War of 1812, they cast cannon and anchors for the navy, and they began making sales and lobbying forays to Washington. After the war, they become an important source of gun iron to the Springfield Armory and to contractors like Eli Whitney.

John's son, Alexander Hamilton Holley, succeeded to the business but was also active in politics, served a term as governor, and was a founding member of the local bank. It was Alexander who finally made the decisive break of "closing the store" to concentrate on the ironworks. He and a local partner, George Merwin, started a knife-making shop in 1844, which was incorporated as Holley Manufacturing in 1854. It was a major area employer until it closed in 1946.

Over time, the Holleys had become the leading family of the town. They certainly lived well, with a gracious house but not a mansion. The children all went to good schools, and they had carriages and some servants. (But American servants in this period had become "help" and tended to think and act like contracted employees.[9]) With all of that, the Holleys were never rich: almost all of them worked hard, and their cash mostly went into their businesses. When Luther died in 1826, he left an estate valued at $34,000, to be divided among six children. Much of it was personal inventory like furniture and silver, and some of the children had already borrowed against their shares. (Several had overborrowed, so their brothers and sisters had to take their notes when the estate settled.) Alexander's correspondence and diary fragments frequently mention money pressures, and the same pressures are also reflected in the letters his oldest son, Alexander Lyman Holley, wrote home from college. (We'll meet Alexander Lyman again, because he became a great figure in the nineteenth-century steel industry.)

Rothenberg's farmers and proto-industrialists like the Holleys dissolve an old interpretive conflict. Historians long divided over whether or the degree to which America's nineteenth-century agrarians were apple-cheeked prelapsarian Jeffersonians, ripe for exploitation by commercially minded interlopers. The reality seems to be that *both* the sons of the soil and merchant-industrialists were intensely commercial, profit-seeking animals, and *both* were deeply rooted in their communities. The behavior of both the entrepreneurial merchant and the farmer was constrained within local webs of obligation: mortgages and mercantile credits were extended, old farm hands kept on, seasonal patterns of work and leisure respected, local celebrations and rituals honored.

The iron districts of Pennsylvania and New Jersey display the same intricate interlacing of farming and industry from early days. The district's iron industries employed an estimated 4,000 workers by the late 1770s, a far denser concentration than any in New England; by 1810 the region accounted for 61 percent of national iron furnace output.[10] Iron was quintessentially a rural industry. With seemingly inexhaustible wood supplies, Americans smelted iron with charcoal, which is far freer of impurities than coal, so blast furnaces were typically located in deep woods.

The Martha Furnace opened in 1808 in the pine woods of southern New Jersey, financed by Philadelphia merchants and iron traders, and has been documented in great detail by the historian Thomas Doerflinger. The furnace proprietors owned timber and bog iron* rights to a section of

---

* Iron is one of the most common elements on earth, and ground water is often rich in dissolved iron. In swamps and bogs, the iron is precipitated by oxidation and bacterial action, forming low-grade ore deposits that sink into the mud. Ore raisers recovered the iron by dredging. It was then roasted and thoroughly dried (steam could explode a blast furnace) and pulverized in a stamping mill to reduce the impurities before smelting. Most ancient iron was from bog iron, but it is no longer used for industrial purposes. New Jersey's iron bogs now produce cranberries.

the pine woods bigger than Manhattan, and its development had the character of a modest-sized town. Based on a lake with a busy dock, it was centered around a thirty-foot blast furnace and a collection of industrial buildings: a bellows house, charcoal storage sheds, and a sand-molding works for casting iron into blocks of pig or end-products like pots and stoves. There were also a grist mill, a saw mill, and a stamping mill, stables, a carpentry shop, and a smithy, plus housing for about seventy workers on a year-round basis, a store, and food warehouse facilities.

The core staff were the skilled artisans who kept the furnace running and executed the crucial annual shutdown, hearth rebuild, and restart. Other skilled men built the cast-iron sand molds, ran the mills, and built and maintained the waterworks and a small fleet of ore boats. The work force was filled out with teamsters, wood cutters, and ore raisers, the nastiest job of all, entailing long, wet days of dredging mud with a clam shovel. All together, there were between seventy and eighty full-timers, all of them resident on-site.

Except for the skilled iron men, the work force was mostly recruited from the local villages. The skilled men tended to be recent immigrants, mostly Irish and Germans, although with a scattering of skilled African Americans. Labor was treated as a scarce resource: the works don't exhibit any of the rigid disciplines of, say, a Carnegie factory later in the century, and bouts of absenteeism and drunkenness were usually overlooked. Camaraderie among the skilled iron men and the management was high—with "days at the beach" and group partying at the local taverns.

Work in general trades like carpentry and wood chopping was scheduled to mesh with the agricultural cycle, so chopping and charcoal making peaked in the winter, much of it with part-time workers from the local farms. Bulk pork and corn supplies were shipped in by Philadelphia-area merchants, but all dairy products, most vegetables, bread, and other meats were sold at the ironworks by the locals. Most of the bigger farmers also had side businesses—tavern keeping, wagon building, and the like—and Martha Furnace was their most important customer. In other words, it was the same industrial-agricultural symbiosis that Rothenberg uncovered in Massachusetts. In early nineteenth-century America, "rural" wasn't synonymous with "agricultural."

As a formula for national growth, it clearly worked. For 135 years, from 1778 to the eve of the First World War, America achieved an average 3.9 percent annual economic growth, in constant dollars. No other country has yet come close to achieving such sustained rapid growth for so long a period of time. The economic historian David Landes attributed Great Britain's sudden rise to commercial and industrial dominance to its culture: its empiricism, its relative social mobility compared to the rest of Europe, its commercialism, its respect for numbers and contracts. By comparison with eighteenth-century Britons, Americans were strivers on steroids.

The sharpest contrast between British and American industry was the intense focus of American companies on large-scale production and distribution of ordinary goods. Historians have from time to time focused on one industry or the other, like gun making, as the quintessentially American industry. But the dominating American characteristic across nearly all major industries was the push for scale—adapting the production methods, the use of machinery, and the distribution to suit the product. This chapter will look at five different early American industries: clocks and textiles in some depth, along with shorter takes on shoes, stoves, and steam engines.

Affordable Clocks

Mechanical clocks had been around for nearly five hundred years in 1800, but it took only a generation for American clockmakers, led by Eli Terry, to show the world how to make decent clocks easily and cheaply and to make them by the million.

The mechanical clock was invented sometime in the late thirteenth century and very quickly reached a remarkably stable basic design. A clock needs a power source, like a falling weight or a coiled spring. It needs a pulsing mechanism, like a pendulum or an oscillating balance wheel. It needs an escapement device that breaks the clock's motion into precisely

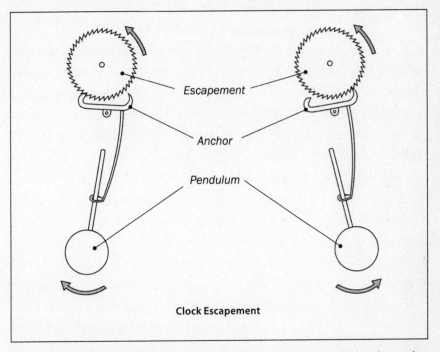

Clock Escapement

The heart of a mechanical clock is the escapement mechanism, a pulsing device that breaks up the gear actions into precisely timed segments. In the illustration, the pulse is provided by the pendulum, which tilts the anchor from side to side to interrupt the turning of the escapement wheel at top. Note the very precise shape and fit of the anchor tips and escapement wheel teeth.

timed segments. And finally it needs a gear train to transmit the timed pulses to the display mechanism.

The evolution of clocks marched to the accelerating tempo of commerce. The workdays of farmers and peasants extended from dawn to dusk, but the quitting whistles at Massachusetts's new textile factories were governed by the clock, and owners tracked output by the minute. Before Terry, American clockmakers worked to order, making expensive products for commercial men, who actually needed them, or for the wealthy, who merely enjoyed them as display and conversation pieces. The standard American clock was a pendulum-driven "tall-clock" design.

Almost all clockmaking was machine-assisted, for few craftsmen could cut out a seventy-eight-tooth gear by eye. Since the machinery was mostly executed in wood, however, only remnants have survived. Turn-of-the-century clockmakers usually powered their tools with hand cranks and foot treadles, although water-powered machines were coming into wider use. Small mechanical saws cut gear teeth. (Jigs were used to clamp several gears together so the saw could cut a number of gears at a time, ensuring that they were uniform.) Indexing devices moved the tool the precise distance to the next tooth. Simple dies were used to draw hot metal into proper-diameter wire. All were supported by a great variety of special-purpose measuring tools and gauges.

Despite Eli Terry's importance in the history of clockmaking, he left a frustratingly sparse record.[11] He was born in Connecticut in 1772 and served as an apprentice to two well-known clockmakers, one of whom, Benjamin Cheney, specialized in wooden clock movements. Hardwood gears, usually of lignum vitae, were quite durable and much cheaper than brass.* In 1793, Terry went into business on his own, making both brass and wooden clocks. In his early years in business, he would make three or four clocks at a time and then take to horse as a peddler, with the clocks strapped around his body on the saddle. He was also an experimenter. In 1797, he was awarded a patent on an "Equation Clock," showing both solar and solar mean time, an impressive achievement,** but too expensive for his market.

It was Terry's disappointment with the Equation Clock that sparked his interest in the trade-off between volume and price. In 1802, Terry

---

* John Harrison used wooden gears in the first longitude chronometers because the oils in the wood made them self-lubricating. Brass was harder and more durable but needed external lubrication, which trapped dust and other contaminants. Harrison feared that their accuracy would degrade on an extended voyage. As he shrank his chronometers, small-dimension machining mandated the switch to brass components. His prize-winning chronometer was watch-sized and had all brass works.

** Because of nuances of the earth's orbit, the length of a day differs from the canonical 24 hours by +16 to –14 minutes throughout the year. Mechanical clocks are based on solar mean time, which treats all hours and days as if they were the same length. When most time was taken from sundials or solar reckonings, mechanical clocks were glaringly out of sync with "real time"—hence, the equation clock. The conversion formula is both complex and tedious, although it is likely that Terry worked it out for himself. As mechanical clocks proliferated, the industrial world quietly chose to forget about solar time.

found sufficient sales outlets to drop his peddling and built a small water-powered factory that employed several apprentices and workmen. When he announced his intention to build clocks by the thousand, a local wag mockingly guaranteed to purchase the thousandth—and was soon forced to make good his bargain.

Then in 1807, Terry made a historic contract with two merchant-brothers, Levi and Edward Porter, to supply them 4,000 clocks over three years. Terry spent the whole first year creating and organizing a larger water-powered factory in a converted grist mill. He produced 1,000 clocks in the second year, and the remaining 3,000 in the third. (Terry produced only the movements, or innards of the clocks, which was normal practice; the Porters contracted with others for the decorative cases.)

And then Terry retired, selling his business and licensing his patents to two joiners who had worked at his plant, Seth Thomas and Silas Hoadly. The Thomas-Hoadly partnership did well, but the two soon went their separate ways. Hoadly became a locally successful clockmaker, while Seth Thomas clocks became a national icon. All of Thomas's early clocks were Terry designs.

But Terry had retired only to rethink his clock designs, and he resurfaced in 1814 in a new factory dedicated to his Connecticut shelf clock, one of the two or three greatest manufacturing successes of the first half of the century. No previous clock had come close to achieving such durability and accuracy in such a portable form at such a low price point. The pendulum and weight hangings were much shorter and cleverly rearranged so they could fit inside a shelf-sized case.

But it was Terry's final iteration of the shelf clock that embodied the truly critical insight. Volume manufacturing requires rethinking product design along with manufacturing processes.* The larger the number of

---

* Americans were painfully retaught that lesson by Japanese manufacturers in the 1970s and 1980s. Japanese products were designed for manufacturability from the start. In America and Europe, by contrast, product design engineers and manufacturing engineers rarely talked to each other. Part counts in Western products were invariably far higher than in Japanese versions, and welds and fittings often in unnecessarily awkward places.

interacting moving parts, the greater the likelihood that small errors will propagate into large outcome variances. The hard way to solve that is to eliminate all the small errors. It's often better and easier to reduce the number of parts or, perhaps easiest of all, if the variances are not too gross, to build in a final adjustment at the last stage of manufacturing. That was the strategy Terry followed in his 1822 five-arbor shelf clock.

The tolerances required for gear trains to move clock hands or strike bells were tight by traditional standards but readily achievable with the current clockmaking technology. The quality of small gear-cutting machines and jigs and gauges had reached the point at which clockmakers could farm out gear making to home craftsmen. Scholars have remeasured stocks of contracted wooden gear teeth from early-nineteenth-century clockmaking shops, and they are indeed interchangeable: not exactly the same, but with variances well within the margins for acceptable performance.

The escapement tolerance, however—the accuracy with which the anchor[*] impinged on the gear teeth of the escapement wheel—was much more demanding. As the motion of the pendulum jogs the anchor back and forth, its two tips slide in and out of the escapement wheel's gear teeth. Even small misalignments disrupt the movement. The most time-consuming task in clockmaking was (and still is in craft-centered watch-making and clockmaking) the depthing. A depthing tool is a complicated vise that allows the craftsman to hold gears in proper alignment to drill their shaft placements on the clock plate. Placing the entire train so the anchor and escapement wheel emerged in near-perfect alignment required a master craftsman and took time.

Terry's breakthrough was breathtakingly simple. He placed the escapement wheel and anchor outside the movement container, so it was accessible just by removing the case. And he placed the anchor on a moveable brass fixture. After the craftsman placed the gear train and closed up the

---

[*] Terry's patents refer to the escapement mechanism as the "verge," an older term that actually referred to a different escapement type but reflected the usage of wooden clockmakers. I've used the modern term to avoid confusion.

movement, he simply moved the anchor fixture to a good alignment, then locked it in place with two small nails. Problem solved—not by increasing manufacturing precision but by increasing the allowable margin of error for producing an excellent clock. A bonus was that if an escapement became misaligned or clogged over the years, it could easily be removed for cleaning and readjustment. It was win-win all around. Costs were cut, and prices fell, but nobody could challenge Terry's advertising slogan that his "Clock will run as long without repairs, and be as durable and accurate for keeping time, as any kind of Clock whatever," because it was true enough.[12]

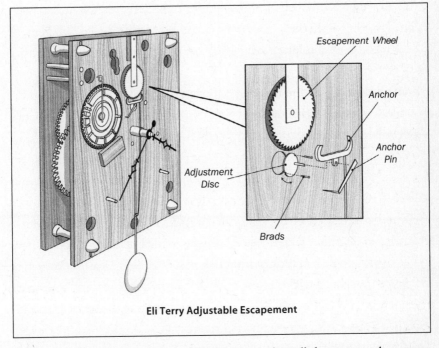

Eli Terry Adjustable Escapement

The central challenge of craft clock-making is to align all the gears so the escapement device works properly. Even in Terry's first mass-produced clocks, it was a time-consuming task for a skilled clockmaker. His most ingenious breakthrough was a simple adjustment mechanism that greatly increased the allowable margin of error in gear placement.

Terry duly patented his five-arbor clock, but any clockmaker could see what he had done. Some major manufacturers, like Seth Thomas, paid him license fees, but the design was widely pirated. The five-arbor shelf clock design became the standard for almost all Connecticut clocks, although with many variations, and production shifted decisively to large-factory modes.

As Terry, Thomas, and other Connecticut clockmakers proliferated inexpensive clocks, peddler networks quickly grew up to handle the distribution. New England tinware makers, who provided all manner of kitchen goods, had extended their peddler networks throughout the country after the turn of the century. Merchants like Levi and Porter seeded new peddler networks for clocks, an ideal peddling product because of its high value to weight. Well-established peddlers paid wholesale prices—often on credit—for their goods, kept the markups, and hired other peddlers on a salary and commission basis. New men often had to post security for their wares.

As markets expanded, leading merchants or manufacturers set up regional operations to supply their peddlers; tinware makers often created satellite factories. Water-powered clockmaking was not feasible in most of the country, but clockmakers, or merchant houses with a strong clock trade, frequently used local merchants as storage points for peddler networks and arranged regional clock-case construction with local cabinet makers.

The Yankee peddler became an iconic figure in the Southern press: readers were regaled with tales of sharpster peddlers hawking goods at a ten-times markup to dim plantation masters. "Peddling" has a derogatory connotation now, but in the national market revolution that took place in the years after the War of 1812, peddling was a reputable, and often a lucrative, first step into a career in merchandising.[13]

The sharp depression of 1837 winnowed the weaker clock manufacturers. Chauncey Jerome, a former Terry apprentice, took advantage of falling brass prices to lead the transition to brass. By the 1850s, his annual production was up to 280,000 movements a year. Jerome was also the first American clockmaker to enter the English market. At first London shops mostly scorned his product, but one dealer took a few on consignment. When they sold immediately—even with duty, they were a lot cheaper than British clocks—the dealer took more that sold just as fast. Jerome therefore sent a large shipment invoiced at $1.50 apiece, which was seized by customs as an obvious case of "dumping" below cost. Customs seizure rules, however, required that they pay the vendor the invoiced amount. Jerome was perfectly happy with that, so he sent another shipment, which was similarly seized and paid for. Delighted, he promptly sent yet another, whereupon customs decided they had their fill of brass movements and let them through.[14] By the 1860s, it was taken for granted that clocks in the average British home had American-made movements.

Terry's brother and three of his sons also went into the clock business; Terryville, Connecticut, is named after Eli Terry Jr., the most successful of Eli's relatives. Terry himself retired from business in 1833 at the age of sixty-one and died in 1852. At retirement, he was rich enough to give away $100,000 and leave sufficient principal to draw an income of $3,000 a year—more than enough to live comfortably, which was the extent of his aspirations. His retirement years were spent working on clocks, mostly new designs for very large church clocks, apparently just for the fun of it.

Samuel Slater
Rips Off the British

American entrepreneurs approached textiles much as Terry approached clocks. The focus from the start was on inexpensive, highly uniform, broadly distributed products of "good enough" quality for the average consumer. In the first half of the century, no other new industry could match textiles in financial returns, employment impact, and technology spin-offs.[15]

The United States never disguised its avarice for British textile technology. It refused to recognize British patents, and American entrepreneurs openly advertised for British power-spinning experts, who were forbidden by law from emigrating. Tench Coxe, Alexander Hamilton's deputy at the Treasury, even sent an agent to England to procure machine drawings, but he was arrested. Great Britain's cotton districts were crawling with surreptitious American agents offering dreams of wealth and preferment for skilled artisans willing to risk prison for flouting the technology embargo.

In fact, few mule-spinning foremen, or even plant managers, were actually able to build working machines, although many would take American money to try. Samuel Slater, only twenty-one, turned out to be the rare individual with the ambition, the intelligence, and the thorough understanding of both spinning and spinning technology to create a working plant from scratch.[16]

Slater was a farm boy who had been put to work in an early Arkwright-style water-powered cotton mill and eventually caught the eye of the mill owner and manager Jedidiah Strutt, who had helped finance Arkwright's first mills and subsequently gone into business replicating them. Strutt opened a new mill when Slater was fourteen and took Slater to the new site as an apprentice, giving him direct experience of the mill construction and start-up process. As he finished the apprenticeship, Slater worried that there was little room for advancement in the British textile industry. So he decided to take his chances in America, embarking in 1789 under an assumed name to evade watchful British emigration officers.

After Slater landed in New York, he worked briefly in a yarn factory, confirming the backwardness of American technology. Hearing that Moses Brown, a Providence merchant and a cofounder of Brown University, was seeking an experienced spinning mechanic, Slater contacted him and traveled to Providence. Brown had been burnt by useless yarn machinery, and an agreement was reached on a partnership to construct an Arkwright-style cotton mill, financed by Brown's advance of $10,000. The partners were Brown's son-in-law, William Almy; Smith Brown, a cousin; and Slater, who had a half share in both the profits and the debt from the advances.[17]

Slater was the genuine article and, within a year, had an operating yarn factory, with water-powered carding (combing the raw cotton), roving (creating rough tubes of fibers), and spinning machinery. While he worked on the factory, he boarded with the family of Oziel Wilkinson, the local machinist who actually built the equipment. He married Wilkinson's daughter, Hannah, who later won a patent on an improved cotton thread, and he frequently partnered with her brother, David, also a machinist, who earned a place in machining history for building a high-precision screw-thread/slide-rest lathe several years before Henry Maudslay.[18]

The first small mill was operated with children, but Slater discovered that he would have to develop a different staffing model. American farmers didn't give up their children as easily as the British, and they kept vigilant eyes on their working hours. Slater's solution was to hire whole families. The father, who often kept working as a farmer on leased, mill-owned land, managed a contract for family production at the mill.

Americans had long-established merchant and peddler distribution systems for British yarns and cloth that Slater could tap into. It took a while for sales to catch on, since American-made yarns had a terrible reputation, but yarn merchants understood value, and word soon spread that Slater was producing basic yarns of British quality at excellent prices.

By 1799, the group had three mills up and running: the original one, another taken over by Almy and Brown and converted by Slater, and a third owned by Slater and Wilkinson—each one bigger than the last. Slater had no patent rights in any of his machines, but it was some years before he faced serious competition. Although the artisans he trained dispersed throughout the northeast, merely understanding the machinery wasn't enough. Cotton varies widely in its fiber lengths and tensile strength, and mill practices, process flows, and thread tensions all needed constant vigilance by experienced supervisors to maintain high-volume production.

Providence soon became the center of a new yarn-making district. Mills often sold both yarns and cloth, although the cloth making was contracted to home weavers using mill yarns. Slater-type spinning mills spread rapidly eastward into Connecticut and Massachusetts—a number of them with Slater capital and technology—and then to New York, where Utica became a major yarn center.

But Lowell Invents
a New Kind of Company

Samuel Slater was a fine technologist, but Francis Cabot Lowell was a visionary who, within just a few years in a sadly short career, created a uniquely American textile industry.[19] Born into one of Boston's elite merchant and shipping families, Lowell did a stint on one of the family merchantmen, concentrated on mathematics at Harvard, went into one of the family countinghouses, and eventually prospered in his own trading business. His health seems to have been delicate, and in 1810, at age thirty-five, wealthy but worn down by the constant stresses of his business,* he took his family on an extended trip abroad. Wartime conditions curtailed plans for a continental tour, so the family spent most of their two-year sojourn in Scotland and England.

Whether Lowell intended to pirate British technology from the start isn't clear, but he made no doubt of his intentions when he met Nathan Appleton, his fellow Bostonian and merchant, in Scotland early in his trip. "Cotton Manufacture" was Lowell's primary focus, Appleton later recalled, for he thought it the kind of business that, if properly set up, could produce a reliable stream of steady, stress-free profits.

Lowell's mercantile friends gained him access to the mills; one can imagine him strolling through the plants, feigning languorous inattention while picking up countless trade secrets—the process flows, the details of gearing, and much else. Before he embarked for America, he also managed to secure copies of machine drawings that he slipped by customs. If that story is true, it seems vaguely dishonorable, and his friends may have been embarrassed when it was revealed what he had been up to.

When Lowell returned to Boston, he set about organizing his Boston Manufacturing Company. Everything about it was bold. The War of 1812

---

* Nineteenth-century upper-class work schedules were generally quite leisurely, but commercial business was inherently stressful because of the large fraction of one's wealth constantly at risk. Ships were lost, commodity prices see-sawed, trade bills defaulted. Cycles of credit expansion and contraction regularly wreaked havoc in all merchant communities.

was just underway, and Massachusetts mercantile houses were staring at economic disaster. (Lowell's return ship, in fact, was taken by a British frigate, and he was briefly held in Nova Scotia.) It was created as a joint-stock company, an unusual form for the time, which preferred partnerships. The initial financing goal was enormous: $400,000, forty times more than the start-up investment in the first Brown-Almy-Slater spinning mill. But Lowell wanted to be absolutely sure of enough capital to carry the business through any reasonable early setbacks. His circular letter proposed an offering of one hundred shares, at $4,000 apiece, $1,000 of which would be paid at closing, with the remainder drawn from time to time as the company required.

The initial investors were an extremely tight group. Lowell's brother-in-law, Patrick Tracy Jackson, with whom he was quite close, took twenty shares, and Lowell himself took fifteen. Jackson was appointed agent, effectively the CEO of the new company.

The remaining shares were very much a "friends and family" offering. Jackson's two brothers took fifteen; two of Jackson's in-laws, John Gore and James Lloyd, took fifteen; while two of Lowell's relatives, Benjamin Gorham and Warren Dutton, took five between them. The roster was rounded out from among their merchant friends. The senior and junior Israel Thorndikes took twenty, and Uriah Cutting took five. The remaining five went to Nathan Appleton, who hesitated considerably before investing. He was probably the wealthiest of Lowell's close friends, and his reluctance evidences the skittishness of the investment climate.

Lowell's mother's family, the Cabots, declined to invest at all. They and other Bostonians, after all, had built fortunes importing British goods. Many of them had been burned two decades previously by the Beverly Cotton Manufactory, an ill-starred, pre-Slater spinning venture that required an embarrassing bailout from the state legislature.

The first critical hire outside the group was Paul Moody, a brilliant young machinist. Lowell had approached Jacob Perkins, a machinist, nail manufacturer, and prolific inventor, to join the enterprise. Perkins recommended Moody, who was an inspired choice, for he had first trained as a weaver—under Scotsmen, who were known for their high-craft weaving tradition—and only then as a machinist under Perkins.

Lowell's strategic vision was as bold as his financing approach. Yarn making and weaving had always been viewed as a separate industries, like flour manufacturing and baking. The two trades had also mechanized at different rates. The Cartwright power loom was patented in 1785, twenty years after the Arkwright spinning frame, and was still an immature technology. British weaving was mostly on the "putting-out" cottage industry basis, and few plants had both power-spinning and power-weaving operations.

But Lowell wanted an integrated production line from the start. He and Jackson bought a vacant paper mill on the Charles River at Waltham and designed a three-story factory in which raw cotton would be cleaned and processed on the ground floor, spun into yarn on the second floor, and woven into cloth on the third. It is an interesting decision, for yarn production multiplied his technology challenges, and good yarns were readily available from established companies quite near his new plant. But Lowell, in true American spirit, was driving for economies of scale and had apparently decided he could not risk *not* controlling the entire production process.

It took nearly a year for Lowell and Moody to get their first loom working. The challenge wasn't conceptual, but as with the English, it was a matter of capturing the micro-motions of weaving without unacceptable breakage. The Lowell-Moody approach was to simplify the problem. Rather than try to create highly flexible power trains, they focused on tough fabrics with sturdy threads.

The first successful Lowell-Moody loom was actually a fairly crude instrument. For instance, there was no stop-action on the batten—the wood piece that banged the weft threads together after each shuttle pass. Instead it was stopped just by the resistance of the cloth. That would have been unacceptable for high-margin, finer-threaded fabrics, but that wasn't the market that Lowell and Moody were interested in.

Where they did lavish attention was on achieving a single flow-through model of cotton cloth making. Moody's 1818 warping and dressing machine was a major advance in that direction. It first sized the threads—rolled them through a starch mixture to strengthen them for the weaving—and then automatically dressed the loom, the once-tedious task of loading each of the individual warp (long) threads into the proper heddle positions. (A stop-action mechanism suspended the operation if a thread broke, so an operator could repair it.) Other innovations, like conical pulleys to adjust thread speeds and faster spindles to increase thread twists for a harder, more durable thread, were all designed to achieve higher processing speeds and fewer interruptions. The narrow range of output also ensured uniform machinery, quicker repairs, and shorter downtimes, exactly the ticket for high-volume manufacturing.*

Lowell made yet another historically original contribution. Both he and Appleton had come away from their trips to Great Britain deeply disturbed by the human degradation in the great textile mills. They feared that Britain was teetering on the brink of social upheaval and did not want to replicate British conditions in America. They were also ready to pay higher than normal wages if they could get the assurance of a reliable work force. Lowell's solution was to create decent mill housing for young farm girls willing to work away from home for a few years to earn their own cash stake—for a dowry, to pay for training as a teacher, or to help out the rest of the family. The hours were long but the work not too physically demanding, and by the standards of the day, the housing was spartan but clean. When Charles Dickens visited the new town of Lowell, the second great development of Boston Company mills, in 1840, he was deeply impressed, even moved:

> I happened to arrive at the first factory just as the dinner hour was over, and the girls were returning to work; indeed, the stairs were thronged with them. . . . [They] were all well dressed: and that phrase necessarily

---

* It does not dim Lowell's accomplishment to doubt the conventional tale that he returned from England with a complete design of a power loom in his head. It is more plausible that he returned with a few sketches and a firm conviction that power weaving was readily achievable, and that Paul Moody then designed and built the looms. Moody, after all, was both a skilled weaver and a great machinist, who probably needed only Lowell's backing to develop a working loom.

includes extreme cleanliness. . . . They were healthy in appearance, many of them remarkably so, and had the manners and deportment of young women: not of degraded beasts of burden. . . . The rooms in which they worked were as well ordered as themselves. . . . In all, there was much fresh air, cleanliness, and comfort as the nature of the occupation would possibly admit of. . . . I solemnly declare, that from all the crowd I saw in the different factories that day, I cannot recall or separate one young face that gave me a painful impression; not one young girl whom . . . I would have removed from those works if I had had the power.

I am now going to state three facts, which will startle a large class of readers [in England] very much. Firstly, there is a joint-stock piano in a great many of the boarding-houses. Secondly, nearly all these young ladies subscribe to circulating libraries. Thirdly, they have got up among them-selves a periodical called THE LOWELL OFFERING . . . [of which] I will only observe . . . that it will compare advantageously with a great many English Annuals.[20]

Dickens's favorable impression would have been reinforced by the design of the mill village. The attractive arrangement of the buildings, the walkways and plantings along the canals, the attention to cleanliness and order, as recently reconstructed, is quite beautiful. (The Scottish "new town" movement was much in the air when Lowell was in Scotland, although he doesn't seem to have visited any sites.) And farm girls who had never been far from their villages were easier to impress than Dickens. They had much more privacy at the mill than on the farm, and compared to mill work, farmwork was dirty, brutally hard, and often dangerous. Farm life could also be isolating, and the girls seem to have taken great delight in meeting and living with so many girls of their own age. It's no surprise that most of them seem to have remembered the mills with fondness.

The first Waltham mill started operations in February 1815 with twenty-three yarn-making machines—carders, rovers, and spinning jennies of various kinds—and twenty-one looms, seven wide and fourteen narrow ones. The initial machinery was rapidly added to, replaced, and rebuilt, as operations expanded and Moody piled on his process improvements. One of Nathan Appleton's firms, a wholesale distributorship, took care of the marketing at a modest 1 percent of sales.

It was hardly an auspicious time for a textile venture. If 1812 had been a bad time to embark on a new venture, 1815 may have been the worst possible time to open a new mill. Manchester textile mills had been amassing unsold yarn and cloth for three years. When the war ended, they poured it into the American markets at rock-bottom prices. Slater survived handily in Providence, but the dumping wreaked havoc among the rash of new textile mills that proliferated during the war. Nevertheless, the Boston Company sailed serenely through. In October 1817, a month after Lowell's death, it declared its first annual dividend, a handsome 17 percent, and for the rest of the first decade it averaged a stunning 18.75 percent.

Lowell died in 1817, just as his great enterprise was getting off the ground. His last contribution to the company was to lobby through a textile tariff bill that basically eliminated British competition in the low-end textile market (predominantly from re-exported and very cheap Indian cotton). Both Appleton and Jackson seem to have adopted Lowell's vision completely as their own, and the company proceeded on an orderly course of steady expansion.

Three mills on the Charles River at Waltham were the most the site could support, so in 1820 the company commenced development on a new site on the Merrimack River, at a location that the directors named Lowell. After the first Lowell mill was up and running, the company made yet another conceptual leap, creating a new kind of organization not unlike the business network the Japanese call a *keiretsu*—an intricate alliance of affiliates and subsidiaries acting as if guided by a single intelligence. The Lowell Locks & Canal Company offers a good window into its operations.

The Locks & Canal Company

The waterwheel is one of the most ancient of mechanical power sources, but it needs reliable rainfall, hilly contours, fast, narrow rivers, and bedrock river bottoms to minimize silting—in other words, countrysides much like those of Scotland, England, and New England.

From medieval times, Great Britain was dotted with water-powered grist mills, saw mills, and fulling mills (washing and pounding woven wool cloth for a tighter finish). In earlier periods they were more often simple paddle wheels sitting in streams, but by the early eighteenth century hydraulic power was transforming into quite serious technology. Mill operators built dams and mill races, or artificial channels, to raise the height and velocity of the water. Gates controlled mill-race water flow and directed surpluses into storage ponds for dry spells. Overshot wheels, in which wheel buckets were loaded from the top, greatly increased power. The water entered the wheel buckets at higher velocity, and because the buckets on the descending side were all full, the wheel's descent weight and momentum were much higher.

New England operators, however, standardized on the "breast-fed" wheel, in which water enters at a point below the apex of the wheel. While it is theoretically not as efficient as the overshot wheel, it worked far better in practice, especially in fast water conditions.* Well maintained breast-fed wheels achieved energy conversion rates in excess of 60 percent. Gating and metering systems were developed to measure and modulate the quantity and velocity of the water flow, and hydraulic engineers in both England and the United States chipped away at the basic mathematics of fluid dynamics and energy conversion.[21] The British, however, were much quicker to shift to steam, since the urban concentration of their industry did not lend itself to waterpower.

The Boston Company's 1820 expansion to Lowell and the Merrimack River was accomplished by taking over the financially strained Pawtucket Canal in East Chelmsford, about twelve miles from the site in Waltham.

---

* The primary advantages of the breast-fed wheel were, first, that it was always moving in the same direction as the water, whereas in the overshot wheel, race water could spill down its back and slow the returning wheel buckets. Secondly, the diameter of an overshot wheel was limited by the height of the mill race, while the breast-fed wheel could be of almost any size, and the water entry point could be adjusted to different levels of water flow.

Although the directors stipulated that they had conducted an extensive search for a suitable property, Patrick Jackson's father was a major Pawtucket shareholder who must have been anxious to unload a white elephant.[22]

The site was nearly ideal for hydraulic power development. The canal had been built to circumvent the falls of the Merrimack River, which had a total head, or drop, of thirty feet within the East Chelmsford area. The river was also fed by several large lakes, so it had an unusually reliable year-round flow, even during dry summers. The existing canal intercepted the Merrimack just before the falls and then circled to the south for about thirteen miles before rejoining the river at its Concord branch to the east of the village. There were two locks to step down barge and other boat traffic. The Boston Company had to maintain those, since the Pawtucket Canal charter required that it be open to public transportation.

After striking an unpublicized deal with the canal company, the directors quietly assembled the land of nearly the entire island encompassed by the Merrimack and the canal, including all associated water rights. (Ransom had to be paid, however, when one sharp-nosed landowner sniffed out what was going on and started buying sites in competition.) Design and development of the site was assigned to Kirk Boott, who had just graduated from Sandhurst, the British military academy. He was good at math, but like most American engineers of the time, he was entirely self-taught in his new profession. Boott did fine, although Moody, who was building the water-mill machinery, was at his side at every stage. Boott also consulted with leading engineers of the day, including Myron Holley, Alexander H.'s uncle, who was one of the senior engineers on the Erie Canal.

The land in the vicinity of the falls was all rocky outcrop unsuitable for mill building, so Boott devised a plan whereby the mills would be located on the relatively flat plain on the western end of the island. The old canal, which was badly deteriorated, was widened and extensively rebuilt, and was intercepted by the new Merrimack Canal running about a half mile across the island to the river. Both canals had good heads, or water drops, followed by long flat runs ideal for mill siting. Work started in the spring of 1822, with as many as five hundred laborers on site at one time.

The first mill wheel, a breast-fed thirty-foot monster on the upper level of the Merrimack Canal, started turning in September 1823. Like Moody's wheels at Waltham, water flow was controlled by gates that were opened and closed by a fly-ball governor. The device consisted of spinning iron balls on a vane driven from the wheel shaft. As the shaft speeded up, the balls extended horizontally, and as it slowed down, they fell toward the vertical, in each case moving a set of levers that modulated the gate settings accordingly. Watt used a similar device on his early steam engines.

Shortly after that first mill opened, the directors made a critical, and as it turned out, brilliantly right decision. Appleton and Moody had calculated that the Merrimack site could support up to sixty mills, but as they began to plan the next few years' development, they were daunted by the potential management and financial challenges of such a massive enterprise. They therefore recommended spinning off the canals and waterworks as the Locks & Canal Company, with a separate but interlocking board of directors. In effect, they created a wholly owned subsidiary operating as a hydraulic power utility, open to any customer who could pass muster within the still tightly knit core group of the original founders and investors.

The directors invented the waterpower unit to calculate a water-leasing rate. They started with the volume of water required to run the first Waltham plant, adjusted it for the greater head at Lowell, and defined that as one waterpower. They estimated how many waterpowers the works could support and set a unit price that presumably would amortize each new extension of the works. The unit price was finally reduced to a per-spindle price, based on the approximately 3,600 spindles in the reference plant at Waltham.

Lowell was also the site of one of Moody's simplest but most important insights: it dawned on him in 1828 that he could connect the main plant's drive shaft to the waterwheel with a broad belt. British mills used cast-iron bevel gearing for drives in both water- and steam-driven applications. The gearing was heavy and consumed a great deal of power. Worse, if a gear cracked, it could take a week or more to get replacement casts. Belts frequently broke but were easily replaced. Over time Moody's drive-shaft belting became standard everywhere.

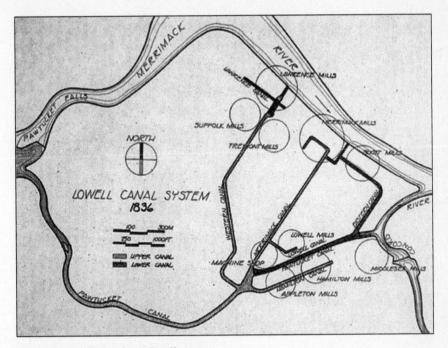

Map of Lowell Canals and Mills, 1836

The Locks & Canal Company was by far the greatest industrial development in the country, and its impact on machining, metalworking, and other industrial technologies is hard to overestimate. George Gibb, the historian of the Lowell machine works, puts the case:

> The manufacture of cloth was America's greatest industry. For a considerable part of the 1813–53 period the manufacture of textile machinery appears to have been America's greatest heavy goods industry, occupying the primary position in point of size and value of product among all industries which fabricated metal. . . . From the textile-machine shops came the men who supplied most of the tools for the American Industrial Revolution. From these mills and shops sprang directly the machine tool and the locomotive industries, together with a host of less basic metal-fabricating trades. The part played by the textile machinery industry in fostering American metal-working skills in the early nineteenth century was a crucial one.[23]

Considered solely as a hydraulic operation, Locks & Canal was world class. By the mid-1830s, it serviced twenty-five textile mills plus a variety of other water-powered businesses, including Moody's machine shops, and by the late 1840s, its waterpower canal network was more than seventeen miles long. Much of its success was due to its long-serving chief engineer, James B. Francis, another self-taught prodigy who assumed his post in 1837 at the age of twenty-two. Over the course of the next half century Francis became arguably the world's leading authority on hydraulic power. His *Lowell Hydraulic Experiments* were masterpieces of adroitly combined theoretical and empirical exposition. They were issued and regularly revised and reissued for a quarter century, especially advancing the fields of flow measurement and hydraulic-power transmission efficiency. Francis was a leader in the conversion of waterwheels into turbines starting in the late 1840s, and his underwater turbines achieved energy conversion rates in excess of 90 percent. A comparison of two advanced mid-century water sites illuminates Francis's contribution to hydraulic engineering.

In 1851, Henry Burden, one of America's great inventors, iron men, and waterpower innovators,[*] built the world's most powerful waterwheel at his works in Utica, New York. It was sixty-two feet in diameter, weighed 250 tons, was beautifully geared for smoothly efficient operation, generated up to 300 horsepower in work output, and ran almost without interruption for a full half century.

Also in 1851, Francis and a superb Lowell Machine Shop mechanic, Uriah Boyden, installed a Boyden-Francis turbine at the Tremont Mill in Lowell. Boyden had done the lion's share of the design and development work, while Francis, as Boyden's primary customer, had created a rigor-

---

[*] Burden was most famous for his horseshoe making machine. A continuous stream of hot bar iron was fed into a round contraption two and a half feet in diameter that executed a dozen high-speed swaging and punching actions that produced a finished horseshoe *every second*. During the Civil War, Burden supplied all the horseshoes for the Union army at a price only pennies above the cost of the iron.

ous design and testing environment to guide the conversion of Lowell waterwheels to turbines. The 1851 Boyden-Francis turbine was five feet in diameter, a twelfth the size of Burden's wheel. It weighed four tons, a sixtieth the weight of the wheel. And it generated up to 500 horsepower in work output, or 60 percent more than that of the wheel.[24]

The high-efficiency Francis turbine* is still used in almost every hydro-electric plant in the world, generating about a fifth of the world's electricity. Francis retired in 1884, although he lived in Lowell and remained a consultant to the company until his death in 1892.

The *Keiretsu* Extended

The "Boston Associates" is the name the historian Vera Shlakman pinned on the founding group of the Waltham-Lowell venture, along with the other investors drawn in as the companies prospered, and it has stuck ever since. Robert Dalzell lists seventy-five members of the Associates between 1813 and 1865. With five Appletons, three Cabots, three Jacksons, four Lawrences, four Lowells, and two Lymans, they were as ingrown as the Hapsburgs.

The durability of the group was partly a consequence of the loosely affiliated nature of the businesses. By spinning off Locks & Canal, the original Associates got diversification—they received their pro rata shares in the spin-offs and could invest further if they chose—and retained a voice in protecting their investment in the waterworks.

Locks & Canal, however, was also a real estate and manufacturing company. It leased land and water sites and, since the spin-off included Moody's machine shops, constructed lessors' waterworks and much of their machinery. Over time, the real estate and manufacturing businesses were spun off as well. Locks & Canal remained Lowell Manufacturing's

---

* The naming convention for Francis turbines was established by others, mostly after his death, in recognition of the consistent impetus he provided over many decades toward smaller and more compact turbine designs with ever higher energy-conversion ratios.

most important client, of course, but Lowell Manufacturing also developed a line of steam engines and was quite profitable in its own right. Intercompany relationships were simplified by the fact that the first wave of independent mills at Lowell were mostly owned by Associates. Kirk Boott had two, for instance, and Appleton was an investor in several.

The Lowell arrangement became a favored venture investing model for the Associates: Acquire water rights on an undeveloped river, construct the required power hydraulics—dam, canals, power supply for the first plant—build a textile factory and a machine shop, then lease the remaining waterpower to other entrepreneurs. James K. Mills, for example, was a prominent Boston merchant and an Associate. He was involved in at least four such ventures both as an investor and a director, two of which, at Chicopee and Mt. Holyoke, have been extensively researched by historians. There was no assurance of great financial rewards. The Mt. Holyoke group raised $2.45 million—a huge sum for the day. Most of it went for a 1,000-foot-wide dam on a river with a 57-foot head, that collapsed on the day it was opened. It was expensively rebuilt and then rebuilt again, and the investors lost every penny. Nevertheless, Mt. Holyoke became a successful paper manufacturing city, partly because of the sunk capital investments of the pioneers. Mills was wealthy and hardly a patsy; one imagines he worked so hard on his start-ups because he enjoyed it.[25]

The Associates also controlled more subtle networks of power. The Massachusetts Hospital Life Insurance Company was not specifically an Associates company. It was chartered in 1818 and awarded a monopoly on the state's life insurance business, so long as one-third of its life insurance profits went to the Massachusetts General Hospital. Only the great and the good are awarded such franchises, and by the time the company was fully operative in the mid-1820s, it was firmly within Associate control. From its founding until mid-century, two-thirds of its directors were Associates, as were all its finance committee members, prominently including Nathan Appleton and Patrick Jackson. There were three lines of business: annuities and life insurance for young men of modest means, life annuities for widows, and trusts for the better off. Profits from the trust

Layout of an Advanced Mid-Century Water Power Plant: Robbins & Lawrence, Windsor, VT, 1846

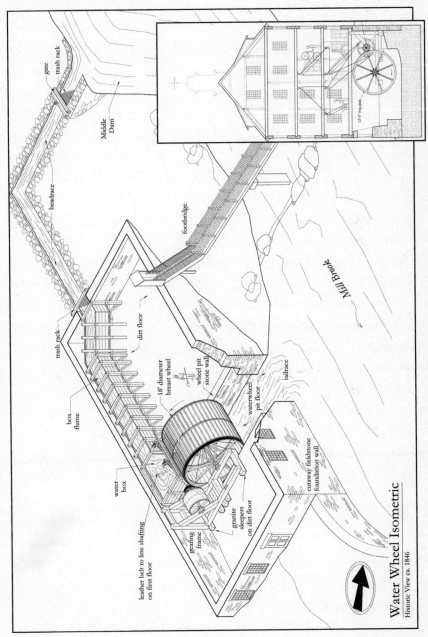

gate
trash rack

Middle
Dam

headrace

footbridge

trash rack

dirt floor

box
flume

water
box

18' diameter
breast wheel

wheel pit
stone wall

waterwheel
pit floor

tailrace

Mill Brook

leather belt to line shafting
on first floor

gearing
frame

granite
sleepers
on dirt floor

cutaway fieldstone
foundation wall

12'-6" engine

Water Wheel Isometric

Historic View ca. 1846

business didn't have to be shared with the hospital, and it filled a real need for Associate families, who were suddenly amassing large sums of cash from textiles.

Within just a few years after it went into operation, Massachusetts Life was by far the largest financial institution in the state, operating almost as an Associate investment club. At first the company followed its charter strictly, limiting its investments to high-quality mortgages, government bonds, and similar instruments, but by the 1830s roughly half of its investments had shifted to textiles. To comply with the charter, textile investments were usually reclassified as personal loans collateralized by small amounts of textile shares. The conflict of interest is stark, since many such loans generated lower returns than less risky blue-chip paper. Loans were also regularly extended or reworked when friends or family of Associates had trouble making payments. It is not likely that any of the Associates perceived a problem. The Massachusetts Life trusts still had decent returns, and since they were mostly funded with Associate money, who could object to their being invested in their own businesses? Similar patterns of ownership and control prevailed in Massachusetts banks and railroads.[26]

The "model village" aspect of Lowell and its mill-town clones came under pressure during the tough economic times of the 1830s. The once-docile mill girls walked off the job at Lowell and other mills when managers imposed wage cuts and rent increases on the mill girls. On the first occasion, in 1834, the Lowell girls retaliated by withdrawing all their savings from the local banks. During another walkout in 1836, one of them took to the stump and made "a neat speech," marking the first time a woman had ever spoken in public at Lowell.[27] Note that these actions occurred *before* Dickens's visit.

By the 1840s, conditions that had appeared enlightened twenty years before were looking considerably harsher to independent observers. A ten-hour-day law was bitterly opposed by the mill owners. The Lowell Female Labor Association was formed in 1844 and led ten-hour petitioning and organizing drives throughout the state. (The fact the mill girls lived together and had developed experience in print publications made them formidably effective.) Although mill organizing was a major advance toward woman's emancipation, the legislature resisted ten-hour-day legislation for another thirty years.

Even deeper problems were coming to the surface. Boston was the epicenter of the American abolitionist movement, and all cotton-related industry was built on slave labor. The entanglement of leading Boston shipping and mercantile families with slavery was a long-standing one, for Boston had been the headquarters of the three-cornered "slaves, molasses, and rum trade," and not a few New England sea officers had captained slavers. The split between Cotton Whigs and Conscience Whigs became irretrievable during the political battles over Texas and the Mexican War. In 1848, Charles Sumner denounced the alliance between "the cotton-planters and flesh-mongers of Louisiana and Mississippi and the cotton-spinners and traffickers of New England—between the lords of the lash and the lords of the loom." Families were riven over the question. Sumner himself was an in-law of Nathan Appleton, the de facto leader of the Cotton Whigs.

Appleton, the last of the original Associates, died in 1861. The *keiretsu* did not survive the Civil War. A number of mills had gone out of business during the financial panic of 1857, and the inability to buy cotton during the war wiped out many others. The younger generations of Associates were generally quite wealthy and in the main not especially interested in textiles. The textile business itself did recover after the war, but it was meaner and much more competitive. Mill working conditions deteriorated dramatically in the second half of the century, as farm girls gave way to immigrant labor. American factory conditions in general, not just at the mills, converged with those in England and in some industries, like steel, became even nastier.

Of Shoes, Stoves, and Steam Engines

America has always been a nation of consumers. Probate inventories from the Middle Atlantic states show how one generation's luxury item, like looking glasses, are middle-class necessities for the next, but simplified and standardized. As higher volumes drive down prices, the same products become commonplace even in poorer homes.[28] Terry's, Slater's, and the Waltham/Lowell experience illustrate how new products could tap into deep peddler networks that ran westward through rural New England, southward down the Hudson to New York and beyond, by packet to Philadelphia, Baltimore, and New Orleans, and in the early days by wagon west of the Appalachians. But there were many other possible models for mass production and distribution businesses.

Lynn, a town about twelve miles north of Boston, traditionally had a small concentration of shoemakers, producing cheap shoes that merchants exported for West Indian plantation slaves. The distribution networks were expanded in the 1780s by a local merchant, a Quaker named Ebenezer Breed, to supply shoes to Southern slaves.

Shoemaking was a craft industry with many specialty tools but few power machines until mid-century. Merchants in and around Lynn organized a massive putting-out manufacturing system. The merchants bought and cut leather and supplied the leather and supplies to home shoe workers: women sewed liners and finishes, while men did the heavy-leather sewing. The Southern slave population exploded with the cotton textile boom of the early 1800s, drawing more and more of the Boston region into the shoe business. As volumes rose, towns began to specialize in specific types of shoes. Higher quality products expanded the market to farmers and working people. Shoe models were standardized, and organization improved, driving down prices and expanding markets even further. As established merchants began to stock standard sizes and models, the peddler network shifted from retail to wholesale distribution. By mid-century or so, the great majority of ordinary people were wearing store-bought shoes, and local shoemakers had been forced to shift their business to the repair of commercially made shoes. By 1860, New England produced about 60 percent of the nation's shoes.[29]

The history of stoves is necessarily different. Stoves were relatively easy to cast at iron foundries but too heavy for peddlers. Still, it was a killer product: every housewife with a bad back and burnt fingers from fireplace-cooking dreamed of life with a "civilized" stove. The challenge was in marketing and distribution. No single manufacturer ever dominated the industry or constructed a Lowell-style master plan, but over fifty-some years, virtually any household that could afford the modest price had acquired a stove.

Clear signs of organization began to emerge in the 1820s in the iron district of Philadelphia and New Jersey. Instead of casting and selling individual stoves, the foundries began to produce stove plate, or the unassembled pieces of a stove, and ship it to Philadelphia for assembly at merchants' establishments. Initial sales were to upper-middle-class households in towns all along the available water routes, a market that was greatly expanded by the opening of the Erie Canal.

Decentralized production and distribution centers sprang up around major water routes—at Albany and Troy for the Erie Canal region, at Cincinnati and Louisville for the Ohio Valley, and at St. Louis for the Mississippi Valley. Local stove foundries, using cupola furnaces to melt scrap iron and steel, shortened transportation networks. As stoves proliferated, stove stores appeared in most medium-sized towns, typically with a catalog of designs and an assembly and finishing shop. Stove finishing became an important subtrade for tinplate craftsmen and simplified quality control at the foundry. Prices steadily dropped even as designs and quality steadily improved. In 1860, stoves accounted for a third of the value of all cast-iron products, with a value-added about the same as rail manufacture. By then, the industry was tilting toward maturity. A postwar shakeout left fewer, larger companies, which paid greater attention to branding and catalog selling, supplemented by retail stores and floor inventory in the biggest markets—in short, a modern industry.[30]

Steam engines, finally, illustrate the extreme end of the transportation challenge in early America. They were also a key to solving the transportation problem by improving water transport and freeing powered industries from water sites.

Oliver Evans was a Delaware merchant who became one of the most prolific of American inventors. (He patented a highly automated flour mill and sold one to George Washington.) He is best known, along with the

British inventor Richard Trevithick, as the father of the high-pressure steam engine. Newcomen and Watt engines condensed steam to create a vacuum and used the vacuum to move the piston. The Evans/Trevithick designs used steam expansively, pushing the piston with steam pressure. Evans came up with his design in 1801, when as one scholar put it, "No more than six engines could be mustered in the whole of the States; mechanical construction and skill were at least fifty years behind those of England." Robert Fulton's steamboats used Boulton & Watt low-pressure engines imported from England.[31]

High-pressure engines used much more fuel but were much cheaper and easier to build. A 24-horsepower Evans engine—powerful enough to run a saw mill—weighed in at about 1,000 pounds, with a piston cylinder nine inches wide and about forty inches long. A Boulton & Watt 24-horsepower engine weighed four times as much and had a twenty-six-inch-diameter, five-foot-long piston. Most good American machine shops could execute an Evans piston by 1820 or so, but only a few in New York and Philadelphia could handle an equivalent Boulton & Watt–scale piston. In the words of Louis C. Hunter, the historian of American power, "The advantages of the simple, compact, low-cost high-pressure engine . . . were so clearly manifest and so appropriate to American conditions—scarcity of capital and skilled labor, scarcity of repair facilities and limited scale of operations—that a wide consensus was early reached, with virtually no debating of the issue."[32]

Unfortunately, high-pressure engines were very dangerous. With boiler pressures routinely as high as 100 pounds per square inch, small construction flaws could result in devastating explosions. Explosions on Hudson River steamboats in the 1820s were frequent enough that passengers sometimes insisted on being towed behind on "safety barges."[33] Improvements came very slowly. It took fifty years to develop accurate steam gauges. Safety valves were often poorly made or poorly maintained, and often intentionally disabled. Riveting was mostly by hand, often with rivets of dubious integrity and boiler plate of poor quality. Steamboat explosions were closely tracked, since they were so public. In the twenty years from 1816 through 1835, there were forty steamboat explosions, causing 353 deaths; 88 percent of the explosions and 83 percent of the deaths were on western steamboats, which were almost exclusively powered by high-pressure engines. Even as much safer designs became available in the last half of the century, they were strongly resisted because of their cost. As steam engines proliferated, disasters kept rising. A study covering 1867–1870 showed about a hundred major explosions a year, killing about 200 people and injuring a similar number.[34] The dominance of efficiency over any other value may have also been characteristic of American industries.

Evans died in 1819; by then his Mars Works in Philadelphia had produced more than one hundred steam engines for both water transportation and industrial power. After his patents expired in 1824, his designs were widely copied and improved on. Robert L. Stevens, an important railroad executive, may have been the most original American contributor to steam-engine technology after Evans.

There was an adroit division of labor in the early manufacturing and distribution of Evans-model steam engines. Eastern manufacturers, who had the most advanced metals operations, constructed the pistons, the flywheel, shafts, and other moving parts, while local contractors, perhaps with on-site supervision from the eastern supplier, executed the heavy castings for the engine housing and boiler and assembled the engine. Even with those arrangements, the distribution of Evans's engines still clearly tracks established waterways and so was likely limited by high overland transport costs. By mid-century, manufacturing of engines was becoming quite decentralized at cities like Pittsburgh, Louisville, and Cincinnati, while the western steamboat had opened many smaller waterways to freight traffic.

———

THERE WAS NO SIMPLE MODEL OF AMERICAN MASS PRODUCTION manufacturing. In clocks, a series of brilliant manufacturing insights of

Eli Terry made it possible to make ordinary clocks on a mass scale. Clocks were a relatively lightweight product and were readily picked up by peddler networks built to distribute buttons and cloth. Textiles were already a mass market in Great Britain when the Boston Company was founded. Lowell and Moody focused on creating a single-line, mechanized-flow manufacturing system tuned to the mass-market, working-class customer using existing distribution networks. Mechanization was not invariably a prerequisite for moving to a mass-market scale: Shoes were a mass-manufacturing industry well before the advent of shoemaking machinery. Stoves and steam engines were mass-scale industries without any mass manufacturers. Both were extremely heavy products, so the ingenuity went into the distribution and assembly. Indeed, it is likely that through much of the first half of the century, as many homes had stoves as had clocks.

The most famous example of American mass production, however, was the manufacture of guns, which will be the subject of the next chapter.

CHAPTER FOUR

American Arms

Whitney, North, Blanchard, and Hall

FOR THE TWO DECADES BEFORE THE WAR OF 1812, THE UNITED STATES was constantly on the edge of being drawn into the escalating conflict between Great Britain and France. The prolonged tension overcame the American aversion to standing armies and triggered a serious round of weapons procurement. The Springfield armory in Massachusetts was directed to commence musket production in 1795, and a new armory in Harpers Ferry, Virginia, was opened the following year with the same mission. A war scare with France in 1798 led to a rush of legislation. Congress voted to create a 15,000-man standing army, with authorization to call up twice that number more in an emergency. Commensurate increases were authorized to beef up naval and harbor defenses. That same legislation authorized the outsourcing of 30,000 muskets to private contractors.[1]

And thereby arose perhaps the most famous story of American industrialization: making small arms by special-purpose machinery to such a level of precision that parts could be freely interchanged between weapons. While the tale has been much embellished, it is mostly true—a prime example of the American impulse toward ever greater manufacturing scale. Gun making is therefore an important thread in the American mass production story. While it is far from the main story as it once seemed, it was still a notable piece of a much larger tapestry.

The gun-making story gained such prominence because it drew accolades from Great Britain in mid-century—a time when British opinion makers tended to react to alleged American achievements with withering scorn. Parliament discovered American gun making as the country was nearing a war with Russia with its small-arms procurement system in a dreadful snarl. An investigative commission gave a ringing endorsement to the American approach, which they dubbed the American system of manufacturing. The full parliament authorized a new small-arms factory at Enfield, outfitted with American machinery and initially staffed with American managers. Enfield was a signal success, and the new machinery greatly accelerated weapons procurement. But while the American accomplishments were real enough, the inevitable exaggerations by parliamentary advocates for their adoption were uncritically taken up by historians for much of the twentieth century (see Chapter 7).

The first American production at Springfield and Harpers Ferry was not machinery-intensive, beyond the use of standard water-powered machines like trip-hammers and lathes. The two armories reached their targeted production rate of about 10,000 muskets a year well before war finally broke out. They also made substantial productivity gains, but it came mostly from work-flow improvement and the creation of specialist teams for specific parts.[2]

A serious policy focus on mechanizing arms production came only after the war. But high-level chatter about the possibility of full-scale mechanization started earlier, much of it generated by Eli Whitney, the best known of the early contractors. But first, a short primer on the complexities of gun making.

The Crafts of Gun Making

Making small firearms—pistols, muskets, and rifles—was one of the most demanding crafts of the preindustrial era. A gun is a precision machine designed to produce repeated, powerful, internal explosions; relatively minor imperfections in the firing apparatus will cause misfires and can even kill or maim the gun's user. Embodying those crafts in machinery, therefore, was a signal accomplishment. Traditional gun-making crafts are still alive in the United States, so to better understand the mechanization challenge, I tracked down a practicing master gunsmith, Steve Bookout of Newton, Iowa, who agreed to let me spend a few days learning about pre–machine-age gun making.

Bookout is a big man, in his early sixties, and heavy in the neck and shoulders. An army helicopter pilot in Vietnam and now retired from May-tag, he makes and sells replicas of vintage guns at his backyard forge, and instructs a loose coterie of apprentices in the crafts. He achieved his master smithing stature not only from his body of work, but by creating a "master piece," the most perfect rifle he could make. It was submitted to a board of master gunsmiths in Alabama, who examined it and certified it as the work of a master gunsmith, engraved it with the place and date of certification, and placed it in a display cabinet with other master pieces as a permanent record.

Bookout has family roots in the trade. All of his handmade guns have an elegant brass "Bookout" sideplate. A rifle on the wall, with the same sideplate bearing the date 1820, was made by a quadruple-great-grandfather. Like his ancestor, Bookout makes his guns with traditional tools and without power machinery. Each one is a minor work of industrial art.

The major components of a flintlock firearm are the lock, the stock, and the barrel.* Traditional gunsmiths usually did the whole job, as do most of the modern practitioners of traditional gunsmithing. But even in the colonial era, craftsmen in larger workshops often specialized in one or the other.

The wooden stock of a rifle or musket is an elegant, complex shape, widest where it supports the barrel, narrowing and sloping down to seat the hand and trigger finger, and fanning out into the shoulder rest at the

---

* The phrase "lock, stock, and barrel" was a favorite of my grandmother, as in "She left and cleaned him out lock, stock, and barrel." I knew what she meant, but the phrase conjured up an odd pastiche of door handles and wooden kegs.

butt end. In Great Britain, where the landed gentry were the largest private gun market, fitting a gentleman's gunstock was as personal as fitting his frock coat. In the hierarchy of woodworkers, gunstockers are on a par with top cabinetmakers. In the early nineteenth century, a skilled man could produce about two stocks in three days.

Barrel making was the most physically demanding task. One of Bookout's apprentices, Tim Crowe, a Wisconsin general contractor, was also visiting when I was there, and the two of them roughed out a pistol barrel for my benefit. They started with an iron skelp, a flat piece of iron that Bookout harvests from the rims of old wooden wagon wheels. After it was heated in the forge to a cherry-red, Bookout grasped it in a pair of long tongs and held it over one of the semicircles cut in the sides of a big chunk of cast iron called a "swage block." Crowe then hammered the bar into the swage shape.* (I was out of harm's way, working the forge blower.) With repeating heatings and hammering, the skelp gradually took the shape of a half cylinder, which they closed by "hot-welding"—hammering the cylinder shut around a mandrel, a steel rod the width of a pistol barrel, to fuse it into a single piece of iron. It is a high-skill task: uneven hammering at any point can leave dangerous weak spots.

Barrels must be straight, and barrel straighteners were among the highest-status craftsmen at military armories well into the twentieth century. Each armory had a window containing a pane with an inlaid horizontal line, and an apparatus for holding new rifle barrels level and perpendicular to the line. In a good barrel, the window line should make two opposite crisp straight shadows on the barrel interior that stay straight as it is rotated. A skilled armory straightener made his adjustments by high-speed tapping with a light copper hammer, instantly spotting the right place to target.[3] Bookout uses the same method for his barrels but starts with a line mounted on a six-foot bow.

Muskets are smooth-bored weapons that early-nineteenth-century militaries preferred over rifles. They were inaccurate and had a short range

---

* Hence the phrase "striking while the iron is hot."

but were much less prone to fouling than a muzzle-loaded rifle. The infantry tactics of the time placed a low premium on accuracy. Opposing lines of soldiers stood within fifty yards, usually in two ranks that alternated firing and reloading in unison. Close-rank volleys could create horrific casualties even if no one aimed at anyone in particular. Drills emphasized formation maneuvers and loading procedures, not target shooting.

The greater accuracy of rifles is the result of spiral barrel grooves that spin the projectile and stabilize its flight. The legendary Kentucky rifle of the Revolutionary War era (which was mostly made in Pennsylvania) was a weapon of uncanny accuracy for its day, and British officers quickly learned to fear American snipers. Bookout is also a sharpshooter and an active competitor in vintage rifle competitions. He has a Montana game warden–certified 760-yard antelope kill to his credit using a replica of an 1874 Sharps. The shot was "off-hand" (without a rifle stand), without special sights, and on a windy day, which is extraordinary. Matt Damon used the same model Sharps for his climactic shot in the movie *True Grit*. (In online chat rooms vintage-gun hunters speak of a Sharps killing range of about 200 to 300 yards, but there is an annual 1,000-yard Sharps marksman contest in Montana.)

Crowe had come to Newton to rifle a new barrel under Bookout's supervision. Bookout has a rifling machine constructed on a long wooden frame. One end has chucks for holding the barrel; at the other is a thick wooden roller holding a barrel-length iron bar with a cutting edge attachment. The roller is incised with five evenly spaced grooves spiraling along its length and passing through a wooden collar with a tooth to fit the grooves. The craftsman positions the cutting bar at the opening of the barrel and fixes the position of the spiral guide in the collar tooth. As he pushes the cutting rod through the barrel, the rod replicates the path of the spiral guide. After each pass, the next groove is fixed in the tooth to cut five evenly-spaced spiral grooves.

Crowe is a fairly skilled craftsman, but the rifling takes him a full day. Each groove requires twenty or thirty separate cuts. Crowe and Bookout made an assortment of shims from postcard stock and cigarette paper to

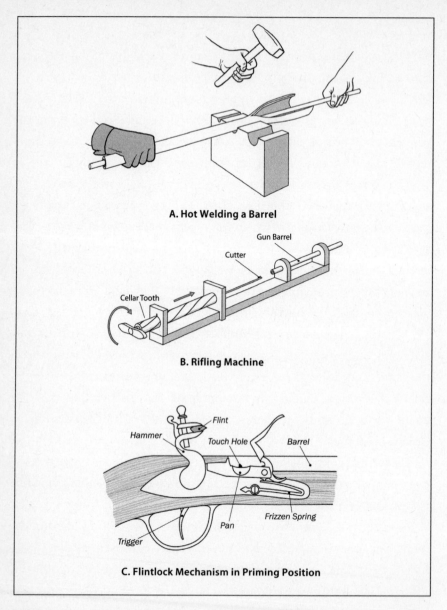

A. Hot Welding a Barrel

B. Rifling Machine

Gun Barrel

Cutter

Cellar Tooth

C. Flintlock Mechanism in Priming Position

Flint

Hammer

Touch Hole

Barrel

Frizzen Spring

Pan

Trigger

A. The hot iron skelp is hammered into semicylindrical shape in the swage block, and then hammered shut around a mandrel. Skilled hammering at the right heat fuses the iron into a single piece. **B.** A wooden cutter holder with incised spiral grooves is placed in a toothed collar, with one of the incised grooves fixed in the collar tooth. As the cutter is pushed into the rifle, it traces the incised spiral. At the end of each pass, the cutter holder is repositioned to move up one groove in the collar tooth to cut the next rifle groove. **C.** With the lock in half-cocked position, the shooter pours powder into the touch hole and the pan. The frizzen is snapped down to protect the powder. Soldiers near an action moved with their muskets primed and in the half-cocked position.

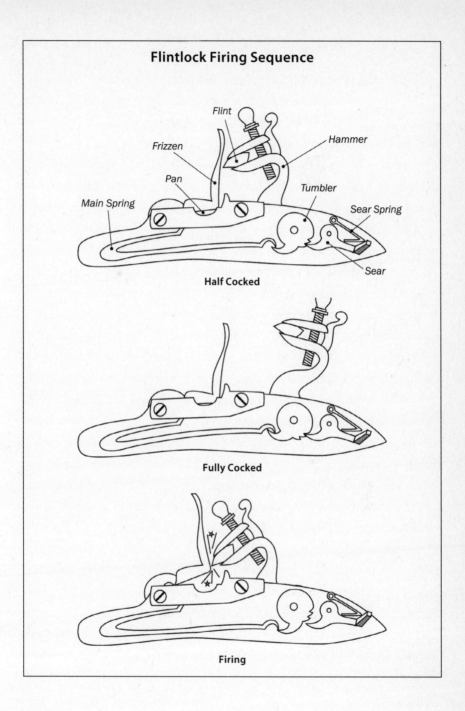

Flintlock Firing Sequence

Half Cocked

Flint

Frizzen

Pan

Hammer

Main Spring

Tumbler

Sear Spring

Sear

Fully Cocked

Firing

gradually raise the cutter bit to deepen the riflings on each pass. The inside of the barrel was also liberally dosed with lubricant to reduce heat and clear shavings. Bookout uses hog lard, both for its verisimilitude to the old days and because Iowa overflows with hog lard. Interrupting a cut in mid-stroke can be a minor disaster, because it is difficult to reposition the tool in a groove partway down the barrel. Worst case, the barrel has to be re-bored to remove the partial grooves and the process started from scratch.

The third major component of a gun is the lock, which presents the most intricate of the gunsmith's challenges. Loading a flintlock musket or rifle required the soldier to stand with his weapon upright, leaving him dangerously exposed on a field of battle for up to a minute or even more for a green soldier. The ammunition used in the War of 1812 came in paper cartridges that contained both a ball and the right amount of pow-der. The soldier opened the cartridge with his teeth, poured the powder down the barrel, pinched the cartridge paper around the ball to make the wadding (so explosive energy didn't leak around the ball), dropped the wad into the muzzle, and ramrodded it tightly in place. Under cover again, he prepared for firing by pulling the hammer into the half-cocked position; then he poured a small amount of additional powder into the pan and snapped down the frizzen to cover the pan. With that, the gun was primed, the pan powder protected, and the hammer in a safe position. Near an action, soldiers moved with half-cocked muskets.

To fire, the hammer was first pulled back to the fully cocked position, which rotated the tumbler backward, compressed the mainspring, and locked the tumbler in place with the sear. When the trigger pull released the sear, the tumbler rotated forward, and the hammer slammed into the frizzen plate, pushing it open and striking sparks. The powder in the pan ignited next to a small touch hole, emitting a large smoke plume into the shooter's face.[*] The explosion ignited the barrel powder through the touch

---

[*] If there was insufficient powder in the pan, or the touch hole was fouled, the powder in the barrel would not ignite—and the soldier would get only "a flash in the pan." If the sear or the tumbler was worn or improperly aligned, a primed, half-cocked gun might discharge by accident—"going off half-cocked."

hole, and the gun discharged. In human time, the trigger pull and discharge are virtually instantaneous.

The lock tumbler encapsulates the lock maker's challenge. It is a complex shape, subject to great stresses, that must operate within a close tolerance range. The tumbler connects to the hammer by fitting a large square-end spindle into a square opening at the hammer base. If the fit is loose, or the corners of the fitting abrade, the hammer stroke will lose force. The surface of the tumbler's high-friction points, like the tumbler notches, must be very hard; if they abrade so the sear slips, the lock is inoperable. But if the tumbler is *too* hard, it will lose tensile strength and be prone to cracking. The steel in the mainspring must be of excellent quality to retain its power. If the pivot fixing the tumbler to the stock is misaligned with the hammer rotation, the torque could twist the lock plate or otherwise interfere with a smooth action of the flint and the frizzen.

A manual craftsman like Bookout starts each lock piece with wrought iron, which is easy to chisel when it's hot, and cuts it into an approximation of the final shape. It is then forged by hammering to expel remaining impurities and to increase its structural integrity and toughness. The forged piece would be further chiseled and filed into the final shape, largely by eye. The last step before the final grinding and polishing would be case hardening at the main friction points, by careful heating and quenching in a carbon bath.[4]

The armories' water-powered lathes saved much time in rough cutting and grinding, while powered trip-hammers removed most of the brute work of barrel welding. (A standard sledge hammer suspended on a fulcrum and raised and released by a toothed wheel could achieve hundreds of steady-force hammer strokes a minute.) Otherwise armory guns were made more or less with the methods Bookout uses, although separate groups of craftsmen worked on each major component. The early-period mechanization chatter was mostly focused on the lock, the hardest mechanization challenge of all—which takes us back to Whitney.

Eli Whitney's
Reputational Thrill Ride

For a century and a half after his death, Eli Whitney was virtually canonized as the Father of American Technology. According to the traditional story, Whitney was the inventor of the cotton gin, which transformed the antebellum South (and unfortunately reinvigorated the institution of slavery); he was the first person to machine-produce precisely fitting interchangeable parts for muskets and was the inventor of critical new machine tools, like the celebrated Whitney milling machine.

The Whitney role in military manufacturing came under withering challenge in the 1960s. The revisionists charged that Whitney's pretension to making arms with interchangeable parts was merely a ploy to justify extensions of his contracts. Indeed, he had little idea of how to manufacture muskets at all, much less how to blaze new trails in making them. He was unconscionably late in fulfilling his arms contract, in part because he spent so much of his time pursuing his cotton gin profits.[5]

That harsh view of Whitney as manufacturer has moderated considerably in recent years. While it's true that Whitney made few contributions to machining technology, most of the extreme claims for his accomplishments were made by others, often long after his death. The traditional source for the story that he claimed to manufacture interchangeable parts appears to be itself a partial fabrication.[6] While he did have a rocky start on his first musket contract, so did many other contractors. The current consensus is that Whitney was quite a competent manufacturer and one of the earliest advocates for mass production by machinery, if not expressly for interchangeable parts—in short, a respectable figure, if not the demigod of legend.

My own view is that in his early career Whitney was indeed something of a flimflam man; some recent work even raises doubts as to whether he invented his cotton gin (see Appendix). And I think the record supports the charge that he dangled the promise of machined interchangeable parts to gain extensions on his contracts. But it's also true that he was a talented artisan and entrepreneur, and once he focused on actually building his weapons—about 1805, when he turned forty—he proved himself to be a good manufacturer and was regarded as such by his peers and armory officials. While it is almost impossible to trace weapon types to specific battles, there is decent circumstantial evidence that Whitney's muskets were used by a good portion of the troops in some of the hottest infantry engagements of the War of 1812 and that they performed as expected.

There is nothing contradictory in such a portrait. Whitney was a hyper-talented farm boy with a modestly connected father. Older than most of his classmates when he entered Yale, he was a good engineer and metal-worker, articulate, a formidable salesman, and desperate to succeed. In the first dozen years or so after graduation, he was very much on the make and sometimes played fast and loose with the truth, but as he matured and focused on a business he was good at, he did well.

Whitney finished Yale in 1792 with a vague idea of becoming a school-master. The president of Yale referred him to a tutoring job on a Southern plantation and introduced him to Phineas Miller, a Yale alumnus of about Whitney's age who had been tutoring on a plantation for several years. Whitney went south with Miller with the intention of acclimating on Miller's plantation before taking up his own duties.

The record is mostly silent on Whitney's first year in the South. But he never made it to his tutoring job, and a year after his arrival, he patented his cotton gin in partnership with Miller. Their business plan was to leverage control over ginning technology to create ginning centers throughout the cotton country, charging 40 percent of the ginned cotton. Whitney returned to New Haven to manufacture the gins, while Miller created and marketed the local centers. Financing came primarily from the mistress of Miller's plantation, Constance Greene, a widow whom Miller eventually married.

The business was a failure. Their pricing was extortionate, and their gin, while a substantial advance, was relatively easy to replicate. The next few years were a nightmare of endless patent litigation, with few victories, rising indebtedness, and the looming bankruptcy of Mrs. Greene. The

French war scare in 1798 came just as Whitney was reaching the end of his rope. As he later wrote to a friend, "Bankruptcy & ruin were constantly staring me in the face. . . . Loaded with a Debt of 3 or 4000 Dollars . . . I knew not which way to turn."[7]

Then Whitney came across a federal circular recruiting gun manufacturers. He wrote to the Treasury secretary, Oliver Wolcott, another Yale man, that his gin factory had been idled by disruptions in trade and that he proposed to "undertake to Manufacture Ten or Fifteen Thousand Stand[*] of Arms."[8] Since the Whitney gin had been widely publicized in the North, Wolcott responded immediately with an invitation to Washington, "knowing your skill in mechanick."[9] Barely a month later, Whitney had a contract for 10,000 stand of muskets on a French pattern, to be delivered in stages over the next two years. The total contract price was $134,000, with a $10,000 advance for tooling: it was the largest of the private gun contracts and the first with an advance. The only objection within the administration was that the schedule was unrealistic, which was true.[10] But the schedule was furthest from Whitney's mind: as he wrote to his friend, in the nick of time he had won a large contract by which "I obtained some thousands of Dollars in advance which has saved me from ruin."[11]

Whitney had minimal acquaintance with gun making, and set off on a tour of arms makers to learn more about the craft. He must have realized early that the delivery schedule was impossible, and as he missed his contract dates, year after year, he defended his tardiness by claiming that he was really engaged in a kind of R&D project: "One of my primary objectives is to form the tools so the tools themselves shall fashion the work and give to every part its just proportion—which when accomplished will give expedition, uniformity and exactness to the whole. . . . In short the tools which I contemplate are similar to an engraving on copper plate from

---

[*] A "Stand" of arms was a musket and necessary auxiliary equipment, which in federal contracts usually included the musket, bayonet and holder, and the ramrod. Other equipment like ammunition and accessories was purchased separately. Musket contracts also often outsourced the bayonet knives to specialists like Nathan Starr.

which may be taken a great number of impressions precisely alike."[12] Each time, he got a pass and sometimes even a further advance.

In Whitney lore, there was a climactic meeting in Washington in 1801 in which Whitney "made a triumphal demonstration of his musket" to a galaxy of top officials including Adams and Jefferson. There, "by allowing the officials to assemble the parts of the locks—selecting the constituent parts at random—he dramatized the concept of interchangeability and made its advantages obvious."[13]

There was such a meeting, and it was indeed a major event, but there is little firsthand information on its details. Whitney merely reported that he went to Washington and "carried on a musket of my manufacture & several samples of Locks &c." Whitney's congressman also attended and wrote that the samples "met universal approbation."[14] But there is no evidence for the story that officials around the table, or anyone else, reassembled locks.

Whatever did or did not happen in Washington, however, Whitney *did* dangle the promise of interchangeability. There's no other way to interpret the "copper plate" letter, and all early accounts cite it in that context.[15] A few weeks before his Washington meeting, moreover, Whitney asked for a reference letter from his friend Decius Wadsworth, a Yale classmate of Miller and the military's head arms inspector. Wadsworth opened by pronouncing Whitney's muskets to be possibly "superior to any muskets for common use ever yet fabricated in any country." And went on:

[Typically] all the similar parts of different locks are so far unlike that they cannot be mutually substituted in cases of accidents. But where the different parts of the Lock are each formed and fashioned successfully by a proper machine and by the same hand they will be found to differ so insensibly that the similar parts of different locks may be mutually substituted. . . . [This concept] has been treated and ridiculed as . . . vain and impractical . . . [but Mr. Whitney] has the satisfaction however, now of shewing the practicality of the attempt.

That is a very large claim and, if taken literally, was simply false. Wadsworth, indeed, having made the requested representation, carefully dissociated himself from it. His next sentence is that "I am of the opinion that there is more to please the imagination than of real utility in the plan yet it affords an incontestible proof of [Whitney's] . . . superior skill as a workman."[16]

Jefferson, in any case, came away with exactly the impression Whitney was hoping for. He later wrote to Madison that Whitney had invented machinery "for making all the pieces of his locks so exactly equal, that take 100 locks to pieces and mingle their parts and the hundred locks may be put together as well by taking the first pieces which come to hand."[17] In short, *something* happened in Washington to convince Jefferson that Whitney had achieved effective interchangeability, and once that impression was made, it was amplified on every retelling.

It is also striking how lightly Whitney wore his promises. He had assured Wolcott, who had been embarrassed by his nonperformance, that "nothing shall induce me to shrink from the task or for a moment divert my attention from its final accomplishment."[18] But he really meant "unless something better comes along." In the fall of 1801, his new advances in hand, he got word of the possibility of a lucrative settlement on the cotton gin patent. Whitney left for the southlands late in the year, did not return until May (long after the gin business was over), and took similar absences for the same reason over the next several years.[19]

A few years after that, it seems, he finally got serious, mostly giving up on the cotton gin litigation and devoting his formidable intelligence and mechanical gifts more or less full-time to the business of producing arms. While there is little evidence of his making any mechanical breakthroughs, he was a good manager and quickly got to a steady-state production of about 2,000 muskets a year. Several musket modifications Whitney made on his own initiative, like making the pan of hardened brass and designing a simplified hammer shape for easier machining, were later incorporated into the standard musket specifications.[20]

How did America's muskets perform on the battlefield? The 1814 theater on the Niagara Peninsula separating Lakes Ontario and Erie was the war's fiercest. From July through November, British regulars and American ground forces were squared off in the bloodiest and most sustained fighting of the war. The battles of Chippawa and Lundys Lane and the siege of Fort Erie were the most intense set-piece engagements, but there was nearly constant hostile contact in the intervals between. The Americans achieved a glorious tie, winning about as many head-to-head encounters as they lost: a performance that weighed heavily in the British decision to back away from the war.

The military historian Richard Barbuto, who has written the closest-to-the-ground history of the Niagara campaigns, told me that he never saw a report of a battle lost because muskets failed. Soldiers took dreadful care of their weapons, and especially broke bayonets. But while repair logistics were often difficult, the absence of postbattle complaints suggests that the muskets mostly performed as expected.[21]

Were any of the muskets Whitney's? It seems so, for in the years just before and during the war, Whitney sold 5,000 muskets to the New York state militia, who were deeply involved at Niagara. In the early days of the war, the New Yorkers had performed poorly, but by 1814 they were battle-hardened veterans who bore a heavy share of the fighting. Unusually, the Niagara ground commander over regulars and militia alike was a New York militia general, Jacob Brown. He had earned the post by his aggressiveness in seeking out and confronting the enemy, and he didn't hesitate to place his own state's soldiers in the thick of engagements. Daniel Tompkins, the New York governor, was a strong supporter of the war, close to Brown, and well informed on events at the front. Tompkins knew Whitney muskets, and in late August 1814, at the height of the fighting, he intervened forcefully to break a bureaucratically imposed blockade on their sale, taking every one he could get at the state's expense and without inspection.* There could hardly be a better reference.[22]

By 1814, Whitney was an established manufacturer with as much experience in musket making as anyone else in the country. He was turning

---

* Two thousand muskets were delivered to the New Yorkers in 1810, another 2,000 in 1813, and the final 1,000 upon Tompkins's intervention in September 1814.

out inelegant, inexpensive, quasi-mass-produced weapons that worked as they were supposed to. The postwar Whitney correspondence with Wadsworth and other armory and Ordnance officials confirms that he had become one of the half dozen or so private contractors they had come to treat as sound and reliable men. Besides Whitney, there was Simeon North, Lemuel Pomeroy, Asa Waters, Robert Johnson, Nathan Starr, and a few others. Ordnance maintained a constant correspondence with all of them, trading information on machines, waterpowers, iron and steel, and other topics of the trade. Whitney's letters are terse and businesslike, with none of the high-flown rhetoric that the younger Whitney used to impress his funders.

In the first flush of revisionism on Whitney in the 1960s, the contractor Whitney was often invidiously compared to was Simeon North. North became a great gun maker, but earlier in his career had some misadventures of his own.

Pistol Maker to the Nation

Simeon North was born the same year as Eli Whitney, and in much the same milieu, on a middle-class but still tightly circumstanced farm in Connecticut. He had a standard farm boy's education—no thoughts of Yale—and was hard at work from an early age. His intelligence is obvious, and from what little else is known of him, he was literate, genial, even-tempered, and taciturn. He enjoyed good health throughout his life and died after a short illness at age eighty-six. In a picture taken late in his life, he looks pure New England oak: erect, strongly built, firm mouth, looking directly at the camera. One vanity was his adoption of the title "Colonel" from a brief, and mostly honorary, stint in the state militia.

North married at twenty-one and took up farming on a sixty-six-acre plot in Berlin, about fifteen miles south of Hartford. He added to his acreage whenever he could, and in 1795, he acquired a tract with a stream, a sawmill, a dam, and waterpower rights. A natural mechanic, he kept the sawmill, added a forge, and started making scythes and other farming

Simeon North in Old Age.

hardware for the local market. It is not known when he gave up farming to concentrate entirely on manufacturing.

North himself left few records, and the standard source is a 1913 biography written by two of his great-grandsons that reproduces many of the key documents relating to his arms business. More recently, the late Robert Jeska, a collector of North pistols, spent years tracking down every North reference in national and state archives to put together a near-complete story of his early pistol contracts, which he privately published along with a large trove of important documents. Along the way, Jeska clears up many gaps and errors in the official records.[23]

North's first pistol engagement came in the spring of 1799, the year after Whitney's first contract. Like Whitney, North had no gun-making experience; he most likely purchased the contract from another craftsman, who was serving as the chief coiner at the Philadelphia mint. The contract was for five hundred cavalry pistols (the 1799s), following a French design, at $6.50 a pistol,* with $2,000 in advance.[24] That was followed up in February 1800 by a second contract for 1,500 pistols (the 1800s) and an additional $2,000 advance. He did not meet his schedules on either contract, and an unduly large portion of the 1799s were marked as "unserviceable."[25] The 1800s were completed nearly on schedule, however, and delivered throughout the country.

In June 1808, North made a new contract with the navy for 2,000 naval pistols (the 1808s), which were heavier and of larger caliber than cavalry pistols, with an eighteen-month delivery schedule and an advance of $4,000. The contract correspondence included North's well-known statement that "by confining a workman to one particular limb of the pistol until he has made the whole two thousand, I save at least one quarter of his labor, to what I should provided I finish them by small quantities, and the work will be much better as it is quicker made."[26]

In the near-term, that strategy caused him no end of trouble. North devoted most of the first contract year to erecting a new factory and acquiring sufficient inventory to make all the components before assembly. In February 1809, the navy asked North if he could expedite the deliveries, because they wanted to increase the order. North responded enthusiastically. He would have "the whole of my barrels made for this contract within eight or ten weeks," and as many as 800 were nearly ready for inspection.[27]

Naval procurement officers were delighted and requested 500 pistols as soon as possible. North was horrified and wrote that he didn't have any pistols, he was still just making *barrels*. The navy sent Isaac Chauncey, a hard but fair man, to inspect North's progress. There were indeed no pistols, and the barrels were disappointing—many were of different sizes and most needed to be rebored. Under Chauncey's pressure, North continued

---

* Pistols were usually contracted in pairs (by the "brace"). North's first contract specified 250 brace of pistols at $13 a brace. References in the sources are not always consistent, however, so I use a single weapon as the basic unit.

to overpromise and underperform. He did not get his production un-tracked until 1810, and finally closed out the contract in early 1811.[28]

It was a black time for North. The navy repeatedly told him that they were "very much disappointed." Indeed, growing frictions with Great Britain had forced them to scramble up and down the coast scrounging up enough pistols to get the fleet to sea. But as the war scare eased, the navy relented, pronounced themselves happy with North's pistols, and in-creased the contract by another five hundred, which were shipped in small batches until 1814. A substantial number of the 1808s went to Chauncey on Ontario, who would not have accepted them if they were defective.

Chauncey's inspection report also makes clear that North had not yet reached the point of making standard parts. Although he made his lock forg-ings in bulk, they still required extensive hand-trimming and fitting work. Like the armories and Whitney, North was still at the stage of exploiting division-of-labor efficiencies, without changing basic craft processes.

By this point, North was well established as a reliable arms manufac-turer, but for some reason over the next few years, his performance slipped badly. As the production of the 1808s got untracked in 1811, North nego-tiated a contract for 2,000 horse pistols (the 1811s) with staged deliveries over the next two years. A few months later, the record shows him solic-iting the navy for further contracts, claiming he was gearing up to produce 4,000 pistols a year.

With the advent of the war, small-arms purchasing shifted to the Commissary-General of Purchases, a new office in the Treasury filled by Callender Irvine, who launched a vendetta with Whitney*[29] and adopted North as a kind of counterexample of a good arms contractor. In the spring

---

* By this time Whitney had long since closed out his initial contract and was steadily turning out muskets under both federal and state contracts. Irvine was pushing a new musket design, in which he may have had a financial interest. Whitney was properly scornful: this was wartime, and supply problems were rife; pressing for a revised musket design was idiotic. The muskets Governor Tompkins bought from Whitney for the 1814 Niagara campaign had been sitting in a warehouse because Irvine and his favorite inspector, who was the designer of the new musket, refused to inspect them.

of 1813, although only a small number of the 1811s had been delivered, North and Irvine executed a huge contract for 20,000 pistols on a modified design (the 1813s). North got an advance of $20,000 and agreed to complete the contract within five years. He also agreed to a clause requiring that "the component parts of pistols, are to correspond so exactly that any limb or part of one Pistol may be fitted to any other Pistol of the Twenty Thousand."[30]

Then, in the midst of a war that was going badly, North's output nosedived. By the end of 1814, when the war effectively ended, North had produced only 756 of the contracted 2,000 1811s, and none at all against the massive 20,000-pistol contract, despite furious letters from Irvine, who was sorely embarrassed. That was most uncharacteristic of North. While he was often late because of unrealistic contract schedules, he usually worked at a steady pace and stayed within shouting distance of the original deadlines.

There are enough straws of evidence to prompt a guess as to what was happening. North had spent $100,000 on a new factory, a high price for the day. He had also indirectly complained to Irvine that the market price of pistols had risen well above his contract price. And there were also several instances of his selling, or trying to sell, pistols to various state militias. Finally, after the war he wrote to a naval procurement officer that he had 1,400 1811s in inventory that had never been inspected.[31] Taken together, the evidence suggests that North may have been in financial trouble and was withholding pistols from Irvine in the hope of selling them on the open market, where he could get a better price without a deduction for advances. That wasn't illegal, but it was the kind of sharp practice not usually associated with North. Nevertheless, as we saw with Connecticut clock salesmen, the rest of the country had learned to be wary when doing business with Yankees.[32]

The war ended in early 1815, with the 1811s in limbo, and the 1813s in complete abeyance.* Irvine was dismissed and Decius Wadsworth central-

---

* Standard sources list some model 1813 production, but Jeska shows convincingly that the apparent 1813s are really 1811s.

ized army weapons procurement within the Department of Ordnance. He renewed North's big 1813 contract, with some design changes (the 1816s), and approved a $25,000 advance (North had asked for $60,000). Wadsworth cautioned North against accepting any other contracts and warned other branches of the government that North had all he could handle. By mid-1817, North was back on track producing the 1816s, although he did receive one sharp warning from Ordnance in 1818 about "the far inferior workmanship" of some deliveries.[33]

Before approving the new contract, Wadsworth asked the superintendents of the Springfield and Harpers Ferry armories to inspect North's plant, where they suggested that North may have made progress on the famous "interchangeability" clause in the 1813 contract—although neither Irvine nor anyone else seems to have mentioned it again. According to the superintendents, North was using a standard die to make all lock plates the same size, or very nearly so, with the various lock pieces individually fitted to the standard plate. Presumably, if part of a lock broke, the whole lock could be replaced by another of the same plate size, and most of the time it would work. That would have been near-interchangeability at the subassembly level, a very intelligent approach. Modern tests of several 1811s, 1813s, and 1816-model pistols produced in this factory, however, did not find that their locks interchanged. But in the longer run, as we will see, North did play an important role in achieving strict uniformity and interchangeability of firearms parts.[34]

The Military Thinks Long Term

The 1815 decision to centralize all small-arms procurement in the Ordnance Department was the product of intense personal lobbying by Wadsworth. He and his deputy, Lt. Col. George Bomford, had been at the epicenter of the wartime procurement chaos—the multiple overlapping lines of authority, the turf wars and infighting, the lack of standards. Irvine at Treasury had been a constant disruption. He seemed almost to enjoy overruling military specifications and frequently refused to pay for emergency field purchases.

Wadsworth, forty-seven years old in 1815, was a member of one of Connecticut's most prominent families, with many high-ranking military men in the family tree. Moderately wealthy, he was a career artillery officer and a creative engineer and inventor. As a young officer, he had worked under the great French artillerist Louis Tousard, the godfather of American artillery practice, author of the American artillerists' field manual, designer of West Point, and a devotée of French pioneers of interchangeability in arms making.

Bomford was twelve years younger than Wadsworth, of obscure provenance. His mother is unknown to history, while his father was apparently a British artillery officer. A chance acquaintance with an influential West Point graduate who recognized Bomford's talents opened the door to an appointment at the academy. Wadsworth recruited Bomford ten years after his graduation, when he had already distinguished himself as a fortification engineer and had invented a new type of cannon.[35] At Wadsworth's death in 1821, Bomford replaced him as Ordnance chief, serving until 1842. He married well, gaining the political connections that were essential for success within the tightly knit ruling circles of the early United States.

Wadsworth and Bomford were bound together by their shared experience of the war. One or the other was constantly traveling during the war years, and their extensive correspondence illuminates the frustrations behind their reform agenda.

In Washington, Wadsworth's desk was awash in matters picayune and crucial alike. He personally ordered a drum, a fife, and dress swords for a recruiting party and then rushed to Albany to inspirit a dithering Dearborn amid the military calamities of the first summer. He created the first working inventory and reporting system for army weapons, oversaw the procurement of artillery carriages at Pittsburgh through a local contractor, intervened with Irvine to get the contractor paid, and then sent Bomford out to customize the carriages. Throughout the war he dispatched a stream of illustrated instructions for younger artillery officers: how to set up a mortar bed, how to organize cannon transport, and much else.[36]

Bomford's letters brim with ideas: designing a standard pattern for cais-sons (munition wagons), creating a new howitzer, proposing standards for shot, for stocks, and for muskets.[37] Constantly lamenting the lack of "Sys-tem," Bomford worked on specifications for musket balls, tried to grade iron quality by its specific gravity, developed empirical standards for pow-der charges to extend musket life, and proved that mobility was to be pre-ferred over throw weight in choosing field howitzers. He raged over the lack of professionalism among the quartermasters—"Waggons picked up here and there," then followed a supply train, and found weapons strewn all over the road. Nearly every letter fumes over one absurdity or another. Repair procedures damaged good weapons. The quality of swords and bayonets was execrable: One sword will "fly into pieces at a blow . . . while another bend to a quadrant." Both he and Wadsworth spent sub-stantial amounts of their own money setting up "laboratories"—repair depots—and tiding over unpaid contractors.[38]

During the very tough 1814 campaign on the Niagara peninsula, Bom-ford ran a musket repair operation, driving the craftsmen to keep up with the flow of arms from the front and complaining of how the soldiers mis-used the equipment.[39] That same summer, Wadsworth prepared the de-fenses on the Chesapeake peninsula and at Baltimore against the raiders who had put the torch to Washington. He was almost certainly involved in arranging the successful artillery defense against a determined British assault on Fort McHenry in Baltimore harbor, the episode immortalized by "The Star-Spangled Banner." Ordnance files don't show his precise lo-cation at the time, but he was on the peninsula and had long been men-toring the McHenry artillery officers. The British mounted a serious twenty-five-hour attack, and the defense is widely acknowledged as a masterpiece.[40]

With the war mercifully ended, and procurement authority consoli-dated, Wadsworth and Bomford set out to fix the mess they had inherited, with the Springfield Armory serving as their primary development labo-ratory.[41] The armory is located at about the geographic midpoint of the Connecticut River, near the Massachusetts/Connecticut border. By 1815, the spinning-mill industry created by Samuel Slater had enjoyed twenty years of development and growth. Lowell's Waltham mill had opened in late 1814, adding to a glut of new mills hoping to profit from the unavailability of British cloth. The mills, along with Terry's clocks, had force-fed the development of a native machine tool industry. David Wilkinson, one of Samuel Slater's first partners, was one of a pantheon of early American machining greats who created the technical substrate for advances in armory and other metal goods production.

That talent pool, the surplus capital in Boston, the fine water sites along the main river and its tributaries, the easy access to the Salisbury iron region, and the convenience of riverboat shipping to and from New York combined to make the Connecticut River Valley a cynosure of an East Coast tradition of advanced precision-machinery manufacturing development.

The armory's new superintendent, Roswell Lee, became the Ordnance point man in the valley and the third critical player on the Wadsworth-Bomford advanced-manufacturing team. Scion of one of the bluest-blood New England families, he had once been engaged by Whitney to maintain his Southern cotton gin establishments. He had been a high-ranking officer during the war, knew Wadsworth, and had lobbied him hard for a postwar civilian position in armory work.[42]

As Springfield superintendent—he served from 1815 until his death in 1833—Lee's wide, active correspondence with the valley's private contractors made the armory a clearing house for technical information, tools development, and hard-to-find skills. A practical mechanic and a competent manager, he maintained a record of steady productivity improvement and good financial controls, and gradually disciplined the armory's unruly workforce.

Wadsworth's and Bomford's goal at the outset was something well short of strict interchangeability of parts. They both talked in terms of "uniformity," which probably meant little more than ensuring that all units of a firearm were built to the same design and dimensions with consistent quality and costs. Achieving even that proved far more difficult than expected.

Wadsworth kicked off the uniformity program with a June 1815 planning meeting in New Haven hosted by Whitney, with Wadsworth, Lee, James Stubblefield (superintendent at Harpers Ferry), and Benjamin Prescott (Lee's predecessor at Springfield) in attendance. After several days of discussions, they agreed on a first step of creating a set of "pattern muskets" for a new model 1816, which incorporated a number of small improvements, including several Whitney had introduced for his militia contracts. (American muskets were based on the French Charleville, a 1763 model supplied to Americans during the Revolutionary War and updated somewhat when production began at Springfield in 1795, becoming the model 1795.) The patterns were to be distributed among the armories and all federal contractors as the template for all future production. As the model number 1816 suggested, they assumed the patterns would be ready the next year.

But it took nearly three years just to produce patterns. The job was first assigned to Harpers Ferry, but Stubblefield botched it, since he had little interest in the idea. Wadsworth reassigned it to Lee, but the squabbling within the armories and with contractors went on for another two years before a design was agreed on.[43]

It had not yet dawned on Wadsworth and Bomford that they didn't know how to specify a pattern.*[44] The modern system of designs on blueprints with precise three-axis dimensioning didn't exist in 1815. No rule with graduated markings, as opposed to a plain straightedge, has been identified at Springfield before 1848. Reasonably priced vernier calipers, true precision measuring instruments, were not available until the early 1850s and were not used on the Springfield shop floor until the 1870s. Ordnance's idea of uniformity at this stage was to circulate several pattern muskets for contractors and armory workers to emulate as best they

---

* Simeon North's 1813 pistol contract, for instance, came with a pattern and a list of exceptions, e.g., "Hammer pin [is] too large . . . the threads on the small lock pins to be increased about one size . . . the cock pin and jaw too loose." Even that was more precise than any of Whitney's contemporary contracts.

could. None of the patterns would be exactly the same at the outset, and variations would inevitably accumulate and multiply.[45]

As Ordnance focused more explicitly on machine manufacturing and true interchangeability, each step forward revealed yet another abyss to be crossed. Achieving their objective would ultimately require reconceiving specification and production systems *all the way down*, in every detail. But one of the great advantages of military R&D is that it can take a long view. For more than thirty years, Ordnance stuck to the mission, steadily refined its objectives, and eventually got within reasonable proximity to its goal. Lee was at Springfield for the first eighteen years of the program, and Bomford for nearly the whole span.

The notion of interchangeability was definitely in the air. Jefferson had been an early apostle and was quick to climb on the Whitney bandwagon.[46] Callender Irvine, as we have seen, made it an express but not enforced part of North's 1813 contract. Pressure to satisfy a political audience is the likely explanation for a peculiar 1818 directive from Wadsworth to all armories and contractors that all musket parts must be made "to fit *every* musket," which he surely knew was not possible.[47] When Lee was pressed by a contractor on the meaning of the instruction, he responded only that his "present station" forbade him from making unfavorable comments except to his superiors.[48]

Line officers were less restrained. Major James Dalliba, who inspected the Springfield Armory for Wadsworth in 1819, wrote in his report that pursuing uniformity "precisely to one pattern in all the detail of parts" was neither attainable nor advisable and would incur a large expense. He also poured cold water on the idea that interchangeability would facilitate field repairs, since weapons became deformed with use.[49]

Wadsworth was already terminally ill by the time of Dalliba's report, but Bomford and Lee never jettisoned the objective of interchangeability, vaguely defined though it was. Their sustained attention, constant cajoling, and alertness in scouting out technologists who might contribute to this or that piece of the puzzle are still characteristic of the kind of successful military development programs that have recently produced the Internet and many developments in semiconductors and other advanced technologies.

A fine illustration of the Bomford-Lee system in action can be seen in the early career of Thomas Blanchard, perhaps the greatest of a handful of outstanding American inventors in the first half of the nineteenth century.

The Machine Geek

Thomas Blanchard was the classic nerd, a technology geek, but since he came of age in the Connecticut River Valley in the early 1800s, he was a machine geek. An indifferent student with limited social graces—he was afflicted with a bad stammer—his father early despaired of turning him into a farmer. As a teenager he was shipped off to work for his eldest brother, who ran a tack factory—and Thomas had found his milieu. His first job was hand-fixing heads on tacks, which he hated. He quickly invented an automatic tack counter to eliminate his record-keeping and then proceeded to eliminate his job by inventing a tack-making machine that turned out five hundred tacks a minute. He patented his tack machine in 1817 and sold the licensing rights for $5,000—a stupendous sum for a young man. That money allowed him to buy his own manufactory in Millbury on a site with waterpower privileges, in an area with some forty water-powered mills and factories already in place.[50] Blanchard must already have had a local reputation. His first patent, for a wool-cloth shearing machine, had been awarded in 1813 when he was twenty-five, and the year after he opened his shop, he was called for a consultation by Asa Waters, one of the region's gun-making elite. Waters had several patents, including ones for a trip-hammer barrel welder[*][51] and a lathe to produce a tapered

---

* Prompting the reasonable complaint from a competitor, "I should not think of gitting a patent for . . . applying a trip to welding a gun barel any moure than plating a scythe or a hoe it seems to me that a strange fanatism has operated on sum peope for gitting patents for some simple things." The complaint anticipates today's controversies over software "business process" patents. The trip-hammer had been around a long time, so Waters appears to have patented the application to barrel welding, rather than the tool.

barrel. He was struggling, however, with the challenge of creating a lathe that could machine the "flats and ovals" required for a musket's breech end.

According to Waters's son, who was later an important manufacturer in his own right, Blanchard listened to the problem and then "glanced his eye over the machine, began a low monotonous whistle, as was his wont through life when in deep study, and ere long suggested an additional, very simple, but wholly original cam motion . . . which upon being applied, relieved the difficulty at once." (A cam is an accessory that can modify a circular motion into an elliptical or linear path.[52])

Blanchard was also well known to Lee. With his ear always to the ground for new technology, Lee quickly learned of Blanchard's flats and ovals machine and invited him to build one at Springfield along with a draw-grinding machine—a new machine type for fine-sandstone barrel grinding just before buffing.[53] Both machines were also later installed at Harpers Ferry. We also know that in 1820, Blanchard had a machine-building contract with the Boston Company, the nine-hundred-pound gorilla of the region's technology buyers.[54] Any Waltham-Lowell machine-building contract would have gone through Paul Moody, arguably the top machinist in the area, who normally manufactured his own machines and also had a profitable sideline selling them to other textile firms. A Moody outsourcing to Blanchard was a gold-star endorsement.

Blanchard's lasting fame is based on the Blanchard gun-stocking lathe, a truly original manufacturing breakthrough with broad implications for all machining of irregular shapes. Once again, the junior Waters tells the story, for the stocking machine arose from his father's new flats-and-ovals lathe. Delighted with Blanchard's solution, the elder Waters exclaimed, "Well, Thomas, I don't know what you won't do next. I should not be surprised if you turned a gun-stock!"[55] When Thomas stammered out that he would like to try, the shop workmen broke into guffaws. Making gun stocks had long been a serious bottleneck at government armories: the variety of curves and the multiplicity of recesses and connection points made it impossible to machine.

As Waters tells the story, Blanchard mulled the problem until one day, on a trip home, "the whole principle of turning irregular forms from a pattern burst upon his mind." A neighbor reported that Blanchard stood in the road shouting, "I've got it! I've got it! I've got it!," while a passing farmer muttered, "I guess that man is crazy."[56]

Blanchard's breakthrough was as simple as it was brilliant. He constructed a lathe with two distinct parts, each separately powered. The first was a V-shaped frame holding on its two branches the target block of wood and a copy, usually in metal, of a finished gun stock, the "pattern." They both rotated slowly and identically while moving back and forth on the horizontal axis. The second part of the machine comprised the cutting tool, geared to revolve at a high speed, connected on a similar frame to a tracer, just a freely moving wheel. The tracer wheel rested against the pattern, while the cutting wheel rested against the wood block. As the pattern rotated and moved longitudinally, the tracer wheel undulated with the pattern shape, imparting the same action to the cutting wheel—and voilà, with just a few passes, the target block assumed the shape of the pattern.[*]

Blanchard perfectly understood that he had solved a general problem— how to machine any irregular shape at all. As usual, Lee heard of it and, even before it was finished, reached out to Blanchard in January 1819. Blanchard responded:

> Yours of the 21 int has come safe to hand you wished me to wright you respecting macenary I conclude you mean a machine I hav recently invented for turning gun stocks and cuting in the locks and mounting. Doubtless you have herd concerning it. But I would inform you that I have got a moddle built for turning stocks and cuting in the locks and mounting. I can cut a lock in by water in one minute and a half, as smooth as can be done by hand. The turning stock is verry simple in its operation and will completely imitate a stock made in proper shape, I shal bring the moddle to Springfield in the cours of three weeks I shall want your opinion of its utility.[57]

---

[*] The frame arrangement described here was used for gun stocks. The original patent application shows a shoe last, a more compact shape, and is arranged differently. The application identified a variety of possible arrangements for different product types.

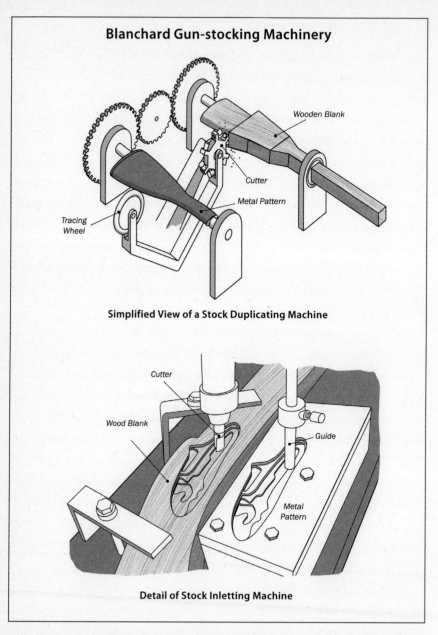

Blanchard Gun-stocking Machinery

Wooden Blank

Cutter

Metal Pattern

Tracing
Wheel

Simplified View of a Stock Duplicating Machine

Cutter

Wood Blank

Guide

Metal
Pattern

Detail of Stock Inletting Machine

The Blanchard profiling cutter was a highly original pairing of a moving high-speed cutting tool and a moving workpiece. In the top drawing, both the workpiece blank and the metal pattern rotate and move back and forth on their horizontal axes, while the cutting tool replicates the motion of the feeling piece against the pattern. Once established, the same concept can be applied in a nearly infinite number of arrangements, as illustrated by the second drawing. The invention was later widely replicated in generations of profiling milling machines.

Blanchard demonstrated the machine at Springfield in March. Lee was much impressed and, along with Wadsworth and Stubblefield, arranged for a demonstration at Harpers Ferry in June. Blanchard took two machines with him: one was installed at Harpers Ferry, and the other hauled to Washington to demonstrate for Wadsworth.

A contract with Springfield, however, had to await the resolution of a patent dispute filed by Asa Kenney, a brass founder across the river from Blanchard. Kenney had reason to be unhappy with the dispute process. The patent commissioner set up a three-man panel that included himself and Lee, who was arguably Blanchard's sponsor. Taking no chances, Blanchard kept Lee closely informed of Kenney's intentions during the pendency of the hearing and hired one of the most powerful lawyers in the state, Levi Lincoln Jr., later a governor and a Congressman, to represent him. The hearing was quickly resolved in his favor.[58]

Blanchard was clearly no naïf, and he always bargained hard with Lee. When he was in Washington with his stocking machine, he even had the effrontery to wangle a letter from Wadsworth ordering Lee to buy it.[59] But then there is a charming series of letters with Lee after Blanchard had begun installing the machine at Springfield. Blanchard pleaded a "grait want of fifty dollars of money," since he'd been buying machine castings. Lee replied that he would be delighted to pay him but needed a bill. A shocked letter from Blanchard shows him to be quite ignorant of billing processes. Lee finally prepared the bill for him and sent it to him for signature.[60] (Clients like Waters probably contracted with a handshake and paid in cash.)

The spring and summer of 1820 was something of a crisis for Blanchard, for the Springfield stockers presented a solid wall of opposition to the stocking machinery. Adonijah Foot, the master armorer at Springfield, reported to Lee in early 1820, "The turning of Stocks progresses very well but I think the Machines for cutting in the lock and the one for jointing the face of the Stock will not be of very great advantage."[61] When Lee passed that on, and expressed his own worries, Blanchard sent an alarmed letter hoping that he had not complained to "head quarters." (Lee in the meantime had been proselytizing hard for the machine to the navy and private contractors.[62]) Blanchard had reason to worry. A turndown at Springfield could kill the machine's prospects throughout the industry, and he promised Lee that he would have early solutions for all the difficulties.[63]

Blanchard did have a serious problem with the locks. His lock-cutting machine probably worked fine, but like all surviving models, it cut a standard seat for a standard lock plate. Springfield lock plates, however, were handmade and varied considerably in size. Oddly, rather than make the lock makers conform to a standard plate—as he had seen at North's plant—Lee left it to Blanchard to machine a standard stock to fit whatever lock plates the artisans turned out, which seems benighted. Conceivably, since Lee's tenure at Springfield had been dogged with labor disputes, he may have been reluctant to precipitate another fight.

Blanchard being Blanchard, he solved the problem anyway. It must have occupied him for the rest of the year, for the first working solution was installed at Lemuel Pomeroy's shop in Pittsfield, where he had gone at the end of 1820 to create a stocking system. The following February he wrote triumphantly to Lee (italics added):

> I have got the Machine in good working order at Pitsfaeld, I have made greate inprovements in cuting in the work, I can cut in the whole lock with great dispatch and exactness *let the variation of the plate be as it may.* I can make a good joint to every lock, I can cut in side plaete and heel plates, *I have discovered a method by which I can vary the jig and set it to evrey lock part* side or heel and make a good joint it is done by a verry simple method I am about to commence building a machine for the above mentioned purpose and will practice on the same in my shop until I can do as good work as can posabily be done by hand.[64]

Charles Fitch, a census analyst who produced a seminal 1883 report on the development of small-arms machinery, described the "curious invention" thusly: "Blanchard devised a combination of dies sprung inward toward a center, so they would conform inside to any shape of lock-plate set in the interior, while the outer ends formed a surface which was used as a former, and *thus every cut in wood was made by machinery to conform with the irregularities of the metal work"* (emphasis added).[65] Unfortunately, no example of the device has survived, but it would have been used at Springfield only until lock-plates were standardized sometime in the 1830s.

The final set of machines Blanchard installed at Springfield, like the one at Pittsfield, "half-stocked" the musket. As Lee described it to Wadsworth: "What we call half Stocking is to face and turn the Stock, fit on the heel plate, let in the barrel, put on the bands, fit on the Lock & trigger plate and bore the holes for the side and tang pins;—the other half is to let in the side plate & guard, hang the trigger, make the groove & bore the hole for & fit the ramrod, let in the band springs, smooth & oil the Stock."[66]

Lee insisted on an extended bake-off at Springfield, pitting Blanchard and his crew and machine against the current stocking crew and standard methods, with the winner to be the one with lowest all-in costs. Blanchard was brought into the armory as an outside contractor, a common arrangement in nineteenth-century factories. He was paid a piece rate and paid for his own workers and machinery, but used armory space, raw materials, and waterpower. Blanchard reconfigured his machinery into fourteen different machines, each dedicated to a single operation, almost all of them completely self-acting, so he could use unskilled hands. He laid them out in a natural production flow. That was still unusual in America, but reminiscent of the Portsmouth block-making production line, which Blanchard had expressly referenced in a patent application.

Blanchard and his machines were the clear winner. Over the life of the contract, he received a gross of $18,500, a large sum for the day. The contract does not appear to have been a full-time occupation, since he continued filing other patents during its operation. His engagement was supposed to end in 1825, but the machinery was destroyed in an armory fire, and Lee strong-armed him to stay on until a replacement line was up and running. It was 1827 before he made his exit, although some of the delay was due to Blanchard's hard bargaining before agreeing to a 9-cent royalty on each musket stock subsequently produced with his machinery.

The Blanchard production line had been completely made over by the early 1850s and extended to incorporate many of the "full-stocking" production tasks. Most of the re-work was done by Cyrus Buckland, a legendary Springfield master machinist. An original Blanchard stock-turning lathe is the only one of Blanchard's own designs to have survived. Over several decades, mostly because of the new machinery, the time for producing a stock was reduced from a day and a half to only about an hour and a half on a timed test.

Freed from his armory obligations, Blanchard became the hardest-nosed, and most innovative, of patent managers, coming up with a great variety of licensing arrangements to accommodate particular situations. His pursuit of infringers throughout the country—in the shoe-last, hat-block, and carriage-parts industries among others—must have kept a small phalanx of lawyers at work. He personally lobbied Congress for patent extensions and won two, bringing him protection through 1862, despite protests from his licensees. He also became something of a showman. To help win his third extension, he used his machine to produce marble busts of congressmen from plaster likenesses. (A wag said Blanchard "turned the heads" of Congress.[67]) He repeated the feat at the Paris Exposition of 1857, executing a bust of the empress Eugénie.

Even while he was at Springfield, Blanchard had become interested in steam transportation and had built a steam carriage before concentrating on steamboats. He built and operated a line of steamboats for the Springfield-Hartford traffic with the shallow drafts for traversing rapids that later proliferated on western rivers. He patented a number of machines for nautical woodworking and created a large pulley-block production line in Burlington, Vermont. A well-known Blanchard wood-bending machine solved a long-standing problem of breakage in objects like plow handles. Blanchard came to the solution by careful study of the internal dynamics of bent wood. Before bending the wood, his machine first compressed it lengthwise to give it greater structural integrity—not unlike forging in metalwork—so it could be readily reformed without cracking.

Blanchard was only fifty-two in 1840, when he was immortalized in Henry Howe's collection of essays, "Great American Inventors." He lived for another twenty-five years, was thrice married and twice widowed, enjoyed a large family, and died a sophisticated and well-traveled gentleman of considerable wealth—even as he long maintained a small workshop to make and sell decorative busts and statues. A eulogy said, "One can hardly go into a tool shop, a machine shop, or workshop of any kind, wood or iron, where motive power is used, in which he will not find more or less of Blanchard's mechanical notions."[68]

The Quest for the Holy Grail

For all the brilliance of Blanchard's machinery, wood was a much more forgiving medium than metal. The challenge of aligning the lock's tumbler and sear was of a different magnitude than that of seating a lock plate in a stock. Achieving consistent interchangeability of metal parts in volume production turned out to be a tougher challenge than the early enthusiasts for uniformity had ever imagined. The practical methodologies evolved over many years, and the most important armory contribution came from John Hall, a gunsmith from Portland, Maine, and inventor of the Hall rifle.

Mastering the interchangeability challenge was not part of Hall's original business strategy. Rather, in the manner of Eli Whitney, when he was anxious to retain a much-needed government contract, he promised he would produce machine-made rifles with interchangeable parts— but he really did it.[69]

John Hall was born into an upper-middle-class family during the waning days of the Revolution. After his father's death, he opened a woodworking and boat-building business, married into a politically connected family, and had a very close marriage with seven children. A stint in his state militia sparked a fascination with firearms, and he switched his business to gun making. In 1811, at age thirty, he applied for a patent on a new type of breech-loading rifle, which eliminated the clumsy process of pushing ammunition down the muzzle at each reload. As Hall described his invention in an 1816 pamphlet: "The Patent Rifles may be loaded and fired . . . more than twice as quick as muskets . . . ; in addition to this, they may be loaded with great ease, in almost every situation. . . . [Since] the

American Militia . . . will always excel as light troop . . . quickly assembling and moving with rapidity . . . these guns are most excellently adapted for them."[70] The critical advantage of the breechloader, of course, was that the soldier didn't have to stand and expose himself to reload.

But nothing came easily for Hall. In contrast to Blanchard, who moved readily from one product or technology to another, Hall was grimly focused, with perhaps a touch of the fanatic, and he could be impatient and confrontational with critics. Nevertheless, after many years of financial struggle, he obtained an armory contract that paid him an average of nearly $2,000 a year in salary and royalties for more than twenty years— a decidedly upper-class income. Total production of his rifles in all versions was about 40,000, and they were widely distributed among both state and federal troops, although their performance was controversial.[71] Scholarly recognition of his achievements was similarly delayed. Until relatively recently, he was merely a footnote in a fable dominated by Whitney and others.

The first harbinger of the stony path ahead came when Hall applied for his patent. The commissioner of patents, William Thornton, notified Hall that there was a prior claim. *From whom?* inquired an incredulous Hall. *From me!* came the reply, although Thornton hastened to reassure him that he was prepared to share the rights.[72] Thornton was a member of Jefferson's circle, the scion of a wealthy American family, educated in Europe, a medical doctor, with artistic and cultural pretensions, and a bit of a scientific dabbler. Standard biographies treat Thornton as an accomplished inventor, for he "held patents for improvements on steamboats, distilling equipment, and firearms." One can imagine how he got them. The story of Hall's patent has the ring of modern machine-politics graft.[73]

Upon receiving Thornton's letter, Hall arranged to see him in Washington, whereupon Thornton showed him an older British breechloader that had never gone into production, and averred, according to Hall that, "he had thought of a plan which would have resembled mine & had given orders for its construction but nothing (except the drawings) had been done toward it (& they were not to be found)."[74] When Thornton made it clear that a patent would not issue unless it was in both their names, an outraged Hall appealed to James Monroe, the secretary of state, requesting a conflict-of-claims hearing under the patent law. Monroe blandly advised him not to rock the boat, because Thornton's influence "in that case . . . would be exerted against me."[75]

To his lifelong regret, Hall caved. In the final arrangement Hall retained manufacturing rights but agreed to share licensing income. In retaliation against Thornton, however, Hall vetoed all licensing deals, which crippled the marketing of the weapon. Thornton thereafter became his nemesis, as Monroe had warned.

The central problem for breechloaders was the gas seal, and the military had great interest in any weapon that could solve it. The rear of the barrel of a muzzle-loader is tightly closed with a threaded breech-plug, so all the explosive power is focused on the projectile. Breechloaders necessarily have a working opening in the rear of the barrel. Unless it is closed quite tightly, muzzle velocity is compromised, and the shooter can be severely injured. The problem was finally solved only when the primer, powder, and bullet were prepacked in self-contained metal cartridges.

Hall's solution placed a chamber in the breech end of the barrel held in place by lugs and a spring lock. When the lock was released, the chamber tilted up above the stock to receive the standard powder-and-ball charge. The rifleman pushed the charge into place with his thumb and then snapped the chamber back into the locked position. During firing, the positioning of the closed chamber had to be exact and tight. Hall managed that well enough to make a barely adequate gas seal. Charles Fitch considered Hall rifles from 1824 not "fine" by 1880s standards, although a great achievement for the day. "The joint of the breech-block [the chamber] was so fitted that a sheet of paper would slide loosely in the joint, but two sheets would stick." An 1837 test at West Point showed that the rifles' muzzle velocity was about three-quarters of that of a comparable muzzle-loaded rifle, and their penetrating power only about as third as high.[76]

Bomford liked the weapons and arranged a small trial in 1816 that gave them high marks, but with the war over, interest waned. Hall then upped the ante with his promise of achieving interchangeability with precision machining, which was sure to get Ordnance's attention. In the meantime, his wife's family had convinced John Calhoun, the new secretary of war, to arrange more comprehensive tests. Two separate trials and a rigorous military board review in 1818–1819 ringingly confirmed Hall's claims. The rifles proved as accurate and powerful as the standard rifle, and even more durable.[*] Both rifle types scored much higher than any musket, but in ease of loading, Hall's rifle had a two-to-one advantage over the standard rifle and three-to-two over the musket. The board rated the ease of loading *"of infinite consequence in the rifle*, the difficulty of loading this arm being the great objection to its more general introduction."[77]

The result was an R&D contract, somewhat like Blanchard's. Finalized in 1819, it would have answered Hall's fondest prayers, but for a near fatal catch-22 that plagued the rest of his days. He was awarded a salaried armory position as director of a "Rifle Works" with an appropriation for equipment and a workforce and, to boot, a $1 royalty for each delivered rifle. But the contract had to be performed at Harpers Ferry rather than at Springfield. Harpers Ferry was the Southern armory, heavily politicized in part because of its proximity to Washington, financially corrupt, and never as technically aggressive as Springfield. The Harpers Ferry superintendents predictably undermined him at every turn—skimming his appropriations, shortchanging him on equipment and space, filing endless complaints about the wastefulness and ineffectiveness of his methods—while Hall slowly and steadily made genuinely important advances in the mass production of precision-metal parts. He later conceded that his own naïve underestimate of the challenge lent credibility to his critics: "I was not aware of the great length of time that would be consumed . . . to effect the construction of the arms with the perfect similarity of all their component parts. . . . I had been told it had been pronounced impossible by the

---

[*] As Robert Gordon has pointed out, interpreting such results is uncertain without knowing all the context of the tests, the target audiences, and hidden agendas. Note the wide variance between this report and the one at West Point.

French Commissioners . . . and I know that all attempts to effect it in Great Britain and this Country had failed; but from an unswerving reliance on my own abilities I expected to accomplish it in a *short* period."[78]

The precise extent of Hall's achievements will never be known, for all of his patent drawings and all of his machinery have been lost. His contributions to the art of specification and inspection, however, are indisputable. Accurate mass production required much more than better machines. It was essential first to define the target product with great precision. Once an ideal model had been constructed, all subsequent specifications should be taken only with reference to that ideal. Hall insisted on special purpose machines for each part and also special purpose machines to make the production machines. Placing and fixing a part in a machine required the same attention as the precision of the machine itself; it was essential, for instance, that every operation on a part be controlled from a fixed bearing point.*[79]

In his drive for exactness, Hall also made substantial contributions to the technology of gauging. Nineteenth-century gauging consisted of molds, or receivers (a good part should fit snugly into the gauge); groove and hole gauging (the gauge fits snugly into the part); thread gauging; and limit, or go/no-go gauging, like barrel diameter plugs (plug 1 must fit, and plug 2 must *not* fit). Under Lee, Springfield was an early leader in gauging systems, but it was still not until 1821 that the armory began to insist on exactitude in barrel bore diameter, outside muzzle diameter, inside diameter of the bayonet socket, and the form, dimensions, and screw-hole placement of the lock plate. And even then, it took another two years to manufacture sufficiently accurate gauging to enforce the rules. By about 1823, Lee had a set of eleven gauges that should have allowed reasonable

---

* Hall hypothesized a man cutting a plate exactly square. Normally he would "Square the 2d side by the 1st, and the 3d. by the 2d., and the 4th by the 3rd., but on comparing the 4th side with the 1st, it would still be found that they are not square; the cause is that in squaring each side by the preceding side, there is a slight but imperceptible variation and the comparison of the 4th with the 1st gives the sum of the variations of each side from a true square. And so in manufacturing the limb of a gun," and he explains the process of measuring every operation on a part from the same fixed point.

control—although he was apparently not yet attempting to enforce uniformity on lock plates.[80]

Hall carried gauging much further. Precision gauges were constructed for every measurement: there were reportedly some sixty-three separate gauges for the rifle, leaving nothing to a workman's judgment. Hall's gauges were always made in three sets, one for workmen, one for inspectors, and a master set in the plant manager's office to monitor wear on the other two.

Hall's influence can be seen in the tenfold increase in the number of Springfield gauges between 1815 and 1845. French influences were involved as well, for Springfield had multiple French contacts, but Lee and Bomford were well aware of Hall's work, and senior artisans rotated through Springfield, Harpers Ferry, and private contractors like North. Hall's final fillip was inspections of inspections, to ferret out any nonconforming part. Hall may also have been unique among the military arms designers of the day in making machinability a consideration in his weapon's design. Better design could have greatly simplified the machining of the Charleville, for instance.

It is generally accepted that Hall made substantial contributions to forging, milling, and cutting machinery, although the details are mostly missing. He greatly expanded the application of drop-hammer die forging—shaping hot or cold metal in a steel mold with blows from a mechanized hammer—which wasted much less metal than rough-forging and grinding, and he worked on techniques to retain the dimensions of the forged shape during cooling. Most notably, Hall created a wide range of cutting machines, including a profiler milling machine* in which the work table was moved in conformity with a profile, similarly to the way Blanchard's gun stocking machine operated.

---

* Milling machines evolved from older rotary filers. A flat workpiece was clamped to a movable table under a fixed vertical spindle-cutter with a rasp end. In operation, the table moved the workpiece rapidly back and forth on one axis and more slowly on the other to achieve an even reduction. Miller cutting tools rapidly evolved into a great variety of shapes including both end cutters and side cutters to cut drill flutings or screw holes. Workpieces could be rotated as they were cut or fixed at various angles against the tool, using either vertical or horizontal spindles. By the 1870s, "universal" milling machines could cut metal into almost any shape at all. Almost all the development took place in the United States.

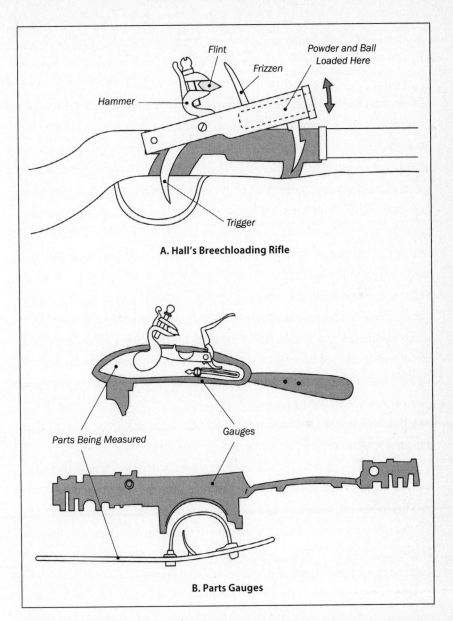

A. Hall's Breechloading Rifle

Flint

Frizzen

Powder and Ball
Loaded Here

Hammer

Trigger

Parts Being Measured

Gauges

B. Parts Gauges

A. Hall invented one of the very first breechloading rifles that had acceptable performance, although its reception was limited by its indifferent gas seal, and maintenance problems associated with rust and powder fouling in the loading breech block. **B.** Far more important were Hall's mechanical contributions in die forging, milling, and in principles of machine construction and management. Hall also pushed gauging practice to new levels of precision and rigor. Note that the gauge in the bottom drawing includes more than a dozen gauging fixtures, each addressing a particular part.

Almost all of Hall's machines were self-acting: after the workpiece was loaded and the power train engaged, the machine moved the tool or workpiece until the operation was complete. Semiskilled young men could often run several such machines at a time under the direction of a "Principal." Hall also lavished attention on dampening vibration and chatter in his machines: they were typically much heavier than standard machines, with bases of iron rather than wood, redesigned drives and spindles, wider belts to improve trueness, and gauging to track drift from accuracy. James H. Burton, a former master armorer at Harpers Ferry, said that the Hall works housed "not an occasional machine, but a plant of milling machinery by which the system and economy of manufactures was materially altered."[81]

It was not until 1824, about five years from his starting at Harpers Ferry, that Hall could finally invite Calhoun and Bomford to examine a production run of rifles manufactured on his principles. They could see for themselves "the manner in which the several parts, promiscuously taken, came together, fitted and adapted to each other." But Congressional complaints driven by the carping at Harpers Ferry forced Bomford to suspend all production activities pending a full field trial of the rifles and an external review of Hall's manufacturing methods.[82]

Two more years were consumed convening the review boards and completing the investigations, but the final reports were stunning vindications of Hall. After a five-month field trial, the military board expressed "its perfect conviction of the superiority of this Arm over every other kind of Small Arm now in use," and supplied a statistical analysis of its great advantages in speed of firing, accuracy, and durability.

The manufacturing review was even more glowing. Hall's system was adjudged to be "entirely novel" with "the most benefitial results to the country." The inspectors, who were all experienced, had never before seen arms "made so exactly similar to each other . . . [that] parts, on being changed, would suit equally well when applied to every other arm." They conducted an experiment of freely intermixing parts from two hundred rifles drawn from different annual production runs and found that "we were unable to discover any inaccuracy in any of their parts." The reviewers also made particular note of Hall's poor working conditions and hoped that he might "receive that patronage from the Government that his talents, science, and mechanical ingenuity deserve."[83]

The board's hopes were in vain, and the sniping from Congress and Harpers Ferry continued, but the report saved Hall's contract. The first substantial order for Hall rifles, in 1828, came from state militias, which the armories by law could not supply, so Bomford directed it to Simeon North, although he deputed Hall as his inspector. To Hall's great frustration, Bomford sent North one of the Hall rifles as a pattern—so even Bomford had missed the point that a "pattern" is a rigorously created and maintained ideal, not just a sample unit pulled from the production line.

The relationship with North got off to a rocky start when Hall arrived at Middletown with his full panoply of gauges and pronounced North's output unacceptable. But North, of all gunsmiths, could understand what Hall was about, and as he came to appreciate Hall's achievement, reproduced the system in his own factory—interestingly, with different machines and different gauges. It took another several years, but by 1834, Hall and North had fully demonstrated to the War Department that parts from both Middletown and Harper's Ferry could be "promiscuously" intermixed and readily reassembled into perfectly functional rifles.

Modern comparisons of Hall rifles confirm that the breech parts, which were the most demanding construct, were in fact interchangeable both between the North and Hall plants and between different rifle vintages. Tolerances on the breech opening among rifles in new condition were between 0.002 and 0.004 inches. In that same period, Joseph Clement was reportedly striving for 0.002 tolerances in constructing the Babbage calculating engines.[84] So Hall and North were working at the very edge of the era's machining technology.

By then Hall was in his mid-fifties and increasingly ill, possibly from tuberculosis. His rifle was slowly becoming obsolete and was soon eclipsed by more modern weapons from gunsmiths like Christian Sharps—the Sharps rifle may have been the favorite of Union troops—and B. Tyler

Henry, whose Henry rifle was a prototype for the long-running Winchester. Hall quietly continued on salary at Harpers Ferry, tinkering with his system until his death in 1841. His place in the story gradually faded into a mere footnote. As one popular history written in the 1950s put it, "by 1820, Hall, using Whitney's techniques of interchangeable manufacture, was turning out his rifles at Harpers Ferry."[85]

Production of the Hall rifle ceased in 1848. Despite some passionate advocates among the officer corps for its accuracy and speed of loading, the weapons seem not to have been much favored by troops. In the Second Seminole War of 1836, which was fought in the Florida Everglades, troops complained that the Hall loading chamber quickly rusted shut and that spilled powder collected in the bottom of the loading chamber, corroding the iron and forcing the chamber out of alignment.[86] In theory, such problems could be easily solved. The military issued small wire brushes to clear chambers of excess powder, and regular application of lubricant would have prevented rusting. But these are precisely the kind of fussy maintenance tasks that soldiers in the field can be depended on to neglect. A large number of the rifles were still in inventory when production ceased, but they were mostly distributed during the Civil War.

The Significance of
Armory Practice

The achievement of Hall and North in manufacturing rifles with fully interchangeable precision parts was a signal milestone toward the final realization of the Wadsworth-Bomford-Lee program of "Uniformity" laid down twenty years before. By about mid-century, practical interchangeability became a fact for virtually all military muskets produced by the armories and private contractors. But legend to the contrary, machines by themselves were still far from being able to consistently achieve such tolerances. A series of microscopic analyses by Robert Gordon showed that precision fitting of firing action components required improvements in *hand-finishing* at least as great as those in machining. And until very recent times, it was rarely cost effective to attempt to replace all hand-finishing with machinery. The achievement of armory practice and high-precision interchangeability, therefore, was the creation of an integrated process of specification, measurement, work flow, and the highest-quality standards in *both* machining and hand work.[87]

The value of mass production processes was proven in the crucible of the Civil War. Firearm production at Springfield in 1860 was a bit lower than 10,000 weapons, but it was ratcheted up quickly during the war. Springfield produced 14,000 weapons in 1861, 102,000 in 1862, 218,000 in 1863, and 276,000 in 1864. Colt was the most important private-sector military arms producer. From 1861 through 1863, its peak year, Colt's output of firearms increased from 27,000 to 137,000—or by a factor of 5—while at the same time Springfield's rose by a factor of 21.8.[88]

But the way in which the military achieved its interchangeability objective suggests its limitations. In the first place, it was a development that took many decades, which is usually possible only in the type of hothouse environment afforded by military settings. The original 1763 French Charleville musket, with only minor modifications became the Springfield Model 1795 and, with another set of small changes, the Model 1816. That was virtually unchanged until the flintlocks were replaced by percussion caps in the 1840s—they worked much like children's cap pistols, although the caps were made of copper. (The unnecessary lock parts were machined away, and a percussion cap receptacle was placed on the breech top with a new touch hole. The hammer remained on the side but was curved to strike the breech-top percussion lug.) With the 1848 advent of the Minié ball, which facilitated muzzle loading without fouling,* the musket barrels were rifled. Civil War troops, therefore, mostly went to war with "rifle-muskets," which were quite respectable weapons, with an effective range of six hundred yards, ten times that of the old smooth bores.[89]

---

* The Minié ball was shaped like a bullet, with a hollow base that expanded on ignition to grip the rifling grooves. Loose-fitting Miniés could be easily pushed down the barrel but still have a tight spin for good range and accuracy.

The basic infantry weapon carried by Union troops in the Civil War, therefore, was still a modified version of the Springfield 1795 musket. Such longevity is not especially unusual in military procurement. The B-52 bomber, launched in 1952 as an anti-Soviet nuclear bomber, has long since been converted to deliver cruise missiles and other standoff precision weapons. There are a number of instances in which sons of first generation B-52 pilots also became B-52 pilots, and some reports of grandsons. Military platforms, in general, like bombers and ships—and the Springfield 1795—tend to have very long lives, so long as their lethality can be steadily upgraded.

While no private company could follow such a strategy, it is well-suited for military technologies. The sheer logistics of maintaining a global military force imposes an extreme conservatism in getting the most out of existing technologies. But by the same logic, the long planning time frame justifies spending resources on promising technologies with a very long payoff. The American military started working on the basic technologies of the Internet some four decades before it finally burst into commercial prominence. In the same way, armory practice in machining laid down a substrate of technologies—including gauging, pattern making, profiling, and milling—that were seized on later and taken in many different directions by private companies.

The apotheosis of armory practice—machine production lines with special purpose machinery turning out fully interchangeable parts with little or no manual intervention—came only with the first Ford Model T assembly line in 1913. That production model dominated much of American manufacturing in the twentieth century. For most of the nineteenth century, however, highly organized production lines using precision special-purpose machines accounted for a very modest share of national output.

The mass-production industries that drove American growth through the nineteenth century were those in which the United States had a massive comparative advantage, and they sprang primarily from the crops, husbandry, and natural resources of the West.

CHAPTER FIVE

The Rise
of the West

F RANCES TROLLOPE WAS FORTY-SEVEN IN FEBRUARY 1828, WHEN SHE disembarked at Cincinnati with three of her five children in tow. She knew no one in the city and had made the last leg of her trip on borrowed money. Two sons, Tom, the oldest, and Anthony, the future novelist, were both in school in England, while her contentious and ineffective husband, a failed lawyer and a failed farmer, remained on their estate near Harrow to stave off creditors.[1]

The notion of publishing what was to be the wittiest, sharpest, and most caustic traveler's account of Jacksonian America was furthest from Trollope's mind. She had come to Cincinnati to repair the family finances by opening a proto-department store offering fine European goods to the grandees of Cincinnati—assuming there were such persons, for her research had consisted only of some pamphlets and conversations with a friend who had once passed through the city.

Despite her dubious judgment in practicalities, Trollope's adventure revealed a woman of rare intelligence, energy, and resilience. Her first year in Cincinnati she made money as the impresario of an elaborate, quasi-mechanical staging of Dante's *Inferno* at the Cincinnati museum. (Her son Henry did the voice of an invisible Oracle in Latin and Greek.) The production was reported as far away as Boston and ran for years. Samuel Colt, nineteen years old and touring the West as "Dr. Coult" delivering laughing-gas exhibitions and science lectures to raise money for his pistols, did a stint with the show in 1833.[2] The humorist Artemus Ward commented on it in 1861.

But Trollope had come to open a store and spent huge amounts of other people's money constructing it. Her "Bazaar" was a pastiche of Gothic and Byzantine architecture, eighty-five feet high. The shipments of expensive French fabrics her husband sent drew no customers, however, so the project was quickly underwater. The day after the sheriff distrained her household goods, Trollope gathered her children and absconded on a steamboat. She had spent twenty-five months in Cincinnati, leaving the Bazaar as her monument or, depending on her mood, her revenge.

With her family in desperate financial straits and her husband of no use, Trollope decided to extend her trip and recoup their fortunes by writing a book. She had never published anything and needed to scrape and scrounge to finance too-short visits to the South and New England. But she wrote beautifully. The book opens with her arrival from England at the mouth of the Mississippi, and she meditates briefly on the difficulty of recording scenery: "The Ohio and the Potomac may mingle and be confounded with other streams in my memory, I may even recall with difficulty the blue outline of the Alleghany mountains, but never, while I can remember any thing, shall I forget the first and last hour of light upon the Atlantic."[3]

Trollope finished her book after she returned to England, working in the mean little farmhouse where her husband, having lost his estate, was sunk in invalidism. The first publisher she favored with the manuscript loved it, and *The Domestic Manners of the Americans* was a best seller on both sides of the Atlantic.

The new fortune was quickly squandered, but she kept writing, turning out 113 volumes of novels and travel books. Because of the Trollopes' financial heedlessness, her first books after *Domestic Manners* were again written under great financial pressure, made the worse by the successive deaths of her husband and two of her children. But she emerged from her crises in full blossom and lived to be eighty-three, hale and active to the very end, finally wealthy, a success throughout Europe, an invitee at royal courts. When she was not traveling, she made her home in Florence, at Villino Trollope, where she was surrounded by her family, artistic friends, and a constant stream of visitors.

Posterity is fortunate in the foreign literary travelers who graced the United States in the crucial decades from the 1820s through the 1840s. Besides Trollope, there were Alexis de Tocqueville and his partner, Gustav de Beaumont, the most famous European rapporteurs on things American. They arrived in 1831 and covered some 3,000 miles in just ten months. Harriet Martineau, one of the world's first female political economists/sociologists, traveled for two years in 1835–1836, living almost everywhere, in both mansions and log cabins, and meeting almost everybody, including Jackson and Madison. Her *Society in America* (1837) is remarkable for both the lucidity of her mind and prose and her de haut en bas lectures on the solutions to America's problems. Charles Dickens compiled his *American Notes* during a four-month tour in 1842. He came to deliver a series of paid lectures and readings in the major eastern cities, but rounded out his trip with flying visits to Washington and Virginia, and to the "West," the rich but thinly populated expanse between the inland slopes of the Appalachians and the Mississippi River.* Trollope was in the United States longer than any of these, but more than half of her stay was confined to Cincinnati.

Each of their accounts is quite different, but there are some common threads. They had all arrived as opponents of slavery but were shocked and horrified when they confronted its reality, and felt the American prating of "liberty and equality" as the deepest hypocrisy. All were variously appalled at the strict separation of men and women in inns and public conveyances; the huge quantities of food consumed by Americans, how fast they ate, and the lack of conversation at meals; and, worst of all, the constant chawing and spitting by American men—spitting indoors and

---

* In this chapter, I use "West" in this sense, for it was the usage of the time. In the next chapter, which is more centered in mid-century, I will call the same region the Midwest, in accord with the newly current usage.

outdoors, on good carpets and bare floors. It does sound awful; Dickens had the misfortune to take the lowest of a stack of bunks on a canal boat and awoke to find his coat drenched with spit from the upper bunks.

At a broader level, all of them understood that they were observing a vast interlacing of the country, as the northeastern and Middle Atlantic states were being drawn into tight commercial relations with the West. They were all stunned at the commercialism and struggled to understand the mechanics of a society without official classes. And, as with many of their impressions of American innovations, they were as dazzled by the beauty and adaptability of the western steamboat as they were appalled by its evident dangers.

Nascent Colossus

In the modern era, an emerging-market country typically industrializes by exploiting cheap labor to become a low-cost manufacturing site for developed country markets, and then moves rapidly up the technology curve to higher-margin output. It was the model followed with great success by Japan in the early twentieth century and has been successfully adapted by most of the Asian Pacific Rim countries over the last thirty years or so.

At first glance, the nineteenth-century American pattern appears to be quite different, because labor was generally more expensive in the United States than in Europe. But only free labor was expensive. The United States had a huge reservoir of cheap labor—slaves—who produced the cotton that accounted for about half the value of American exports from 1820 through 1860. Over the same period, only about 15 percent of American exports were manufactured or semimanufactured goods. Everything else was extractive or farm-related—wheat and tobacco (which taken together were dwarfed by cotton), lumber, ores and metals, and processed foods.[4]

America's primary imports, on the other hand, were heavily tilted to manufactures, altogether about 63 percent of all imports during the period. Some of those comprised luxury goods, like gowns, mirrors, fine china, and the like, but a very large share was the high quality steel, engines, rails, tools, and other capital goods needed to power America's leap into the industrial age. America had chronic trade deficits, but except during financial disruptions, they were typically small. The accumulated deficit during the whole 1820–1860 period was about $175 million, or a little over $4 million a year, but it still had to be financed.[5]

PREBELLUM FINANCE

The United States was not a capital-rich country, and its annual trade deficits had to be covered by shipping gold, by increasing exports, or from inflows of foreign investment. Mega-projects, like canals or railroads, were normally financed by state bond issues, which were sold through American and English banking houses. (The last of the federal debt was discharged in 1835, so there was no Treasury bond market.) A sample of American state bond yields in London and New York from the first half of the 1830s shows spread differentials only in the few hundredths of a percent, suggesting tight integration of the two countries' capital markets.

The splendid success of the Erie Canal, which had been financed with New York bonds, created an eager British market for American canal and railroad bonds. To the British upper classes sitting on inherited low-yielding British consols, American bonds were attractive investment-grade, high-yield paper, so about half of all American canal and railroad-related bonds were held in Great Britain. A spate of canal and railroad building from 1836 to 1842 drew at least $60 million from abroad and was a substantial factor in the American recovery from the 1837 recession.

The ease of bond sales created something of a canal and railroad bubble. A substantial number of newer state bonds, from Indiana, Michigan, Illinois, Arkansas, and Florida, defaulted. They had been mostly issued in the later stages of the market cycle, and most were eventually repudiated. Eastern state bonds continued to perform well, with the exception of Pennsylvania's. That state's businessmen, alarmed by the withering competition from the Erie Canal, had pressured the government to finance hundreds of miles of canals just on the eve of the railroad age. While almost all American bonds took a reputational hit, differential spreads in London suggest that foreign investors were well able to discriminate between sound offerings and junk.[6]

Entrepreneurial capital mostly came from personal or family savings, as it still does today. Business startup costs were certainly lower than today, and a skilled craftsman could often make most of his tools and equipment himself. Local merchants also provided capital for likely entrepreneurs, while more expensive startups, like a substantial forge, might get the support of an informal consortium of leading men of an area. The Holley family and their partners financed most of their businesses from their own resources but joined with other leading merchants and business men to found a local bank.

The commercial banking industry of the day was mostly about trade, in accord with the prevailing "real bills" doctrine, which held that bankers should lend only against goods moving in trade to bridge the cash-flow gap between a sale and the receipt of payment. As raw materials production shifted to the West, trade finance was a major development bottleneck. Local banks naturally sprang up to meet the challenge, but often with indifferent results. In theory, farmers could contract with coastal merchants' agents for the sale of their crop at a future date and receive a "bill of exchange," equivalent to a check, payable in the future when the crops were delivered. A local bank would discount the bill—that is, buy it from the farmer for cash at a discount from face value to cover collection costs—and collect on the bill from the merchant house when the crops were shipped.

In reality, the combination of the distances, the extended performance periods, and the limited liquidity of local banks made the process highly prone to breakdown. Since illiquid local banks would of necessity quickly rediscount their bills, and often pay penalty discounts themselves, all of those costs were deducted from the initial payment to the farmer. Much of the time, the farmer's discounted proceeds did not cover his real costs, trapping him in a continuing debt spiral. The system's instability was greatly aggravated by the refusal of foreign traders to accept American bills, so import payments had to be made in scarce coin. Hard-money Republicans increased the funding pressure by insisting on accelerating the payment of the public debt. The debt was payable in specie, and much of it was held abroad, so debt retirement drained away gold reserves.

For a relatively brief period, however, through much of the 1820s, when Nicholas Biddle was at the helm of the Second Bank of the United States,* the country's internal monetary system functioned as well as any in the world. Biddle was a dilettante, a Philadelphia nouveau-aristocrat, a dabbler in painting and poetry, and the compiler of the popular edition of the Lewis and Clark journals. He was also very intelligent and arguably the first to understand both the regulatory and the monetary roles of a central banker.[7]

First and foremost, Biddle was a careful manager of his own bank's positions, and he maintained a strong relation with Barings, so within a year or so after his ascendance, the notes of the Bank of the United States (BUS) were accepted almost everywhere near par. More important, the high reputation of the Bank's notes gave Biddle de facto regulatory leverage over local banks. Since the BUS applied strict and consistent standards before accepting local bank note issuances, the merchant community quickly learned to accept only notes approved by the BUS. At a stroke, BUS notes and approved local notes became a national mercantile currency. And since Biddle was willing to provide BUS notes to well-managed local banks, interior liquidity was greatly increased, the steep interior discounting rates shrank dramatically, the pace of commerce quickened, and interior incomes rose. A related benefit was an easing of the specie shortage. Once the discount demanded by foreign acceptors of BUS notes fell below the cost of shipping specie, they stopped demanding payment in coin.

Biddle also understood a central bank's role of easing credit at times of temporary market stress. (During this period, the Bank of England reflexively

---

* The Bank was a private, federally chartered, institution, with a fifth of its shares held by the government. Biddle assumed the presidency in 1822.

pulled back credit to protect its own specie at the barest hint of problems, displaying in the words of one authority, "an inexcusable degree of incompetence."[8]) Biddle, by contrast, tuned his collection procedures to the state of the economy. Rather than increase pressure on merchant houses when credit was tight, he would let his notes remain uncollected until conditions eased—effectively expanding the money supply. Similarly, when animal spirits were on the boil, he would reduce his discounting activity and speed up on collections. In 1825, 1827–1828, and 1830–1831, he steered the United States through major credit contractions caused by typically benighted specie-hoarding policies at the Bank of England.[9]

That happy state of affairs existed for most of the 1820s, a period labeled in elementary history texts as the Era of Good Feelings. It ended when Andrew Jackson, in a triumph of prejudice and ignorance, vetoed a bill reauthorizing the BUS. (It had passed both the House and the Senate by good margins but was two short of the votes required to override a veto.) Jackson was heavily influenced by people like Amos Kendall, his postmaster general, an early telegraph entrepreneur, and a radical advocate of laissez-faire, who believed the BUS to be a near-biblical scourge. Another close banking adviser, William Gouge, a former newspaperman who was knowledgeable in finance, insisted that banking "was the principal cause of social evil in the United States."[*] Gouge and Kendall held their views sincerely, but many of the businessmen in the Jacksonian Kitchen Cabinet were tied to bankers who greatly resented the BUS's restraining hand.[10]

Biddle didn't help his case by his aristocratic style or his dismissiveness of people less intelligent than he. His reputation was finally destroyed by his hopeless and ultimately vindictive rearguard action against Jackson's veto, which succeeded only in creating a political firestorm and rattling the entire economy. Once the BUS's charter expired in 1836, he rechar-

---

[*] Gouge insisted that Biddle's success in managing monetary crises was a compelling argument for withdrawing the BUS charter, since it necessarily implied an excess of power and discretion vested in a single individual.

tered it in Pennsylvania and seems to have deluded himself that he could replicate the position of the old BUS from a state platform. He was quickly overextended and not only destroyed the Bank but hastened the collapse of the state's canal-stretched finances. It was a time when the transatlantic financial system was badly strained by excesses in western land, in canals, in cotton, and much else. If the BUS had survived with Biddle as president, he might have considerably ameliorated the American crisis, but in his new incarnation as an overreaching head of a state bank, he materially contributed to the excesses. It took more than a century before historians discovered his earlier accomplishments.

With the demise of the BUS, state banks once again came into their own. "Free banking" legislation spread, especially in the West. Some, indeed, were sober and well-run institutions, but in many states they were mere engines of chicanery, shipping the same small trove of gold coin from one bank to the next to stay ahead of auditors, and pumping out notes beyond reason. "Wild cat" banking referred to some bankers' hiding "in the woods where the wild cats are" to avoid having to redeem their notes. The key to success, counseled one banker, was to create such gorgeous notes that the rubes would never redeem them: "a real furioso plate, one that will take with all creation—flaming with cupids, locomotives, rural scenery, and Hercules kicking the world over." While there appears to be no truth in the tales of western farmers hauling wagons full of bank notes on provisioning trips, the shutdown of the BUS ushered in a long period of financial instability. Remarkably, it does not appear to have interfered much with the average rate of growth, although the stomach-churning year-to-year ups and downs must have inflicted great hardship.[11]

THE SOUTH AND THE REST

As an industrial boom took hold in the rest of the country, the South slipped into the position of an internal colony. In effect, the South exploited its slaves, while the rest of the country exploited the South. Cotton prices were generally strong from the 1830s until the Civil War, and virtually all the South's resources were sucked into cotton production. Cotton was very profitable, but the first large slice of cotton profits accrued to Northern finance houses in the form of hefty trading, marketing, shipping, banking, and insurance revenues. The earnings that did flow to the South mostly flowed right back out again, for food from the West and for western and northern manufactures. By the 1840s, the everyday clothes and shoes worn by Southerners were made in Massachusetts, Rhode Island, and New York. The steam engines, farm tools, grain, and packed meats they needed came down the Ohio and Mississippi from Cincinnati, Louisville, and Pittsburgh. The schools the planter elite chose for their children were in New Jersey, New York, and New England.[12]

By 1860, the West, New England, and the Middle Atlantic states were rapidly evolving into an approximation of a unified commercial and industrial economy. Erie Canal traffic is a good proxy for the integration: after it opened, the traffic was primarily between western New York and the coastal cities, but by 1860 the eastward traffic originated primarily in the West.[13]

Unlike the South, the West invested its agricultural surpluses in businesses and public infrastructure, like railroads. Much as in Massachusetts a few decades before, the intense commercialization of agriculture was creating larger, mechanized farms, and the agricultural workforce was shifting to higher productivity industrial employment. By mid-century, the United States had the second-largest GDP in the world, and the second-largest per capita GDP. Great Britain was still far ahead, with nearly three times the output as America. But the United States had the fastest growth rate in industrial production by far than any other country, on both an overall and per capita basis, and with a rapidly growing adult population besides.[14]

Striving

Foreign travelers in America were uniformly stunned by the commercialism. Tocqueville wrote, "I know of no country, indeed, where wealth has taken a stronger hold on the affections of men."[15] But the full reality didn't dawn on him until he was in Ohio, when he wrote, "The entire society is a factory!"[16] Harriet Martineau noted that bad roads limited the availability of some goods in the interior, but still, she wrote: "When a few other neighbors besides frogs, gather round the settler, some one opens a grocery store. [On the Niagara peninsula] . . . there is a store on the borders of the forest. I saw there glass and bacon; staylaces, prints, drugs, rugs, and crockery; bombazeens and tin cans; books, boots, and moist sugar, &c. &c."[17]

Trollope found the source of American industriousness in "the unceasing goad which necessity applies to industry." During her stay in Cincinnati, she reported, "I neither saw a beggar, nor a man of sufficient fortune to permit his ceasing his effort to increase it."[18]

She was ambivalent, at best, about the constant drive for advancement. A young, energetic, illiterate farmer she knew made a favorable impression. He and his family had "plenty of beef-steaks and onions" three times a day. Besides tending his farm, he cleared forests, split rails and built fences, built a new house, rented half of it, contracted to build a bridge, and opened a store. Trollope had "no doubt that every sun that sets sees him a richer man than when it rose." The farmer hoped his son would become a lawyer, and she supposed he would, and would "sit in congress" besides, and "the idea that his origin is a disadvantage, will never occur to the imagination of the most exalted of his fellow-citizens."[19]

But in her heart of hearts, she thought a society *needed* proper class divisions to function, and their absence in America was disorienting: "The greatest difficulty . . . is getting servants, or as it is there called, 'getting help,' for it is more than a petty treason to the Republic, to call a free citizen a *servant*. . . . Hundreds of half-naked girls work in the paper-mills, or in any other manufactory, for less than half the wages they would receive in service; but they think their equality is compromised by the latter." When Trollope finally found "a tall, stately lass" she liked, she asked what "I should give her by the year." The girl laughed out loud. "You be a downright Englisher, sure enough. I should like to see a young lady engage by the year in America!"—and explained that she might get married

Mᴿˢ TROLLOPE

Mrs. Trollope. Engraving executed in 1845 after an oil painted around 1832 by a young French artist, Auguste Hervieu. The Trollopes had acted as Hervieu's patrons in England, and he traveled to America with the family as part of the household.

or decide to go to school. Her work proved satisfactory enough, but she resigned in a huff when Trollope refused to lend the price of a ball gown— "Then 'tis not worth my while to stay any longer."[20]

"All animal wants are supplied profusely at Cincinnati," Trollope conceded, "and at a very easy rate." But the leveling tendency left no room for "the little elegancies and refinements enjoyed by the middle classes in Europe," and she missed them. "Were I an English legislator," Trollope wrote, "instead of sending sedition to the Tower, I would send her to make a tour of the United States. I had a little leaning towards sedition myself when I set out, but before I had half completed my tour I was quite cured."[21]

Dickens rather enjoyed the leveling, because it made good copy. But it was behavior he would have regarded as "impertinencies" in England— like the inn proprietor walking in and out of his rooms with his hat on, or that worthy's practice of starting conversations "in a free-and-easy manner," or lying down on Dickens's sofa to read his paper. In America, it was all just part of being a "good-natured fellow," he wrote, with more than a tad of sarcasm.* But he clearly liked "the funny old lady," who, "when she came to wait upon us at any meal, sat herself down comfortably in the most convenient chair, and, producing a large pin to pick her teeth with, remained performing that ceremony, and steadfastly regarding us meanwhile with much gravity and composure (now and then pressing us to eat a little more), until it was time to clear away. It was enough for us that [the service] . . . was performed with great civility and readiness, and a desire to oblige."[22]

Martineau, who was of Radical politics in England, urged Europeans to adjust their manners to the Americans':

It should never be forgotten that it is usually a matter of necessity, or of favour, seldom of choice (except in the towns,) that the wife and daughters of American citizens render service to travellers. Such a breaking in upon their domestic quiet, such an exposure to the society of casual travellers, must be so distasteful to them generally as to excuse any apparent want of cordiality. . . . [Look instead for] the cordiality which brightens up at your offer to make your own bed, mend your own fire, &c.—the cordiality which brings your hostess into your parlor, to draw her chair

---

* Dickens's description of America and Americans is much more savagely satirical in *The Life and Times of Martin Chuzzlewit*, which began serialization in 1843, not long after his return.

and be sociable, not only by asking where you are going, but by telling you all that interests her in her neighborhood.[23]

It was Tocqueville, the royalist, a child of the ancien régime whose family had been decimated by the guillotine, who thought most intensely about the leveling impulse and penetrated the deepest. He and Beaumont took the steamboat to Albany and attended a Fourth of July ceremony, where they were moved by the solemn reading of the Declaration of Independence. They had planned to spend time there investigating the workings of state government. But as Tocqueville wrote to a friend, "The offices and registers were all open to us, but as far as *government* goes, we're still looking for it. Really it doesn't exist at all." There had been no police attending the ceremony they had witnessed; but while it was humble by European standards, it was still perfectly orderly. The parade marshal was a volunteer with no official status, yet everyone obeyed him.

Comprehension dawned in Ohio. This, Tocqueville understood, was democracy without limit, "absolutely without precedents, without traditions, without customs, without even prevailing ideas." For his own class in France, "the family represents the land and the land represents the family . . . an imperishable witness to the past and a precious pledge for the future." But Americans "flee the paternal hearth . . . to chase after fortune—nothing, in their eyes, is more praiseworthy."

"An American taken at random," he went on, "will be ardent in his desires, enterprising, adventurous, and above all an innovator." And when they meet each other, though they may differ greatly in wealth, "they regard each other without pride on the one side and without envy on the other. At bottom they feel themselves equal, and they are." And he explained why:

> Imagine if you can, my friend, a society formed from all the nations of the world—English, French, German. . . . All of these people have different languages, beliefs, and opinions. In a word, it's a society without roots, memories, biases, routines, shared ideas, or national character, and yet it's a hundred times more fortunate than our own. More virtuous? I doubt it. So there's the point of departure: What serves to bond such diverse ele-

ments? What makes a people of all of this? *L'intérêt!* That's the secret: the interest of individuals that comes through at every moment, and declares itself openly as a social theory.

For Tocqueville, Ohio demonstrated "one thing I had doubted until now, that the middle classes can govern a state. . . . They do definitely supply practical intelligence, and that turns out to be enough." As he put it in *Democracy in America*: "The doctrine of interest, properly understood does not produce great sacrifices, but day by day it prompts little ones. By itself it cannot make a man virtuous, but it shapes a multitude of citizens who are orderly, temperate, moderate, foresighted, and masters of themselves. And if that doesn't lead directly to virtue through the will, it advances gradually closer to virtue through the habits."

So the leveling imperative—the assumption of equality that led to the easy familiarity that bemused Dickens and unsettled Trollope; the casualness toward rank that had a president, to European astonishment, shaking hands with anyone who approached him—was not a social disorder. Rather, it was the clue to the country's success. Tocqueville admitted that he himself could never be completely comfortable in such a society, but few contemporaries understood it so well.[24]

The Western Steamboat

At a much less abstract level, all of our travelers, like most Europeans, were deeply impressed with the western river steamboat, a uniquely American invention that was a critical breakthrough for the region's development. Martineau wrote:

The ports of the United States are, singularly enough, scattered around the whole of their boundaries. Besides those on the seaboard, there are many in the interior; on the northern lakes, and on thousands of miles of deep rivers. No nook in the country is at a despairing distance from a market; and where the usual incentives to enterprise exist, the means of transportation are sure to be provided. . . .

The steam-boats of the United States are renowned as they deserve to be. There is no occasion to describe their size and beauty here; but their number is astonishing. I understand that three hundred were navigating the great western rivers some time ago: and the number is probably much increased.[25]

The eastern seaboard was blessed with a more or less continuous system of tidal waterways linking almost all the major cities. Rivers like the Hudson and the Connecticut were broad, deep, and relatively straight. For a skilled captain with a good boat, sailing upstream was almost as easy as sailing down. As a teenager, Cornelius Vanderbilt ran a Staten Island–to–Manhattan ferry service with a small sailing sloop. By his early twenties he owned a string of twenty- to thirty-ton fast sailing vessels running freight traffic up and down the East Coast. He could sail up the Delaware during shad season, picking up fishermen's catches to sell in New York City. Fast, easy, waterborne freight transport facilitated commerce on the eastern seaboard from the earliest days.[26]

The new steamboats developed on the East Coast early in the century were therefore targeted at passengers rather than freight. The standard boats were large, usually well built, and commodious to the point of grandiosity. Fulton used imported Boulton & Watt–style low-pressure engines from the start (they were long since off patent). Some operators experimented with high-pressure designs, until a rash of boiler explosions pushed the bigger operators into the Boulton & Watt camp until much later in the century. (When a low-pressure boiler failed, it might inundate the deck, but no one got hurt.)

The waterways that so densely veined the interior of the West, by contrast, were shallow, narrow, and winding, often with swift currents. Sailing vessels were close to useless, so downstream shipping was commonly by flat boat, with the craft broken up and sold for lumber at its destination. There were also keel boats that made round trips, but the week or two trip downstream from Louisville to New Orleans was a brutal three- to four-month slog of poling and shoreline towing to get back. Western exports therefore mostly went downriver to New Orleans, while the region imported little back, relying on wagon trekkers crossing the mountains with essential eastern or English manufactures.

The practical effect was that westerners were consigned to a kind of preindustrial self-sufficiency. In 1815, Mt. Pleasant in Jefferson County, Ohio, about ten miles from the Ohio River, was home to "between 80 and 90 families and about 500 souls." There were some forty different craft establishments—saddlers, hatters, blacksmiths, weavers, bootmakers, carpenters, tailors, cabinetmakers, wagon makers, a baker, and an apothecary. Within a radius of six miles, there were at least two dozen mills of various kinds.[27] These were not isolated settlers, and the town must have been a hive of activity, with almost everything it needed within a convenient wagon ride. Measured by the basics of nutrition and shelter, the standard of living was good, but in such a small-pellet economy, technology was stuck at a handicraft level. The river network could support some regional production, but to exploit it required steam.[28]

Building a western steamboat network took about twenty years, and involved two East-West face-offs: one between rival entrepreneurs and another between rival designs. Both were won by the West.

Eastern interests made the first move in 1811, when the Livingston-Fulton combine, which owned the profitable Hudson River franchise, acquired an exclusive steamboat franchise from Louisiana. Robert Livingston was one of New York's richest men. He had been a member of the Committee to Draft the Declaration of Independence, a minister to France, and a key negotiator of the Louisiana Purchase. He had met Robert Fulton in France, where the younger man was experimenting with a military submarine. The two agreed to cooperate on a steamboat venture in New York, and Fulton eventually married Livingston's niece. Their first successful run, from New York City to Livingston's Clermont Manor estate on the Hudson took place in 1807. (The boat was officially named *Steam Boat* but became known to popular history as the *Clermont*.)

Fulton's first western boat, the *New Orleans* (371 tons), left Pittsburgh in October 1811 for the 2,000-mile trip to the Gulf down the Ohio and Mississippi, arriving in New Orleans the following January. The group put three more boats into operation in 1814 and 1815. They were all roughly the size of the *New Orleans* and mostly concentrated on the much shorter (300 miles) but very lucrative Natchez–New Orleans trade. (Livingston and Fulton died in 1813 and 1815 respectively, which likely slowed the combine's move into the West.)

Monopoly franchises were pervasive in Great Britain and fairly common in the East, but westerners were outraged at the Louisiana grant. New Orleans was the gateway to the entire West, so a Louisiana monopoly imposed tribute on steamboats from any other riparian territory. The fact that the franchise had gone to easterners only added to the anger. A Pennsylvania group operating out of works in Brownsville on the Monongahela River, some fifty miles south of Pittsburgh, decided to ignore it. The group was headed by two excellent mechanics and engineers, Daniel French and Henry M. Shreve.* Their boat, the *Enterprise* (75 tons), with Shreve at the wheel, made it to New Orleans in 1815. Over the next couple of years, Shreve became locally famous for his clever cat-and-mouse games with New Orleans authorities both on the *Enterprise* and on the much bigger *Washington* (403 tons).

Everyone sued, and an 1816 federal court decision held that territories could not grant monopolies. By 1818, with all appeals exhausted, the western rivers became open to all comers. By 1819 there were a reported thirty-one steamboats operating in the West, mostly on the 1,350-mile stretch between New Orleans and Louisville, just above the Mississippi–Ohio River junction.

Having banished the monopolists' business methods, westerners now had to rethink their equipment. The boats launched by the Livingston-Fulton group all followed their Hudson patterns. They were strongly constructed with relatively deep, rounded hulls and were powered by

---

* Besides his engineering accomplishments, Shreve spent fifteen years as superintendent of western rivers. In that capacity, he invented several large engines for clearing debris from river channels. His greatest accomplishment was to clear the Great Raft, a 150-mile-long tangle of submerged logs and fallen trees that closed off the Red River to navigation and, as it silted, threatened to turn the river basin into a giant swamp. Shreveport, located where the far end of the raft had been, was founded and named in his honor.

low-pressure engines.* It was possible for them to navigate western rivers, as the *New Orleans* had proven. But achieving reliable, economic transportation over the vicissitudes of river high and low points required reconciling a number of conflicting demands: the ideal steamboat would be a very light, shallow-draft vessel but one able to carry very heavy loads. It also had to be nimble, with a high power-to-weight ratio for quick response to rapids and other river hazards.

Power-to-weight requirements ruled out the Boulton & Watt–style engines. The engine on a Fulton boat launched at New Orleans in 1815 weighed one hundred tons and generated 60 horsepower, while the one on an 1816 French-Shreve competitor weighed only five tons yet generated a full 100 horsepower. Captains also preferred the high-pressure engines in difficult water because they could generate sudden thrust—a fast "wad of steam"—by tossing a handful of pitch into the firebox. Power in a Boulton & Watt engine was limited by the size of the condenser, regardless of the steam pressure. It also had almost twice as many moving parts and was harder to repair and maintain. The final bonus, of course, was that especially early in the century, the west didn't have the technical base to build the outsized Boulton & Watt components. A series of extremely simple and elegant engines from French and Shreve steadily increased efficiencies and gradually became the standard for the whole western industry.**

The high-pressure engines of the era, as we have seen, were dangerous fuel hogs. But fuel costs in the West were too low to really matter. Trollope described the squalid woodcutters' cabins lining the river banks and the spavined families carrying wood down to the fueling dock for a few coins.

---

* Ironically, the *Clermont/Steam Boat* was of a western-style flat-bottom design. Fulton, indeed, seems to have targeted the western rivers from the start. But as the Hudson trade expanded, Fulton/Livingston adjusted designs to fit the local market and then transferred them wholesale to the West.

** Although Oliver Evans was the co-inventor of the high-pressure engine and opened a Pittsburgh factory in 1812, he and his son, who ran the western business, won little steamboat business. The Evanses dominated western mill and factory engines, but Shreve and French, who were steamboat men first and engine makers second, were far ahead in adapting engines to the special demands of western steamboats.

And the advantages of the new steamboats were so overwhelming that Americans, and hordes of foreign travelers, chose to live with the risk. Bad as the safety record was, travelers' reports often exaggerated it. In an 1831 letter, Tocqueville wrote, "Thirty [steamboats] exploded or sank during the first six weeks we were in the United States"—a rate of attrition that would have wiped out the entire American fleet in hardly more than a year.[29]

A high-efficiency, lightweight engine was just a first step. To achieve the shallow draft, the shape and structure of the steamboat had to be radically reconfigured to present a broad flat surface to the water. Holds were done away with and cargo storage moved to the deck, with lightweight—critics said "flimsy"—superstructures for passengers and pilot house. Paddle wheels were moved higher to accommodate the reduced draft, and they were made larger for greater circumferential speed. The standard boats on arterial rivers typically achieved three- to four-and-a-half-foot drafts empty and five-and-a-half-foot to eight-foot drafts fully loaded. A special breed of "light" boats, able to carry fifty- to two-hundred-ton freights on two feet of water, were built to service tributary rivers that were often sandbar obstacle courses. A wag wrote that the first mate on a light boat could open a keg of beer in front and sail for four miles on the suds. An 1851 British survey of American steamboats reported: "the steamers built for [western] waters carry a greater amount of freight and accommodate a larger number of passengers upon a given draught of water than those constructed in any other part of the world; at the same time, their *cost* of construction and outfit per ton of freight capacity, or for passenger accommodation, is very much less."[30]

As boat and engine designs stabilized, shipping times dropped markedly. In the early days, the upstream trip from New Orleans to Louisville took about a month, which was a threefold to fourfold improvement over human- or animal-powered upstream times. By the end of the first decade of western steamboating, that same trip was down to about two and a half weeks, and by mid-century, fully loaded business trips to Louisville with normal stops were routinely accomplished in a week or less. Important marginal gains were squeezed out by river improvements, like clearing snags (submerged tree trunks that could destroy a hull) and building canals around strategic obstacles, like the Ohio Falls at Louisville—really a stretch of rapids with a twenty-six-foot fall over two miles. The falls were readily navigable by shallow-draft boats, but standard boats could make it upriver only at peak water levels.

Comparable improvements were made in travel on the Upper Mississippi, to St. Louis and beyond to St. Paul, and on the Upper Ohio from Cincinnati to Pittsburgh. The major tributary water systems were fully integrated into the network in the 1830s, and by the 1840s almost all significant rivers throughout the West, and many throughout the Southeast and Southwest, had some steamboat service. By the late 1840s, important river cities like Cincinnati, St. Louis, and Pittsburgh all averaged about 3,000 steamboat landings a year.

The jump in trip frequencies and freight capacity released an explosion of goods on the West. Western prices had been dominated by transport costs, including for local products. The West was rich in salt mines, but with steamboats on the rivers, the price of salt dropped from $3 a bushel in 1817 to 75 cents by 1825; sugar went from 24 cents a pound to 9 cents. Country stores in the West suddenly had full shelves of glass, hardware, nails, dry goods, and even luxury items, like Wedgewood's "queen's ware." Westerners could also afford imports because they were exporting so much more, like grains, dried or salted meats, and even some steam engines.[31]

Improved market access spurred the commercialization of farms and accelerated the use of money. Trollope described a farm family she visited in 1828. It was a well-run farm by all indications, and the family was amply provided for, with chickens and other animals, several acres of corn and other crops, well-constructed housing, beds, chests with drawers. "Robinson Crusoe was hardly more independent," Trollope reported, for they grew all of their food, spun all of their cloth, and made their own shoes. They had no need for money, the wife told her, except occasionally for coffee, tea, or whiskey, and she could get that by sending a "batch of butter and chicken" to market.[32] But such families were a dwindling minority. Ohio farmers were embarked on the same rapid rural-industrialization path that Winifred Rothenberg's Massachusetts farmers had traversed earlier in the century, but the transition would be much faster.

Building steamboats became a major industry in its own right. After 1820, western factories built an average of one hundred big steamboats a year for nearly the rest of the century, three-quarters of them at Pittsburgh, Cincinnati, and Louisville. Steamboat building jump-started the Ohio and western Pennsylvania iron and coal industries, and the big river cities were soon dotted with large-scale foundries and forges, rolling mills, and heavy machine shops. Glass, paint, and fine furniture industries developed in their wake. New England peddler networks spread out in almost seamless conjunction with every extension of transportation. The big Connecticut brass founders and clock and tinware makers retained their manufacturing dominance by decentralizing their distribution and sales networks, much as the Boston Associates had done in textiles.[33]

The western population soared from a mere scattering of adventurers in 1800, to 1.6 million in 1830, and to 9 million in 1860, or about 30 percent of the national population. Cincinnati, the queen of western manufacturing cities before the Civil War, saw its population jump exponentially from 2,500 in 1810, to more than 20,000 when Trollope visited, to 46,000 the next decade when Dickens made his stopover, and 115,000 by 1850.[34] While Trollope thought the city rather disorganized and dirty, Dickens implicitly gave it high marks for managing its growth: "Cincinnati is a beautiful city; cheerful, thriving, and animated. I have not often seen a place that commends itself so favourably and pleasantly to a stranger at the first glance as this does: with its clean houses of red and white, its well-paved roads, and footways of bright tile. Nor does it become less prepossessing on a closer acquaintance. The streets are broad and airy, the shops extremely good, the private residences remarkable for their elegance and neatness."[35] But however smooth and seamless the West's boom appears almost two centuries later, such huge shifts in population centers, technology, wealth, and hierarchies were terribly stressful for ordinary people.

Anxiety

Mary Graham was a farm wife in Sudbury Massachusetts, struggling to make a go of it in the explosive local industrial economy. As she wrote to a friend in 1837: "Here we are all in comfortable health. L and myself have had to work as hard as we have been able, and a good deal harder than we wanted to I have shoes aplenty to bind, from 6 to 8 and 12 pairs a week—and with all the rest have got four as dirty, noisy, ragged children to take care of as any other woman, they look as though they would do to put out in the cornfields . . . to keep away the crows."

Life was hard in an economy without safety nets, but she had her health and wrote in good humor. There was no humor in a letter she wrote seven years later: "Some news not very pleasant to me . . . Lucius has sold us out of house and home with the privilege of staying here until the first of June. If he can rake and scrape enough after paying his debts to set his family down in Wisconsin he is determined to go. So you wonder that I feel sad. Nothing but poor health and poverty to begin with in a new country looks dark to me."[36]

She had much to fear. Trollope especially noted how drawn, tired, and lonely western farmwives looked, and she also understood that, high nutrition notwithstanding, the population was sick. For all its attractions, the riverine West was a sink of malaria. One farmwife who "seemed contented, and proud of her independence" conceded "that they had all had ague in the fall."[37]

Trollope was a great walker and loved getting out of Cincinnati with her children to enjoy the scenery around the river or to picnic at a cherished woodland glen with a small waterfall.

> It was indeed a mortifying fact, that whenever we found out a picturesque nook, where turf, and moss, and deep shade, and a crystal stream, and fallen trees, majestic in their ruin, tempted us to sit down, and be very cool and very happy, we invariably found that the spot lay under the imputation of malaria. . . .
>
> We had repeatedly been told, by those who knew the land, that the second summer was the great trial of health of Europeans settled in America. . . [and] I was now doomed to feel the truth of the above prediction, for before the end of August I fell low before the monster that is for ever stalking through that land of lakes and rivers, breathing fever and death around.[38]

The "ague," a debilitating fever attack that is a symptom of malaria, often recurs throughout one's life. Trollope's first bout kept her in bed for nine weeks. The following year, not long after she had left Cincinnati and was anxious to start her book, the ague returned and "speedily brought me very low, and though it lasted not so long as that of the previous year, I felt persuaded I should never recover from it." Her son Henry had contracted it as well.[39]

Social anxiety is often reflected in social unrest. On the East Coast, where employment relations were much more structured than in the West, there was a wave of strikes. The most famous were in New York, where "Workeyism," akin to later European laborite political movements, showed its organizational power. The commercial sailors, the riggers and stevedores, the building laborers, the tailors, the coal heavers, the hatters, and other trades all went out on strike—often more than once. At times the port was completely shut down, and in 1836, the city was on the precipice of a general strike. The recession that followed the Jacksonian banking crises quelled labor unrest for a time, and the inundation of destitute, mostly unskilled, famine Irish, in all major eastern cities shifted the organizing focus to nativism.[40]

Outside of the major cities, anxieties were more likely to be expressed in revivalism. Charles Grandison Finney evangelized much of western New York in the 1820s, preaching a more user-friendly brand of Presbyterianism, emphasizing salvation through repentance. Finney was among the entrepreneurs of a newer, more professional, form of revivalism, all carefully choreographed and marketed—with advance men, handbills, and arrival parades. Revivalism intersected with Temperance drives, and together harkened back to Jeffersonian notions of a republic of sober, stalwart, independent, virtuous, farmers and mechanics.

Especially in the West, Methodist and Baptist circuit riders mastered the camp-meeting revival form, turning it in into a welcome mode of mass entertainment like a rock concert, as well as a splendid release valve for mass anxiety.[41] Our reporter Frances Trollope was on the scene. She had "long wished" to attend a camp meeting and jumped at an invitation to accompany "an English lady and gentleman" in their carriage, to a "wild district in Indiana" finding themselves among a great crowd of curious spectators that mixed with the faithful.[42]

They "reached the ground about an hour before midnight," parked their carriage in care of a servant, and made their way through three circles of fire and tents. There were fifteen preachers in attendance; they would preach in rotation from Tuesday through Saturday. No one was preaching outside when Trollope and her party arrived, but "discordant, harsh, and unnatural" sounds were coming from the tents. They entered one and saw "a tall grim figure in black . . . uttering with incredible vehemence an oration that seemed to hover between praying and preaching." The circle of people kneeling around him responded with "sobs, groans, and a sort of low howling inexpressibly painful to listen to."

"At midnight a horn sounded through the camp," and people flocked from all over to the central preacher's stand. Trollope and her hosts estimated that there were about 2,000 people in attendance, and they found a place right next to the preacher's stand. A space in front of the stand was called "the pen," and after a harangue that "assured us of the enormous depravity of man," one of the preachers invited "anxious sinners" who wished "to wrestle with the Lord to come forward into the pen."[*]

When few people moved to come up, the preachers came down to the pen and began to sing a hymn.

> As they sung they kept turning themselves round to every part of the crowd, and by degrees, the voices of the whole multitude joined in chorus. This was the only moment at which I perceived any thing like the solemn and beautiful effect, which I had heard ascribed to this woodland

---

[*] Trollope was "forcibly" reminded of Milton's lines:
Blind mouths! That scarce themselves know how to hold
A sheep-hook, or have learned aught else, the least
That to the faithful herdsman's art belongs!
—But when they list their lean and flashy songs,
Grate on their scrannel pipes of wretched straw:—
The hungry sheep look up, and are not fed!
But swoln with wind, and the rank mist they draw,
Rot inwardly—and foul contagion spread.

worship. It is certain that the combined voices of such a multitude, heard at dead of night, from the depths of their eternal forests, the many fair young faces turned upward, and looking paler and lovelier as they met the moon-beams, the dark figures in the middle of the circle, the lurid glare thrown by the altar-fires on the woods beyond, did altogether produce a fine and solemn effect, that I shall not easily forget.

But soon the "sublimity gave way to horror and disgust," as Trollope was fascinated and repelled by the undertone of sexuality:

Above a hundred persons, nearly all females, came forward, uttering howlings and groanings, so terrible that I shall never cease to shudder when I recall them . . . and they were all soon lying on the ground in an indescribable confusion of heads and legs. They threw about their limbs with such incessant and violent motion, that I was every instant expecting some serious accident to occur. . . .

Many of these wretched creatures were beautiful young females. The preachers moved among them, at once exciting and soothing their agonies. I heard the muttered "Sister! dear sister!" I saw the insidious lips approach the cheeks of the unhappy girls; I heard the murmured confessions of the poor victims, and I watched their tormentors, breathing into their ears consolations that tinged the pale cheek with red. . . . I do [not] believe that such a scene could have been acted in the presence of Englishmen without instant punishment being inflicted.

Eventually, "the atrocious wickedness of this horrible scene increased to a degree of grossness, that drove us from our station." Trollope and her friends repaired to their carriage to snatch some sleep (on beds prepared by the servant) and "passed the remainder of the night in listening to the ever increasing tumult at the pen."

But as morning broke, the show-business aspect of it all began to dawn:

The horn sounded again, to send them to private devotion; and about an hour afterward I saw the whole camp as joyously and eagerly employed

Trollope camp meeting. Lithograph by August Hervieu. Trollope is in the foreground (with illuminated bonnet). Hervieu is behind her with his sketch pad. Note the discreet distance maintained by Trollope's entourage from the scene before them. [43]

in preparing and devouring their most substantial breakfasts as if the night had been passed in dancing; and I marked many a fair but pale face, that I recognized as a demoniac of the night, simpering beside a swain to whom she carefully administered hot coffee and eggs. . . .

After enjoying an abundance of strong tea, which proved a delightful restorative after a night so strangely spent, I wandered alone into the forest, and I never remember to have found perfect quiet more delightful.

The Coming of the Railroads

Steamboats did an effective job of tying together the interior of the country west of the Alleghanies, but as the Erie Canal had shown, the real bonanzas came from linking the West with the eastern seaboard. Chicago, Cleveland, and New York could be linked by water, but common-carrier transportation from interior cities like Pittsburgh and Baltimore would have to cross some formidable mountains; all skeptics notwithstanding, that required railroads.

Canals and railroads are both forms of low-friction transportation and were much in competition in the first third or so of the nineteenth century. "Low-friction" also includes horse-drawn trolleys, which were common in nineteenth-century cities. One of the earliest of commercial railroads, the Baltimore & Ohio (B&O), was horse-drawn during its first couple years of operation but switched to steam in 1830. The cost and difficulty of constructing canals and railroads were not greatly different,[*44] but railroads were generally much faster and therefore came to be preferred by passengers.

Great Britain had used steam locomotives in mines from the early 1800s, but the two countries got off to a roughly neck-and-neck start in

---

* In a famous analysis, Robert Fogel made a case for the potential economic equivalence of railroads and canals. The capital costs of canals were considerably less than railroads, but they externalized their equipment and services costs. The Erie Canal was almost as long as the Erie Railroad, but was completed in less than half the time—which speaks more to the turmoil at the railroad than the inherent difficulty of the projects.

The deWitt Clinton Locomotive. The *deWitt Clinton* was the first steam locomotive to run in New York state, in 1831, on the Mohawk and Hudson line between Albany and Schenectady, a run of sixteen miles.

commercial railroads. George Stephenson opened the first commercial British railroad, the Stockton and Darlington, in 1825. The first commercial steam railroad in the United States commenced operating either in 1828 or 1829. The first American railroad entrepreneurs bought their engines from Great Britain, but British engines were designed for the highly engineered British rail system, with its heavy tracks, level runs, and minimal curves. They destroyed American tracks and were easily derailed.[45] Robert L. Stevens, head of the Camden and Amboy, invented the T-rail, which still prevails today. It's easy to lay and very durable. A New York engineer, John Jervis, invented the rail-hugging swivel carriage for the front of the locomotive. Even in the mid-1830s, Jervis's engines could routinely hit sixty miles per hour. Also by then, American locomotives had acquired their bell-shaped stacks—to reduce the flying sparks from wood-fueled engines—and the cowcatchers, which allowed killing a cow without a derailment. They were also the first to incorporate lighting—at first just a fire-bearing cart pushed in front, later replaced by a kerosene lamp with a mirror to project a beam.[46]

Harriet Martineau traveled by one of the first train lines in the South. She took an overnight stage to Columbia, some sixty miles, to meet a train due to arrive at eleven the next morning, which would take her to Charleston, another sixty-two miles, in time for dinner. The carriage hit a stump and was very late, but the train had had its own minor accident and was even later, so the passengers still had a several-hour wait. Martineau wrote:

> I never saw an economical work of art harmonize so well with the vastness of a natural scene. From the piazza [where they were waiting] the forest fills the whole scene, with the railroad stretching through it, in a perfectly straight line, to the vanishing point. The approaching train cannot be seen so far off as this. When it appears, a black dot marked by its wreath of smoke, it is impossible to avoid watching it, growing and self-moving, till it stops before the door. . . .
>
> For the first thirty-five miles, which we accomplished by half-past four, we called it the most interesting rail-road we had ever been on. The whole sixty-two miles was almost a dead level, the descent being only two feet. Where pools, creeks, and gullies had to be passed, the road was elevated on piles, and thence the look down on an expanse of evergreens was beautiful. . . .
>
> At half-past four, our boiler sprang a leak, and there was an end to our prosperity. In two hours, we hungry passengers were consoled with the news that it was mended. But the same thing happened again and again; and always in the middle of a swamp, where we could do nothing but sit still. . . .
>
> After many times stopping and proceeding, we arrived at Charleston between four and five in the morning; and it being too early to disturb our friends, crept cold and weary to bed, at the Planter's Hotel.[47]

Despite a wild English railroad-building bubble in 1845–1848, the United States quickly outstripped the United Kingdom in total rail mileage.

The construction boom of the 1850s was nothing short of stupendous. Mileage increased by half in New England, doubled in the Middle Atlantic states, quadrupled in the South, and increased eightfold in the West. By 1860, the West was becoming the center of gravity of the national population and had the greatest extent of railroad mileage. Locomotives got

Railroad Miles in Service[48]		
Year	United Kingdom	United States
1840	1,650	2,760
1850	6,100	8,600
1860	9,100	28,900

much bigger, faster, and more complex, while bridge builders like John Roebling achieved new milestones in suspension bridge technology, as in his Niagara River Suspension Bridge connecting the United States and Canada, which was opened to train traffic in 1855.

A concerted national program of internal improvements, with a heavy focus on transportation to knit the country together, had long been the dream of Henry Clay and the Whigs. Jefferson himself had favored turnpike and canal building, but Andrew Jackson had put an effective end to federally supported internal improvements with a famous 1830 veto, incidentally foregoing the opportunity to establish national standards for items like road gauges (track widths) to ensure connectivity.[49]

Trollope visited Washington as the debate over internal improvements was at its zenith, and attended several of the debates: "I do not pretend to judge the merits of the question. I speak solely of the singular effect of seeing man after man start eagerly to his feet, to declare that the greatest injury, the basest injustice, the most obnoxious tyranny that could be practised against the state of which he was a member, would be the vote of a few million dollars for the purpose of making their roads or canals; or for drainage; or, in short, for any purpose of improvement whatsoever." A few days later, she witnessed the elaborate funeral cortege of a deceased congressman and learned that all members were entitled to be "buried at the expense of the government (this ceremony not coming under the head of internal improvement)."[50]

The practical effect of the improvements veto was that extensive development of the roads was almost always a combined public-private enterprise, with private investors contributing equity, while the states sold revenue bonds and facilitated the assemblage of the necessary rights-of-way. One of the most ambitious of the early projects was a hybrid Philadelphia-Pittsburgh connection largely financed by the state of Pennsylvania and comprising canals on either side of the Alleghanies, with a "Portage Railroad" to cross the mountains. When it opened in 1834, a traveler could board a train in Philadelphia and proceed 82 miles by rail to Columbia, on the Susquehanna River; shift to a canal boat for 176 miles to Hollidaysburg, near Altoona; then cross the Alleghanies to Johnstown via a series of wooden inclined planes, with an average slope of about 10 percent. The distance of the traverse was 36 miles as the crow flies, with railcars pulled up by stationary steam engines on the ascent and coasting free on the downslope. Johnstown was the terminus for a final 104-mile canal connection directly into Pittsburgh. The highest point on the Portage road was 2,300 feet above sea level, and the vertical distance of the ascent and descent on the inclined planes were 1,100 and 1,300 feet respectively.[51]

Dickens took that route on his trip west and wrote, "Occasionally the rails are laid upon the extreme verge of a giddy precipice; and looking down from the carriage window, the traveller gazes sheer down, without a stone or scrap of fence between, into the mountain depths below. . . . And it was amusing, too, when . . . we rattled down a steep pass, having no other moving power than the weight of the carriages themselves." One enterprising sailor took a boat from eastern Pennsylvania via river and canal to the Portage Road and, after it had been hauled to Johnstown, sailed all the way to New Orleans.[52]

The Portage road cut the cost of moving goods across the mountains to a fourth the cost of the old wagon routes. But it was never a financial success, in large part because it was very expensive to maintain and to staff. The frequency of "breaking bulk" was also an annoyance. Merchants of the day took for granted that they had to unload and reload their goods at each change of railroads, or from railroad to canal boat. But the Portage road required reloading at each new inclined plane—ten times altogether at each crossing. In 1854, the state sold the road to the Pennsylvania Railroad, a private entity that the state had taken the lead in organizing in 1846. It began working on an Alleghany rail crossing shortly after it was incorporated, even as it consolidated dozens of smaller roads on both sides of the mountains and forged the links required to supplant the old canal legs of the journey. The unified Philadelphia-Pittsburgh rail line opened in 1855, a two-track road completed according to the high engineering standards the Pennsylvania became famous for. The most striking engineering feature was the Summit Tunnel, 3,600 feet long, running through the summit of the highest mountain traversed, about 200 feet below the peak. The construction required four shafts, two of them 300 feet deep. Winter operating conditions were sufficiently severe that the western tunnel portal was fitted with doors that were opened only for a train passage.[53]

Elsewhere, line development was rather more harum-scarum, although often punctuated with feats of virtuosic engineering. The Erie, completed in 1851 and linking New Jersey's Hudson River piers to Lake Erie and the West, may be the best example.

The Erie's slogan was "between the Ocean and the Lakes," and when it opened, it was the longest continuous train route in the country. The construction had taken almost twenty years, and completion came only months shy of exceeding a twenty-year franchise limit that would have triggered a reversion of the railroad to the State of New York, which could have sold it to the highest bidder.

It was a challenging route, wending through the Catskill and Pocono mountains, necessitating ravine-spanning bridges and difficult cuts and grading through granite terrain. Most impressive, perhaps, was the Starrucca Viaduct, consisting of Roman-style stone arches, 1,090 feet long, 25 feet wide, and between 90 and 100 feet high. When asked if he could build it, an engineer affirmed that he could, and could finish on time, "provided you don't care what it costs."[54] But the true miracle was navigating the shoals of politics and finance in a notoriously corrupt age, while fending off Wall Street's banditti. For comparison, the transcontinental railroad authorized by Congress the next decade was completed in about one-third the time, even though it crossed the Rockies.

There were multiple close calls. Several times the planned route turned out to be impassable, and by pure luck, another acceptable path was found.[55] And the road was often on the verge of bankruptcy. At one of the darkest moments, in 1846, the company was running out of money, the British were ratcheting up the price of the line's iron rails, and late British deliveries were making the completion deadline unattainable under almost any circumstances.

The rescue came from two brothers, George and Selden Scranton, who ran a floundering little iron business—a furnace, a forge, and a rolling mill—in the woods of northern Pennsylvania. The Scrantons volunteered to supply the rails, a product they had never manufactured, for slightly more than half the British price. The Erie gambled on the Scrantons, and they somehow produced adequate rails on schedule, hauling them as much as sixty miles through the forest. The Scrantons' precarious iron venture, relocated to Lake Erie and dubbed the Lackawanna Iron and Coal Company, became a major industry player in the second half of the century. Their coal business remained in Pennsylvania, and the village near their woodland factory is now the city that bears their name.[56]

Actual completion of the line was decidedly a matter for celebration, in an era that had grandiloquent tastes for such doings. The main event was a train trip from the railroad's Hudson River docks to Dunkirk, the small town on the southern shore of Erie that served as the line's western terminus. A two-train excursion party included President Millard Fillmore, who was born in the lake region and had practiced law in Buffalo; Secretary of State Daniel Webster; other members of the cabinet; presidential hopefuls like William Seward and Stephen Douglas; executives and bankers of the railroad; and nearly three hundred other notables.

The party assembled on May 13 at the Battery at the southern tip of Manhattan and moved in stately procession to city hall, where they were entertained by multiple military marching bands and hours of speechifying. Promptly at six the next morning, they reassembled at the Battery for the twenty-five-mile steamboat ride to the Erie terminal at Piermont, New York. There they disembarked and were directed to two trains leaving just five minutes apart. Remarkably, both were actually underway only a few minutes later than the scheduled departure.[57]

The steamboat trip was necessitated because some years before, the directors had inexplicably passed up an offer from the tiny Hudson and

Harlem Railroad for an inexpensive direct rail link into the city—a mistake that dogged them for the next century, not least because of the necessity to break bulk on arriving at the Hudson and restow goods on a freight ferry. Another catastrophic decision was to use the six-foot British rail gauge, when most American lines were standardizing on a gauge of four feet, eight and a half inches. The wider bed increased the labor of cutting track beds in granite, the heavier trains burdened bridge building, and it cost many millions to finally bring the Erie to standard a half century later. The choice of the British gauge was both intentional and utterly wrong-headed, for it was expressly intended to make it difficult for other lines to connect with the Erie—to its great disadvantage as the national network steadily integrated after the Civil War.[58]

The celebratory trip itself came close to fiasco. Almost as soon as the train reached steeper terrain, the first engine proved inadequate to its load. (There had been a bitter factional argument over engines within the engineering staff.) After a considerable delay, the second train's engine was linked to the rear of the first, which solved the problem. According to the testimony of the conductor, engineer, and several passengers, the trains then traversed a thirty-four-mile stretch from Port Jervis to Narrowsburg in just thirty-five minutes, an extraordinary speed for the time. Some passengers were sufficiently alarmed to leave the party. Webster must have had the ride of his life. To get a full view of the scenery, he had insisted on riding in a rocking chair tethered to a flat car, protected only by a steamer blanket and a bottle of rum.[59]

In the event, the party reached Elmira, 283 miles from New York within minutes of the scheduled 6:09 PM arrival time. They were greeted there with a seven-hour banquet but were off again the next morning at 6:30 and arrived at the scheduled 1:45 PM at Dunkirk, where they tucked into yet another enormous meal. The bill of fare was preserved for posterity: "Chowder, a yoke of oxen barbecued whole, 10 sheep roasted whole, beef a la mode, boiled ham, corned beef, buffalo tongues, bologna sausage, beef tongues (smoked and pickled), 100 roast fowls, hot coffee, etc."[60]

The broad outline of the modern railroad network east of the Mississippi was more or less in place by 1860. There were four large east-west

networks. Two originated in New York: the Erie and Cornelius Vanderbilt's New York Central, an 1850s consolidation of ten connecting roads.
Both the Pennsylvania and the B&O offered through service to Pittsburgh
and beyond from Philadelphia and the Chesapeake region respectively.
The outline of a rail network emanating from Chicago was in place, with
multiple connections both with the four east-west lines and to Cincinnati,
St. Louis, and most other western cities besides.

American development was still very inconsistent, much like the quality of its trains, but the breadth and power of the economic surge was un-
mistakable. But if British investors seemed almost irresistibly drawn to
American bonds, elite British opinion remained dismissive of "Jonathan's"
pretensions.

Two other European travelers visited the United States shortly before
Trollope did. One, a British military man and travel writer, had the same
caustic tone as Trollope but with none of her natural empathy. He was especially entertained that the New York legislature consisted "chiefly of
farmers, shopkeepers, and country lawyers, and other persons quite unac-
customed to abstract reasoning." Unlike Tocqueville, he did not believe
the middle class could run a country. A German traveler, Duke Bernhard
of Saxe-Weimer-Eisenach, like Tocqueville a noble from one of the most
royal European lines, was critical of a great deal of what he saw, especially
in the South, but much more favorably impressed than British travelers.

A British journal reviewed the two books together in 1829 and decided
that the German's views could only be accounted for by the fact that most
of his previous travels had been on the continent: "The rapidity of the
progress made in [America] must be the more striking to one who com-
pares them, as the Duke would do, with the cities [on the continent] . . .
than to a native of Great Britain. . . . So the differences between our two
authors may be easily accounted for by the different tenours of their previous experiences and habits." The reviewer concluded happily that there
is "nothing in [America] . . . to excite envy or jealousy."[61]

CHAPTER SIX

America Is
Number Two

B Y 1860, THE UNITED STATES WAS HOME TO 31 MILLION PEOPLE, OR NEARLY as populous as Great Britain and France. Until the 1830s, population growth had been dominated by the rate of natural increase. Immigration accelerated in the 1830s, and from the 1840s until the 1920s consistently accounted for a quarter to a third of the total growth in population. As the country grew, its center of gravity also steadily moved west.

The country was urbanizing. At the turn of the century, three-quarters of employed Americans worked in agriculture, but by 1860, only 56 percent of workers toiled on a farm. Agricultural employment accounted for fewer than a third of jobs in the Northeast by 1860 but still more than 60 percent in the Midwest, and a nearly unchanging three-quarters in the South, which remained dependent on King Cotton.[1] The Northeast still commanded about half of the country's total income, but average incomes in the Northeast and the Midwest had begun to converge and would be approaching parity by the end of the century.[2]

The Northeast's large income advantage reflected both its lower reliance on agriculture and greater concentration of good-paying, white-collar, service employment—banking, insurance, accounting, wholesale and retail trade. The white-collar pay advantage was particularly strong in the nineteenth century. Edward Tailer was twenty in 1850, when he started work as an assistant clerk for a New York dry goods importer while complaining of his $50 annual salary. But within two years, and after two

TABLE 6.1 Population by Region, 1790–1860[a]			
	1790	1830	1860
Northeast[b]	50.1%	43.1%	33.7%
Midwest	N/A	12.5%	28.9%
South	49.9%	44.4%	35.4%[c]
West	N/A	N/A	2.0%

  a Michael R. Haines, "The Population of the United States, 1790-1920," in *The Cambridge Economic History of the United States,* vol. 2: *The Long Nineteenth Century,* ed. Stanley L. Engerman and Robert E. Gallman (New York: Cambridge University Press, 2000), 189.
  b The census districts are: Northeast = New England and Middle Atlantic; Midwest = East North Central and West North Central; South = South Atlantic, East South Central, and West South Central; West = Mountain and Pacific.
  c Figure includes 4 million slaves. Free southerners made up only 22.8 percent of the population.

job changes, he was making $1,000—a solid middle-class income. He then went on the road as a traveling salesman at $1,200 and had his own business when he was twenty-five.[3]

Americans were the best-fed people in the world—already by the mid-eighteenth century their nutritional intake was about the same as that of 1960s Americans. They were taller by several inches than the average European and commensurately heavier. The average work output of Americans was plausibly larger than that of Europeans, an effect that was partly offset by the Europeans' adaptive smaller stature.[*4]

Oddly, although American incomes and dietary provision continued to rise, height and mortality data suggest a major decline in Americans'

---

* Data assembled by Robert Fogel show that in 1700 an average American male consumed 2,300 calories over and above that required for basal metabolism and vital maintenance functions, like eating. A French or British worker's diet would have furnished only 400–750 "extra" calories, respectively, if they had been the same size as Americans. How much their smaller statures compensated for the gap is not known. Anecdotally, British sailors noted their own superior staying power against French sailors during the Napoleonic wars, presumably because of the poor diets of the Frenchmen.

health over about a thirty-year period starting in the 1840s. The causes have not been definitively pinned down. Rapid urbanization and the westward migrations are obvious culprits. The exploding population in the West was a feast for malarial mosquitoes, while runaway growth in coastal cities overwhelmed public water and sanitation infrastructure, triggering wave after wave of typhoid, cholera, tuberculosis, and other crowd diseases. The poor health of many arriving immigrants, especially the famine Irish who flooded the eastern cities in the 1840s, was undoubtedly also a factor.

Recent research points to cataclysmic health consequences from the Civil War, which "produced the largest biological crisis of the nineteenth century, claiming more soldiers' lives and resulting in more casualties than battle or warfare, and wreaked havoc on the population of the newly freed." Freedpeople were particularly vulnerable as they were crowded into refugee camps and poorly fed and sheltered. Smallpox, cholera, and other diseases were rampant. To make matters worse, the Freedmen's Bureau spread epidemics by frequently moving its charges from camp to camp over large areas of the country. Similar consequences appear to have followed the forced Native American migrations of the 1870s. Whatever the reason, Americans were still slightly shorter than the English and Swedes in the 1880s, although they recovered their advantage in the twentieth century.[5]

Finally, ordinary Americans, at least outside the South, were better educated than Europeans. The New England public school movement was well underway by 1820 and rapidly spread through the Middle Atlantic states and then to the Midwest. A study of national census return figures shows a quintupling of the population's average lifetime days of school instruction. By the 1830s, about 70 percent of the white population ages five to nineteen in New England and the Middle Atlantic states were enrolled in school, including more than half of the children of paupers. The Midwest made spectacular gains starting a decade or so later and reached equivalency of provision with the Northeast well before the Civil War. Southern states increased their spending sharply in the 1850s, but enrollments were far lower than in the rest of the country, so only favored groups benefited from the spending increases. The spending increases were concentrated on the common schools in the early days of the movement, but as states approached near-universal literacy and numeracy among school-age children, reformers shifted their attention to high schools. By 1860, Massachusetts had nearly 120 public high schools.[6] The great British industrialist Sir Joseph Whitworth suggested that the receptivity of American workers to productivity-enhancing machinery was a consequence of their comparatively high levels of education.[7]

Even with the slippage in health-related indicia, the overall favorable demographic and economic trends were such that the country was growing very rich. In 1800, the United States was a struggling ex-colony, wrestling crops and wood products from a resistant nature either for subsistence or to export to its erstwhile mother country. A half century later, it was the second biggest economy in the world, with output per worker virtually even with that in Great Britain. Isolating just manufacturing productivity, the United States was probably already ahead of Great Britain by the 1820s, and by 1850, according to a recent analysis, the average output of American manufacturing workers was plausibly 75 percent higher than that of the British.[*][8]

Economy-wide, Great Britain still had a small edge in output per worker, as a result of substantial advantages in services and agriculture. All of Great Britain's commercial services industries—shipping, railroads, delivery services, banking, and finance—were far in advance of America's, even as the very large share of agricultural workers in the American labor force—three times that of Britain—pulled down average worker output even further.

---

* The study I am relying on here is a careful one, by two respected economic historians, an Englishman and an American. Inevitably, as data are collected and filtered and run through spreadsheets, they produce output at second-decimal precision. But given the nature of the data sources, any such conclusions are very approximate. Their study concludes that American worker productivity across all industries was about 95 percent that of British workers, which is tantamount to equality within reasonable margins of error.

By 1860, there was already visible a rough map of American industry that would prevail into the 1930s and beyond, leaving aside developments in the far West. Both the Northeast and the Midwest were becoming industrial powerhouses, but each with its own development pattern. Industry in the Midwest was closely tied to its natural resources, while the eastern patterns of development were more the result of history and specific skill bases. We will look at each in turn.

The Queen City of the West

By the time of the Civil War, about a third of the free population lived in the nonslave states west of the Appalachians. For a couple of decades in mid-century, the region's economy revolved around the city of Cincinnati. Its population was on an exponential curve that reflected the growth of commerce—2,500 in 1810 to 161,000 in 1860. By then it was the seventh largest city in the country, just a hair behind New Orleans, with fast-growing St. Louis and Chicago nipping at its heels.

For a vivid journalistic tour through Cincinnati in the 1850s, we are indebted to another Englishwoman, Isabella Lucy Bird, just twenty-four at the time but as intrepid as Trollope and as gifted a writer. She was the sickly daughter of a minister, visiting American relatives but traveling solo for much of the time. Although she was pious, the "sickliness" seemed to occur only when she was living in the parsonage or later with her spinster sister. She desperately longed to travel and finally convinced her father to allow her to go to America. He gave her £100 for her trip, with his permission to stay as long as the money lasted. She stretched it for nearly a year in 1854–1855, a journey she described in her first book, *The Englishwoman in America*. For the rest of her life, the inevitable sickliness induced by sojourns in England was magically cured by travel—to the Rocky Mountains, Japan, Tibet, much of South Asia. Back in England, and turning fifty, she finally acquiesced to a pathetically long courtship by a respectable doctor some years her junior. Marriage greatly worsened her health, but her husband's providential early death effected a complete cure. After training as a doctor to justify continued travel, she spent the rest of her life in the remotest parts of the world, mostly in Asia and the Near East. There were eighteen more books after her first American account, the last of which, on Morocco, she produced in 1901, when she was seventy.[9]

Lucy Bird on the road was nothing like the neurasthenic creature haunting the parsonage halls. For one thing, she liked men. Her first encounter with "prairie men" on a train from Cincinnati to the Mississippi, made her giddy:

> Fine specimens of men they were: tall, handsome, broad-chested, and athletic, with aquiline noses, piercing gray eyes, and brown curling hair and beards. They wore leathern jackets, slashed and embroidered, leather smallclothes, large boots with embroidered tops, silver spurs, and caps of scarlet cloth, worked with somewhat tarnished gold thread, doubtless the gifts of some fair ones enamoured of the handsome physiognomies and reckless bearing of the hunters. Dulness fled from their presence. . . . Blithe, cheerful souls they were, telling racy stories of Western life, chivalrous in their manners, and free as the winds.[10]

We get a fuller picture of Lucy Bird from her second American trip eighteen years later, ostensibly to seek the curative air of the Colorado Rockies. By now, the twaddle about infirmities was a comic tic, for the trip was the last leg of a jaunt through Australia and Hawaii, where she had climbed Mauna Loa. Her "cure" over a long winter high in the Rockies, included serious climbing and eight hundred miles of horseback travel, some of it alone in mountain blizzards. She rode astride the saddle like a man and was strong enough on a *"broncho"* that she was drafted to work as a cowboy during a difficult, weeks-long, end-of-winter roundup of cattle scattered through snowed-in ravines. Her most reliable companion was her "dear desperado," "Mountain Jim" Nugent, who was missing an eye from an encounter with a bear. He was a legendary trapper and formidable gunfighter, with a dark past as a Kansas-Nebraska War bushwhacker. She was out riding one morning and saw him standing by his cabin.

[He was] a broad, thickset man, about the middle height, with an old cap on his head, and wearing a grey hunting-suit much the worse for wear . . . a knife in his belt, and a "bosom friend," a revolver, sticking out of the breast-pocket of his coat. . . . His face was remarkable. He is a man of about forty-five, and must have been strikingly handsome. He has large grey-blue eyes, deeply set, with well-marked eyebrows, a handsome aquiline nose, and a very handsome mouth. His face was smooth-shaven except for a dense moustache and imperial. Tawny hair, in thin uncared-for curls, fell from under his hunter's cap and over his collar. One eye was entirely gone, and the loss made one side of his face repulsive, while the other might have been modelled in marble.[11]

Even better, her mountain man was well spoken and courtly; he wrote poetry and knew the classics, although nothing is known of his roots. While her account gives no direct hints, some suspect a serious romance. One hopes it's true. But Nugent was also an episodic alcoholic, and whiskey could make him a monster—and she does record her pleading with him to swear off drink. "Too late," he always replied.[12]

When she finally left for home, Nugent rode down the mountain with her to the stage. It arrived with an Englishman, a land speculator, whom she had met previously on her trip: "He was now dressed in the extreme of English dandyism, and when I introduced them, he put out a small hand cased in perfectly-fitting lemon-coloured kid gloves. As the trapper stood there in his grotesque rags and odds and ends of apparel, his gentlemanliness of deportment brought into relief the innate vulgarity of a rich *parvenu*."*[13]

---

* Nugent and Bird remained in touch after she left. Within a year, however, Nugent was shot and killed by Griff Evans, another friend of Bird's, whom she had characterized as "weak." Evans was hoping to open a tourist hotel; Bird was his first and possibly only guest. The lemon-gloved Englishman who had arrived on the stage represented a British investor, the fourth Earl of Dunraven, who hoped to create a private British hunting preserve. Evans became his agent and was strongly opposed by Nugent and the majority of the locals, who justly regarded it as a land steal. Evans was reportedly drunk when he killed Nugent, and the shooting has been labeled "cowardly," although the details are murky.

Bird's youthful trip to Cincinnati occurred in the early fall of 1854, so she was able to travel from Boston entirely by rail. The trip covered about 1,000 miles in forty-two hours, with just a couple of train changes and a few brief stopovers to allow passengers to hurriedly purchase meals from station vendors. She recorded her arrival thus: "It was a glorious morning. The rosy light streamed over hills covered with gigantic trees, and park-like glades watered by the fair Ohio. . . . And before us, placed within a perfect amphitheatre of swelling hills, reposed a huge city, whose countless spires reflected the beams of the morning sun—the creation of yesterday—Cincinnati, the 'Queen City of the West.'"[14]

The city reminded her of Glasgow, "the houses built substantially of red brick, six stories high—huge sign-boards outside each floor denoting the occupation of its owner or lessee—heavily laden drays rumbling along the streets . . . massive warehouses and rich stores—the side walks a perfect throng of foot passengers—the roadways crowded with light carriages." And all of this "life, wealth, bustle, and progress" are on a "ground where sixty years ago an unarmed white man would have been tomahawked as he stood."[15]

Cincinnati's population had multiplied fourfold since Trollope's visit, with about half the increase from newly immigrated Germans and Irish. But it was a crossroads city, and Bird saw "dark-browed Mexicans, in *sombreras* and high slashed boots, dash about on small active horses with Mamelouk bits—rovers and adventurers from California and the Far West, with massive rings in their ears, swagger about . . . and females richly dressed . . . driving and walking about, from the fair-complexioned European to the negress or mulatto."[16]

Trollope had been a generation too early with her dream of a department store featuring European luxuries, for Bird found that although store windows featured "articles of gaudy apparel and heavy jewelry, suitable to the barbaric tastes of many of their customers," inside she found "the richest and most elegant manufactures of Paris and London," while a bookstore, "an aggregate of two or three of our largest, indicated that the culture of the mind was not neglected."[17]

Despite her hitherto sheltered life, Bird had a quick grasp of economics:

Cincinnati is the outpost of manufacturing civilization, though, large, important, but at present unfinished cities are rapidly springing up several hundred miles farther to the west. It has regular steam freighters to New Orleans, St. Louis, and other places on the Missouri and Mississippi; to Wheeling and Pittsburgh, and thence by railway to the great Atlantic cities, Philadelphia, and Baltimore, while it is connected with the Canadian lakes by railway and canal to Cleveland. Till I thoroughly understood that Cincinnati is the centre of a circle embracing the populous towns of the south, and the increasing populations of the lake countries and the western territories, with their ever-growing demand for the fruits of manufacturing industry, I could not understand [the basis for all the vast enterprise].[18]

Bird closes her descriptions of the beauty of Cincinnati's streets and the "astonishing progress, and splendour of her shops" by divulging:

that the Queen City bears the less elegant name of Porkopolis; that swine, lean, gaunt, and vicious-looking, riot through her streets; and that, coming out of the most splendid stores, one stumbles over these disgusting intruders. Cincinnati is the city of pigs. As there is a railway system and hotel system, so there is also a *pig system*, by which this place is marked out from any other. Huge quantities of these useful animals are reared after harvest in the corn-fields of Ohio, and on the beech-mast and acorns of its gigantic forests. And at a particular time of the year they arrive by thousands— brought in droves and steamers to the number of 500,000—to meet their doom, when it is said that the Ohio runs red with blood![19]

Porkopolis

Bird was correct about Cincinnati's annual hog-processing volume, which had expanded by a factor of ten in just twenty years. "It was

Cincinnati," a wag said, "which originated and perfected the system which packs 15 bushels of corn into a pig, packs the pig into a barrel, and sends him over the mountains and over the ocean to feed mankind."[20] Besides its favorable siting as an Ohio River entrepôt, Cincinnati was conveniently near the large salt deposits required for a packing center. During the antebellum period, western meatpacking was all about hogs. Beef cattle were easier to drive, and their meat harder to preserve, so they usually traveled to eastern markets on the hoof.

To ease the hog traffic in the city streets, local merchants and traders organized stockyards just upriver of the main city through the 1830s. Butchers who had doubled as hog slaughterers relocated around the stockyards and gradually consolidated into several dozen industrial-scale operations—"something on the plan of the abbatoirs of Paris," Bird suggested.[21] Most of them were sited on the Miami-Erie Canal, so slaughtering waste could be dumped to float away on the once-blue Ohio. A last rationalizing step was the integration of slaughtering, packing, and by-products processing to create the first midwestern high-volume, continuous-flow factories.[22]

The scale of the industry was enormous. A contemporary survey showed 96 packing points throughout the Midwest during the 1843–1844 season, shipping the meat of 1.25 million hogs. A decade later 216 packing points processed 2.6 million hogs. Cincinnati was the highest-volume producer throughout the prewar era, although its volumes stabilized near the half million mark. Cincinnati's efficiency and the competitive forces in the industry suggest that they were probably operating near an economic maximum.

Slaughtering was a manual process, so efficiencies were derived primarily from work rationalization and topped out at lower volumes than in, say, the Waltham-Lowell textile mills. The biggest antebellum hog packers packed around 20,000 animals a year. Since the point of maximum efficiency in postbellum beef packing plants has been estimated at 100 animals a day, hog packers were running their plants at a high level.

Transportation was the next critical factor. Cincinnati was well positioned for distributing the finished product to market, but its access to the live animals was limited to the number that could be raised within droving range. As local railroads proliferated through the Midwest, it became more economical to shorten droving times by building stockyards and Cincinnati-style slaughterhouses at interior rail depots, and then rail-shipping the processed meat to the closest Ohio River ports. The internal logic of the industry led to a broad decentralization of efficient but medium-sized packing plants.*[23]

The rationalization of slaughtering evolved over more than a quarter century. In the late 1850s, an English traveler reported that it took hardly two hours "from the first hammerstroke until [the carcass] was singed, cleaned, cut up, placed in brine, and packed in a cask for exportation."[24] A skilled team could separate a carcass into its constituent parts in less than a minute.

Since time immemorial, slaughtered animals had been hung upside down on hooks to drain and for most cutting and cleaning operations. In the early Cincinnati "disassembly line," slaughterhouse workers lifted the animals from one worker's station hook to the next. (Pregutting, a standard Cincinnati hog weighed about two hundred pounds.) In the 1840s, the hooks were attached to a wheeled chain to move carcasses from the slaughtering floor to cooling rooms. It took another twenty years to finally evolve the continuously moving hook array traversing all the slaughtering and trimming steps. Henry Ford later remarked that the meatpacking disassembly line had been one of the inspirations for his famous Model-T plant.[25]

The Cincinnati disassembly line was a signal achievement. It was not nearly as complex as a New England cotton mill, but rethinking the sequence and content of manual operations to fit the space-time units available to each worker was a big step toward the rational factory. A decade later, the beef disassembly lines in Chicago had up to seventy-eight processing steps. A knocker stunned a steer with a sledgehammer, and it was

---

* Business historians have shown that Chicago's giant postbellum meatpacking plants were far larger than scale efficiencies warranted. Competition should have led to a redistribution of slaughterhouses around interior rail centers, closer to the herds. The packing oligopoly led by Armour and Swift colluded to forestall such a redistribution.

swept up on a hook and sped past gutters, slicers, splitters, skinners, rump sawyers, hide droppers, and trimmers. It was fast, hard, dangerous work, and the blur of wickedly sharp instruments exacted a fearful toll among the workers. The Chicago plants became a lurid wonder of the world, a tourist attraction that the famed actress Sarah Bernhardt pronounced "a horrible and magnificent spectacle."[26]

As volumes expanded, Cincinnati's packinghouses were regularly reengineered to keep pace. A favored design was a multistory packinghouse. The animals were driven up a ramp and slaughtered on the top floor, cut and dressed on the next, with hams, ribs, bacon, and other cuts dropped into chutes leading to their various curing and salting tanks in the cellar. Over time, rendering of the lard and other wastes became part of a seamless flow. As the scale of investment increased, the packers moved to year-round operations. Packinghouses were rebuilt with giant ice cellars: during the winter they were loaded with tons of river ice that was covered with layers of sawdust. As the weather warmed, fans circulated air over the ice and through vent systems to the operating floors.

By the 1830s, Cincinnati slaughterers were learning to harvest more and more of the valuable hog by-products—selling "all but the squeal," as the slogan went. Hides went to tanners, bristles to brush makers, bones to eastern button factories, and newly arriving German butchers took the intestines for sausage casing. Packers began to pay drovers for the privilege of slaughtering, cutting their deals well in advance of the season. Rendering plants sprang up alongside the slaughtering and packing clusters around the stockyards. The variety and quality of marketable by-products grew steadily as processing innovations conferred better and better control over outcomes.

America's First Chemical Industry

Hog lard is one of the most desirable animal fats. Gourmet pastry chefs still prefer it as shortening, and it's actually healthier than butter or hydrogenated vegetable fats.[27] Lard contains multiple fats and oils that are important constituents of soap, candles, waxes, and lubricants.[28] The annual lard rendering for soap and candles was the most exhausting, dirty, and dangerous of the farmwife's tasks, exposing her to caustic lyes. But rising American wealth and production efficiency gradually brought store-bought, scented, noncaustic soaps and long-lasting candles within the reach of the average home. Lard-based lubricating oils—odorless, nonexplosive, with excellent viscosity in cold weather—were ideal for finely meshing mechanical parts, while lard-oil illuminant was much cheaper than the ever-scarcer spermaceti oil, and its bright flame made it the first choice of lighthouse operators on foggy shores.

A signal invention came from a Cincinnati meatpacker, Ebenezer Wilson, in 1844. Industrial lard rendering had been just a larger-scale version of the farmwife's lard boiling: the same open-flame cooking, but in 100-gallon kettles. Quality control was spotty at best, and the lard was easily scorched. Wilson reduced the lard with superheated steam in 1,200- to 1,500-gallon pressure cookers. With experience, he learned he could reduce virtually the entire carcass—offal and all—and still produce a highly purified lard with minimum residuum, as well as a variety of oils and glue. By 1847, he was operating four processing tanks in Cincinnati, was turning out 35,000 tons of prime lard annually, and had opened plants at meatpacking centers in Kentucky and Indiana.

Wilson may also have been the first to integrate slaughtering, disassembly, and rendering in a single plant. By 1851, the newest and largest integrated plant, in Covington, Kentucky, packed 23,500 hogs, more than all of Chicago's packers. The entire operation, including nine curing cisterns and a Wilson rendering system, ran within a single building the size of a football field, sited on its own wharf so the packed meats went directly from the plant into riverboat holds.

New soap-boiling apparatuses developed by a Baltimore chemist combined the mixing and boiling steps while preserving the best qualities of the lard. Cincinnati soap makers naturally adopted the same kind of continuous-flow factory principles as the meatpackers. Steam-heated conduits piped the soap through each step in the manufacturing process. After cooling into blocks, wire machinery cut and shaped uniform soap bars; fancier soaps could be poured directly into molds.

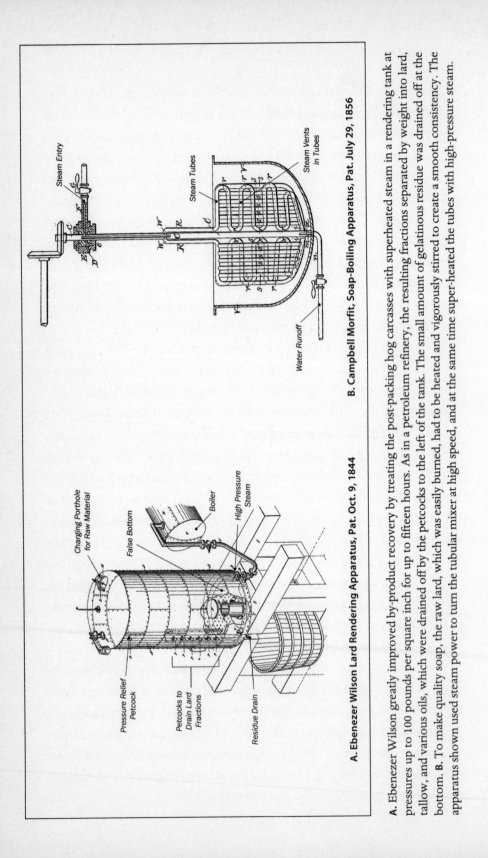

A. Ebenezer Wilson Lard Rendering Apparatus, Pat. Oct. 9, 1844

B. Campbell Morfit, Soap-Boiling Apparatus, Pat. July 29, 1856

A. Ebenezer Wilson greatly improved by-product recovery by treating the post-packing hog carcasses with superheated steam in a rendering tank at pressures up to 100 pounds per square inch for up to fifteen hours. As in a petroleum refinery, the resulting fractions separated by weight into lard, tallow, and various oils, which were drained off by the petcocks to the left of the tank. The small amount of gelatinous residue was drained off at the bottom. **B.** To make quality soap, the raw lard, which was easily burned, had to be heated and vigorously stirred to create a smooth consistency. The apparatus shown used steam power to turn the tubular mixer at high speed, and at the same time super-heated the tubes with high-pressure steam.

Mastery of the chemistry of lard facilitated the production of pure glycerine for a host of applications. It was important to tanners, a useful solvent, and widely used in the production of pharmaceuticals and food. Purified stearine, another lard derivative, was far superior to the farm-wife's tallow for candle making. It was odorless, maintained its shape much better under heat, and could be easily molded and dyed—clear "opal" candles were a Cincinnati specialty. From the mid-1840s to the mid-1850s, Cincinnati's soap exports increased twentyfold, while candles, chemicals, lubricants, and other lardoil products jumped at comparable rates. As Cincinnati's processing sophistication rose, the area sprouted a number of industrial chemical plants making inorganic acids, pigments, dyes, and other chemicals used in metal and food industries.

A major consumer company was born in Cincinnati when an English candle maker and an Irish soap maker, named William Procter and James Gamble respectively, married sisters, and their new father-in-law convinced them to go into business together in 1837. By 1859, their turnover passed the $1 million mark.[29] Their timing was perfect, for they were selling into a new middle-class gentility boom. About a century before, the English gentry had become interested in personal cleanliness. Regular bathing, though rarely with soap, became commonplace. Upper-class Americans, always eager for cultural clues from England, began to emulate the custom. When Boston's elegant Tremont Hotel opened in 1829, it included "eight bathrooms" in the basement. America's new and ever-alert middle class were quick to jump on the cleanliness bandwagon. Horatio Alger's Ragged Dick, who "had no particular dislike of dirt" as a street urchin, was transformed by a good bath and clean clothes. Missionaries to more benighted lands began to insist that the natives wash.[30]

The processing of lard and its derivatives was America's first true chemical industry. (New England textile makers generally bought their bleaches and dyes from the British.[31]) Lard processing also offered a prototype for the postbellum oil-refining industry. In its early stages, oil refiners were an assemblage of mom-and-pop operations, not much different from whiskey distilling. But they rapidly morphed into the same kind of large-scale continuous-flow operation as lard processing, with the additional benefit of a good native base in academic chemistry.[32]

. . . And Mass Production of Furniture

Lucy Bird spotted another Cincinnati specialty besides pigs when she stopped at a mass-production, machine-based furniture factory, which she recognized as something new under the sun:

> There is a furniture establishment in Baker Street, London, which employs perhaps eighty hands, and we are rather inclined to boast of it, but we must keep silence when we hear of a factory as large as a Manchester cotton-mill, five stories high, where 260 hands are constantly employed in making chairs, tables and bedsteads.
>
> At the factory of Mitchell and Rammelsberg common chairs are the principal manufacture, and are turned out at the rate of 2500 a week, worth from 1l to 5l a dozen. Rocking chairs, which are only made in perfection in the States, are fabricated here, also chests of drawers, of which 2000 are made annually. Baby rocking-cribs, in which the brains of the youth of America are early habituated to perpetual restlessness, are manufactured here in surprising quantity.[33]

Lumber and finished wood products were one of America's leading industries in 1850, well behind textiles and cotton but in an approximate tie for second place with leather and its products, metal and its products, and transport equipment and machinery. From colonial days, there was industrialized logging in Massachusetts, Maine, New York, and Pennsylvania, both for coastal ship builders and for export to England.[34]

Commercial exploitation of the great forests of the Midwest was underway by the 1830s and, like all of the region's industries, was heavily reliant on the high-pressure steam engine. A characteristic innovation was the development of large, portable circular saws packaged with a steam engine that could be trucked from one logging area to another.

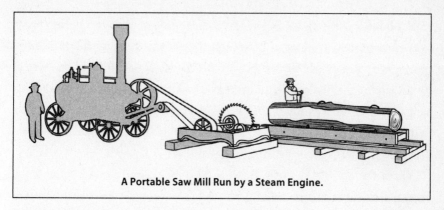

A Portable Saw Mill Run by a Steam Engine.

Rough-sawing raw logs at the logging site greatly improved transportation efficiencies. Midwestern loggers developed steam-powered portable saws that could handle logs up to thirty feet long.

Rough sawing in the forest greatly reduced transport costs. A portable forest mill, with a crew of two or three men and a 40-horsepower engine, could process 15,000 to 20,000 board feet of timber a day. One such mill, manufactured by a Cincinnati company, Lane & Bodley, could handle logs up to thirty feet long and forty-eight inches in diameter.

A survey in an 1872 British text noted that such forest mills in the Midwest had become

a vast business; not less than two thousand workmen are, in the state of Ohio alone, engaged exclusively on portable circular-saw mills, with the steam engines to drive them. . . . At first sawyers who had, by observation and experience, mastered the circular-saw mill, were in great demand at high wages. In fact, it is a feat of no mean pretensions to keep a large circular saw at work on rough timber; yet experience has done much to overcome the mystery of "running" a circular mill. . . . Portable circular-saw mills have not yet been to any extent built in England. There is, however, a colonial demand springing up for them.[*][35]

---

[*] The normal practice was to use reciprocating (up-and-down) blades, which could not cut nearly as rapidly. The large surface area of the circular-saw blade, its high speeds, and temperature differences between the center and the periphery created sufficient complexities to require a highly skilled operator.

All Europeans criticized the wastefulness of American lumbering practice. Running big logging saws at high speeds and keeping them true required very heavy, thick saw blades, so the kerf, or width of the wood ground up by the blade, was as much as a half inch.[36] Big timber-producing states like Maine, Michigan, and Wisconsin each processed routinely 200 to 300 million board feet a year, so those half inches added up. To forest-deprived Britons, it was a continuing scandal.

From the earliest periods, Boston, New York, and Philadelphia were centers for fine furniture making, much of it exported to wealthy planters in the West Indies. Americans showed great imagination in chair making; the rocking chair is apparently an American invention. The *Niles Weekly Register* recorded a shipment of 12,000 chairs dispatched from Baltimore in 1827 for a trip around the Horn, with delivery points up and down both of the South American coasts.

Before the 1820s, furniture was a small-shop, mostly handcrafted product. Fine cabinetmaking was almost entirely a bespoke business. Some local carpenter shops might make modest quantities of workaday furniture for sale but would otherwise produce to order. By the 1830s, New York craftsmen were already complaining that machine-made product was driving down the price of common furniture, but the most intensive development of furniture factories was pursued in the Midwest after 1840. Whitworth also reported on the American furniture industry, but it was only in the eastern states. He does not report on any large factories but details several "interesting machines," like an apparatus for shaping the arms and legs of chairs.[37]

The Mitchell and Rammelsberg plant memorialized by Bird offers a fine case study of the industry's evolution. The company's founders, Robert Mitchell and Frederick Rammelsberg, were two successful Cincinnati cabinetmakers who joined forces in 1847. The factory that Bird visited was steam-powered. Rough plankings were delivered and finished on the first floor; manufacturing processes took place on the middle floors, with finishing, varnishing, and drying on the top floor and roof.[38]

There is a surviving equipment list from a factory expansion in 1859. Two basement steam engines drove all the machinery, which included sixteen lathes, dovetail cutters (for joining the corners of drawers), planing machines, varieties of rip saws and crosscut saws, mortise and tenoning machines, routers, boring machines, and a variety of trimming equipment—scroll saws, friezing machines, and a molding machine.

A number of these machines, like the mortising machine, date from the Brunel-Bentham-Maudslay Portsmouth block factory a half century before. (The mortise is the female joint of the mortise-and-tenon system for joining wooden corners; the machine is a steam-powered chisel preset to the desired cut.) Most decorative machines, like the friezing machine and various carvers, are developments of the original Blanchard principle of a profiler/carver: an independently powered cutting tool directed by tracing a pattern of the finished product.[39]

The 1859 factory had thirty-six carvers for decorative work, working both by hand and with the aid of powered equipment. The scroll saw was a narrow reciprocating blade passing through a table and held in tension by a spring. A carver could draw a pattern on a workpiece and make a manually guided rough cut with the scroll saw before finishing it by hand. More advanced profiling carvers were developed after the Civil War, but precise effects usually required a dozen or more progressively finer cutting tools and tracing styluses, and the tool changes were time-consuming. Spindle carvers were small, fixed rotary cutters projecting horizontally from a base. The carver would hold a workpiece against the cutter and manipulate the piece to create decorative flourishes. The blade type determined the nature of the cut, but the carver free-handed the pattern.

The nineteenth-century American furniture industry is sometimes cited as an example of the armory tradition of manufacturing interchangeable precision parts with specialized machinery. But that seems a stretch. The Mitchell and Rammelsberg achievement is best understood as a brilliant product/marketing strategy—creating a cornucopia of styles and price points to suit both the newly well-to-do nonconnoisseur and the middle-class clerks, craftsmen, and hog farmers brightening their homes with a nice-looking table-and-chair set. In an age of heavy, ornately decorated furniture, different-size wooden orbs, flat squares, and cubes with beveled edges could be combined into a near-infinity of treatments of newel posts, leg bases, bed headboard posts, and other ornamentation. A variety of machine-molded edges added finish and style to flat shelving. Standard engravings, friezes, and carved crests were combined on beds and sideboys. Headboards could be flat with simple crests or have inset panels with contrasting veneers and more ornate flourishes. Veneers were widely substituted for expensive hardwoods, while stains turned oak into rosewood. Manufacturing tolerances were not highly demanding, but machinery construction was technically challenging since the machines typically ran much faster than metal-cutting machinery and had heavier blades, which stretched the limits of current ball-bearing technology.[40]

A Philadelphia architectural magazine sneered in 1861:

> An immense trade has sprung up in the last few years in a cheap and showy class of furniture, of mongrel design and superficial construction. . . . [Demand in the South and West is such] that a number of large steam factories are engaged in this trade exclusively. They make furniture of a showy style, but with little labor in it, and most of that done with the scroll saw and turning lathe. . . . This furniture is easily detected by examination, as it consists mostly of broad, flat surfaces, cut with scroll-saws into all imaginable and unimaginable shapes, and then by a moulding machine the edges are taken off uniformly: this gives it a showy finish.[41]

The critic did not name any specific manufacturers, but the article's descriptions of both furniture types and manufacturing processes, absent the sarcasm, was a dead-on portrait of Mitchell and Rammelsberg. By that time, the company seems to have been the trendsetter for the industry and had opened substantial stores throughout the major cities of the region.

An English observer had a better understanding of what was afoot, however, when he wrote in a catalogue of an American exhibition in London a decade earlier: "The absence in the United States of those vast accumulations of wealth which favour the expenditure of large sums on articles of mere luxury, and the general distribution of the means of procuring the

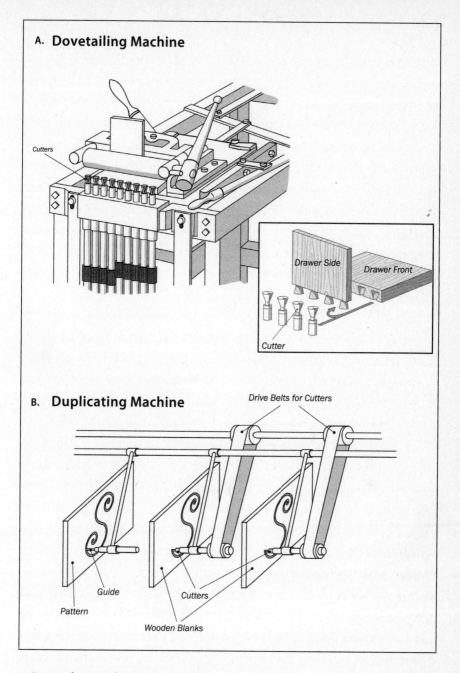

A. Dovetailing machinery was proliferating in mid-century, judging by a caustic reference in an 1872 textbook. They were a standard fixture even in modestly-sized furniture factories by the 1880s. **B.** Nineteenth-century furniture factories in the Mitchell and Rammelsberg tradition were quick to exploit Blanchard's concept of duplicating profiler/carvers. For inscribing cuts like the one shown, up to a dozen cutters might be driven off a single pattern guide.

more substantial conveniences of life . . . [directs American industry] to increasing the number or the quantity of articles suitable to the wants of a whole people, and adapted to promote the enjoyment of the modest competency which prevails among them."[42]

By 1860, the Midwest was a major manufacturing center in its own right, mostly centered around the big Ohio River cities like Cincinnati and Louisville. Chicago was gaining rapidly in population—110,000 to Cincinnati's 161,000—but Cincinnati still had a nearly six-to-one edge in manufacturing employment. Food processing and its by-products were the largest single industry, but the Midwest was developing a large transport sector: steam engines, steam boats, and, increasingly, rails and rail cars.

In the first few decades of the Midwest's rise as a manufacturing power, the east-west transportation barrier acted like a protective tariff. Trade between the eastern states and the Midwest was dominated by easy-to-transport goods: the West sold packed meat and lard products and bought shoes, clocks, and textiles. At the same time, improving riverine transit, the construction of nearly 1,000 miles of canals in the 1830s and 1840s, and the spectacular burst of 1850s railroad construction welded the Midwest into a large and more or less cohesive economic unit that could support its own substantial manufacturing base. By the time a national railroad network nearly eliminated transport barriers, Midwest manufacturers were able to hold their own, especially in piping, valves, steam engines, agricultural equipment, and other heavy machinery.[43]

The skill-based industries of the East, by contrast—shoes and textiles, brass clocks and fine instruments, the light machinery of the Connecticut River Valley—were there mostly by accidents of history. That deepening skill base created a regional advantage in newer industries like sewing machines, typewriters, and watches. But skill-based eastern manufacturing also included very heavy fabricated products—locomotives, large mill machinery, and large printing presses. We will look at those in the rest of this chapter, along with the one eastern industry that was driven purely by locational factors—open ocean–sailing vessels.

Steamships

The steamship industry may be the only instance in which the United States plausibly seized, or was in position to seize, leadership from Great Britain but quickly gave up its advantage and for all practical purposes exited the business.

Competition in the East Coast steamboat industry was ferocious. By the 1830s and 1840s, the boats were of oceanic proportions, roughly twice the size of Fulton's *Clermont/Steamboat* and far heavier and faster. Competing lines raced, and occasionally jostled, each other on the water, rather like NASCAR racers. There was no dominant owner, but the active presence of Cornelius Vanderbilt kept all the lines at a knife-sharp point of tension. His strategy was to move into and out of the trade opportunistically—launching price wars against complacent operators to gain control of their routes, then selling out at a profit. Vanderbilt had become by far the richest of the operators and the only one who could order and pay for major steamboats from his own resources—rich enough even to shrug off the loss of a major new boat, *The Atlantic*, a 321-foot behemoth. (It was driven on rocks during a fierce storm in Long Island Sound, with the loss of fifty of the seventy passengers and crew.) Unlike many buyers and sellers of companies, Vanderbilt was also a superb manager and nearly always turned lackluster properties into profit machines.[44]

Since almost all the steamboats were built locally, the New York–New Jersey harbor was lined with massive foundries and engine and machine shops, as well as shipyards of the largest dimension. By 1850, they had produced thirty-eight major steamships, including two for foreign governments. William H. Brown was the biggest yard, accounting for about a quarter of the hulls. Other important yards included William H. Webb, Westervelt & Mackay, Simonson's, and Jacob Bell. There were also multiple dry docks. Webb's, built in 1854, was the biggest at 325 by 99 feet with a 38½ foot depth; it had twelve pumps and was operated by two large steam engines, one on each side, each with a locomotive boiler. About half of the steamboat engines were made by the Allaire Works on the East

River, a pioneer of the marine compound engine,[*] with the Novelty Works likely in second place. (Vanderbilt gradually absorbed both the Allaire and Simonson businesses to improve his profit margins.[45])

Transatlantic shipping was largely the province of American sailing ships until two British steamships, the *Sirius* and the *Great Western*, arrived in New York Harbor within twelve hours of each other in the spring of 1838. The *Great Western* was much the more formidable ship—it had twice the tonnage of its rival and was a third greater in length and much faster (it had left England three days later). It had been designed by Isambard K. Brunel with an engine from Maudslay Sons and Field—respectively the sons of Mark I. Brunel and Henry Maudslay, who created the great pulley-block factory at Portsmouth. As was the convention until well into the second half of the century, both ships were under steam power and sail the entire voyage to conserve fuel. A number of other British competitors jumped into the fray, and the Cunard Lines won the premier position by virtue of a coveted mail subsidy—a generously calculated payment for handling British-American mail.[46]

E. K. Collins of New York, scion of a generation-old transatlantic packet-boat and freight operator, responded by launching four steamships in 1849–1850, all of them built in New York harbor, buttressed by an even more lucrative mail subsidy from the American government, justified on "national interest" grounds. The first two, the *Atlantic* and the *Arctic*, had engines from the Novelty Works, while the engines of the *Pacific* and the *Baltic* were from Allaire. The engine cylinders were all ninety-five or ninety-six inches in diameter, while the pistons had nine- or ten-foot strokes. There were other steamship lines, but the Collins and Cunard ships were on the same routes and even used the same terminal in New York, so they were most visibly engaged in a head-to-head competition. On the early matchups, the Collins ships—besides being much bigger— proved much faster. Cunard commissioned two big new ships, the *Asia*

---

[*] A compound engine, often called a "double engine" in this period, combined both a high-pressure (expansive) and low-pressure (vacuum) engine. The excess steam from the high-pressure component was piped into a Boulton & Watt–style apparatus, improving the power-to-fuel consumption ratio.

and the *Africa*, which were a marked improvement. But they did not decisively trump the Americans until the launch of the very large and very fast *Persia* in 1855.[47]

Cornelius Vanderbilt, in the meantime, had been gaining experience as an ocean steamship operator by running a lucrative Pacific line to take advantage of the California Gold Rush. The route went from New York to a port on the coast of Nicaragua. Passengers then embarked on a combined river-lake-transit road trip across the peninsula to meet steamships to San Francisco. His first ship commissioned for the East Coast leg was the *Prometheus*, which in 1850 made the 5,600-mile run, including stops at Havana on the way down and at New Orleans on the way back, in the extraordinary time of nineteen days, while consuming about a third less coal than any comparably sized ship would have required.[48]

The secret of the *Prometheus*'s performance was the engine. All of the oceanic steamships were side-wheelers. British design dogma, which had been adopted by Collins, required that oceanic ships have their engines located low in the hull for stability, so operating the side wheels required complex gearing with poorer operating efficiency. Vanderbilt insisted on a traditional walking beam engine, with the beams on the deck and the drive shafts connected directly to the side wheels, and proved the naval architects wrong. The walking-beam engine was much lighter and more efficient, and the ship, like most side-wheelers, was very stable.[49]

Vanderbilt launched the *North Star* in 1853, and in a slow market, he adopted it as his personal yacht. At 2,500 tons, with 260 feet at the waterline, 34-foot side wheels, and two walking-beam engines, it was among the largest and most capacious, most lavishly outfitted, and fastest commercial-scale ships in the world. He took his family and retainers on a world tour, in part just to introduce himself to the international scene but also to advertise the capabilities of American shipping and to underscore his challenge to the Collins mail franchise, which Vanderbilt bragged, doubtless correctly, that he could operate at half the price.[50]

Vanderbilt returned from his tour, refitted the *North Star* as a passenger ship, and began work on the *Vanderbilt*, even bigger and faster than the *North Star*. Plausibly, the United States looked poised to seize shipping supremacy from the British. It didn't happen. By the eve of the Civil War, the Collins line had collapsed, and Vanderbilt had sold off most of his steamship interests, turning over his larger ships to the government for war transport.

What happened? The immediate causes were economic. Congress decided to make drastic cuts in the Collins subsidy, just as the economic crisis of 1857 devastated freight and passenger revenues. More subtly, the British, acting on pure free-trade doctrine, had opened their registries to foreign shipping in 1849. As British shipping interests had predicted, the Americans, with their unmatchable clipper ships, quickly dominated international freight shipping, most especially the lucrative China and India trade.

But theory for once was triumphant. All sensible American investors plowed their money into the wooden sailing-ship industry. When the Crimean War ended and the British began a full-scale transition to iron ships[*] and propeller drives, Americans were simply not in the game. And at the end of the day, compared to the opportunities in the American West and in railroads, ocean steamships did not look like an especially attractive business, since it was so heavily dependent on subsidies.[51]

After the Civil War, the Pennsylvania Railroad attempted to re-create a steam-based merchant marine industry by building four creditable ships, but it finally merged them into a Belgian combine in 1884. In 1902, at the height of an American leveraged buyout boom, J. P. Morgan led a roll-up of two American and two British shipping lines. The new entity, International Mercantile Marine, was arguably insolvent on its first day of business, and as an investment, was an unmitigated disaster.[52]

Baldwin Locomotive

Matthias Baldwin was a Philadelphia jeweler, a whitesmith—a metalworker in silver, pewter, and tin—and clearly a gifted mechanic. When he

---

[*] High-quality iron was much more expensive in the United States than in Great Britain, making iron ships uneconomic except for military uses. Rough iron and steel price/quality parity was not achieved until sometime in the 1880s.

and his partner moved to a bigger shop in 1824, he built a stationery steam engine to power their machinery. Although it was his first engine, it was remarkably efficient and had enough useful innovations to attract a number of orders from other Philadelphia workshops. When the partnership broke up in 1829, Baldwin opened his own workshop as a jobbing machinist and specialist in steam engines.[53]

This was at the dawn of the railroad age, and in 1830 Baldwin was commissioned by the Franklin Institute to build a realistic working model of a steam-driven railroad. That led to contract from the new Philadelphia-Germantown Railroad to build a full-scale engine. A second contract with another line followed a few months later, and others after that; in the single year of 1835, he built fourteen locomotives.

From the time Baldwin entered the business, he pushed the product boundaries. The second engine he produced incorporated Jervis's four-wheel swiveling truck at the front of the engine, which improved its performance on curves. Baldwin followed that up with a bigger three-axle engine, including the truck, and then added a power train to the truck. In both 1836 and 1837, Baldwin sold forty locomotives, employed some three hundred men, and became one of the wealthier Philadelphia manufacturers. An 1838 Treasury survey showed that there were 350 steam locomotives in the United States, 122 of them from Baldwin. Since 78 engines had been imported, Baldwin had 45 percent of domestic production, and had begun to win contracts on the European continent.[54] Among some twenty-two other American locomotive producers, Baldwin was clearly the dominant player.

When the 1837 Bank Panic shut down most railroad construction, Baldwin was exposed to the perils of big-ticket capital goods production. Since he supplied much of his customers' financing, he found himself desperately squeezed for cash, scraping through by stonewalling suppliers and groveling to creditors. He preserved the company by working out an informal receivership with his creditors that allowed him to retain control until markets recovered, although he lost his position as industry leader. For Baldwin, a deeply religious man with high business principles, it was a time of terrible strain.[55] The half-century-long railroad boom that followed the Civil War finally put the company on a solid footing, and by the 1880s, it was the world's largest locomotive maker.

Despite the financial headaches, between 1850 and 1870 Baldwin made extraordinary productivity gains, as shown in Table 6.2.

TABLE 6.2 Baldwin Output, 1850–1870[a]

	1850	1860	1870	Multiple 1850–1870
Employees	400	675	1,455	3.6
Locomotives	37	79	273	7.4
Average Locomotive Wt.	44,661	51,812	64,513	1.4
Total Weight	1,652,457	4,093,148	17,612,049	10.7

[a] Brown, Baldwin Locomotive, 166.

That accomplishment is the more impressive if one considers the much greater complexity of the 1870 over the 1850-vintage locomotive, plus the fact that dominant railroads like the Pennsylvania and the Baltimore & Ohio were increasingly specifying highly customized designs.

How did they do it? The original Baldwin manufacturing strategy was, at heart, that of the classic machinist's job shop. But superimposed on that was a prototype for the modern systems integrator, like Boeing. Boeing has great manufacturing skills and is arguably the world leader in mega-wing design and production, but the vast majority of the millions of components in one of its planes are sourced from outsiders, including many of the most critical, like the engines and the avionics. The ability to manage that complexity is the deep skill that makes Boeing such a successful company.

Baldwin's challenge was similar. By the 1840s, standard locomotives weighed 40,000 tons and had some 4,000 parts, far more than Baldwin could make itself. Many of the components, moreover, like boiler plates, axles, wheel castings, and large flues, were beyond Baldwin's shop capacities. From the earliest days, therefore, Baldwin formed strong relationships with key vendors. Each new contract produced a flood of parts orders that could usually be specified by the variations from a previous order. On a standard engine delivery schedule of sixty days, the first four to six weeks were devoted to making, or purchasing and finishing, the components, followed by two weeks of building the engine. Several engines could be worked on simultaneously, but each one, along with virtually all its components, was essentially built from scratch, and few of the engines were ever completely identical. Throughout the decade, depending on the market, Baldwin turned out a locomotive every ten days to two weeks.

Baldwin did that with almost no management to speak of. As the company entered the 1850s, Baldwin was the sole owner and chief executive. He had elevated a shop foreman, Matthew Baird, as the de facto number two, although Baird spent most of his time with customers. The rest of management consisted of a general superintendent, George Hufty, who oversaw day-to-day production, and one more executive, a shop floor veteran with a flair for numbers who took care of the accounts. Baldwin, besides managing day-to-day financing issues, was immersed in tooling strategies and product design, a major source of the company's reputation. And that was it—four managers in a four-hundred-person company, two of them in sales and accounting rather than line positions, supported by a handful of clerks.

Operating management lay with the shop foremen. There were seven shops in 1850: foundry, boiler, smith, painting, and three machine shops. Each foreman was effectively the master of his house. Baldwin and Hufty would establish a production schedule, set the timelines for each of the shops, and order the required components and raw materials. From that point, the shop foremen were on their own. In effect, they were running sizeable businesses with about fifty workers each, and like Baldwin, they had mastered every detail of their shop work, hired and fired their workers, purchased their own shop supplies, and organized their internal work flow as they saw fit—with the major difference that they had only a single customer. The relation with major suppliers was somewhat similar. Over the years they must have developed high levels of trust, and Baldwin could not have met its schedules without top-priority treatment by all its vendors.

But as the 1850s opened with a surge of new sales, the company's productivity could not keep pace. Locomotives were bigger, and part counts were rising—so were mistakes and missed deadlines. Baldwin and Baird began to rethink operations, and over the next twenty years the company became a model of a modern, World War I–vintage, capital goods manufacturer.

The first step was the installation of a piecework payment system. That wasn't a matter of turning a switch, for there was no documentation on the discrete tasks performed in each shop or the value of each major process completed. It took a couple of years, but they worked it through. In general, the men liked it because they earned more. (Baldwin, unlike an Andrew Carnegie, did not use piece rates to reduce wages; if output was rising, he was happy to see the men earn more.) The foremen hated it because the implicit task standardization invaded the traditional independence of the shops.

The next challenge was the proliferation of locomotive designs.* Parts counts were becoming unmanageable, and the craft-shop manufacturing culture meant that standard parts were rarely identical anyway. So-called standard parts emerging from the machine shops couldn't be fitted into standard boilers in the boiler shop without extensive reworking. To make matters worse, customers were complaining about the work required to make even the simplest repairs. Other shops had the same problems, but a high-volume producer like Baldwin** could strangle on them.

Solving the parts snarl took more than a decade and required a complete rethinking and upgrading of the production system. The first step

* The "Master Mechanic" problem was the industry's name for the proliferation of design shops at the larger railroads. In fact, few of the customization demands were frivolous but rather reflected the steadily improving engineering capabilities at the bigger lines. Different lines operated over quite different terrains, often with different average-weight loads. Procurement engineers were learning to specify optimum power outputs and other features to suit their operating environments.
** I have so far used "Baldwin" as if the man and the company were the same. After his death in 1866, however, the company had many different names, as the successive partners changed. "Baldwin Locomotive Works, Inc." was adopted only in 1909, but for convenience I use "Baldwin" throughout the text.

Baldwin Shop. After all parts had been manufactured or received from its vendors, Baldwin typically devoted two weeks to assembling each engine. Since every engine was different, the erecting shop workers had to embody a broad range of skills. Even standard parts that were nominally "interchangeable" were likely to require fitting just as gun parts did. The workers by the windows are filing parts. The erecting shop was expanded to accommodate multiple engines in the early 1850s, and was regularly further expanded as volumes increased. There are at least seven engines being worked on in this picture from 1869, which suggests the complexity of the parts acquisition and tracking challenge.

was to identify all the parts used in production and eliminate any unnecessary variation. All boilers have multiple water taps, for instance; absence a specific justification for a variance, all such parts should be identical. But to achieve that, the company had to choose the default tap, carefully specify it in a set of dimensioned engineering drawings, and then repeat that exercise for a couple of thousand or so more standard parts. By the early 1870s, there were standard, dimensioned drawings covering all important standard parts, with a comprehensive parts catalog. When a job was being laid out, all standard parts were specified by their catalog number.

The last step was to gradually adopt armory-style gauging. Baldwin had a large cadre of skilled machinists and had long made almost all of its own machines, so it's likely that it made its own gauges as well. By the 1880s, locomotive makers were claiming that all their parts were "interchangeable," although only subsets, like critical gears and power train parts, demanded the kind of high precision required by watchmakers or gun makers. All major railroads had sophisticated machine shops to manage repairs, and since replacement parts were typically installed in heavily used machinery, some fitting was almost always required.

The striking advances in productivity speak for themselves. But they had much more to do with management than with machines—simplifying designs, rationalizing the production and assembly process, and taking control of parts, specifications, and work sequences. Improved specification also allowed the company to experiment with "insourcing" the shops: bidding out contracts, usually to foremen, for delivering annual production according to a negotiated price schedule. On the whole, the experiment worked out well and was retained for many years, but the ground had been prepared by the years of work on standardization and work rationalization.

Baldwin offers yet another model of mass-production manufacturing. Like the Mitchell and Rammelsberg plant, it has a number of affinities with armory practice. But although it took full advantage of improvements in gauging, cutting tools, and materials quality, its operations were highly labor-intensive well into the twentieth century, with heavy reliance on general-purpose machinery in the hands of skilled workers.

The real story at Baldwin was not mechanization but its operations management—the product of an ultralean top management with deep experience on the shop floor. There were no outside "efficiency experts." In the early twentieth century, indeed, Baldwin executives were extremely critical of Taylorism and the so-called scientific management movement. An 1879 visitor noted: "Owing to the magnitude of the establishment, a stranger would naturally suppose that it would require almost a regiment of Bosses and any amount of 'bossing,' but such is not the case by any means. There are very few lookers on to be seen in the shops. . . . The proprietors, superintendents, gang, and track bosses all work themselves so there are very few, if any, drones in the hive."[56]

And it stayed lean for a long time. In 1910, when Baldwin had grown to 14,500 employees turning out 1,675 locomotives, most of enormous weight and complexity, the president, William Austin, normally spent half his working day in the drafting room checking drawings.

Corliss Engines

George H. Corliss was a dominant figure in steam-engine technology in the second half of the nineteenth century. The son of an upstate New York physician, he had no university or technical training and is said not to have seen the inside of a machine shop before he was eighteen. But Corliss had the gift. Bored as a clerk in a country store, he invented a machine for sewing leather and patented it in 1843, when he was twenty-six. Hoping to develop prototypes, he went to Providence, a machining center, in 1844 and took a job as an assistant in a machine shop. The partners appreciated his acumen and encouraged him to shift his interest to steam. Within two years he was a full partner. By then Corliss had already conceived the mechanisms that one of his rivals, who later became an industry historian, called "the most famous steam engine that has appeared since the time of Watt."[57]

One of the machine-shop partners capitalized a new company to develop Corliss's ideas. Corliss got one-third interest plus royalty payments on sales, in return for his patents and a small capital contribution. The first engine sold that same year for $8,600 without the boiler, and its success quickly led to several more sales. By the time of the final patent award in 1849, they were already building a new and expanded factory. The company was renamed the Corliss Steam Engine Company in 1857, and by 1864 Corliss had purchased full ownership.

The standard American high-pressure steam engine of the 1840s was based on the slide valve. There is a steam chest along one side of the cylinder: as the slide valve moves back and forth, it alternately admits and vents steam on both sides of the piston. After the success of the engine in river steamboats, it spread rapidly throughout industry, freeing mills and forges from the dependency on waterpower. Even in waterpower-rich New England, rising power demands and winter production losses forced the shift to steam. The Lowell Locks and Canals Company acquired its first steam engine in 1850 and had thirty-nine by 1870.

But as the stationary steam engine became the factory power source of choice, its gross deficiencies became the more apparent. For one thing, standard engines were prodigal consumers of coal. Fuel was usually the biggest factory expense after personnel. Just as important, the energy output from most engines was very irregular. In small shops, that was rarely an issue, but in a large textile mill, where high gearing often ran looms at extreme speeds, power variations were amplified to violent effect. Even with steady power, if several big looms went down at the same time, the drop in power load could cause the other looms to spin at destructive speeds. In a big iron rolling mill, the sheer weight of the machinery made variations in power especially damaging. A skilled operator could throttle steam up or down, but the inherent lag between the action and its full effect made it hard to prevent major plant disruptions.

Corliss's first patent addressed both fuel consumption and speed regulation as related problems. The operations of a standard slide valve exposed each end of the steam chest to alternate doses of fresh and expanded steam. The temperature differentials were wide enough that much of the heat in the fresh steam was spent on rewarming the steam chest. Corliss's first innovation was to completely separate the intake and exhaust operations to minimize the need to reheat the apparatus on each cycle.

The second innovation was to rethink the throttle. In the slide valve engine, the throttle limited the steam entering the piston cylinder from the steam chest while venting any excess—thus wasting good steam. Instead, Corliss regulated the engine with an automatic variable cutoff valve. To reduce or increase power, Corliss reduced or lengthened the period of the valve that admitted steam directly into the cylinder. Since just the right amount of steam was delivered, none had to be vented, so energy waste was greatly reduced. The regulation of the valve cycle was performed by the traditional spinning-ball governor. As the engine changed speeds, centrifugal force would change the plane of the balls' rotation, and an apparatus connecting the governor to the valves would modify the valve settings proportionately. An important fillip was that as the balls approached horizontal, the valve connection was dropped—in the words of the patent, the valve was "liberated"—so it would shut almost instantaneously. (A clever latch arrangement automatically reconnected a closed liberated valve, while a shock absorber prevented any damage from too hard a closing.) The inventions, moreover, were adaptable to any type of steam engine.

Modern analyses show that Corliss's valves and valve management systems improved fuel efficiency by about 30 percent. Since Corliss's early sales were almost all to replace older engines, the savings were usually 50 percent or more. British observers were inclined to mock the awkward-looking rods on the outside of the machine[*] but were converted by its performance at the Paris Exposition of 1867, where it won the gold medal. A British engineer wrote of the Paris engine that it was "refined, elegant, most effective and judicious . . . spares steam to the utmost but develops what it uses to most effect." The governor was "sensitive to the most delicate changes of speed, and feels the slightest demand upon the engine for more or less work and steady speed." In sum, the review concluded, "everywhere tells of wise forethought, judicious proportion, sound execution, and exquisite contrivance."

---

[*] The Corliss arrangement did look ungainly, but that was partly because he put almost all the connections outside the engine, where they would be easier to adjust and repair.

Corliss's first innovation was to save steam by separating the entry and exhaust valves on each side of the piston. (A conventional slide valve both admitted and expelled steam leading to wide temperature variation both at the valve and within the steam chest, so steam was wasted on reheating engine parts.) The exterior drawings show how the Corliss wristplate and the valve rods manage the valve actions, while the interior drawings show the separation of the steam intake and expulsion actions. The second innovation was that the intake period could be precisely timed to accommodate shifting power requirements. Conventional engines tuned power through a throttle that slowed the rate of steam admission, necessarily wasting excess steam. The drawing on the next page illustrates the Corliss timing mechanism.

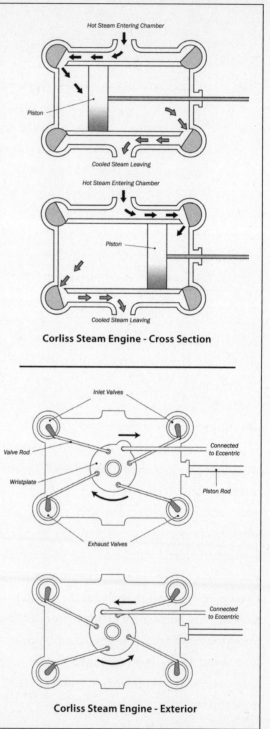

Hot Steam Entering Chamber

Piston

Cooled Steam Leaving

Hot Steam Entering Chamber

Piston

Cooled Steam Leaving

Corliss Steam Engine - Cross Section

Inlet Valves

Valve Rod

Wristplate

Connected to Eccentric

Piston Rod

Exhaust Valves

Connected to Eccentric

Corliss Steam Engine - Exterior

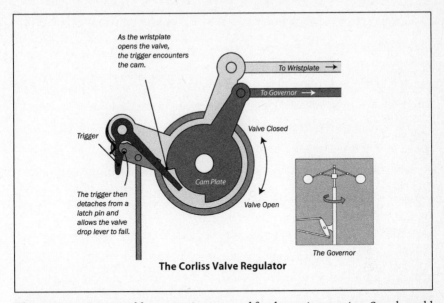

The Corliss Valve Regulator

The power engineer could set a maximum speed for the engine rotation. Speed would be measured by the rotating flyball governor in the inset. When the governor reached the preset speed, it triggered the valve regulator, and a drop lever instantly shut the intake valve. If a number of looms went down in a large mill, the Corliss would instantly reduce power to the point where they continued to operate at a constant speed, and would make a comparable adjustment as the failed looms were brought back on line.

Corliss marketed his machine in the early days by offering customers an option of a fixed price or a sum geared to actual fuel savings. Customers who chose the contingent price always paid much more. Fuel savings were even higher than raw fuel consumption data suggest, because the intrinsic regularity of the operation allowed the use of lower-quality coals. Textile mill operators most valued the "extreme regularity" of the Corliss. The reductions in thread breakage made it almost a must-have in the industry. In its first fifteen years of operation, up to 1862, the company sold 480,000 horsepowers, or about 480 separate engines. (At the time, engines were only about 30 percent of its sales.) Sales over the next seven years more than doubled the installed horsepower, reflecting both sales growth and a trend toward larger engines. By the time his patents expired in 1870, Corliss had collected $213,000 just in royalties, mostly from his own company.

Corliss's great success was marred by bitter and prolonged patent litigations. In truth, almost every important feature of his engine had been anticipated by previous patents, although none had presented a comprehensive, integrated, new plan for an engine the way Corliss had. In later patent filings, he acknowledged the priority of other designers for specific pieces, although the designs themselves were quite different. While he didn't win every case—he bemoaned the unpredictability of lay jurors—he carried all the essential ones, and Congress granted him a seven-year extension to compensate for his loss of revenue while the litigations were underway.

Corliss's most famous engine was produced as the showpiece for the 1876 centennial celebration in Philadelphia. It was an unreserved bash, attracting 10 million visitors from all over the world with some 30,000 exhibits spread over 236 acres in Fairmount Park. But the center of attraction was the goliath Corliss steam engine powering thirteen acres of machinery in Machinery Hall. It comprised two one-cylinder walking-beam engines. The beam centers were 30 feet off the floor; the beams themselves were 27 feet long and 8 feet deep at their center. The cylinder was more than 3 feet in diameter, and the great flywheel weighed fifty-six tons. Visitors were most impressed, however, by the machine's near silence, which attests to the very high quality of manufacturing at Corliss. The power shaft driving the Hall's machinery was 352 feet long, and its major distributing gears were all 6-foot-diameter bevel gears. The trueness of the drive shaft and the lack of chatter in the enormous gears exemplified the precision of Corliss's products.

Unlike a Baldwin, Corliss usually made *every* part in his own factory, which had been constructed to build to monumental size. Besides his engines, he made a wide range of heavy machinery and parts, like heavy wheel and shaft castings. His plant could pour single castings of as much as thirty-two tons. There were also four in-plant locomotive turntables with two railroad spurs connecting to commercial lines. (A locomotive could enter the plant, take a load, and be turned around on the table.) A fair summary of the Corliss operation is that it was one of the world's best

British-style heavy manufacturing operations, working on a craft basis at every stage of production.

In the mid-1880s, Corliss closed down his plant with the thought of converting it to a more mechanized, assembly-line-type operation, but he died suddenly in 1888, at the age of seventy-two, and the plans were never implemented. The business declined after his death, for he had not provided for a successor. One of his great engineers, Edwin Reynolds, had joined the E. P. Allis Company of Milwaukee (later Allis Chalmers) in 1877, after serving as Corliss's general superintendent for six years. With Corliss gone, Allis became the leader in innovation in very heavy machinery. By then, nearly the whole industrialized world had converted to Corliss-type machines for heavy steam plants, until they were superseded by the steam turbine and new valve configurations around the period of the First World War.

Hoe Printing

Robert Hoe, an apprentice carpenter, emigrated from England to the United States in 1803, when he was nineteen. In New York City, he and two brothers-in-law, a joiner and the inventor of a hand press, formed a company to make wooden presses and later saws. After his brothers-in-law died, Hoe continued the firm under the name of R. Hoe & Co. When he died in 1833, he was succeeded by his eldest son, Richard March Hoe, who became one of the great figures in nineteenth-century printing technology.[58]

Hand printing presses had changed little since the days of Gutenberg, and the conventional designs were maintained through the early generations of power-driven presses. A bed of type—the form—was inked, and then a piece of paper held tightly in a frame was forcefully pressed into the form by a flat metal or wood platen. Thus the first powered cylinder press, invented by a Saxon, Friederich Koenig, and installed at the London *Times* in 1814, was something of a landmark event. In Koenig's machine the set type lay flat and was moved back and forth. A cylinder held the paper sheet and had three positions: one for loading the sheet, one for the actual printing, and one for removing the sheet. Sheet loading and removal was by hand, but with skilled feeders the presses could produce up to four hundred pages an hour. The machine was widely adopted by the British, who made a number of improvements, especially in the paper handling.[59]

The Hoes learned about the cylinder press only in 1832, when the senior Hoe was already ill. Richard produced his own version in 1833 and sold them by the hundreds. By the 1840s, his double-cylinder press achieved speeds of 4,000 pages per hour on one side, with two feeders.

The cost of paper fell rapidly after the introduction of the Fourdrinier paper-making machinery from France. In the world's most literate and information-hungry nation, cheap paper was like crack cocaine; the bottleneck was only the speed of the presses. Hoe's response was the patented Hoe Type Revolving Machine. Instead of a flat bed of type with the paper turning on a cylinder, Hoe put the *type* on a large central cylinder, with the paper fed in flat and taken up by a stationary roller. The major technical challenge was learning how to fix the type securely in the form of a nearly perfect circle.

The new machine incorporated a number of important paper-handling improvements: the feeder simply slid the sheets down a ramp, and mechanical contrivances positioned them correctly on the roller, unloaded them after printing, and stacked them in the correct piles; the inking apparatus was built into the central cylinder. The beauty of the arrangement was that one could position a number of separate feeding slots and printing rollers around the central roller. The biggest, and fastest, model sold was the Ten Cylinder model shown on page 235, with feeders positioned on both sides.

The Ten Cylinder machine achieved output of 20,000 pages an hour and was an essential enabler of the vast proliferation of newspapers of all kinds in the mid-nineteenth century. Most of the large presses in the world adopted the Hoe revolving press. Great Britain was the sole holdout, until the London *Times* finally purchased two Ten Cylinder presses in 1856. That was an especially sweet victory for the Hoes, for in 1848, when the *Times* purchased a conventional press, it had pointedly editorialized on

Hoe Ten-Cylinder Printer. Printing presses achieved very high speeds when Richard Hoe managed to create a cylindrical type holder that could retain the heavy type at a high rate of rotation. The inking apparatus was inside the cylinder, so fresh newsprint could be introduced at multiple points on the cylinder. Young boys could serve as feeders, since advanced paper-handling apparatus made the final paper placements. Note that six feeders are working on the near side of the machine and four on the other.

the absurdity of the Hoe claims: "No art of packing could make the type adhere to a cylinder revolving around a horizontal axis and thereby aggravating centrifugal impulse by the intrinsic weight of the metal."

Not much is known of the details of Hoe's manufacturing processes, but what is known suggests that they ran rather as Baldwin's did. All makers of heavy equipment were necessarily major uses of power-assisted machinery, much of it made in their own factories, as it was with Baldwin and Corliss. Precision requirements were increasing in all branches of industry, and a machine like Hoe's Ten Cylinder press included thousands of small parts and had to be exquisitely calibrated to maintain proper print registers at speed. Hoe also developed its own large-form depthing micrometer for precise manufacturing measurements, which put them in the forefront of the gauging movement.[60] Because of their scale and complexity, major products did not lend themselves to mass-production engineering.

Like a locomotive, each big press would be custom-built, but with considerable standardization of key parts to simplify servicing and maintenance.

R. Hoe & Co. was a dominant player in large-scale printing through the rest of the century; among its many other innovations, it invented the first newspaper-folding presses. Almost weirdly, it never dropped the saw business that the senior Hoe and the Smiths had picked up in the company's earliest days. Mocking any business-school notion of "focus," Hoe was a major competitor in large industrial saws well into the twentieth century.[61]

———

B UT THE NORTHEAST WAS HOME TO ANOTHER STREAM OF INDUSTRIAL development: the true armory practice tradition of mass production of complex, high-precision products, with special-purpose machinery and high-precision hand finishing to such a level of accuracy that parts can be freely interchanged from one unit to the other. In mid-century, the exemplar of armory practice was Samuel Colt's great gun-making plant in Hartford. The British discovery of Colt and of armory practice manufacturing, and their decision to purchase American arms-making equipment for their own military, marked the first recognition by influential Britons that the United States was proceeding about its business in some quite original ways.

CHAPTER SEVEN

On the
Main Stage

L ONDON'S GREAT CRYSTAL PALACE EXHIBITION OF 1851 WAS ORGANIZED
by Prince Albert and his circle, and officially titled the Great Exhibition of the Works of Industry of All Nations. That "All Nations" in the title
was merely politesse, for no one could mistake that the event was a festival
of self-admiration, a celebration of the global triumph of empire, British
industry, and British culture.

The construction of the Exhibition Hall in London's Hyde Park was
itself a great feat of engineering. More than a third of a mile long and
housing 13,000 exhibitions, it was constructed of more than a million
machine-fabricated, iron-framed glass sheets and set among gorgeous
plantings and 12,000 fountain jets spurting as high as 250 feet. (The great
engineer Isambard K. Brunel designed much of the exhibition's water system.) The plate-glass components, sufficiently interchangeable to be simply bolted together, were as astonishing as anything in the displays,
pointed testimony to the continued march of British technology. They
were the product of a new plate-glass rolling and annealing process
patented in 1848 by James Hartley, one of Great Britain's largest glass manufacturers.[1] The massive edifice was erected in only twenty-two weeks,
for just a six-month run from May through October, during which it accommodated more than 6 million visitors. When the exhibition closed in
the fall, the hall was dismantled and reconstructed in a London suburb,
where it remained until it was destroyed by fire in 1936.

The Crystal Palace. The great hall of the Crystal Palace during the inauguration ceremony. It was the first large-scale prefabricated ferrovitreous (iron and glass) structure in the world, perfectly suited to illustrate the preeminence of British technology.

Countries with little industry to speak of paraded their treasures. The Greek exhibit displayed figures from the Parthenon and some ancient statuary, while Russians offered fabulous jewels, massive bronze candelabras, and Chinese vases that appear to be booty. Compared to such extravagances, the ragtag collection of homely objects in the American display drew quiet British jeering. *Punch* sniffed that America's "contribution to the world's industry consists as yet of a few wine glasses, a square or two of soap, and a pair of saltcellars." In disgust, the *New York Herald* editor, James Bennett Forbes, suggested adding P. T. Barnum's "happy family" exhibit, displaying "owls, mice, cats, rats, hawks, small birds, monkeys . . . and what-not, all in one cage, and living harmoniously together."[2] Then the gods of coincidence came up with a boat race, forever after designated the America's Cup, which quite unintentionally became a major side event of the Great Exhibition.

The Great Race

The notion of an American-British sailing race originated with an innocuous letter from a British merchant to John Cox Stevens, the president of the New York City Yacht Club. The merchant professed himself an admirer of American pilot boats. They were descendants of the famed Baltimore Clippers that so bedeviled the British during the War of 1812, and considered the fastest sailing ships afloat. The gentleman hoped that the club might send a few at the time of the exhibition, so Englishmen would have a better opportunity to assess their merits.[3]

John Cox Stevens was the son of John Stevens, the inventor and steamboat and railroad entrepreneur, and the elder brother of Robert, who was an entrepreneur and technical genius like their father. Stevens père earned enough from his enterprises to be a rich man but had also married into the super-rich Livingstons, allowing John Cox to spend most of his time with his boats and horses. He and his yachting friends quickly decided to take up the merchant's idea but chose to construe it as a challenge to race, rather than as a simple invitation.

The Club contracted with the big William H. Brown shipyard and a young designer George Steers to construct a racing schooner to their specifications. (Much of the risk was borne by Brown and Steers; if the boat didn't pass a series of trials in the United States and go on to win the race in England, they would be paid nothing.)

The bargain made, the new boat, named *America*, was built and passed its trials in the United States. It was captained by Dick Brown (no relation to the builder), who ran the fastest pilot boat in New York Harbor and brought his own crew.[*] *America* sailed to Le Havre in July. It was a difficult crossing, marked by alternating storms and calms, but was accomplished in nineteen days, well under the average for fast packet ships.

Their arrival in England, at Portsmouth, was preceded by tales from the Le Havre pilots about the American craft that sailed so smoothly and so fast. A racing cutter from the Royal Yacht Squadron met *America* on the Channel, offering to escort them into the harbor. Brown accepted and immediately found himself in an impromptu race. After a brief tacking duel, *America* sailed into the harbor with the cutter far in its wake.

Stevens was warmly welcomed by Britain's sailing establishment and richly entertained. Although the talk was dominated by the *America*, no one offered a race. After making several direct challenges, Stevens was fobbed off with the suggestion that he enter *America* in an upcoming regatta for "all ships" of "all nations," around the Isle of Wight, a fifty-three-mile run. It was clearly not the race he was looking for. *America* would be competing with speedy light cutters as well as schooners, with much of the race in light winds in the lee of the island, far from the conditions it had been designed for.

Irritated, Stevens took his boat out day after day intentionally showing up British yachtsmen, to the point at which the British press, always happy

---

[*] Pilot boat captains provided pilots to guide large ships into the New York Harbor. Each captain had a stable of pilots and competed by being the first to the best customers. The trade was well-paid, so large rewards went to the daredevil captain with the fastest boat. Brown's *Mary Taylor* was a sixty-six-foot ocean schooner.

to tweak the idle upper classes, was getting interested. A reporter from the *Times* watched a club race that the *America* shadowed, and wrote:

> As if to let our best craft see she did not care about them, the *America* went up to each in succession, ran to the leeward of every one of them, as close as she could, and shot before them. . . .
>
> Most of us have seen the agitation which the appearance of a sparrow hawk in the horizon creates among a flock of wood pigeons or skylarks, when . . . [they] are rendered almost motionless by fear of the disagreeable visitor. . . . Although the *America* is not a sparrow hawk, the effect produced by her apparition off West Cowes among the yachtsmen seems to have been completely paralyzing.[4]

Anxious to get home, and with no other options besides the all-comers regatta, Stevens swallowed his frustration and acquiesced to the regatta.

The day of the race, Friday, August 22, dawned with enough wind to at least give *America* a chance against the lighter cutters. At the cannon signal, *America* was caught by a sudden gust and got tangled in its cable, requiring it to strike its sails and restart. Brown still caught the first stragglers within five minutes, sailing aggressively through the pack, and within fifteen minutes was behind only three schooners and several light cutters. Shortly thereafter, the leaders entered a stretch more open to the channel winds, and *America* was finally in its element. After the second hour, it had left all the schooners in its wake and was running down the cutters one by one. Even many of the steamers carrying sightseers were having trouble keeping up. When *America* made the turn into the lighter winds for the final run, no other boat was in sight. Queen Victoria and Prince Albert were watching from their yacht but, with the race obviously decided, took off for home. One steamer passing a dock was hailed from the shore: "Is the *America* first?" "Yes," came the reply. "What's second?" "Nothing."[5]

The apparent runaway victory by *America* dominated the accounts of the race, although in reality it won by the slimmest of margins. With only five miles to go, the wind died, and *America* could barely creep forward, as a lightweight cutter, the *Aurora*, slowly closed the gap—"bringing the wind with her," in Brown's rueful phrase.[6] That last five miles may have taken three hours, but the wisps of breeze finally stiffened enough that the *America* slipped over the line with just eight minutes to spare.

The British were as magnanimous in defeat as they had been reluctant to engage. For the yachting community, however, according to the *Times*, the loss had been like "a thunderclap . . . the sole subject of conversation here, from the Royal Yacht Commodore . . . to the ragged and barefooted urchin." A wealthy American commented to a lady on British courtesy and the lack of mortification her friends seem to feel. "'Oh,' said she, 'if you could hear what I do, you would know that they feel it most deeply.'"[*7]

O N THE SAME DAY AS *AMERICA'S* VICTORY, AN AMERICAN SUCCEEDED IN opening a famous, exquisitely crafted, and "unpickable" British Bramah lock—meeting a challenge that had stood for forty years. (Joseph Brahma was a great British machinist, yet another graduate of the Henry Maudslay school of advanced precision manufacturing.) The lock breaker was Alfred C. Hobbs, a talented huckster with an excellent understanding of machine manufacturing. He adroitly downplayed that his lock-breaking feat took more than two weeks and then offered $1,000 to any British locksmith who could open his own machine-made locks. When no one could meet his challenge, he collected the exhibition's lock medal and almost immediately made plans to open a factory in England.

Hobbs's demonstration came just a few weeks after Cyrus McCormick's reaper had decisively bested a feeble array of local competitors in a series of field tests. The usually anti-American *Times*, which had earlier derided McCormick's machine as "a cross between a flying machine, a

---

* They got used to it. Stevens's syndicate donated the cup to the New York Yacht Club in 1857, on the condition that the club would accept international challenges from time to time, with the cup to be held by the winning nation under the same stipulation. The first challenge, from a British syndicate, was in 1870. Competitions continued intermittently, usually against British challengers. The Americans turned away all comers, until an Australian team captured the cup in 1983, ending a 132-year winning streak.

wheelbarrow, and an Astley chariot," abruptly changed its tune: "The reaping machine from the United States is the most valuable contribution from abroad, to the stock of previous knowledge that we have yet discovered," predicting that it would "amply remunerate England for her outlay connected with the Great Exhibition."[8]

But the praise heaped on reapers and locks were far eclipsed by the plaudits for Sam Colt's repeating firearm exhibit; even the Duke of Wellington, a regular visitor to Colt's booth, was heard proclaiming the virtues of repeating firearms. Another gun maker, the Vermont firm of Robbins and Lawrence, conducted a well-attended demonstration showing how its machine-made rifles could be disassembled, their parts mixed up, and then randomly reassembled by an unskilled workman using only a screwdriver—a feat that British gunsmiths had long declared impossible. Robbins and Lawrence won the exhibition's firearms medal, while Colt, like Hobbs, let it be known that he too would open a plant to bring American technology to Great Britain.

It was sweet turnaround for the Americans. Even *Punch* gleefully switched to mocking punctured British pride:

> *Yankee Doodle sent to town*
> *His goods for exhibition;*
> *Everybody ran him down,*
> *And laughed at his position;*
> *They thought him all the world behind;*
> *A goney muff or noodle,*
> *Laugh on, good people,—never mind—*
> *Says quiet Yankee Doodle*
> Chorus *Yankee Doodle, etc.*
>
> *Their whole yacht squadron she outsped,*
> *And that on their own water,*
> *Of all the lot she went ahead,*
> *And they came nowhere arter*

Your gunsmiths of their skill may crack,
But that again don't mention;
I guess that Colt's revolvers whack
Their very first invention. . . .
But Chubb's [another British lock maker] and
      Bramah's Hobbs has pick'd,
And you must now be viewed all
As having been completely licked
By glorious Yankee Doodle.
CHORUS Yankee Doodle, etc.

While the public was impressed with the sailing race, a portion of the British cognoscenti had become extremely interested in American gun manufacturing methods, which they often referred to as the "American system of manufacturing," by which they meant manufacturing to an idealized model, with special-purpose machinery, to such a level of precision that parts could be freely interchanged between weapons without loss of performance. And it was Sam Colt who, deservedly, most captured their imagination.

Inventors had tried their hand at making repeating firearms for centuries. Colt spent a great deal of money and invested some three decades of his life to the challenge, and when he came up with a viable solution, he displayed true marketing genius in making it a reality. His correspondence shows that he had a good grasp of manufacturing processes, but the man who turned the Colt pistol into a triumph of mass production was Elisha King Root.

Elisha K. Root

Elisha Root was a Massachusetts farm boy who went to work in a cotton mill at age ten or twelve. He then apprenticed as a machinist and in 1832, at age twenty-four, was hired as a journeyman lathe hand by the axe maker Collins & Company at Collinsville, a new postal subdistrict in Canton, Connecticut. After just a few months on the job, he was given a two-year contract to build and repair machinery at a wage 75 percent higher than that of the average skilled worker. Sam Collins, the company's primary owner and manager, had a nose for talent.[9]

The axe was a critical tool for the land clearing that enabled the spread of American agriculture. The intensive employment of axes since the first American settlements had evolved the world's most efficient axe, with head weighting and balance that greatly reduced strain on the woodsman. In the early nineteenth century, axes were usually made by local smiths. Sam Collins started his company in 1826 on the bet that a superb factory-produced axe would command an enormous market. (Axe makers made only the axe head; local distributors procured and fit the handles.)

Collins was right. Although he was financially overextended from time to time, when Root joined the company it was already the largest and fastest growing American axe maker. Collins may also have had the ideal businessman's temperament—even-tempered but running a tight ship, possessed of a fine sense of strategy and organization but staying close to the shop floor—and his axes quickly earned a reputation for quality.

The Collinsville plant used traditional methods: a hot skelp, or iron bar, was flattened with a trip-hammer and folded around a set of pins to form the eye, where the handle was inserted. A second bar piece, the plate, was welded into the space between the two ends of the fold, and the whole piece hammered, filed, and ground into the proper axe-head shape. The cutting edge, or bit, was made of high-grade steel—it still had to be imported from England—that was welded into a V-shaped seating on the business side of the head. That was followed by multiple tempering, grinding, polishing, and other finishing steps before shipping.[10]

Collins was constantly pushing for manufacturing improvements and maintained a cadre of first-class creative mechanics to that end, although Root outshone them all. By the time he left the company to take over the design and construction of Colt's new Hartford factory in 1849, he had created and fine-tuned a nearly completely mechanized production system that enabled Collins to become a true global supplier.

Root's most important patent, filed in 1838, was a fundamental change. Instead of folding the skelp around pins, he invented a machine that punched an eye through a solid block of hot iron. That gave the head far more structural integrity than the folding and welding method.[11] He followed that invention with a number of others to mechanize the finishing process—shaving and shaping machines, mass tempering on revolving racks, and consolidating operational steps to reduce machining stations.

Rather than introduce the inventions piecemeal, which would have unbalanced the production lines, Collins waited until Root's entire line of machinery was sufficiently proven, then converted the whole company in one swoop, by elevating Root to the superintendency of the shops and building a new plant to accommodate the new mechanized system.

Root's new building was up and running by 1847. An 1859 *Scientific American* article reports a machine array right from Root's patent book, although greatly multiplied—there were twenty-six shaving machines, for instance. Root's achievement was widely recognized by aficionados, and job offers had been coming his way for years. He always refused them. Root was well paid, lived modestly, and enjoyed the luxury of a boss who was willing to take major financial and production risks to put his ideas into action. His own building, designed from scratch, was worth more than the pay offers he was receiving.

But when the plant was up and in full production, the equation changed. Sam Colt had tried to hire Root years before but had been turned down.* In 1849 he was back, planning a major new plant in Hartford, anxious to bag Root as the plant designer and manager, and willing to let him name his price. Sam Collins, who greatly admired Root, proved himself a true friend by telling him that he should jump at the chance.

The Amazing Samuel Colt

Samuel Colt was born in straitened circumstances but far from the poverty that he liked to allege. The Colts were one of the oldest of New England

---

* Root and Colt had met when Root was still an apprentice. Colt was giving a demonstration of an underwater torpedo, which then went awry and sprayed water and mud on the crowd. Root prevented the crowd from inflicting bodily harm on Colt. Colt also paid a visit to Collinsville before he set up his first gun venture and took notes on the machinery, so he would have formed a good impression of Root's capabilities.

families, with many successful merchants and entrepreneurs in the family tree, and the men had a knack for marrying into rich families—the Olivers, the Lymans, the Caldwells. Colts made fortunes supplying American and French troops in the Revolutionary War and were original partners with Alexander Hamilton in his Society for Useful Manufactures, a proto-industrial park in Paterson, New Jersey. At Paterson, the Colts were pioneers in developing and leasing water rights years before the directors at Lowell adopted the strategy.[12]

The family also had a streak of instability, and its financial annals are littered with bankruptcies. After the Paterson venture failed, Sam Colt's uncle Roswell, a master promoter, fund raiser, lobbyist, and string puller, bought a controlling position and used it as the base for his ventures, most of them disreputable. Huge volumes of money ran through his fingers, much of it diverted to lavish homes and entertainments or misappropriated to support his private ventures.

But the most lurid family highlight was provided by Sam's brother John in 1842. He killed a colleague with an axe in a dispute over money, then chopped up the cadaver and attempted to ship it to New Orleans. When the ship was delayed, odor betrayed the corpse, and John was arrested and convicted in a sensational New York trial. The grisly details drew tabloid interest throughout the country, which only increased with the revelation of a triangle with a woman, who had become pregnant to boot. John died in his cell before he was hanged, possibly a suicide. Sam paid for the legal defense but also managed to work in pistol demonstrations during the course of the trial.[13]

In 1829, when Sam was fifteen, he had been sent to Amherst Academy but was quickly expelled for pranks and for allegedly setting off an explosion. He then went to sea, as the story has it, where he conceived of the idea for a repeating firearm. (All such stories of Colt's early years must be taken lightly, for they usually originate with Colt, an inveterate tale spinner.) In any event, by the time he was seventeen, Sam was actively canvassing his firearm ideas, borrowing from his uncle Roswell and his financially pressed father to finance prototypes. An alliance with a Baltimore gunsmith, John Pearson, produced some beautiful sample guns, most of them long guns. Colt, typically, stiffed Pearson on his invoices, and for the rest of his life, Pearson justifiably insisted that the original Colt guns were his design.

Colt was a natural showman. Whenever he was really desperate for money, he transformed into Dr. Coult, traveling the boondocks giving natural science lectures and demonstrations of laughing gas and explosives. One wishes that Frances Trollope had still been in Cincinnati to give us a portrait of the youthful Dr. Coult when he did a turn at her "Inferno" show.

Colt acquired patents on his revolvers in both Great Britain and the United States, and in 1836, with the help of Roswell, he incorporated the Patent Arms Manufacturing Company in Paterson, raised capital, and, like his uncle, proceeded to run through enormous amounts of money. Colt mostly concentrated on sales and was constantly on the road, spending lavishly as he chased down state militias and wooed federal military brass. (Just his tailoring bills are astonishing.) He did get promising sales interest from Latin American governments and sold several thousand guns to the Texan independence forces and to Americans troops fighting Florida's Seminole wars. The factory was under the supervision of Pliny Lawton, a respected mechanic recommended by Colt's father who got a decent production line up and running. But the company was always at the financial edge in part because of Colt's spending. It was probably doomed by the 1837 financial crash, but it was already in turmoil because of a serious split between Colt and his investors. The business was insolvent by 1841 and shut down the next year.[14]

The breakup with the investors may have had less to do with money than the fact that Colt still couldn't produce reliable firearms.*[15] The

---

* The investors complained that Colt had fraudulently concealed the problem that multiple firing chambers often ignited simultaneously. The board was dominated by Dudley Selden, a friend of Colt's father, who had acted as Sam's lawyer in forming the company. He engineered a cash call among the investors, and cut off Colt's salary. Colt had no money, and his failure to meet the call would have triggered the loss of all his stock and control over his patents. (Venture capitalists often resort to such devices to squeeze out inconvenient founders.) Colt's alleged fraud was to demonstrate his weapons with only a single chamber loaded. But these were all professional investors, and Colt was a fast-talking twenty-two-year-old. If they were gulled that easily, it is hard to feel sorry for them. The dispute petered out after the bankruptcy, and Colt kept control of his patents.

weapons he was flogging in the 1830s may have been more dangerous to the user than to the target—which testified less to Colt's incapacities than to the gnarliness of the challenge. For a century or more, the world's most talented gunsmiths had been making runs at making repeating weapons without much success. Colt was not the first to try the revolving cylinder; all ran aground on the problem of multiple cylinders firing at once. Colt's early revolvers were loaded much as muskets were: the gunman used a tool to remove the cylinder and pushed powder and ball into each chamber; ignition was by a percussion cap. If loose powder leaked around the cylinder, chambers could ignite indiscriminately, which could cause the weapons to explode. In early Colt models the chambers were open in the rear and would occasionally fire backward.

But Colt worked through it, which may be the most surprising part of his story. One half of Sam Colt was the buncoing fabulist, the walking bonfire of other people's money, the drinker and carouser; the other half was a truly gifted inventor, not so much a mechanic as a man of fine mechanical intuitions, diligent and perseverant in pursuit of his objectives. An 1839 patent showed major strides on all fronts—preventing ignition contamination, simplifying the handling of the percussion caps, significantly reducing the part count.[16] Those were the kind of micro-modifications that require long periods of experimentation and testing, and at the time, Colt was about the only person working on the problem. (Lawton executed Colt's ideas in hardware, but there is no suggestion that he played a significant role in designing them, as Elisha Root later did. At one point, Lawton requested Colt to return a sample of a newly designed pistol so he could see how to make it.[17]) The combination of patient midnight-oil tinkerer with raucous huckster and con man is almost oxymoronic.

When his Paterson venture shut down, Colt removed to New York City, an ideal stage for his multiple talents. For six years, he lived in high style, if always from hand to mouth, spewing out a string of inventions. He developed a system of mines detonated by telegraphic signals to augment coastal defenses. The idea won military financing, allowing Colt to blow up giant ships in New York Harbor and the Potomac to the cheers of thousands-strong crowds. But it was peacetime, and the military wasn't in a spending mood. He patented waterproof cartridges and actually made some money on them, and he started a telegraph company. Colt also stayed active in New York's scientific societies, worked hard on a self-education in chemistry and physics, won a number of awards, and made a host of useful contacts, like Samuel F. B. Morse.

The 1846 war with Mexico brought both opportunity and allies. The war was a chapter in the American drive to push its western border to the Pacific and was triggered by the agreement to annex the newly independent Texas as a state. The Texans who had fought for independence loved Colt's pistols and had passed them on to the newly organized Texas Rangers. An encounter in which a small force of Rangers with Colts decimated a much larger, conventionally armed band of mounted Comanches was already legendary. The famous Ranger captain Sam Walker insisted on Colts for his men in the new war. The actual sales were modest—only about 1,000—but it was still splendid publicity. Walker participated in the design, and the new pistol emerged as a saddle-carried weapon, one of the heaviest and most powerful Colts ever made.

It took all Colt could do to deliver on them. He had no time to build a factory, and his old financial network was in tatters, but after a frenzy of money scrounging, he put together a production consortium. Some parts—apparently barrels, chambers, and brass parts—were outsourced, with the rest of the manufacturing and finishing performed by Eli Whitney Jr. in New Haven. In the meantime, Colt returned to Hartford and raised money for his own factory on Pearl Street near the banks of the Connecticut River, which opened in the fall of 1847. From that point, the handguns were the stars of Colt's product line. They were ideal for close combat after cavalry charges, for ship boardings, and for countering the close-quarter tactics of Native Americans or of the "Kaffirs" bent on complicating Great Britain's imperial ambitions.

The year 1849 was a banner one for Colt. Intense lobbying and barefaced bribery finally secured a patent extension. It was also the year of the California gold strike, and the beginnings of a vast population movement to the West and Southwest, where guns were almost workaday tools. For the first time, Colt was in position to catch a very tall wave, and he made the most of it. In that same year, he produced the most successful single product of his lifetime: the 1849 .31 caliber pocket pistol, which eventually sold 325,000 units. It is a measure of how well he understood his business, and his own limitations, that he put on such an all-court press to nail down Root.

Colt's first Hartford plant employed about thirty men and was in temporary space. The production was likely a small-scale version of that at Springfield. Much of the machinery came from Nathan Ames, who had long been selling knockoffs of the Springfield equipment; most of the rest were the lathes, dies, tools, patterns, and a furnace that Whitney had bought for the Mexican War contracts. (Naturally there was a prolonged spat over Colt's past-due bills before Whitney released the equipment.)

Within months of getting his temporary plant underway, Colt began construction on a much grander plant that opened in early 1849. The *Hartford Courant* reported that it was "a museum of curious machinery." For its time, it was a big building, 150 by 50 feet, with "long lines of shafting and machinery . . . performing difficult work and shaping irregular and intricate forms of solid steel as though it were soft as lead." That same year, the credit service R. G. Dun's reported Colt as "making money, large business, employs 100 hands, good credit." He completed a new armory in London in 1853 and started work on his last, and most spectacular, plant in Hartford, which opened in 1855. Production soared in the new plant and jumped again with the coming of the Civil War. Colt died in 1862, at only forty-seven, so he missed most of the wartime boom that made his descendants among the richest of Americans. By his death, however, he had sold a quarter million guns.[18]

The last years of his life were satisfying ones, for he had finally created a stage equal to his self-conception. He married a wealthy young woman in 1856, built a lavish estate on the grounds of his new plant, held forth in Turkish costume at Newport summer soirées, and traveled the world with his wife, sightseeing, art collecting, and selling arms to distant potentates—

all the while badgering his managers for details of their operations. The cause of his death was variously listed as "gout" or "rheumatism" but was probably a result of three decades of hard living combined with the day's lethally ignorant doctoring.

The London Armory

Most of the information on Colt's most advanced production processes comes from his London factory. A few months after being lionized at the Crystal Palace Exhibit, Colt became the first American to be invited to speak at the prestigious British Institution of Civil Engineers, and he was later awarded an engineering medal. The talk, in November 1851, was heavily attended, with both British and American government and military luminaries in the audience. The discussion following the presentation extended over two evenings. Opinion was virtually unanimous on the virtues of the weapons, as was the amazement that they had been made by machinery. In Colt's words: "Machinery is now employed by the Author, to the extent of about eight-tenths of the whole cost of construction of these fire-arms; he was induced gradually to use machinery to so great an extent, by finding that with hand-labour it was not possible to obtain that amount of uniformity, or accuracy in the several parts, which is so desirable, and also because he could not otherwise get the number of arms made, at anything like the same cost, as by machinery."[19]

The intense interest in Colt's talk stemmed from an evolving crisis in British military arms procurement. Weapons requirements had dropped off sharply during the aristocratic stability that followed the Napoleonic wars. But as black war clouds gathered at mid-century, the military small arms industry had become slothful and stagnant, quite unequal to the task before them. Military gun making was concentrated in Birmingham and organized into forty-eight different trades and subtrades, all of them working by traditional methods. Each trade made its particular pieces and shipped them to the government for inspection. The proved work then went to highly skilled fitters, who assembled guns by hand-filing. While many of the craftsmen were superb, the process was wasteful, and the quality of work had deteriorated considerably. Nor was there much hope of reform, for the crafts were in full control of the shop floor.[20]

Desperate for a solution, the doyens of British engineering grasped at the idea of attacking the problem with machinery, vaguely defined as the American system of manufacturing. James Nasmyth was one of the witnesses before a parliamentary committee looking into the advisability of greater reliance on machinery in arms making. Asked how he could be so sure that the British trade would benefit from more machinery, Nasmyth retorted:

> Then I should ask why are the gunmakers of Birmingham so much at the mercy of their men; if they have that quantity of machinery that I think is applicable to gunmaking, they ought to be quite independent of those men, and not be knuckling down to them as they are. . . . I may quote Mr. Brazier as giving me that information.
>
> [Committee] What account did Mr. Brazier give you?—That he has been tormented out of his life by his men striking.[21]

To Colt, the undisguised British admiration for American machinery looked like Opportunity writ large. When he left London in 1852, he was determined to return and open an armory. In the meantime, John Anderson, a senior civil servant with Ordnance responsibilities, created an expert delegation to travel to America to inform themselves on American applications of machinery, especially with reference to firearms. The fact that it was coheaded by Joseph Whitworth attests the high importance accorded the investigation. The group spent the summer and early fall of 1853 in the United States, with Whitworth focusing on metal trades and gun making, while the other cohead, George Wallis, one of Great Britain's leading educators, investigated a broader rage of industries.

Moving with his usual alacrity, Colt had his London plant up and running on the banks of the Thames by January 1853, and it quickly became something of a tourist attraction for the British intelligentsia. By the time the Whitworth and Wallis groups returned from the United States and produced their initial reports, the new armory had been open for a year and was a convenient reference point for the parliamentary hearings that commenced in the spring of 1854.[22]

The best available description of the armory is in a two-part 1855 article in the *London Journal of Arts and Sciences* that includes detailed line drawings of the major machines. The opening sentence says it all: "The establishment of a fire-arm manufactory at Thames-Bank Vauxhall, by Colonel Colt, is a fact from which we shall ere long have to date an entire revolution in the production of small arms in this country."[23]

The new armory was in a leased brick building, some 350 feet long, with a deep basement and three stories. The basement space was devoted to the heavy machinery used to make the factory's machine tools; the first and second floors to multiple turning, boring, and milling machines; and the top floor to polishing, fitting, and final assembly. Large sheds in the yards were for carpenters and smiths, and housed a row of steam hammers, the drop forge, and associated furnaces. The steam engine was in the basement connected to a separate boiler house. Next to the plant was a well-kept garden area and a sales office and showroom.[24]

The factory was a pinnacle for Root—a marked advance over his Collinsville machinery, with the same attention to detailed process flow. In the smiths' sheds, for example, the forges allowed two smiths to work on a furnace at the same time, and the grates arrangement did not immerse the bars in fire, so their color could be readily observed. The barrel forging machines, built for octagonal barrels, each comprised four consecutive barrel-length dies and a cutter. The worker took a steel bar at the proper heat, placed it and pressed it in each die in sequence, and trimmed it—"shaping out the barrels, one after the other, with great rapidity."[25]

Of the machines in the shed, the drop forger drew the most comment. It was built as a rectangle with V-bar slides for drop hammers on each vertical corner. Two workers were normally in attendance, each managing two hammers. The heavy screw drive in the center was constantly in motion, lifting the hammers. A simple latch device allowed the attendants to place each hammer to any level on the slide to tune the force of the blow.

After a hammer was released and dropped, it automatically reengaged with the drive and was lifted to either a preset height or the top of the forge, where it disengaged and remained in place until released again. Cast dies on the hammer and its drop site closed completely around the hot metal to minimize irregularities. The very heavy construction and extreme precision of the screw drive and the V-bar slides produced highly exact forgings, minimizing milling and filing.

That same intelligence was displayed throughout the plant. Colt's barrels were bored, rather than hammer-welded or rolled, for greater integrity. The barrel-boring machine had a lever device that allowed the bore to be withdrawn straight out for lubrication, in place of the usual slow reverse rotation. The rifling machine rifled four barrels at a time, automatically resetting the tool placement for the six or seven grooves that were standard for Colt pistols. The breech cylinders were bored in two machines: the first made three progressively finer bores in each chamber location; the second involved four separate boring and finishing tools operating on the six chambers of eight target cylinders on a rotating wheel. All the tool placements and workpiece adjustments were accomplished by self-acting cams. There were dozens of other machines operating on similar principles.

Great Britain's wide-eyed reaction to the London armory was fully warranted. Colt's plants in London and Hartford were the most advanced precision-manufacturing operations in the world, far in advance of any of the American armories. When the British investigators toured the Springfield Armory, for instance, they were much impressed with the Blanchard stocking machinery. But they were surprised that the line was not set up for a true process flow. When the great machinist Cyrus Buckland reconstructed the Blanchard line, he used fifteen different machines. The times required for the different machines to do their specific tasks naturally varied, so the slower machines were bottlenecks. At Collinsville, and at Colt, Root naturally multiplied the slower machines to keep the flow even and all machines occupied, which seems just common sense. But for thirty-five years, the armories either didn't notice or, since they were working to a quota, not a profit line, had no incentive to run full.

Colt London Armory Machines:
from 1855 *London Journal of Arts and Sciences*

A. Two-dimensional end view of forging engine. A hot bar was rapidly forged and cut in the row of tools indicated.

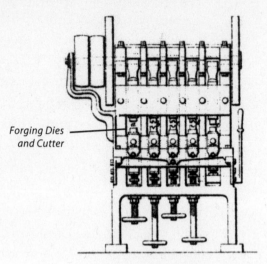

Forging Dies and Cutter

A. Barrel Forging Engine

B. The drop hammers and dies (indicated) manufactured near-finished forgings. Note the different drop heights of the two hammers shown. An airburst cleanses the dies after each pass.

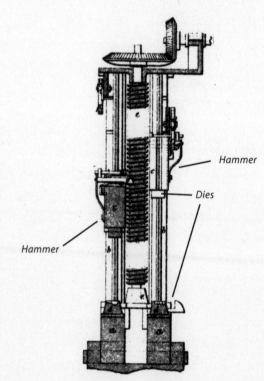

Hammer

Dies

Hammer

B. Drop Hammer

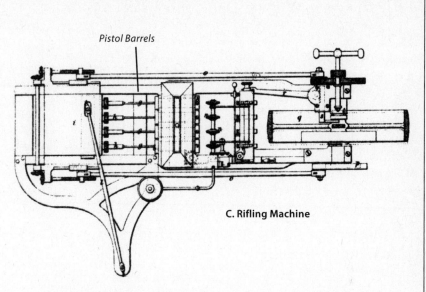

Pistol Barrels

C. Rifling Machine

C. The rifling machine rifled four barrels at a time, automatically re-setting to each of the six or seven grooves in a pistol.

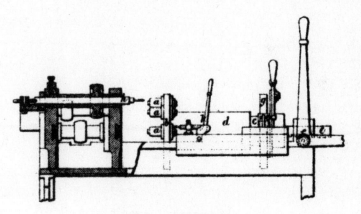

D. Breech Cylinder Borer

D. The machine applied four separate finishing operations to each of the six chambers of eight cylinders mounted on a wheel. Tool changes and workpiece management were all self-acting, except that an attendant pulled a lever to move a fresh cylinder to the cutting tool station.

The Colt Armory's effect on the British cognoscenti was quite powerful. Nasmyth said: "In those American tools there is a common-sense way
of going to the point at once, that I was quite struck with; there is great
simplicity, almost a quaker-like rigidity of form, given to the machinery;
no ornamentation, no rubbing away of corners, or polishing; but the precise, accurate, and correct results. It was that which gratified me so much
at Colonel Colt's, to see the spirit that pervaded the machines; they really
had a very decided and peculiar character of judicious contrivance."[26] John
Anderson, the civil servant driving the reform of military procurement,
himself a talented engineer and a prolific inventor, testified on his visit: "I
went to Colonel Colt's factory with high expectations . . . and I did not
leave with disappointment. . . . So far as an old building would admit of,
the work in this manufactory is reduced to an almost perfect system. . . .
There is also much that is new in England, and abundant evidence of a vigorous straining after a large and accurate result, which is well fitted to in-
spire us all with healthy ideas; indeed it is impossible to go through that
work without coming away a better engineer."[27]

Charles Dickens, who visited in 1854, was inspired to even more
vaulted reflections:

> To see the same thing in Birmingham and in other places where fire-arms
> are made almost entirely by hand labour, we should have to walk around
> a whole day, visiting many little shops carrying on distinct branches of the
> manufacture. . . . Mere strength of muscle, which is so valuable in new so-
> cieties, would find no market here—for the steam-engine—indefatigably
> toiling in . . . the little stone chamber below—performs nine-tenths of all
> the work that is done here. Neat, delicate-handed little girls do the work
> that brawny smiths do in other gun-shops. . . . Carpenters, cabinet-makers,
> ex-policemen, butchers, cabmen . . . are steadily drilling and boring at
> lathes all day in the upper rooms. Political economists tell us that the value
> of labour will find its level as surely as the sea: and so, perhaps it will: but
> [rarely] . . . quickly enough to prevent a great deal of misery. Perhaps if
> men who have learnt but one trade . . . could be as easily absorbed into

another . . . as these new gunsmiths are, the working world would go more smoothly than it does.[28]

The dénouement of the hearings was that the British pressed ahead and opened a government armory at Enfield, the source of the famed Enfield rifle, and furnished it with American machinery. They naturally inquired of Colt for machinery, but he was in the middle of launching his 1855 plant in Hartford, which consumed all of his machine-making capacity. The final sourcing was primarily from Nathan Ames (for Blanchard-style equipment) and Robbins and Lawrence for most of the milling and other metalworking machinery. At full production, Enfield regularly turned out 1,000 rifles a week.

Once again, one is struck by the British obliviousness to the broad possibilities of the new mechanical age they had so recently inaugurated. Time and again, in the British commentary on the Colt factory, or some other American mechanized plant, someone would say more or less, "Well, that's simply another type of the old Brunel-Maudslay pulley-block factory"— which, of course, was so. The final report of the parliamentary Committee on Machinery struck a similar note in its comment that in the United States, "a considerable number of different trades are carried on in the same way as the cotton manufacture of England, viz., in large factories, with machinery applied to every process, the extreme subdivision of labour and all reduced to an almost perfect system of manufacture."[29] The British, of course, had been the first to mechanize cotton production but had been surprisingly torpid in attempting similar revolutions in other industries. It's not that they were reluctant to adopt machinery—British shipbuilding factories were the most advanced in the world, employing massive, very precise machines that mid-century Americans could not yet replicate. What was missing, perhaps, was the American instinct to push for scale, the conviction that the first objective of any business should be to grow larger.

In any event, the success of the Enfield factory made no more impact on British industrial practice than the Portsmouth pulley-block factory had. In 1908, Cadillac won the British Thomas Dewar automobile prize.

Three Cadillacs were given a test drive, taken apart and disassembled, their parts mixed up and reassembled, and subjected to another test drive, which they passed handily—and the British still found it amazing.[30]

The Colt Armory in London was closed down in 1856 because it was unprofitable. The government had opened its Enfield plant and was not willing to send enough orders Colt's way to keep so productive a plant running full. Colt tried for a while to use it as a base for servicing all of Europe, but it was cheaper to ramp up his new Hartford plant and service his export markets from there. It was also a convenient way for Colt to shed an emotionally and financially taxing relation with his younger brother James, an unreliable whiner and malcontent whom Sam had foolishly appointed to head the London operation. While he continued to support James, he did it in ways that wouldn't put his business at risk.[31]

Colt capped his career by joining with Root to come up with their "most perfect design," the model 1860 .44 caliber army, navy, and police revolver. Very powerful but much lighter than its predecessor, sleek and streamlined, with a price point designed to sell, it dominated its market long after the Colt patents had expired.[32] The final evolution of small arms into their modern form came with the introduction of the self-contained, metal primer-powder-bullet cartridge, which was adopted in larger caliber handguns about ten years after the close of the Civil War. Beginning in the 1870s, most handgun and all long-gun revolvers were gradually supplanted by varieties of magazine-fed, spring-driven mechanisms like those in the famed Henry and Spencer rifles during the last years of the Civil War.

Good as the Colt-Root machinery was, Colt never strove for interchangeability of the most demanding precision parts, like those involved in the cylinder alignment and firing action. The machinery of the day was not up to the task, and there was little point in striving for interchangeability of such parts in any case. To serve a private market required many models and frequent model changes; redesigning machinery for each part change would have been prohibitively expensive.

But the machinery was good enough that probably the great majority of parts would have been effectively interchangeable with only minimal filing cleanup from the machining. So Colt was exaggerating, but not strictly lying, when the old medicine-man persona resurfaced in his address to the British Civil Engineers. Knowing the British fascination with inter-changeability, he naturally fibbed a bit: "All the separate parts travel inde-pendently through the manufactory, arriving at last, in an almost complete condition, in the hands of the finishing workmen, by whom they are as-sembled, from promiscuous heaps, and formed into fire-arms, requiring only the polishing and fitting demanded for ornament." Later, having been undercut by his own employees on the point and pointedly questioned by the parliamentary inquiry, Colt somewhat testily fell back on the claim that his pistol parts were "very nearly" interchangeable.[33]

The Expansion of Armory Practice

What the British called the "American system" of manufacturing was more accurately American armory practice. The great Colt plants were the most perfect exemplars of the methodologies first pursued by Decius Wadsworth, Simeon North, and John Hall decades before. In mid-century, besides clocks, there were just a few modestly sized industries that fit the model. And, without the luxury of producing exactly the same product year after year, as the armories did, they all had to reach various accom-modations with the demands of a private sector market, much as Eli Terry had done by creating a last-step adjustment device to ease the requirement for absolute dimensional precision.

Three other precision-manufacturing industries were in their relative infancy in the years just before the Civil War: sewing machines, typewrit-ers, and watches. The three followed different strategies for achieving high precision in complex, high-volume products. Sewing machines came closest to the armory-practice paradigm, although the market leader, Singer, reached high volume levels before it finally adopted rigorous man-ufacturing methods. The typewriter and watch industries each followed routes more reminiscent of Terry's than of Springfield's.

SEWING MACHINES

Sewing machine inventions proliferated from the eighteenth century on, but the core patent, which included a needle with the eye at its point, a shuttle to form a lock stitch, and an automatic feed, was filed in 1846 by Elias Howe, a former cotton-mill apprentice. A poor man with a family, he failed to raise enough capital to start a business in America and failed again in England. Upon returning, he found that his patent had been appropriated and improved on by others. A successful lawsuit ended with all the infringers agreeing to contribute their patents to a patent pool, freeing them to compete while Howe assembled a substantial fortune from his royalties.

One of the competing firms was Willcox & Gibbs. Their market share was always modest, but they are of special interest because they contracted their manufacturing to Providence's Brown & Sharpe, a firm that made fundamental contributions to high-precision manufacturing. Joseph Brown, as the American pioneer of near-perfect screw threads and thousandths-of-an-inch measurement instruments, might be considered the nearest American equivalent of Henry Maudslay. Brown was also a key developer of the universal milling machine, which was able to cut metal into any shape by manipulating the workpiece and the cutter along multiple axes.

Lucien Sharpe, who had apprenticed with Brown before becoming his partner, managed the sewing machine contract, and from the start chose to apply the whole armory practice treatment: a precise model, complete gauging, and special-purpose machinery. It was much harder and more expensive than he expected, but the firm had extraordinary mechanics, and they got it right. Collectors today treat the Willcox & Gibbs machines as a superb example of Victorian-age engineering. They ran very fast, were durable, and were known for their near-silent operation. The business was a success in the sense that it made a profit and lasted into the 1950s, although primarily as an industrial sewing-machine vendor. Brown & Sharpe remained their manufacturer, and a number of their more important machine tools, like the 1877 universal grinding machine, were developed in the sewing-machine plant. Henry Leland, the brilliant mechanic who ran the Brown & Sharpe sewing-machine plant for eighteen years, went on to found the Cadillac Automotive Company. It was his engineers who amazed the British with the interchangeability of their automobile parts at the 1908 Royal auto show.

The runaway winner in the sewing-machine competition, however, was Isaac M. Singer, an actor, theater manager, occasional inventor, and genius promoter who had little interest in manufacturing but knew how to sell. Singers were produced by traditional handcraft methods well into the 1880s, when sales regularly topped a half million a year, fifteen times the production in Willcox & Gibbs's best year. It was only at such volumes that traditional machine-artisanal processes could not keep pace, and Singer finally brought in talented manufacturing professionals who, over time, created the kind of streamlined, highly mechanized production system that accorded more closely with the armory practice paradigm.[34]

TYPEWRITERS

Typewriter startups proliferated through the 1850s and 1860s, but most were far too slow to compete with handwriting. (A common device was a letter wheel requiring the user to turn the wheel to strike each letter.) The idea of an individual key for each letter was turned into a working solution primarily by a former newspaper editor, Christopher Sholes, in Milwaukee. On a third try, he produced a small number of working machines that outpaced manual scribes, one of which, from 1872–1873, survives. It is recognizably a modern mechanical typewriter, complete with a QWERTY keyboard. (The original keyboard was in alphabetical order, but Sholes realized that when closely spaced keys, like *s* and *t*, were struck in sequence, they tended to jam. The QWERTY sequence was the random outcome of multiple key rearrangements to reduce high-frequency, closely spaced sequences. The DFGH sequence in the middle row is a remnant of the original layout.)

Successful though they were, the Milwaukee prototypes highlighted the severity of the manufacturing challenge, for typewriters were "the

Early Surviving Scholes Typewriter, c. 1872–1873.
The typewriter developed primarily by a Milwaukee
editor, Christopher Scholes, was the first to look like a
recognizable modern typewriter. Note the QWERTY
keyboard. Schole's first keyboard was alphabetical, but
closely-spaced frequent companion letters tended to
jam. The new keyboard arrangement was the random
outcome of Schole's trial-and-error method of addressing the problem.

most complex mechanism mass produced by American industry, public
or private, in the nineteenth century."[35] Sholes and a financial partner
had the good sense to seek a professional manufacturer; they settled on
E. Remington & Sons, an important small arms maker in central New
York. Remington was nominally an armory-practice production shop: they
understood models, gauging, and special purpose machinery. But their operations were a mess, with typewriters, arms, pumps, cotton gins, and
other production lines tangled together in the same shops. Remington did
succeed in making thousands of typewriters but was unable to ramp up
production to meet demand. After a number of financial reverses, it spun
off the typewriter business to the biggest distributor in 1886. The new
company, the Standard Typewriter Company, renamed itself Remington
Typewriter in 1902 and was later part of Sperry Rand.

By the 1890s, there was a host of competitors—Hall Typewriters, American Writing Machine, Oliver, L. C. Smith & Brothers—and the industry, unlike sewing machines, evolved into a manufacturing competition. Major advances were made in ball bearings, in the use of new materials—vulcanized rubber, glass, sheet metal, cellulose—and in new machinery, like pneumatic molding devices and "exercise machines" that would put the finished products through grueling tests of high-speed typing. All of the critical parts were interchangeable to a high degree, but given the large number of parts, assembly and adjustment was one of the most important steps in the manufacturing sequence. Parts were not filed to fit, as in the old armories, but were manufactured for easy adjustment by screws or other devices. It was the same principle as the adjustable escapement setting in Terry's shelf clock, but carried to the nth degree.[36]

WALTHAM WATCHES

Although watchmaking seems a natural extension of the brass clock industry, the required precision at very small dimensions created an entirely different order of technical challenge.

The father of the American watch industry was Aaron Dennison, an entrepreneur and skilled mechanic who, in 1849, together with clockmaker Edward Howard and a small coterie of investors, set out to mass-produce quality watches. At the time watchmaking was the province of British handcraft artisans. Individual parts were farmed out to subspecialists to be later fitted and assembled by masters of the trade. Although he was committed to machine manufacture, Dennison recruited a number of British craftsmen for their know-how and their highly specialized tools.

The company started in a corner of Howard's clock factory, but in 1854 Dennison built a factory in Waltham and dubbed the company the Waltham Watch Company. By the time he ran out of money in 1857, he had produced some 5,000 watches. Most of the output was by traditional methods, although the company worked on developing new machinery from the earliest days. An investor bought the company at auction and supplied the capital to maintain its development. A new factory super-intendent hired in 1859, Ambrose Webster, created a highly rational, lightly mechanized, new production system just in time for a boom in watch sales from the sudden Union military demand and the disruption of British trade. By 1864, with 38,000 watch sales in a single year, the company was solvent and had capital to spare.

From that point, Waltham Watch commenced a single-minded, three-decade drive to fully automate watch production. Various competitors entered the industry from time to time, most of them falling by the wayside as Waltham relentlessly drove down prices and improved its quality, along the way creating entirely new swathes of production technology. The Elgin Watch Company, founded in 1864 by former Waltham mechanics, was the only one of the era's start-ups to survive in the long term.

Among Waltham's many process inventions, they were the first to adopt dimensioned gauging—based on precise measurements instead of tests of fitting—since the small size of watch parts made traditional gauging imprac-tical. Needle gauges tested the diameters of jeweled hole collars, eventually to accuracies of $1/17,000$ inch. By the 1880s, all screws, by far the most com-mon watch part, were produced internally with automatic screw-cutting machines. Escapement wheel-cutting machines carried fifty blanks at a time and were completely self-acting, making ninety cuts per wheel with three steel and three sapphire cutters. (The hardness of sapphire eliminated the need to polish the finished escapement teeth.) The list of new machining and control processes could be extended almost indefinitely.

Much as in typewriters, the final adjustment and tuning of the watch was a critical step. Tiny shifts in the ratio of balance weight and hairspring strength affected accuracy. Multiple set screws tuned the balance between all the critical parts. Adjustment of the cheaper watches was often left to dealers, but adjustment on top of the line products could take months. Among other things, they had to assure consistent time keeping at temper-ature extremes. With sales of 18 million watches by 1910, steadily falling prices and costs, and the most precise production machinery in the world, Waltham wrote a unique chapter in the annals of automated manufacture.[37]

A RMORY PRACTICE-STYLE OF MANUFACTURING WAS AN IMPORTANT THREAD of American industrial development, but it became a major feature of the economy only with the mass manufacture of automobiles, kitchen appliances, and other complex national consumer products in the twentieth century. As we have seen, the intense interest of the British in American gun making, their dubbing it the American system of manufacturing, and American pride in making such a positive impression naturally led industrial historians, at least implicitly, to treat armory practice as an important driver of nineteenth-century growth.*

The real story is that in a labor-short country, Americans were quick to resort to mechanized solutions to a wide range of production problems, like the portable sawmills in midwestern forests, or the high-pressure lard-processing systems, or the steam-powered threshers of the 1870s, processing 5,000 bushels a day on Great Plains factory farms, pouring them directly into freight cars lined up on the farms' own rail spurs.

The overwhelming proportion of nineteenth-century American mechanization efforts went into basic processing industries, not precision manufacturing. Food and lumber processors were 60 percent of all power-using manufacturing industries in 1869. Add textiles, paper, and primary metal industries like smelting, and the number rises to 90 percent. Industries that would plausibly lend themselves to armory practice methods—fabricated metal products, furniture, machinery, and instruments—accounted for only 7.5 percent of 1869 manufacturing power demand. And the mere use of power machinery doesn't qualify as armory practice. It's safe to say most furniture and metal fabrication shops stuck with craft-based methods. There are only small differences in the data in the 1889 census.[38]

All industries were moving to higher levels of precision as the century passed the halfway point. Continuous-flow processing, as in lard, grains,

---

* I helped perpetuate the mistake in my book *The Tycoons*.

and later petroleum, imposes requirements for precise valves, gauges, temperature control devices, and protection from contaminants. And those requirements mount exponentially as volumes and levels of customer sophistication rise in tandem. It took new generations of superb machinists, and superb new tooling, to meet those standards, but for the most part, it had little to do with armory practice.

One index of the pervasiveness of armory practice is the sales of precision metal-shaping machinery from Brown & Sharpe, the quintessential armory-practice vendor. The company sold almost 24,000 machines between 1861 and 1905. Of that total, it took until 1875 to sell the first 1,000 and until 1883 to sell another 1,000. That is consistent with the picture of armory-practice industries expanding very late in the century before its apotheosis in the Model-T plants.[39]

Mid-century America was still a predominately agricultural country. On the eve of the Civil War, only 16 percent of the workforce was in manufacturing.[40] They worked in grain milling, meatpacking, lard refining, turning logs into planks and beams, iron smelting and forging, and making steam engines and steamboats, vats and piping, locomotives, reapers and mowers, carriages, stoves, cotton and woolen cloth, shoes, saddles and harnesses, and workaday tools. These were the industries in which America's comparative advantage loomed largest and were the ones that dominated American output. It was the drive to mass scale in those industries, by a wide variety of strategies and methods, that was the real American system, or perhaps the American ideology, of manufacturing.

America in 1860: On the Brink

The Civil War violently disrupted economic growth, but by finally resolving the sectional conflict, and excising the cancer of slavery, it removed the last important obstacle to continental expansion and vigorous industrialization. Abraham Lincoln came out of the old Whig tradition of Henry Clay—egalitarian, pro–manufacturing and protective tariffs, pro-education, and pro–canals, roads, and interior development. His favorite speech in a pre-election lecture tour was on discoveries and inventions. In his famous

1858 debates with Stephen Douglas, Lincoln stressed the economic perils of the extension of slavery as much as he did the system's moral depravity. Extending slavery into western territories, he insisted, would inevitably drive the wages of free working men to the slave standard. Those were not trumped-up fears. Throughout the border and "blue grass" states, like Kentucky, Tennessee, and Virginia, there were at least a hundred major iron plantations, with predominately slave labor, turning out quite decent iron. The admixture of white workers, often about a quarter of the workforce, were themselves virtually enslaved by the proverbial company store and the hard-driving boss characteristic of the plantation culture.[41]

During one of the darkest periods of the War, in 1862, the Republican Congress passed one of the great development programs in American history. The Homestead Act allowed any citizen, including single women and freed slaves, to take possession of virtually any unoccupied tract of public land for a $12 registration and filing fee. Live on it for five years, build a house, and farm the land, and it was yours for just an additional $6 "proving" fee. Over time, the act helped settle some 10 percent of the entire land mass of the United States. Senator Justin Morrill's (R-VT) 1862 land-grant college act awarded each state a bequest of public lands that it could sell to finance state colleges for the agricultural and industrial arts. No other country had conceived the notion of educating farmers and mechanics, and the Morrill Act schools are still the foundation of the state university systems.

The 1862 Pacific Railway Act made yet another lavish grant of public lands to finance a railway line from the Missouri River to the Pacific Ocean, a dream of the pro-development party for more than twenty years. The project was scarred by financial problems and scandal but was actually completed more or less as its promoters promised and surprisingly close to the original schedule. Over time, its development impact justified the airiest promises of its supporters. The Republican/Whig agenda was rounded out with major tariff increases and a federal banking act that, for all its flaws, got the country through the war and its financial aftermath.

Development economists speak of a "takeoff" point when an economy is poised for a long-term ratchet upward in growth. The United States was clearly at or approaching such a point in 1860, but the progression was violently disrupted by the war. When growth resumed at the end of the 1860s, it was accompanied by dramatic turns in the economy that are still not completely understood. The 1870s was a time of jagged economic ups and downs, including a steep railroad-led crash in 1874 and an equally sharp recovery late in the decade. But over the full decade, nominal growth (not adjusted for inflation), was 3.9 percent, or about the long-term average.*

The surprise came when economic historians adjusted the 1870s data for price inflation. In the modern era, we assume moderate price inflation is a normal condition, so "real" (inflation-adjusted) growth is always somewhat lower than nominal growth. But when the price adjustment was applied to the 1870s data, output *rose* by nearly 60 percent. In other words, prices *fell*, and quite substantially, through most of the decade even as output soared. The deflation was felt by almost everyone as a dreadful, and extremely disruptive, experience. It was a period of extraordinary social unrest. The year 1877, for reasons that are obscure, saw riots in most major cities, and Pittsburgh mobs put the torch to virtually all the main installations of the Pennsylvania Railroad. The phenomenon of real prices falling even as real output rose continued through most of the 1880s.

As Japan has painfully shown, generally falling prices now tend to be associated with stagnation or depressions. But in the 1870s, wholesale prices fell by about 25 percent, the population grew by about 25 percent, employment grew by 40 percent, and real output grew by a blazing 67 percent. All real indices were up strongly. Fuel consumption doubled, metal consumption tripled, and the real value of manufacturing output was up by 40 percent. Food production showed the same picture. Home consumption of grains and cotton rose by half, and per capita beef consumption increased by 40 percent. Wheat exports were up 250 percent, and beef exports rose eightfold. Total agricultural exports more than doubled, and railroad freight loadings were up strongly. At the end of the decade, Amer-

---

* In the nineteenth century, with the notable exception of the 1870s, there was usually little difference between nominal and real, or inflation-adjusted, growth rates. Long-term prices were quite stable although year-to-year fluctuations could be quite sharp.

icans were better fed, better clothed, and better educated, with bigger farms and higher output, and with access to a much broader range of products like stoves, washtubs, new farm machinery, and much else. Real growth in the decade, at 6.2 percent, is among the fastest in the country's history, although real people, it seems clear, mostly felt awful.*[42]

The evidence suggests a "supply shock," a rare event on an economy-wide basis. Supply shocks frequently occur in individual commodity markets: the recent success in exploiting large shale-based natural gas fields in the United States has sent natural gas prices plummeting and may ultimately affect all fossil-derived fuel prices. But a supply shock in a large nation that occurs more or less across the board implies a far-reaching increment in national capacity.

A reasonable speculation is that in the United States, after the Civil War, the combined impact of a deepened national transportation network and the spreading application of mechanized, rational production methods to every kind of industry triggered new economies of scale, in both production and distribution, across a wide swath of industries. Both factory productivity and labor productivity registered a sharp jump upwards in the mid-1870s and maintained that level for the rest of the century.

The jump in per capita output is consistent with the large accretion of capital in the United States in this period. Per capita consumption roughly doubled from mid-century to 1900, but savings increased by two and a half times, to nearly 30 percent of household incomes by the century's end, possibly its highest ever. The country's capital stock tripled from the Revolution to 1799, but from 1800 to 1860, it multiplied sixteenfold, albeit from a relatively small base, and then grew another eightfold from 1860 to 1910. Over the entire run, American capital stock increased 388 times, and compared to Europe's, it was much newer.[43] The falling prices seen

---

* The explanation for the apparent distress as the real economy boomed probably lies in the temporary distribution of the adjustment pain. The better-off, who were likely to be creditors, would have greatly benefited from the rise in monetary values, and it is likely that wage cuts applied first to the most vulnerable workers. The question has recently drawn much interest, but definitive answers will require a great deal of scholarly digging to reconstruct data on wage levels and household balance sheets to match the generally good census data on physical output.

throughout the economy were especially sharp in capital goods, like machinery and tooling, which further amplified the impact of increased savings and rising capital investment. Since the transportation sector was by far the most capital-intensive of the day's industries, as well as a major productivity enhancer, a virtuous circle of savings, investment, and greater productivity came to dominate the entire economy.*

The increase in capital was paralleled by a great expansion of American territory, and continued strong population growth. But although the population tripled between the Civil War and the eve of the First World War, the stock of capital per citizen continued to grow. Finally, the contribution of immigration to American population growth was generally strong in this era, and immigrants punched above their weight. They were disproportionately young adults with few dependents—adventurous risk takers who had come to work.

Great Britain, in the meantime, continued to grow at about its long-term rate, or roughly 2 percent, while United States grew twice as fast. A curve of a steadily compounding advantage sufficiently prolonged inevitably starts to turn in a near-vertical direction. Sometime in the last quarter of the nineteenth century, the United States moved past Great Britain on nearly all major economic indicia, and by the eve of the First World War, US output was larger than that of Great Britain, France, and Germany combined.

That takes us to the close of the main portion of the story: how America built the economic platform that allowed it to replace Great Britain in the global economic catbird seat. To bridge the gap between the creation of the platform and the climactic event, the next chapter is a compressed account of the vast American industrial expansion in the second half of the century.

---

* The shift is apparent in a mid-century leap in American worker productivity. Even as its manufacturing sector grew rapidly, American labor maintained its roughly 2:1 edge over British workers for the rest of the century. At the same time, American transportation productivity jumped sharply, doubling that of the British by century's end, while wholesale and retail trade made gains nearly as great. Aggregate data somewhat muffle the shift, in part because as an older population, Great Britain had a considerably higher percentage of its people in the work force.

CHAPTER EIGHT

The Newest
Hyperpower

HE 1886 BLOOMINGDALE'S CATALOG—160 PAGES, STUFFED WITH SOME
1,700 products, from ladies' corsets to pistols—advised its clients to
send a follow-up inquiry if they had not received an order confirmation
within ten days after they had posted it, but to allow fifteen days if they
lived on the Pacific Coast. Consider the billions of investment that underlay that offer. Just twenty years before, at the end of the Civil War, there
had been only a few hundred miles of railroad track west of the Mississippi.
Even in the 1870s, vast regions of Bloomingdale's 1886 catalog market had
been reachable only by wagon train. But by 1886, the backbone of the national rail system was already in place, along with fast-freight forwarding
companies, telegraph-based delivery tracking and financial settlement systems, insurance, and newly invented bills of lading that guided a delivery
through the railroad maze.

And therein lies the secret of the American surge in per capita growth.
It wasn't advanced technology. Throughout the nineteenth century,
Americans were students to the British in steelmaking and most other sci-
ence-based industries. Where the Americans wrote the rulebook, however, was in mass production, mass marketing, and mass distribution.
The great nineteenth-century American economic invention, in short,
was the first mass-consumption society. The invention proceeded in
stages. The first was to create the infrastructure for a continent-wide, first-
class economic power.[1]

Infrastructure

Railroads and the telegraph were symbiotic businesses. The roads offered clear graded routes for stringing telegraph lines, and station managers conveniently doubled as telegraph operators; the benefit for the roads was that the telegraph, for the first time, allowed them to track and manage their far-flung freights and rolling stock.

There were other, less obvious symbioses. The western railroads were typically built far ahead of traffic—"If You Build It, They Will Come." The roads benefited from both state and federal land grants in wide swaths on both sides of their tracks. In order to create future freights, they frequently transferred their land to farmers on highly advantageous terms. Much of the early risk capital came from the British, who regarded American railroad bonds as the equivalent of today's high-yield paper: defaults were to be expected, but the returns were still attractive. So the railroads opened the great American grain belt west of the Mississippi, and innovative factory-farmers created a Saudi Arabia of food.

It was a prodigious accomplishment but deeply flawed: thousands of miles of track were poorly constructed, curves were dangerous, bridges flimsy. Even today's takeover titans might be embarrassed at the reckless financial leverage at many of the lines. Speed to completion and revenue collection were the constant imperatives. Leverage drove behavior in other ways. With huge volumes of shares and bonds in play, takeover battles raged around nearly all the lines, exhausting the resources of courts and grinding up investor dollars. The takeover wars were yet another accelerant for the track laying: you achieved local dominance, and earned the cash for debt service, by controlling access to all the prime business centers. So expansions proceeded in a series of flanking and counterflanking lurches. Chaotic as it was, the rails and their piggy-back telegraph lines pulled together the country commercially. The country had less than 9,000 miles of track in 1850, nearly 50,000 miles by 1870, and 164,000 in 1890. By 1910, the national rail network, with 240,000 miles, was roughly the one we have today.

At least four major industries were enabled by the railroads: factory farms, meatpacking, steel, and petroleum.

BONANZA FARMS

Jay Cooke may have been the most respected banker in the country, until the insolvency of his Northern Pacific railroad precipitated the Great Crash of 1873.[2] In 1873–1874, more than one hundred railroads failed financially. All of them had borrowed too much, built too far ahead of customers, and couldn't pay their debt service and dividends. The Northern Pacific, however, had a valuable asset—some 39 million acres of federal land grants—and creditors often took land in settlement of their loans. The president of the Northern Pacific, George Cass, had the idea of organizing the absentee owners' lands into productive farms; he hoped the new freights would reinvigorate the line. He tapped as his manager a failed farmer-entrepreneur and Yale graduate, Oliver Dalrymple. Dalrymple's attraction was that he was a visionary who had failed in a promising way—he had run out of capital trying to transform the nature of farming.

Cass provided the capital and the steady hand, while Dalrymple laid out an industrial-style, multiyear production schedule, which included sod busting and plowing 5,000 acres of land each year, with specific land-improvement and planting schedules thereafter. The whole idea would have been infeasible before the advent of quality steel plow blades to cut through the thick tangle of prairie grass roots. Harrowing, seeding, harvesting, threshing followed in quasi-military sequence, and the land was replowed before freezing set in. By the 1890s, gang plowing was being executed with seventy-horse plow teams arrayed in a 45° angle to the plowing line, so the lead team could lead a great wheeling maneuver at the end of each mile-long run.

Dalrymple's first producing parcel, in 1878, had 126 horses, eighty-four plows, eighty-one harrows, sixty-seven wagons, thirty seeders, eight threshing machines, and forty-five binders. By the 1881 harvest, with thirty-six threshers, he was loading three freight-car loads, or 30,000 bushels every day—at an average cost of 52 cents a bushel in a market that was paying $1. That's why they were called "Bonanza" farms. By 1890, American wheat farms west of the Mississippi were producing about 30 percent to 50 percent of the Western world's supply, incidentally jump-starting the

Minneapolis flour milling industry. The Pillsburys were among the first to construct modern, mechanized, flow-through flour milling plants and underwrote many of the railroad extensions into Minnesota.[3]

CHICAGO MEATPACKING

Consumers were accustomed to eating salted pork in the form of bacon and hams, but beef consumers preferred their meat fresh. Since the largest markets for fresh beef were in the East, so were the herds. Unfortunately, they were concentrated in the Southeast and were decimated during the Civil War. Entrepreneurs noticed that the seemingly limitless Texas grasslands were full of semiwild longhorns, and European capital flowed into big-ticket ranching. Barbed wire was the critical invention. The XIT ranch, organized in the mid-1870s with 3 million acres and 6,000 miles of barbed wire, was the largest in American history. At first, the cattle had to be driven to train connections in Abilene for delivery eastward to local slaughterers. Within about twenty years, thickening train connections in cattle country consigned the romance of the cattle drive to the pages of dime novels.

Shipping dressed meat was obviously cheaper than shipping steers, but the distances required refrigerated railroad cars. Various experiments with ice-packed cars were unsatisfactory until Gustavus Swift, a Massachusetts butcher, added a forced-air circulatory system. But he was stonewalled by the railroads, which had invested heavily in new fleets of cattle cars and expensive stockyards and watering sites. Swift scraped up enough money to finance ten cars for a Canadian railroad line and started delivering fresh beef to Boston. The transport savings allowed him to undersell the local slaughterers and still book very high profits. He plowed the profits into expansion and started selling fresh "Western Beef" up and down the East Coast. The railroads dropped their opposition, and within just a few years, meatpacking was concentrated in Chicago, where it quickly sorted down into four or five major houses, most of which consolidated vertically into stockyards, ranches, and distribution centers, with American beef transshipping as far as Tokyo and Shanghai.[4]

STEEL

Western railroads required steel rails to support their high speeds and heavy freights, but when the postwar railroad boom got underway, American mills still did not mass-produce quality steel, so the roads used British rails. Steelmaking was an ancient craft. The high-carbon iron that emerges from a blast furnace is suitable for casting into stove plate, anvils, and the like but is very hard and brittle. Easy-to-work malleable or wrought iron was created by removing all the carbon, usually by puddling, a tedious craft process. Steelmakers recarburize the iron just enough to hit a sweet spot between hardness and malleability.

Alexander Lyman Holley, scion of the Salisbury Holleys and son of Alexander Hamilton Holley, the forge owner, edge-tool maker, and Connecticut governor, almost single-handedly dragged America into the steel age. As a young man, Lyman negotiated iron contracts with Springfield's Roswell Lee, frequently visited the Collinsville Axe works, and counted Sam Collins's son among his close friends. Graduating from Brown with an engineering degree, he went to work for George Corliss and then, though still young, shaped a career as an engineering consultant and a science journalist, focused on machinery and metallurgy. A brilliant draftsman and a fluent writer, he was a regular in the pages of the *New York Times* and the editor of several technical journals. On a European trip studying ordnance, he encountered the Bessemer process that had revolutionized British steel production, and arranged with Bessemer to act as his American agent. That required mediating substantial patent challenges, which were resolved by the formation of a patent-pooling trust to oversee compliance and collect royalties.[*]

---

[*] Henry Bessemer, a prolific British inventor, had discovered that injecting a blast of cold air into a container of molten iron touched off a violent reaction that decarburized the iron within minutes. Adding a small amount of carbon back into the mixture produced excellent steel, as the chemical violence within the container ensured total mixing. A technical problem, which took some time to overcome, was that the process worked only with low-phosphorus ores. Fortunately, the vast Mesabi ore range around the Great Lakes was ideal for the Bessemer process.

90-ton Ingot. By the end of the nineteenth century, American steelmakers, led by Carnegie Steel, had far surpassed the British in total steel production, and with the exception of some specialty products could match the British in steel quality. The picture shows a 90-ton steel ingot poured at the Carnegie Homestead plant in 1892.

Holley then designed most American steel plants. Of the eleven Bessemer plants in America, six were entirely his design, on three others he was a design consultant, and the remaining two were copies of his other plants. His signature piece was Andrew Carnegie's Edgar Thomson plant, the ET, near Pittsburgh. Opening in 1875, it was the first Holley was able to build from scratch, and he made it a model of continuous-flow processing. Pig iron was melted in twelve-ton cupolas and poured directly into a giant Bessemer converter. After the conversion had been completed, the converter was tipped and poured the steel into a moving train of ingot molds on an internal rail. The rail system transported the ingots to cutting and trimming machinery and then to mechanical rail rollers, where they were "pressed with uniformity and precision . . . by hydraulic fingers [and therefore] . . . cool almost perfectly straight," which Holley contrasted to hand straightening "which cannot, of course, be precise and uniform."[5]

Subordinating the plant design to the requirements of the internal work flow was a Holley mantra. At the ET, the plant was "a body shaped by its bones and muscles, rather than a box into which bones and muscles had to be packed."[6] Work-in-process always moved from one station to the next by rail, loading and unloading was always mechanical, and the direction of loading was always down. Other innovations, like snap-out converter bottoms for brick relining, were all designed to maximize production uptime.

Integration was pushed much further just a few years later, when the blast furnaces that smelted iron ore were moved to the steel plant. The new iron was then charged directly from the furnaces into the Bessemer converters, eliminating the necessity of transporting and remelting the pig— a step akin to Paul Moody's integration of textile spinning and weaving. Finally, the ET plant site was at the intersection of two rivers and two major rail lines, all with direct connections to the plant's internal rail system to simplify loading and unloading.

Carnegie was America's greatest steel tycoon. He had started as a telegraph boy at the Pennsylvania Railroad, working directly for Tom Scott, the boss of operations. He rose quickly as the fair-haired boy of both Scott and Edgar Thomson, the road's president; along with Scott and Thompson, he grew rich by looting the company. The three formed a series of businesses headed by Carnegie, with Scott and Thomson as silent partners, selling sleeping cars, iron, bridges, and other gear to the Pennsylvania on preferential terms. Scott was nearly fired when the board discovered their game. Cut adrift, Carnegie cast about for a new career; on a trip to England, he visited its vast new Bessemer plants and saw his future.

Carnegie remained remote from the factory floor, although he loved to dabble in the details. His plants were run by a succession of great managers and steel technicians—"Captain" Bill Jones; Henry Frick, who had created the coke industry before joining Carnegie; and Charlie Schwab. But Carnegie was the ideal client for Holley. His management target was always market share, not profits, so he kept a laser focus on through-put, mechanization, and reduced manning—so-called hard-driving. Bill Jones, who patented a number of steelmaking processes, created a stir just six years after the ET opened by telling a meeting of British engineers that his plants got twice the output from a comparable converter as the British did. Holley, whom the British viewed as an honest broker, confirmed the claim. The secret wasn't faster processing—the laws of physics determined that—but much less downtime.

As Carnegie's market share grew, he acted as the industry price disciplinarian. If markets turned down, he was the first to cut price and increase share. By the mid-1880s, the industry's rail-pricing standard hovered around the long-outdated tariff level of $28 a ton. (British export prices, pretariff, were about $33 a ton for rail-quality steel.) During a collapse in the rail market in 1897, Carnegie drove prices all the way down to $14 a ton to keep his plants running full, and *still* made record profits. Elbert Gary, later the president of US Steel, observed that Carnegie had been on the brink of "driv[ing] entirely out of business every steel company in the United States." By the time of the 1901 US Steel consolidation, Carnegie controlled about a quarter of American steel production, which was equivalent to about half the total British output.[7]

STANDARD OIL

Far more than any other big American industry, the rise and dominance of American petroleum in the nineteenth century is the story of one company, Standard Oil, and one man, John D. Rockefeller. Rockefeller, from middle-class farming stock, started his career in dry goods and, in 1861, invested with his dry-goods partner in a new oil refinery in the booming new "rock oil" district of western Pennsylvania. Upon a firsthand inspection, he found the business so attractive that he took over as day-to-day manager. Four years later, he bought out his partners, opened his second refinery, and built oil-shipping facilities in New York. (About 70 percent of oil was exported from the earliest days.) From the start, Rockefeller seems to have envisioned the industry as a single, integrated, continuous-flow process operation from the wellhead to final user, and he moved directly and inexorably to make that a reality. By 1870, when he reorganized as the Standard Oil Company, he was already the biggest refiner in the world.

Rockefeller won his markets by concentrating fanatically on reducing costs and increasing efficiency. Refining was already developing a strong technical base, with good temperature controls, use of super-heated steam, much larger-scale equipment, and increased focus on capturing waste for useful by-products, like cold creams. After joining with the Pennsylvania's president, Tom Scott, in a misconceived attempt to create an oil shipping cartel, Rockefeller quietly bought up nearly all of the other Cleveland refiners. He was never a haggler and was happy to pay premiums for transactional speed. Just showing a target Standard's books was usually enough to close a deal, for no competitor ever came close to matching Rockefeller's profit margins. Targets always had the choice of being paid stock or cash, and Rockefeller always recommended taking stock. Most opted for the cash; the ones who took stock and held on to it became very rich.

Once he owned all the Cleveland refiners, Rockefeller scrapped them all and built an entirely new refinery complex comprising six state-of-the-art production sites, each concentrated on a single distillate for processing efficiency. (Kerosene for lighting dominated sales in the nineteenth century, but there were also lucrative markets in lubricants, naphtha, benzene, and other distillates.) The new plant equated to about a quarter of the country's refinery capacity and was almost certainly the most efficient. At roughly the same time, Rockefeller began to take over the major railroads' oil collection, loading, and dock facilities. He also generally stood ready to finance upgraded tank cars or help fund important line extensions, and he was willing to guarantee shipping volumes in return for lower shipping prices.

With the Cleveland consolidation behind him, Rockefeller quietly proceeded to take over almost all the rest of the nation's refineries. It happened very fast. Rockefeller simply visited each of the top regional refineries, in New York, Philadelphia, Pittsburgh, and Baltimore, and nearly all of them agreed to merge with Standard. These were all powerful businessmen, with giant egos, who had built nearly the same scale of operations Rockefeller had. But without any obvious strife they joined Standard under Rockefeller's leadership, dramatic testimony to the power of the Rockefeller personality at first hand.

All of the acquisitions were executed in secrecy—there were no laws about such things in the 1870s. They all kept their names and current executives, but they all took strategic direction from Rockefeller. With Standard's coffers behind them, they all stepped up the pace of acquisitions within their own operating regions, again with few signs of the changes afoot. The immense consolidation became known only in 1879, when Henry Rogers, a Standard distillation expert, was asked during congressional testimony to estimate the share of national refining capacity owned by Standard Oil. He thought for a minute and guessed that it was "from 90 to 95% of the refiners of the country"—as jaws dropped throughout the hearing room.[8]

Standard's global near monopoly was not challenged until the mid-1880s, when the Nobel brothers' Russian Baku fields began exporting into Europe. But it was still in a class by itself. From 1887 through 1896, Carnegie's collection of steel, iron, iron ore, coke, and related businesses earned a cumulative $41 million; over the same period, Standard Oil earned $189 million, about four and a half times as much.

Rockefeller and Standard played very rough when they were building their franchise. Doing business in nineteenth-century America was much like selling airplanes in today's Middle East. Bribing local officials was standard practice, and there is at least one documented instance in which Rockefeller clearly committed perjury on a witness stand. But the broader story that Rockefeller's Standard Oil won its position by "secret railroad rebates" and other illegal monopolistic practices has little basis. The United

John D. Rockefeller. This portrait of Rockefeller was painted when he was in his fifties and at the height of his powers. It captures some of the powerful aura that for several decades allowed him to utterly dominate a major industry without, it seems, ever raising his voice.

States had no laws against railroad rebates or monopolies when Rockefeller was building his business, and claims by the contemporary muckraker Ida Tarbell and many subsequent Rockefeller biographers that they were "against the common law" are not supported even in the Supreme Court's 1911 decision breaking up the company.

Once Rockefeller eased out of day-to-day management by about 1895, "administrative fatigue" seems to have set in at Standard.[9] John Archbold, Rockefeller's successor, visibly began to monetize Standard's position. Equity returns jumped about two-thirds, from the rather modest average 14.3 percent in Rockefeller's day to 24.4 percent under Archbold. As the company lost its entrepreneurial aggressiveness, its refinery market share dropped to only about 65 percent. Standard was also late to recognize either the opportunities in gasoline or the threat that electricity posed to its kerosene franchise. The 1911 Supreme Court decision mandating the breakup did Rockefeller a favor. Freed from the lassitude at the Trust headquarters, the thirty-four erstwhile subsidiaries almost all greatly improved their performance. Adjusted for inflation, their rocketing stock prices made Rockefeller possibly the richest man in history.

Rockefeller's primary achievement was to create the world's first global consumer product, with market shares in Europe, China, and Russia, akin to those in the United States. Hamlin Garland, writing of his hardscrabble childhood on a Great Plains farm, told of coming home from the fields in 1869 to the amazing transformation effected by a kerosene lamp on the table. Magazines like *America's Women's Home* extolled the advantages of a "student lamp" for late-night studying. The bright white light of the kerosene lamp, in every apartment and farm house, was a hallmark of modernity, just as the Standard Oil blue five-gallon kerosene can marked one of the earliest presence of modern markets in some of the remotest sections on earth.

The First Middle-Class Nation

Michael Spence is a New York University economist who has been studying the processes by which emerging markets, like Brazil and India, make the leap into the ranks of advanced countries. He suggests that there is a critical point he calls the "middle-income transition," when a sufficient mass of the population become future-oriented, are able to plan and to save, and consciously set out to improve their positions. The United States,

indeed, may be one of the few nations that was middle-class from the start.*
The act of emigration itself suggests the presence of Spence's middle-class
mind-set. Tocqueville may have been the first to use the term "middle-
class" in this sense, and Trollope was continually struck by the striving,
go-ahead impulse among her midwesterners. Nobody they encountered,
other than Southern slaves, reminded them of the peasants of England
and France.

A key feature of a middle-income transition is the shift from infrastructure spending to consumer-oriented production. That transition was in
full blast in the United States by the 1880s. Underlying the shift was the
country's pervasive social mobility. The very bottom and very top layers
were probably more stable than Tocqueville believed, but the top ranks
were far from impenetrable. Cornelius Vanderbilt, Andrew Carnegie, and
John Rockefeller all came from modest backgrounds. Mobility was especially high within the middle three quintiles, probably higher than anywhere else. A number of studies show quite high rates of farm laborers
becoming farm owners, blue-collar workers becoming managers, and
countinghouse clerks rising to very senior positions.[10]

Real incomes grew steadily after the 1873–1874 recession and continued to grow through the 1880s, and it was reflected in people's housing.
The typical house got bigger and, in urban areas, was separated from the
workplace, becoming a locus of family bonding after the day's activities. In
other words, it became a "home." On farms as well, farmhouses evolved
from a family factory into a civilized retreat from the animals and the
odors. With the opening of the Brooklyn Bridge in 1883, Brooklyn became
a bedroom suburb of Manhattan, and the "lunchroom" dotted the business district.

The midwestern "balloon" house, a wooden self-supporting frame
hung with weather-proofing walls, became the American standard and

---

* All such statements reserve the significant exception of African American slavery. Even after
the Civil War, freed slaves and their descendants—particularly, but not just, in the South—
were kept in a state not unlike that of Russian serfdom for nearly another century.

may have inspired the steel-cage structure of the new office skyscrapers. Midwestern factories churned out machine-made doors and windows, and by the 1870s, machine-made mail-order kit houses were available in a wide range of prices and styles. Inexpensive, machine-made carpets and drapes and new methods of grinding paint pigments allowed people of quite modest incomes to add a touch of color or personal style to their home. Home spaces were divided into a semiformal parlor or sitting room, a dining room and a scullery, and bedrooms. Children increasingly had their own beds. Middle-class families regularly supplemented incomes by taking in boarders, who also supported the cost of household help.

The focus on the home space drastically changed the role of women, who became society's officially designated civilizing force, arbiters of domesticity—"homemakers" who, as *Harper's* noted, "legislate for our dress, etiquette, and manners without fear of veto." Home economics, advice columns, home management, etiquette, and cookbooks proliferated. Being middle-class was a life strategy, a continuing campaign, mostly managed by women. Tactics included smaller families, more intense child rearing and education, budgetary management and savings plans, and training children in prudence and deportment.

The new respect for the purchasing power of women was reflected in the blossoming of the department store. The first establishment by that name was John Wanamaker's, which opened in Philadelphia in 1876 as the "largest space in the world devoted to retail selling on a single floor." Occupying a full city block in midtown, it was all about women. Lighted by a stained-glass ceiling by day and hundreds of gas lights by night, it was arranged in concentric circles, as much as two-thirds of a mile long, with 1,100 counter stools, so a lady could sit and discuss her purchase. Displays featured "Ladies' Furnishings Goods," "Gloves," "Laces," and "Linen Sheeting." The 70,000 people who showed up on opening day were naturally almost all women, as were the counter assistants—although the lordly, formally dressed floor walkers were all male. The department store became a fixture in every sizeable city. New York had its Macy's, Bloomingdale's, Lord & Taylor, and B. Altman; Brooklyn its Abraham & Straus;

Boston its Filene's; Chicago its Marshall Fields; San Francisco its Emporium. Even much newer, rawer cities, like Detroit, Indianapolis, and Milwaukee had their Hudson's and Gimbels.

Beneath the surface gloss, urbanization brought serious problems, especially in sanitation, which lagged population growth by several decades. Water-borne diseases like cholera and typhoid remained dangerous killers well into the twentieth century, accounting for a quarter of all infectious disease deaths in 1900. Wives, or servants, were still lugging water from pumps in the 1870s, but by the end of the decade most larger cities were piping (unfiltered and unchlorinated) water into homes in most of their residential areas. Privies were not connected to sewage systems. The backyard latrine—or in many working-class areas, the neighborhood latrine—gradually gave way to indoor toilets. Water closets, which flushed into a pit, were suitable for less settled areas, while urban designers experimented with a host of "earth closet" contraptions.

Many cities had gas lighting, at least in better neighborhoods, and almost everyone had a kerosene lamp. Over time, the expanding national wealth readily financed a great burst of municipal investment in clean water, sewers, garbage collection, transit, street lighting, police and fire services, and parks, stretching from the 1880s well into the twentieth century. Local water systems became a major market for Corliss's big-ticket steam engines.

The clinching proof of the consumerization of America was the sudden explosion of brands. History had never seen a burst of new products like that in the America of the 1880s and 1890s. Store shelves offered Cream of Wheat, Aunt Jemima's Pancakes, Postum, Kellogg's Shredded Wheat, Juicy Fruit gum, Pabst Blue Ribbon Beer, Durkee's salad dressings, Uneeda Biscuits, Coca-Cola, and Quaker Oats. Pillsbury and Gold Medal wiped out local flour millers. (Wives started buying cake mixes in the 1890s, but baking one's own bread was still a badge of honor.) Advertising flourished right alongside. (N. W. Ayer, one of the first of the big advertising companies, got its start with John Wanamaker's.) So Jell-O was the "quick and easy" dessert; Schlitz Beer was made with "filtered water"; Huckin's soups were "hermetically sealed"; no human hands had touched Stacey's Workdipt Chocolates. H. J. Heinz created a fifty-foot-tall electric pickle with 1,200 light bulbs in Times Square in 1896. The sign blinked Heinz's "57 Good Things for the Table," listing each one in lights. You'd "Walk a Mile" for a Camel and hum the jingle for Sunny Jim cereal. The Great Atlantic and Pacific Tea Company, A&P, was the first national grocery chain, and Frank Woolworth's "nickel stores" swept through the country.

The speed of the branded-food triumph could have been due to the naïveté of consumers or perhaps to the execrable quality of local stores' barrel food. One suspects it was both; nostalgia buffs too readily assume that consumers were fooled. Packaged brands brought people in much of the country their first access to more varied diets. Local grocers were often sinks of poor hygiene, bad storage conditions, adulteration, and outright misrepresentation (hog fat for butter). The packaged food industry had its own scandals, especially in meat, but safety and consistency were probably a great improvement over the general store.

A vast range of products made life simpler—Bissell carpet sweepers, Gillette "safety" razors with disposable blades, rubber boots and shoes, zippers, ice boxes (often with an opening on a house's outer wall, so the iceman could fill it), Levi's for workers. Or made life more fun: roller skates were a craze in the 1870s, bicycles in the 1890s. James Bonsack's automatic cigarette-making machine went into production in James Duke's factory in 1886. By 1900, Americans were buying more than 4 billion cigarettes a year, almost all of them from Duke, including still-current brands, like Lucky Strike. A pre-Duke cigarette maker invented the baseball card. Young women were discouraged from smoking but had a "mania" for cosmetics. Handbag stores prestuffed their bags with branded lipsticks and rouge. Helena Rubinstein and Elizabeth Arden, between them, dominated the business by the early 1900s. Household walls were festooned with chromolithographs: color facsimiles of American painters like Audubon, Bierstadt, and Winslow Homer. Currier and Ives were among the first to produce paintings specifically for chromolithography. Mark Twain's Connecticut Yankee knows he is in a strange place because the medieval castle has no "chromos" on the walls.

Residential mail service triggered a postcard craze and then a greeting card craze. Postcards with photographic scenes were popular collectibles—one company produced 16,000 different views. Thomas Edison invented the phonograph in 1879, but Emile Berliner came up with the popular gramophone and the flat record in 1889; his system could make thousands of records from a single master. Versions of the modern juke box proliferated in the 1890s, and it was a natural accompaniment to the drugstore soda fountain—a pharmacist could pull in $500 worth of nickels a week. Both were an index of the increased leisure time of young people. Middle-class parents kept their kids in school, instead of sending them off to the factory, and were discovering that the demographic between child and adult was a previously undreamed-of species.

Home entertainment sales boomed—lawn tennis and croquet, board games, and stereoscopes. Two stereoscopic slides viewed in front of a light source produced a three-dimensional scene. Millions of slides were produced—natural wonders, stories, religious matter. Oliver Wendell Holmes once boasted that he had seen more than 100,000 stereo views. George Eastman introduced the celluloid film roll for his Kodak in 1888. A Kodak-sponsored photography contest in New York in 1897 drew 26,000 people. By 1900, the country had more than 1.5 million telephones. Improvements in printing technology produced an outpouring of magazines, inexpensive novels, and city newspapers. Plant lighting made morning papers possible, and publishers pulled in readers with sports pages, comics, puzzles, women's pages, and advice columns. Dorothy Dix's column started in 1896. Professional entertainment—baseball, boxing, vaudeville, burlesque, Barnum's circus—and the amusement park were fixtures even in smaller cities. The Ferris wheel at the 1892 Chicago Exposition was 264 feet high, each of its cars was larger than a Pullman coach, and the fully loaded wheel handled more than 2,000 people at a time.

The great investment banks that had financed the railroad and steel industries—J. P. Morgan and Jacob Schiff's Kuhn, Loeb—were supplemented by newcomers like Goldman, Sachs, and Lehman Bros. They were mostly Jewish, ascended from the earlier urban "rag trade," and provided industrial-scale financing for consumer industries, which the Morgans and the Schiffs did not understand. Julius Rosenwald, a true retailing genius, took operational command of a struggling Sears and Roebuck in 1895 and, through Goldman's, launched the first-ever public stock offering in a retail company. The purpose of the offering was to finance a mechanized rail- and roller-based goods assembly and distribution system, not unlike those pioneered by Alexander Holley for the steel industry. By the turn of the century, virtually every consumer was within reach of a Sears or Montgomery, Ward catalog. Delivery times almost anywhere in the country were thirty days or less, which prevailed until air-freight deliveries became widespread three-quarters of a century later. In order of magnitude, the gains in distributional efficiency were probably greater than those from the Internet in our own day. And with consumers as the driving force behind growth, the American economy was roaring ahead at a rate faster than any country had ever sustained over so long a period.

Leaving Britain Behind

American industrial output steadily closed the gap with Great Britain throughout the nineteenth century and then exploded to the top rank. In 1800, the output of American factories and mines was only a sixth that of Great Britain; by 1860, it was a third, and by 1880, two-thirds. American industrial production pulled ahead of Great Britain's sometime in the late 1880s and by the eve of World War I was 2.3 times larger. In 1860, Great Britain accounted for about 20 percent of world industrial output and the United States only about 7 percent; by 1913, the American share was 32 percent, while Great Britain's had slid to 14 percent.[11]

Strikingly, despite the country's high rate of population growth, per capita industrial production grew faster in the United States than anywhere else in the world. Industrial output per head grew sixfold in the United States from 1860 to 1913, compared to only 1.8 times in Great Britain. Only Germany among the major powers showed a per capita growth rate (5.6 times) comparable to that in America, and the Germans started from a much lower baseline. (On the eve of the Great War, decades of hyper-rapid growth had pulled German output to Great Britain's level.) By the end of the 1870s, America dominated international trade in grain, enjoyed a near monopoly of the world meat trade with a 70–80 percent share, and enjoyed at least as great a share of the burgeoning global petroleum market. As for the other Great Powers, France steadily lost ground to both Great Britain and Germany, while Russia remained a sink of despondency.

Late nineteenth-century British savants were mesmerized by the relentless American advance. A near-obsessive search for the causes of the relative British decline spurred a century's worth of economic history on both sides of the Atlantic that offers a superb lens for tracing the sources of American advantage. The divergent paths followed by the American and British steel industries were the most intensively researched, because they were among the few that readily lent themselves to direct comparison.

Loss of leadership in steel was especially painful for Britons. Steel was the foundation industry for the late-Victorian period, much as information technology is today. Nor was there any question of British ability to produce the world's finest steel. Sheffield steel set the quality standard for the world, and its crucible steel had almost the status of a semiprecious metal. Almost all the era's steelmaking advances came from the United Kingdom: the hot-air blast furnace, the Bessemer process, and the Thomas-Gilchrist basic lining, enabling the use of high-phosphorus ore. Charles Siemens invented the furnace used for the Siemen-Martin open-hearth method of steelmaking that competed with Bessemer's, especially in nonrail applications. Siemens belonged to the great German industrial family but spent most of his life in England and eventually became a citizen.

The American challenge lay in the vast growth of its steel-making *capacity*. Stephen Jeans, secretary of the British Iron Trade Association, and the steel engineer Frank Popplewell both wrote book-length surveys around the turn of the century seeking the reasons for the American success.[12] As Jeans put it, just the increase in the American output over the six years from 1895 was "considerably larger than the total output of steel of all kinds throughout the world in any one year prior to 1890, and is about half a million tons more than the total make of steel in Great Britain in any two years prior to 1897."[13] Jeans glumly noted that American annual steel and pig-iron output was already twice as large as Great Britain's and greater than the total of Great Britain and Germany combined.

Popplewell and Jeans each make it clear that the American advantage involved no fundamental breakthroughs but was rather about methodologies, work organization, and mechanization. Popplewell's list of the characteristic features of an American plant were all in place at Carnegie's Edgar Thomson Works by the early 1880s. There were some splendid British steel plants; indeed, Holley had extolled several as models for the United States. But there were many more older, smaller plants and a lower degree of mechanization. Continuous processing through the entire ore-to-steel cycle was rare, and smaller plants could not afford expensive equipment like the chargers that injected the chemical and mineral additives into the converter mechanically. Popplewell commented on the "very conspicuous absence of labourers in the American mills."[14] American rail and rod mills routinely produced three times the output of British mills with fewer than half the men.

The cost advantage once enjoyed by the British industry from its conveniently located ore and coal supplies gradually disappeared as Americans mechanized ore mining and transport through the 1890s. Great Lakes Mesabi Range ore was surface-mined with giant steam shovels, and Popplewell was awestruck at lake port ore handling: huge mechanical clamshell shovels unloaded 5,000-ton ore boats into moving lines of freight cars, at rates over 1,000 tons per hour. Carnegie Steel's own Pittsburgh-to-Erie railroad, with some of the largest cars and the most advanced loading facilities, had driven ore transport costs as low as a seventh of a cent per ton.

The big American production runs were facilitated by a high degree of product standardization. Holley had pressed hard to standardize rail patterns before his death in 1882, but it was not accomplished until 1898, compressing some 119 different rail designs down to just 10. Carnegie Steel accomplished a similar result in structural steel at about the same time, with the publication of its structural steel handbook, which was soon adopted by the whole industry. The British found standardization much more difficult, in part because so much of their product was exported and in part, as in the case of rails, because of the resistance of smaller railroads and the manufacturers that serviced them.

The British still led the world in the scale and quality of their ship-plate production and in other high-end products, and no other country, Jeans felt, could match the British in ultralarge steam forges for ship components. Although American locomotives from Baldwin were spreading throughout the world, Jeans did not think they came up to British quality but conceded that they were cheaper.

Jeans's overall conclusion, that American steel "can compete with Great Britain and Germany in the leading markets of the world,"[15] was sugar coating for his parliamentary audience. The scale, the aggressiveness, the modernity of the American plants that he so painstakingly documents leave little doubt that the contest was over. Indeed, just about the time Jeans completed his review, Great Britain was transmuting from the world's dominant steel producer into the largest steel importer. Both American and German steel, it seemed, were underselling Great Britain in its home market.

The failure of the British to keep pace is a classic example of the disadvantages accruing to a technological first mover. By the time American and German competitors appeared on the scene, the structure of the British industry already had a settled character. The prevalence of smaller companies, many specializing just in iron or just in steel, was not conducive to American- and German-scale processing efficiencies and mechanization, for they were not cost-effective for any but the largest works.

Just as important, a competitive late entrant usually starts with the most modern plant, and if it enjoys a high growth rate, requiring constant plant additions, its advantage in facilities will steadily grow. Older competitors, with flat or falling shares, will find it commensurately hard to finance plant upgrades. By the 1880s the British industry was clearly behind the Germans and Americans in production technology. A number of

Britons understood that only a root-and-branch reconstruction of the industry could restore its competitiveness, but the financial and organizational obstacles, in a country committed to laissez-faire economic principles, made it practically impossible.

A long finger of suspicion points at both British workers and British managers. Most fair-minded observers conceded that American and German workers and bosses were better educated and more open to scientific advances. Worker recalcitrance and union resistance were major obstacles to mechanization throughout British industry. But British managers also played a big role in the deterioration. The entrepreneurial drive of the 1840s and 1850s had markedly ebbed. Old-school managers, consciously or not, connived with their workers to stick with what they knew: the smaller plants, the old methods, the clubman's version of genteel competition. As one expert put it, "outside England people say, 'What is the saving?' In England, the first question is, 'What is the cost?'" A sympathetic American was struck by the "pessimism and lack of courage" among British iron and steel men.[16]

The same slippage can be seen in the British chemical industry. In midcentury, Great Britain led the world in inorganic chemicals (ammonia, caustic soda, sulfuric acid) but failed to adjust when the new Solvay technology emerged in the 1870s; within a decade German and Belgian manufacturers had perhaps a 20 percent cost advantage, with far less environmental damage. The Americans came on strongly in the late 1890s, starting with the Solvay process and the even newer electrolytic technology. Similarly, in electrical power generation, the steam turbine engine, one of the critical enabling technologies, was invented by an Englishman, Charles Parsons, in 1884. But the industry was quickly dominated by America's General Electric and Westinghouse and Germany's Siemens. Some failures seem cultural. In reaction to a wave of machine-made American shoe imports in the early 1900s, British industry switched to American shoemaking machines yet somehow never realized American productivity levels.

Jack Brown, an industrial historian at the University of Virginia, supplies a striking example of the British cultural difference. British rail lines typically made all their equipment—not just their locomotives and cars, but everything else, including tapestries, table-settings, ticket-blanks, and furniture. That was not absurd: each was seeking to express a specific company personality to its employees and customers. U.S. rail lines, by contrast, outsourced almost everything—George Pullman owned and maintained virtually all the lines' luxury sleeping cars. The only value being served was economic rationality. When British lines were forced to turn to American suppliers during a long 1895 strike, they were shocked to find that they were saving 30–40 percent on their own costs of production.[17]

Finally, the vulnerability of the British industry was increased by the country's ideological commitment to free-trade dogma, in face of steep protective steel tariffs in both the United States and Germany—and on the part of the Germans, flagrant, predatory, below-cost "dumping," as they attacked Great Britain's steel markets everywhere. (An important distinction is that US trade policy was protective but not predatory. It artificially obstructed British imports, but almost all of its steel production was consumed at home. Germany's strategy was predatory: it dumped most of its production overseas, making up the losses by charging high prices at home.)

It is all the more remarkable, therefore, that the British political and business establishment emphatically rejected a return to protectionism in the early 1900s, even though it was labeled, reasonably enough, as "fair trade" retaliation against predators. The politics and interests involved were complicated, but to a striking degree, the rejection was based on a web of highly abstract arguments. As the *Times* put it, "Protection . . . brings its own punishment. Nature will retaliate upon France whether we do or not."[18] The flower of the British economics establishment, the legendary professors Marshall, Pigou, and Jevons, all pronounced on the folly of trade restriction, insisting that the British industry was merely undergoing a "natural" adjustment. Winston Churchill worried how ministries and Parliament, "hitherto chaste because unsolicited," might behave once the protectionist bawd ran free.[19]

In the United States, the usual penalty to the protective nation—excessive prices—did not apply in steel because of Carnegie. By economic rationality, if British steel was selling at $25 per ton pretariff, American steel makers would price as close as they could to $53 ($25 + $28). That is why tariffs were often called the "mother of all trusts"[20]—the windfall profits were so high that American firms would quickly reach market-sharing agreements, as happened in sugar, whiskey, tin plate, and other industries.

But it didn't happen in steel. From 1886 through 1899, the British export price averaged $23 per ton, or $51 to the customer after the tariff. But the average selling price from American Bessemer mills was only $28. In other words, the Americans left $23 of available tariff protection on the table; in 1897 and 1898, the average American price was actually lower than the British pretariff price. In steel, in other words, the tariff had only minimal impact on final prices, because of Carnegie's persistent drive to steal share from his competitors.[21]

The primary driver for J. P. Morgan's purchase of Carnegie Steel in 1901, and the roll-up of most of the rest of the industry in a new conglomerate, US Steel, was to reestablish the cartel. With Carnegie safely dispatched to the fields of philanthropy, Morgan could finally slow the march of technology to staunch the drain of capital spending, and keep steel prices at whatever level was needed to service his massive acquisition debt. From then on, most new advances came out of railroad or automobile company labs, or from overseas. US Steel settled into the sleepy dominance that came to characterize nearly all big American industries until the Japanese and German assaults of the 1970s and 1980s.

While England Slept

By the end of the century, the United States, almost inadvertently, was poised to make inroads into Great Britain's dominant position in global finance. The British branch of the great Rothschild banks was run by "Natty" Rothschild, grandson of old Nathan. The London house's founder was accustomed to be lead finance house to underwrite British overseas adventures. When the South African war broke out in 1899, Rothschild was shocked to learn that the government planned to grant half the financing mandate to an American syndicate led by Morgan. After fierce lobbying by the financial elite, Morgan was given only a very minor role during the first round of fund raising. But as drawn-out war pressured British gold reserves, the Exchequer had no choice but to give Morgan an equal role. Worse, it was forced to yield to Morgan's peremptory demand that he get twice the commission as the British consortium. Niall Ferguson, the historian of the Rothschild family, writes, "It was an early sign of that shift in the centre of financial gravity across the Atlantic that would be such a decisive—and for the Rothschilds fateful—feature of the new century."[22]

The underlying tidal shift was that the United States was transmuting from a debtor to a creditor nation. America's long history as a debtor was the inevitable result of its persistent trade deficits on top of the strong inflow of investment capital, primarily from the British.

The trade deficit began to shrink in the latter part of the 1870s, primarily from a big jump in exports of grain, flour, meat, and animal fats. Purely in merchandise trade—that is, excluding services like finance and transportation—the United States was nearly always in surplus after 1876 and finally flipped into surplus in both goods and services in the mid-1890s. By the end of the century, its finished manufactured exports had a dollar value greater than either cotton or wheat.[23]

A country's international credit/debtor position is the difference between all American claims on the rest of the world and vice versa. Foreign claims on America include not only outright borrowings, but any foreign ownership of stock, land, or any other American asset. The United States was a net debtor nation through the entire nineteenth century, primarily because of foreign investment flows, as in the late 1830s, 1850s, and post-Civil War booms in railroads, cattle ranches, and other real assets. America first became a net overseas investor in the late 1890s, mostly in Canada and Latin America. The huge surpluses earned during WWI made the United States by far the world's largest creditor nation.[24]

And now, as everyone knows, America is itself in danger of being pushed off the top-dog pedestal. In the next chapter we will look briefly at the looming contest for economic dominance between China and the United States, and its similarities and differences compared with the one between Great Britain and America a century and a half ago.

CHAPTER NINE

Catching Up
to the
Hyperpower

A Reprise?

━━━━━

THE RAPID GROWTH OF THE CHINESE ECONOMY IS ONE OF THE MOST portentous phenomena in the world today.[1] Chart 9.1 shows the data comparing the total economic output of China and the United States from 1980 through 2011, and projected through 2017, as compiled by the International Monetary Fund (IMF).

Some comments on the data. The comparison is measured in "purchasing power parity" dollars (ppp$). Official dollar/RMB exchange rates do not fully capture the pricing differences between China and the United States, especially in labor-intensive services, which are typically very cheap in a low-wage country. Using ppp$ inflates Chinese output by about 50 percent over currency market values. No one would claim that ppp calculations are accurate, but most analysts accept that they provide a better fit to reality. Projecting economic growth based on official currency rates tends to show that it will take well into the 2030s before Chinese GDP catches up with America's. All such comparisons, however they are adjusted, are only gross approximations of reality, given the radical differences between the two economies. Even taking the IMF forecasts at face

CHART 9.1 Chinese and US GDP ppp$: 1980–2017 (est)

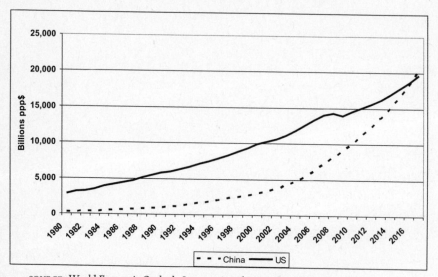

SOURCE: *World Economic Outlook,* International Monetary Fund, April 2012.

value, China will hardly be a rich country in 2017, since it will be distributing approximately the same purchasing power as the United States among four times as many people.

China's rapid growth, however, is already triggering another crucial process, Michael Spence's middle-income transition, introduced in the last chapter. About the point at which per capita incomes rise to between $5,000 and $10,000, a broader middle class begins to take control of its future and define the tone of economic life. Since self-directed people are often unwilling to accede to petty officialdom in matters they deem important, the transition can be particularly treacherous in a state-driven economy like China's.[2]

We will come back to that point, but first we will look at some of the broad similarities between America's tactics against Great Britain in the nineteenth century and China's catch-up strategies today.

The Pleasures of
Starting in Second Place

THE JOY OF THEFT

The United States had a fine record of innovation from its earliest post-colonial days, but its inventiveness was mostly lavished on large-scale production and distribution techniques for established products. The nineteenth century's iron and steel technology—the blast furnace, Bessemer conversion, the "basic" process, the Siemens open-hearth furnace, the cast steel of Sheffield—nearly all came from Great Britain, with some important but lesser contributions from France and elsewhere on the continent. Roughly the same could be said of textile technology, coal and coke, steam engines, chemicals, and precision machinery. Britain's policy was to keep such technologies out of the hands of its North American colonies, which were supposed to serve as the rural hinterland of industrializing England, supplying scarce timber, grains, and ores and providing a captive market for home-country manufactures.

But once independent and determined to industrialize on their own, Americans saw this immense hoard of technology as theirs for the asking—or for the stealing. Tench Coxe was Alexander Hamilton's deputy in the first Treasury Department, and he had no compunction about offering cash awards for stolen British textile technology and paying bounties high enough to induce craftsmen to risk prison for emigrating with trade secrets. Americans viewed Great Britain as a semihostile power, and understood that their own poorly diversified economy was a source of vulnerability. Conventional ethics do not apply in the game of nations, and the United States set out to steal whatever it could. Knowledgeable Chinese occasionally cite that history when they are criticized for their disregard of intellectual property rules.

Japan adopted a similar strategy vis-à-vis the United States in the post–World War II era, even though it was among America's closest allies. Companies like Cummins Engine subcontracted production to companies like Komatsu in the 1960s to take advantage of Japan's low labor costs. Within a few years, Cummins's home diesel market was attacked by inexpensive but disconcertingly high-quality Cummins knockoffs from Komatsu.

China's relationship with America is much like that of the fledgling United States with Great Britain. China is both the United States' second largest trading partner (after Canada) and an avowed rival. The American navy is an intrusive presence close to its shores, and smaller countries that it views as within its sphere of influence pointedly take shelter in America's shadow. Relations have an extra edge because the United States stands for the kind of raucous, self-indulgent democracy that China's leaders fear could destabilize their own fragile ruling compact. So with respect to technology, much as America did, China is stealing all it can, not only from the United States but from all Western advanced economies.

A recent roundup by *Businessweek* listed nineteen recent convictions under American economic espionage laws for intellectual property theft by Chinese agents and company moles. The roster of victims reads like a Who's Who of corporate America: Apple, Boeing, Chicago Mercantile Exchange, Dow Chemical, DuPont, Ford, General Motors, Goodyear, Motorola, Northrup Grumman, Sanofi-Aventis. The targets ranged from formulas for industrial fireproof paint to detailed specifications for the space shuttle and a wide range of military aircraft; from derivative trading software and algorithms to polyethylene shielding; from titanium pigments to trash management software; from advanced display technology to automobile design specifications and advanced wind turbine management software. Some of the evidence included records of government officials supplying shopping lists and offering encouragement.[3]

All of those cases involved Chinese agents on site in the target companies, often in responsible positions, physically stealing or copying sensitive material. Far more widespread, most experts agree, are cyber-invasions by government-sponsored or protected hackers. For nearly a decade, Chinese hackers thoroughly compromised the data systems of the erstwhile Canadian telecommunications giant Nortel, seizing more or less complete access to all of the company's product designs and other trade secrets. Disquietingly, there is a distinct possibility that after Nortel was broken up and sold in bankruptcy to several other technology companies, the infections were transmitted to the new hosts.[4]

Data from the US Cyber Command in the Department of Defense tabulate more than 50,000 malicious cyber-intrusions per year in recent years. It does not break out the data by country of origin, but China is clearly a major contributor. In 2011, for example, RSA, a leading vendor of security technology for corporate data systems, was itself hacked into. Subsequent analysis showed it be an extremely sophisticated attack, dubbed an "Advanced Persistent Threat." Although it had been routed through several countries and continents, the attack appeared to emanate from China. One apparent object of the attack was to compromise the security-key systems for accessing confidential company databases, possibly including those of RSA's customers. If it had been successful—the company said it was "confident" that it had not been, but who knows?—it would have operated as an open sesame to acres of sensitive, and highly valuable, material.[5]

EXPLOITING PARTNERS

In the early days of independence, the United States was almost entirely dependent on Great Britain for manufactured products beyond the capabilities of local seamstresses and blacksmiths. British products were consigned to coastal merchant houses that distributed them throughout the country. Typically, it was those merchants who provided the capital for local artisans to create knockoffs of the British designs and keep the profits at home.

The Chinese behave the same way. But since today's high-value products are often far too complex to readily knock off, they exploit the eagerness of Western companies to gain entry to the vast potential Chinese market. Recently GE, anxious to land a large avionics contract (flight management software and technology) for a projected Chinese jumbo commercial jet, agreed to transfer technology developed for the Boeing 787 Dreamliner to a fifty-fifty joint venture in Shanghai. Since the technology has obvious military applications, GE says that Chinese military personnel will be excluded from the joint venture and that there will be limits on ex–project employees transferring to Chinese military programs—protections that one congressman called "laughable."

GE stresses that the deal was vetted by both the Commerce and Defense Departments. But a deal valued at $300 million and creating at least a few hundred jobs in the United States, but many more in China, was hardly likely to be turned down in the midst of a "jobless recovery." Four other aviation technology companies will also benefit from the contracts, and for GE, the deal came bundled with the promise of additional deals in coal gasification, energy, locomotives, and a high-speed-rail joint venture that could be worth another $1 billion.[6] Imagine the row GE would have kicked up if the deal had been turned down.[*]

If the past is portent, the likelihood of the joint venture working out well for GE is not high. Siemens and ThyssenKrupp worked closely with a Chinese high-speed-rail consortium supplying maglev technology to its Shanghai bullet trains. China is now proceeding with maglev development elsewhere in the country without the German partners, and it may soon be competing with them for global sales. That same prospect is looming in a number of other industries—solar power, batteries, aviation, automobiles, chemical manufacture—in which Germany has supplied advanced technologies to Chinese customers and partners.[7]

Incidents like these are not random occurrences, the kind of occasional flaps that are inevitable when two companies with different cultures and languages engage as close partners in complex undertakings. Ever since the end of the Maoist Cultural Revolution, China has made no secret of

---

[*] A GE official pooh-poohed the idea that they would allow such critical technology to be exploited by China: "Why would we give away our future?" he asked. But senior bankers made that same argument in the years just before the financial crash. In most cases, they readily sold their firms' futures for the sake of temporarily higher revenues, higher stock prices, and higher bonuses.

its intent to move rapidly up the technology ladder by virtually any means, fair or foul. Specific plans offered as part of the regular five-year national planning cycle emphasize "indigenous innovation," which is defined to include "enhancing original innovation through co-innovation and re-innovation based on the assimilation of imported technologies," and states that "the importation of technologies without emphasizing the assimilation, absorption and re-innovation is bound to weaken the nation's indigenous research and development capacity." The US Chamber of Commerce said that the technology plans taken together amounted to "a blueprint for technology theft on a scale the world has never seen before."[8]

The Chinese patent regime, according to the Chamber, has been perverted to facilitate technology theft from outsiders. Authorities expressly encourage—and even underwrite the cost of—filing "utility" patents claiming intellectual property in the application of someone else's technology to a particular narrow use. It has become a pointed tactic for punishing Western patent holders who file suits against Chinese infringers in Western courts.

Schneider Electric is a mid-size French company with a global business in high-tech power management products and a rich patent portfolio. In the late 1990s, Chint, a small Chinese company that supplied the Chinese market with products similar to Schneider's, opened shop in Europe and was sued by Schneider for a number of infringements. (Schneider won a number of cases but not all of them.) Chint had filed a utility patent on a product in Schneider's portfolio and retaliated with an infringement suit in a Chinese court. The court found for Chint, imposing a $54 million fine. Schneider was eventually forced to merge with another local company, founded by two of the original partners in Chint. Such are the devices that go under the name of "re-innovation."[9]

UNFAIR TRADE PRACTICES

In nineteenth-century America, the Southern secession allowed the newly dominant Republican party to push through a highly protective tariff scheme, covering iron, steel, textiles, and most manufactured products, as well as a host of commodities, including wool, sugar, flax, and others to benefit the agrarian Western interests. Such tariffs were maintained long after there was any validity to "infant industry" arguments, although the effect of the tariffs were mitigated, at least in steel, by competition between American vendors.

China joined the World Trade Organization in 2001, with the support of the United States, and does not maintain unusually onerous tariff schedules. But as Japan did during the period of its rise, China maintains a host of nontariff trade barriers and subsidies. State-owned industries typically benefit from highly subsidized electricity and fuel prices and can acquire land at far less than free-market prices. Customs barriers are intentionally Kafkaesque. Even minor changes in a product currently sold in China—like a new shade in a line of lipsticks—can be held up for months awaiting inspection and certification. Or customs rules are turned into a tool for intellectual property theft. High-technology products like firewall and smart-card software cannot be sold unless officials first examine and certify the source code, which most Western companies will not permit.

There have been a number of cases in which the government has attempted to impose Chinese-specific software solutions or standards on foreign products, so far without much success. Advanced technology vendors have frequently refused to depart from established international standards. In the few instances in which they have agreed to include the Chinese standard as an option, customers typically don't use it, or it doesn't work acceptably. China, however, is far from an incompetent country in high technology. One database of peer-reviewed, high-quality scientific journals shows the Chinese paper count to be in third place, behind the United States and the United Kingdom. It is abundantly clear that the government understands the importance of controlling basic architectures in most high-tech products and is resolved to move beyond the role of passive acceptor of Western paradigms. In the 1980s Japan had similar aspirations, which it has largely failed to fulfill. China, however, may be a much more entrepreneurial country than Japan, with a potential home market big enough to establish standards with global impact.

In broad strokes at least, China has been following much the same catch-up tactics as nineteenth-century America, although adapted to today's utterly different technology environment. But Americans still had an advantage that China cannot replicate. The United States was founded in an immense, richly endowed, and barely populated new country. In effect, a select group of ambitious and adventurous people, informed by centuries of the European experience, got the chance to start over. China is in an entirely different position. Despite the talents of its people and its outstanding economic successes, the speed of its growth is beginning to throw up what may be fundamental obstacles of place and time.

Challenges

NATURAL RESOURCES

America's fast-track development in the nineteenth century was based on prodigal consumption of resources. Much of the westward settler movement was an exercise in land spoliation. Farmers would clear land, wear it out in just a few years, pull up stakes, and move on. Forests were decimated to feed blast furnaces and steam engines. Industrial cities like Cincinnati dumped all their wastes—human, animal carcasses, iron filings, chemicals—directly into local rivers and lakes. Disease epidemics forced better sanitation toward the end of the century, but serious attempts to mitigate environmental damage got underway only in the 1950s and 1960s. The air in mid-twentieth-century Pittsburgh was much like that in most Chinese cities today: on a clear day you could see to the next corner.

Nineteenth-century Americans might be forgiven for believing that the country's resources were inexhaustible. As the populace pushed across the Appalachians into Ohio and beyond, one of the most dangerous maladies, as Frances Trollope acutely observed, was sheer loneliness. Whatever damage early settlers inflicted on the environment seemed like mere pinpricks amid the primeval vastness.

China, by contrast, had a billion people before it began to industrialize. It is not a resource-poor country. It has ample coal and has recently virtually cornered the market on rare earths, a vital component in most semiconductor manufacturing. But it still must import vast amounts of commodities to feed its industrial machine. China now accounts for approximately one-fourth of world demand for zinc, iron and steel, lead, copper, and aluminum, and is the world's second largest importer of oil after the United States. With its current history of trade surpluses, however, it can easily afford the external commodities required to feed its industry.

But China is running out of water, and without extraordinary action, the lack of water could jeopardize all of its economic ambitions. The country's per capita water supply is only a quarter of the world average, and most of it is in the wrong place. Northern China produces half of GDP, contains most of the arable land and 40 percent of the population, but gets only 12 percent of the rainfall. Despite persistent water shortages, Chinese industry is a profligate consumer of water, using four to ten times more water per unit of output than other industrial countries. The biggest water consumers are agriculture, mining, and hydropower; between them, they account for more than 80 percent of national consumption and are famously inefficient. Less than half the water used for crop irrigation, for instance, actually reaches the fields. The growth of cities has also greatly increased the rate of personal water use, including display uses like lawns and golf courses, in keeping with the aspirations of the country's nouveau riche. Hastily extended urban water systems leak away about a fifth of the supply. To make matters much worse, Chinese industry is notoriously polluting, so large portions of the available water supply is becoming unusable—a quarter of it is so polluted that it is unsuitable even for industrial purposes.

Official Chinese forecasts suggest that the country's available water will be at the World Bank's "scarcity" level within the foreseeable future. Already, only half the rural population has access to safe drinking water. Extreme levels of surface-water pollution has forced heavy exploitation of ground water, which is lowering water tables, causing land subsidence with collateral damage in built-up areas, and speeding the country's desertification. Forced-draft projects to reroute rivers to divert water to agricultural and industrial areas are only making the problems worse, even as they raise tensions around the exploitation of transnational rivers and continue the destruction of the environment. One current mega-project, twice as expensive as the famous Three Gorges Dam, is diverting water from the Yangtze River in the south through three major new channels some eight hundred miles to Beijing. It has been compared to "channeling water from the Mississippi River to meet the drinking needs of Boston, New York and Washington." It will involve forced relocations of hundreds of thousands of people, will work environmental havoc along most of its route, and will worsen already worrisome drought conditions in the south.

The Three Gorges experience does not instill confidence. Required relocations may be four times higher than original estimates, seismic activity has risen sharply, and large areas of reservoir banks have been lost to landslides. At the same time, the Three Gorges reservoir water is becoming dangerously polluted. The government is far behind on wastewater treatment for the cities surrounding the reservoir, and tens of millions of tons of industrial and urban waste are dumped into the reservoir every year. Many of the same observations could be made with respect to China's astonishing levels of air pollution.[10]

DEMOGRAPHICS

The Western press has recently highlighted a potential demographic crisis in China. The *Economist* magazine called it a "deadly point of unseen weakness."[11] The increased health and longevity of older Chinese, along with the long-standing national one-child policy, will inevitably create a sharp ramp-up in the aged "dependency ratio," the number of people over age sixty-five per hundred workers. By 2050, the Chinese dependency ratio will nearly quadruple, from eleven to forty-two, while in the United States, despite the aging of the baby boomers, it will increase from the current twenty to only thirty-five.

In isolation, this indeed looks like a serious problem, but it exaggerates by using the United States as the comparison. Because of its relative receptivity to immigrants and relatively high fertility rate, America is in better shape than most advanced countries on issues of generational dependence.

As Chart 9.2 shows, the projected Chinese dependency ratio is not unusually high among advanced countries. Japan is the country facing a true
demographic crisis, which is arriving now, while the Chinese transition is
still some time off. While China has a much less developed social security
system than the advanced countries, it has been rapidly expanding the population's access to government pensions, retirement savings plans, and
health insurance, at a rate that Nicholas Lardy, a Chinese expert at the Peterson Institute, calls "impressive." Coverage is still far narrower than it
will need to be, but the current government seems determined to continue
the programs' expansion. Pension amounts are quite small by advanced
country standards, but China does not yet have the per capita GDP to live
up to the norms of rich nations.[12]

Changes that evolve over forty years rarely warrant the term "crisis."
Population projections are perilous, of course, but even assuming they are
correct, China has ample time to prepare. If China manages to avoid a national breakdown, even if there is a marked slowdown for some time, the
country should still achieve advanced-country level of per capita income
by the 2030s or 2040 and should be well able to support decent lives for

**CHART 9.2 Old-Age Dependency Ratios, Selected Countries: 2010
and FC2050**

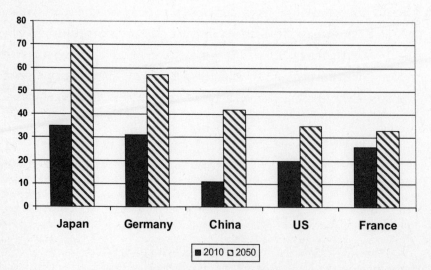

the aged. The Chinese will also have learned from watching how the Japanese and Germans deal with their elder booms. The Japanese in particular are seeking technological alternatives to intensive hands-on caretaking of the frail elderly. And if technology disappoints, all richer countries with large populations of dependent elderly will one way or the other increase their immigration rates.

The coming shift in the Chinese age structure, then, is likely to be a serious problem only if the country's economic progress is arrested to the extent that it fails to complete its transition to a wealthy country with a well-established, middle-income, working class. Unfortunately, China appears to be entering a dangerous stage of development fraught with risks to its continued economic success.

ECONOMIC DISTORTIONS

The Hu Jintao / Wen Jiabao government,[*] at least since 2007, has warned that Chinese economic growth has been "unsteady, imbalanced, uncoordinated, and unsustainable,"[13] implicitly accepting Western criticisms along much the same lines. There appears to be substantial agreement in principle on the part of the government, and among most Western economists, that over the last decade or so, China has tilted inordinately toward its manufacturing export-driven sectors at the sacrifice of building up the consumer and services sectors characteristic of countries making the middle-income transition. It should be noted, however, that loose credit policies in the United States, especially related to home equity lending during the housing bubble, played a big role in enabling the Chinese

---

* Hu Jintao is the "paramount leader," holding the posts of general secretary of the Communist Party, president of the People's Republic of China, and chairman of the Central Military Commission. Wen Jiabao is the premier of the State Council, which oversees the day-to-day operations of the government. The members of the Party Politburo and the State Council all come from a relatively small body of senior leaders, who make all important policy and personnel decisions. All important positions are filled by party members. At this writing, the Hu-Wen government will complete its second five-year term in office in 2013 and will cede its positions to a new team that has not yet been officially designated.

addiction to exports. (Between 2002 and 2007, America's current account deficit and volume of net home equity withdrawal each increased in parallel by more than $4 trillion.)

Regardless of blame, the Chinese macro numbers look seriously distorted. Investment accounts for more than half of all national spending, up from about a third in 2005. All East Asian "tiger" countries invested heavy shares of national spending in investment, but never more than about a third. (United States savings rates also rose to 30 percent in the second half of the nineteenth century.) Some economists defend the very high rate of investment on the grounds of the country's daunting infrastructure deficits. The relevant question, however, is not the scale of the infrastructure deficit but the practical limits on the number of mammoth projects a government can manage at one time. Evidence of shoddy construction and insufficient safety precautions on the new high-speed rail lines and the Three Gorges hydropower project are not reassuring.

A side effect of the investment surge is that it is yet another force repressing consumer spending. Consumption is still rising in real terms, but it has been shrinking as a percentage of GDP. Household consumption was only 34 percent of GDP in 2010, down from 50 percent in 2005, and "by far the lowest rate of any major economy in the world." The suppression of consumer spending has been accomplished primarily at the expense of services. Since expansion of services—health care services, legal services, financial services—is usually a reliable sign of a country making a successful middle-income transition, current policies may actually be retarding the economy's maturation.[14]

Patrick Chovanec, a business professor at Tsing Hua University in Beijing and a long-time China watcher, has become a leading voice in a growing chorus of analysts who are distinctly bearish on China's near-term economic future. Chovanec suggests that the country's response to the financial crash, while effective in the short term in maintaining employment, may have deepened the underlying problems. National banks vastly increased the supply of credit—by about 40 percent, Chovanec estimates—and much of it went into new urban apartment housing, vast swaths of which now stand empty.[15]

That may not be as bad as it sounds. Completed apartments in China typically contain few if any improvements like kitchen appliances, and there are no real estate taxes, so the cost of carrying vacant housing is lower than in most other countries. Private citizens have few opportunities to invest in appreciating capital assets, so the apartments may be intentionally held as a store of value. If real estate prices fall, however, which Chovanec thinks likely, the repercussions would be profound.

Chovanec's fear is that an accumulation of real estate that is not returning any income to the owners, along with the great expanse of hasty new, stimulus-related investments undertaken by deeply corrupt local governments, has created a giant layer of zombie assets. In a true market economy those conditions would trigger a financial crash similar to the recent experience with the popping of the asset bubble in the West. That is unlikely to happen in China. Instead the banks will probably roll over the loans, which are mostly now coming due. To the degree that the huge stimulus-related credit expansion was poured into such zombie assets—it's likely that most of it was—they will act as a long-term drag on the country's credit capacity and inhibit the required rebalancing between investing and consumption. Attempting to submerge the problem with another big credit expansion, Chovanec suggests, could ignite dangerous inflation. He suspects that official data on national debt and price inflation already seriously understate the true picture.[*16]

Whether or not the bearish views of China's near-term outlook are correct, the economy continues to be seriously unbalanced, even as it faces a potentially disabling crisis in water supply, serious environmental degradation, and possibly a major real estate bubble. And those challenges loom as the nation is trying to make the difficult transition from a premodern society to a modern economy grounded in a successful middle class. Given

---

* Chovanec worries that the government can manipulate inflation data by managing prices on goods tracked in the official consumer market basket. Impressionistically, the prices he sees every day in Beijing are rising by double-digits, but taxi fares, which are in the basket, have been held flat, causing a visible diminution of taxi service. Other data, based on physical movement of goods and the like, suggest that important sectors of the economy are contracting, even though reported growth continues to be strong.

the extreme centralization of formal power, the critical question is whether the government is up to the challenge.

Can China Cope?

In the spring of 2012, Chinese politics were roiled by the sudden scandal of Bo Xilai and his family. Bo had been an up-and-comer, a charismatic outsider who had been forcing himself into consideration for a seat on the Party Politburo. As party chief of Chongqing and previously as mayor of Dalian, he mounted vigorous anticorruption campaigns and won favor among the masses by adopting redistributionist policies out of the Maoist playbook. Bo's career crashed when a top lieutenant, the Chongqing police chief Wang Lijun, asked for asylum in the American consulate in the nearby city of Chengdu. He believed that his life was in danger because he had uncovered the possible involvement of Bo and his wife in the murder of an English businessman, who had served as a family retainer and fixer.

That triggered a flood of noxious revelations. The famous corruption crackdowns may actually have been a wholesale looting of local businessmen, abetted by torture, arbitrary imprisonment, and other atrocities. Bo receives only a modest salary, but a large number of close relatives, including his wife, are hundred-millionaires, while his son leads the high life at Western universities. For the time being at least, Bo has disappeared.

Those stories, while not proven, are consistent with allegations surrounding a peasant uprising a few months before in Wukan, a fishing village in Guangdong Province. The villagers barricaded the roads and faced down the police and local village and party leaders, alleging that officials had been selling the peasants' common land and fishing rights, impoverishing the people and keeping the sales proceeds for themselves. Premier Wen himself criticized the local leadership, and China's State Council has admitted that in 2011, some 700,000 hectares were transferred illegally.

There are as many opinions about the current path and future prospects of China as there are Western scholars. China's system of producing leaders, murky though it is, has a record of producing a number of outstanding men—well educated and well informed, quite capable of holding their own in international settings.

But there is still widespread concern that the government is too remote, too corrupt, too riven with infighting to govern effectively. For example, despite the Hu-Wen rhetorical commitment to more balanced growth, the crucial macro steps, like readjusting the relative shares of investment and consumption, may have been blocked by the industrial barons and their representatives on the Politburo and State Council. The monolithic character of the party machine, moreover, is likely to forestall significant change. Regardless of shifts in policies at the center, anything far-reaching must be accomplished through the local officialdom. All local officials have been trained for decades in a uniform way of doing business: Build! Grow! Never miss your numbers! Helping to implement a shift to a more market-driven economy, stepping away from financing decisions, no longer picking local favorites, and becoming merely neutral regulators may be beyond their capacities and likely contrary to their financial interests.

The looting and rapaciousness disclosed by the Bo episode, moreover, may not be especially unusual. High position in the party is a royal road to riches. The big Hollywood studio DreamWorks Animation recently opened a major studio in China. Its partner in the deal is Jiang Mainheng, who is the son of the former Communist Party leader Jiang Zemin. The younger Jiang has also been awarded serendipitous partnerships in joint ventures with Microsoft and Nokia. Big business in China involves a lot of palm-greasing with the relatives and retainers of politicians. A financial executive suggested that the way to get along with the leadership was to "just make them part of your deal; it's perfectly legal."

So Hu Haifeng, the son of President Hu Jintao, heads a conglomeration of technical firms spun out of Tsing Hua University, benefiting from a string of government contracts. Wen Jiabao's son, Wen Yunsong, is CEO of Unihub Global Networks, a large Chinese networking company and a partner in a Chinese private equity firm that frequently works with Western investors. The son and daughter of former premier Li Peng chair, respectively, China's largest power company and an electricity monopoly, while Levin Zhu, son of former prime minister Zhu Rongji, has long run one of China's biggest investment banks. Any important capital raise for a Chinese company in the West will nearly always have relatives of the leadership involved in the deal. Ninety-one percent of the country's multi-millionaires, according to the Chinese Academy of Social Sciences, are the children of party influentials. Victor Shih, a China expert at Northwestern University, has said, "There are actually a lot of princelings out there. You've got the children of current officials, the children of previous officials, the children of local officials, central officials, military officials, police officials. We're talking about hundreds of thousands of people out there—all trying to use their connections to make money." An inheritance-based economic nobility coupled with the depredations of local party officials, as in Wukan, reminds one of prerevolutionary France.[17]

The world has an enormous stake in China's successfully completing its transition to a modernized, middle-class-based country with per capita incomes and opportunity structures in the same range as other advanced countries. America has no stake in China staying poor, and the sooner it reaches true advanced-country status, the better for all of us, despite the fact that its total GDP will inevitably be greater than America's.

The next decade is likely to be a crucial one in Chinese history, for it may determine how well they can make the transition and how long it will take. The consequences of their failing could be terrible. A successful transition does not necessarily mean that the Chinese have to evolve governing structures on the pattern of Western-style liberal democracies. Francis Fukuyama, in his recent study of the evolution of modern governments, suggests that governing forms are inherently contingent. The possibility of a new type of polity "with Chinese characteristics," in the party's phrasing, should not be ruled out. Whatever it is, Fukuyama speculates, it will have to retain some form of effective accountability of the government to the governed—which is the major advantage of democratic forms, however clumsy and slowly reacting they may be.

This brings us back to America. Perhaps the greatest advantage it had in the early days of its rise as an economic power was that it was born as a middle-class country, settled primarily by people looking to better their lives and achieve economic independence, delighted to be freed from the encrusted ways of the countries and fellow-citizens they had left behind. In effect, the country never had to accomplish the middle-income transition because most of the first generations of immigrants had already made it simply by choosing to come—and once they got here, there were no important entrenched interests to stand in their way.

No large country with a deeply controlling, top-down government has ever successfully accomplished a middle-income transition. The struggles of Russia, with its vast natural resources, its world-class kleptocracy, and the quiet wars between the new industrial oligarchs and the *siloviki*—the Putin-linked Party stalwarts—are similar to the struggles in China, with the difference being that the Chinese have a much more entrepreneurial society. The recent history of China suggests that when the government makes mistakes, they tend to be doozies. It hadn't been that long since the Maoist Cultural Revolution. It will likely take at least another decade or so to see whether China can accomplish the national transition to a true middle-income society. The rest of the world can only hold its breath.

APPENDIX

========

Did Eli Whitney Invent the Cotton Gin?

ANGELA LAKWETE IS AN AUBURN UNIVERSITY HISTORIAN WHO HAS devoted a career to the antebellum cotton industry. In a recent book, she argues that Whitney's gin was of only minor importance in generating the explosive growth of the King Cotton plantation culture in the South; for as she concludes, "ginning was not a bottleneck as the nineteenth century dawned."[1] But although she never makes the specific charge, Lakwete also lays out an impressive prima facie case that, rather than invent the new gin, Whitney and Phineas Miller, his cotton gin partner, stole a gin design and patented it as their own. I've added a few details that, looked at anew, seem to strengthen the case.

The Whitney Cotton Gin Revisited

There is no question that Whitney was a talented craftsman. Although many stories of his youthful inventing prowess are probably apocryphal, he was blacksmithing by his early teens and was a skilled metalworker.

When Whitney secured his tutorship in South Carolina in 1792, he traveled south with Miller. They were close in age, though Miller had graduated from Yale seven years before. Miller had gone to Georgia as the tutor of the children of Gen. Nathanael and Catherine Greene, who lived on a rice plantation. When the general suddenly died, Miller took over as overseer of the plantation. Miller invited Whitney to stay at the plantation for a few weeks in October, before taking up his tutoring position in November. Whitney was utterly infatuated with Greene.[2] (But so apparently was Miller: he and Greene married in 1796, with George Washington and his wife as witnesses.)

Nothing further is heard from Whitney until April 1793, when he reported to a friend, Josiah Stebbins, that he had not taken up his tutoring position, had never left the plantation, and had no prospects and no money. A letter to his father on the same day told the same sad tale, adding apologies for his debts. Just a few weeks later, however, on May 1, Whitney wrote another letter to Stebbins announcing that "Dame Fortune" had made him "very expert in the Hocus-Pocus line," and that he expected shortly to have plenty of money.[3]

That sets the stage for Lakwete's case. The new gin, to begin with, is a "technical marvel," a radical rethinking of current gin technology. Each element of it—an iron-toothed wooden rolling cylinder, a grated breastwork to filter seeds, a breastwork cleaner, and a seed hopper—had to be of a precise design, precisely aligned. That is impressive, for cotton processing was a strongly empirical craft. Gins had evolved over many years, with improvements typically coming from people deeply involved in the industry. Yet by Whitney's account, he had by chance heard men speaking of ginning problems "and struck out a plan of a Machine in my mind." Once conceived, it took him only "about ten Days" to build a model.[4]

Lakwete underscores the role of the breastwork in the Whitney gin. Its thickness matched the average length of a cotton fiber, and the spacing of the grate and teeth was designed to block most cotton seeds. "There is no precedent for that anywhere," she writes, "including any carding machines anywhere at any time."[5] In operation, the cylinder rotated the teeth through the grates in the breastwork, pulling seeded cotton from the hopper, as the seeds fell from the grate. A rapidly revolving cleaner on the other side of the breastwork helped pull through the now-seedless cotton and freed it from the wire teeth. In a letter to his father in September 1793, Whitney said that after quickly building his first model, he had spent the rest of the previous winter "perfecting the Machine," completing a working version "that required the labor of one man to turn it."[6]

Greene knew Thomas Jefferson, who as secretary of state held the patent portfolio. Miller wrote him on May 27, recommending Whitney and his new machine, which Whitney had devised "without tools or workmen." A few days later, he urged Whitney, who had gone back to New Haven, to expedite the patent application, for there were "two other claimants for the honor of the invention of cotton gins, in addition to those we knew before." Whitney delivered the patent petition on June 20 and followed with detailed specifications and drawings in mid-October.[7] To complete the filing, he still had to provide a working model of the new gin,* which took him another six months, apparently because of difficulties in fixing the shaped wire teeth in the wooden cylinder. But it was finally delivered in March 1794, and Jefferson issued the patent, retroactive to the previous November, when he had received the drawings and descriptions.

Without waiting for an accepted filing, Miller launched a preemptive business strategy. The plan was to create ginning mills throughout the cotton areas, charging 40 percent of the cotton ginned, while at the same time fighting off any competitive gins with litigation. The struggle that ensued would be tedious to recount. Suffice it to say that the Miller-Whitney strategy prompted a wave of competitive gins, some of which were patented, and litigation dragged on for years. Whether Whitney ever made any money out of it isn't clear. The venture appears to have been funded almost entirely by the Greene estate, which was financially troubled to begin with. Miller died suddenly in 1803.

---

* The patent system then in effect required a petition with a short description, separate detailed descriptions and drawings, and a model if the secretary required it, which Jefferson did in this case. The secretary did not "approve" patents: he officially accepted completed filings to give notice to other inventors. A filing conferred fourteen years' exclusive production and use subject to challenges in courts.

The most formidable competitive gins, some of which were also patented, substituted fine-toothed circular metal saw blades on a shaft for the toothed wooden cylinder—a lighter, easier-to-build solution. The "saw gins," as they were called, spread rapidly, forcing Miller to shift his patent strategy to include the saw gin, on the grounds that it was indistinguishable from Whitney's wire-toothed version and—what was crucial under then-current law—that it was part of Whitney's original conception, simply one of several approaches he had always considered as interchangeable.

To back up that story, Miller asked Whitney to depose his friends on "the subject of ratchet wheels." Whitney duly asked Stebbins to write a statement that said: "Whitney repeatedly told me that he had originally contemplated making a whole row of teeth from one plate or piece of metal."[8] Stebbins never furnished such a statement, although Whitney and Miller stoutly maintained that position. (Another friend, Elizur Goodrich, a congressman, Whitney's adviser, and an investor in Whitney's later enterprises, did testify in support of their claim.) Whitney's version in the court was that, while building his first model, "not being able to procure sheet iron or sheets of tined plates"[9] on the plantation, he fell back on using wire teeth emplaced in wood.

The Case Against Whitney

The various Miller-Whitney accounts are riddled with inconsistencies. To begin with, it is hardly credible that Whitney, with no experience in the cotton industry, more or less immediately conceived such a complex solution upon a chance overhearing of a conversation. The claim that he quickly built a pilot model—including the iron breastwork with its long row of precisely aligned, smaller-than-a-cotton-seed grating slits—also stretches credulity, the more so when compounded with Miller's statement that he did it without "tools or workmen." Further, if Whitney had really spent the winter of 1792–1793 "perfecting" a working model of his gin, as he told his father, it is hard to explain why he didn't simply ship it to Jefferson's office. And if the saw gin had been Whitney's first choice all along, as he claimed, it's even harder to explain why he struggled to make the wire-toothed solution when he was under time pressure to deliver a model and even later, through the first several years of the business.

The wire-toothed cylinder was a simple component but a fussy manufacturing challenge. The original Whitney patent material was lost in the Patent Office fire of 1836, but an 1803 copy of Whitney's description, certified by James Madison, then secretary of state, was later recovered by the Whitney family and is available at the patent office. It does not specify the number of teeth but recommends that the wooden cylinder be from two to five feet long and from six to nine inches in diameter; that the spaces between the rows of teeth "ought not to be less than seven sixteenths of an inch," and that the spaces "between the teeth in the same row must be so small as not to admit a seed or a half seed; they ought not to exceed one twelfth of an inch, and I think about one sixteenth of an inch the best."[10] The patent drawings suggest fifty-two teeth, which would be about a third of an inch apart on a six-inch diameter cylinder. Even at that number, with half-inch spacing, a two-foot long cylinder would still have nearly 2,500 teeth. The drawing shown in Figure A.1, which the patent office argues is an original one, has fifty-two teeth per row but apparently a very large number of rows. (See images 1 and 6 in Figure A.1.)[*][11]

Such a device could only be fashioned by hand. The placement of the rows on the cylinder and the gratings on the breastwork had to be a precise

---

* After the fire, the Patent Office solicited families and other sources for old records to reconstruct lost filings. The family provided Whitney's written specifications but not drawings. The drawing shown in Figure A.1 is a copy of drawings, certified as accurate in 1804, which were found in the records of one of the cotton-gin patent cases. The Patent Office later made a model of the Whitney gin and apparently made drawings from that, which are now bundled with the original specifications. A 1960 article by a senior patent official confirms that the patent office commissioned a model of the Whitney gin in 1845, and that the drawings now on file "are merely drawings of the cotton gin made in 1845" and include "the addition of some figures . . . showing alternative forms of teeth." But it adds, "Whitney is known to have made a model showing three different forms of teeth." The original description, on the other hand, nowhere mentions other forms of teeth. Instead of clearing up the record, therefore, the Patent Office may have merely made it conform to the legend.

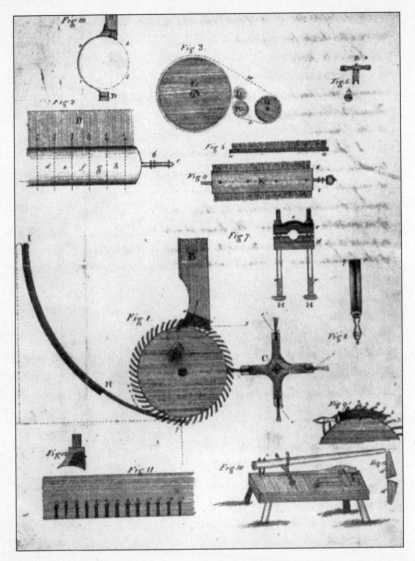

Figure A.1., the Patent Drawings for Whitney Gin. This drawing was found in the records of a Savannah lawsuit, one of the many that ensued after Whitney's patent was filed. It bore the certificate of James Madison, dated 1804, and was published in a 1960 article by a senior patent official, along with evidence for its accuracy and originality.

match, and all the teeth in each row had to be so aligned that they could rotate at speed through the grating. (I assume Whitney used a stencil to place the teeth.) Then the teeth had to be properly bent and sharpened to engage the cotton. In the patent description Whitney described how he drew out the wire to strengthen it, cut it into approximately one-inch lengths, and used a tool and a gauge to shape each one. He then flattened one end of each and drove them into the cylinder with "a light hammer" before trimming them to the right length with "a pair of cutting pliers." The cylinder was then "secured in a lathe" and the teeth filed to "a kind of angular point" and finished off with a polishing file.[12] A major problem, Whitney told Stebbins, was that placing so many teeth split the cylinder, until he finally figured out a way to place them across the grain.

The saw gin was much simpler to make. Manufacturers could first cut out the separate blades, cut in the teeth, place them on a shaft, and use spacers to align each blade with the breastwork slits. Whitney was known as a skilled metalworker, and New Haven was a metalworking center. If metal saw blades were truly his first choice of construction, it made little sense to stick so stubbornly with the wooden cylinder and wire teeth.

Connect all those dots: The sudden shift in Whitney's self-assessment of his prospects in the second half of April 1792. The urgency to perfect the patent before other multiplying potential claimants, including "those we knew before." The inconsistencies between the tales of where and how easily the plantation model was built and Whitney's labors to construct one in New Haven. The glibness with which the two appropriated the saw gin, and the blatant appeal to Stebbins. Any one of them might easily be explained away, but taken together, they raise a dark suspicion that Miller and Whitney, for all their talents, were dishonest young men on the make, trying to profit from a claim-jumping patent.

The ensuing years of litigation blighted Whitney's life, although Catherine Greene suffered the most financially.*[13] At the very least, however, the episode suggests the need for cautious skepticism in evaluating controversial episodes in Whitney's later career.

---

* Miller wrote Whitney in 1797 that "We"—presumably referring to the gin business—"have been literally bankrupts for one year past—and I have been reduced to the cruel and mortifying necessity of appropriating the Property of the Estate to prevent this Bankruptcy from becoming public—In consequence of which a Plantation belonging to the Estate of Gen. Greene of Carolina will this spring be sold for half its value." Whitney in the meanwhile was complaining to Stebbins that Miller was skimming too much money, and there is a later very bitter letter from Miller to Whitney.

IMAGE SOURCES, CREDITS, AND PERMISSIONS

Page 33 HMS *St. Lawrence*, with permission of the Royal Ontario Museum © ROM.

Page 43 Newcomen's Pumping Engine, Science Museum / Science & Society Picture Library / All rights reserved.

Page 66 The Babbage Difference Engine No. 2, Science Museum / Science & Society Picture Library / All rights reserved.

Page 77 Erie Canal, from the Collections of the New York City Public Library.

Page 101 Lowell Canals, courtesy of the Library of Congress: Historic American Engineering Record.

Page 105 Robbins & Lawrence Waterworks, courtesy of the Library of Congress: Historic American Engineering Record.

Page 129 Simeon North, from the Collections of the New York City Public Library.

Page 170 Frances Trollope, National Portrait Gallery, London.

Page 185 Camp Meeting, from Frances M. Trollope, *Domestic Manners of the Americans*, 1832.

Page 187 DeWitt Clinton Locomotive, courtesy of the Library of Congress.

Page 225 Baldwin Shop, courtesy, Pictorial Collections, Hagley Museum and Library.

Page 235 Hoe Printer, from Robert Hoe, *A Short History of the Printing Press*, 1902.

Page 238 Crystal Palace, Science Museum / Science & Society Picture Library / All rights reserved.

Page 264 Scholes Typewriter, courtesy, Milwaukee Public Museum, Carl P. Dietz Typewriter Collection.

Page 278 90-Ton Ingot, courtesy, University of Pittsburgh, William J. Gaughan Collection.

Page 283 Eastman Johnson portrait of John D. Rockefeller, courtesy of the Rockefeller Archive Center.

ACKNOWLEDGMENTS

As the book's dedication suggests, I owe a large debt to Bob Gordon and Carolyn Cooper for their willingness to take questions, suggest sources, act as sounding boards, even read and criticize lengthy drafts. Bob, a former chairman of the Yale metallurgy department, knows everything about iron and steel and is a founding father of industrial archaeology. Carolyn, who is also at Yale, is the go-to authority on nineteenth-century American woodworking and an expert on Thomas Blanchard. I imposed myself on Carolyn when I was working at the Whitney archive at Yale. She was helpful and introduced me to Bob to clear up some metallurgical point. I sent each of them additional questions from time to time, at first cautiously and infrequently, but since they always responded so generously, I was soon quite unconscionable in my impositions.

I've always been impressed with the willingness of academics, even the most senior, to take over-the-transom questions from outsiders. Scholars and curators who have been helpful in ways great and small include, in no particular order, Winifred Rothenberg, Patrick Malone, Richard Barbuto, Angela Lakwete, Barbara Tucker, T. J. Stiles, Stanley Engerman, Mark Hilliard, Don Hoke, Liz Economy, Matt Pottinger, Jack Brown, Richard Colton, Bill Brown, Quintin Colville, and Doron Swade. Gary Beam, a former tall-ship sailor, helped me on naval matters, while Steve Bookout and Tim Crowe taught me enough to evoke my sincere admiration for their nearly-lost craft. Needless to say, neither Bob nor Carolyn, nor any other of the good people I imposed on, bears any responsibility for the errors and deficiencies in the final product.

Friends who read and commented on all part of versions of the manuscript include Gordon MacInnes, Jon Weiner, Chris Reid, and Charles Ferguson. And although I don't have their names, archival staff at Yale, Princeton, University of Pennsylvania, the Connecticut State Library, the Connecticut Historical Society, the National Park Services archives at Waltham and at the Library of Congress, and the Public Library of Scoville, Connecticut, always took an interest in what I was doing and were helpful in guiding me to sources. The MaRLI Scholars program at the New York Public Library gave me more convenient access to that institution's great collections, plus full access to the libraries of Columbia University and New York University. It is an experimental program, one I hope is made permanent.

A special pleasure of this book was working with my daughter-in-law, Jenn Morris, who interrupted her burgeoning artistic career to execute the illustrations for this book. A bonus was that she has a better mechanical eye than I do and saved me from a number of errors.

I have long been spoiled by the people at PublicAffairs, so thanks yet again to Peter Osnos, Susan Weinberg, Clive Priddle, and especially Melissa Raymond, who does the dirty work to ensure a book really happens. Beth Wright of Trio Bookworks was a careful and considerate copy editor.

And finally, but never least, a special thanks to my wife, Beverly, who has the best nose for pretentious jargon of anyone in my acquaintance.

NOTES

CHAPTER ONE

1. Robert Gardiner, ed., *The Line of Battle: The Sailing Warship, 1650–1840* (London: Conway, 1992); and Brian Lavery, *Nelson's Navy, The Ships, Men, and Organization, 1793–1815* (Annapolis, MD: Naval Institute Press, 1995), 245ff. My thanks to Quintin Colville of London's National Maritime Museum for confirming the count of active British first-raters in 1815. (They were the *Caledonia*, the *Ville de Paris*, the *Hibernia*, the *Impregnable*, the *Ocean*, and the newly launched *Nelson*.)

2. Henry Adams, *History of the United States during the Administrations of Thomas Jefferson and James Madison (1801–1817)* (New York: Library of America, 1986), 2:447–448. For the chronology of the war, I used, among others, Jon Latimer, *1812: War with America* (Cambridge, MA: Harvard University Press, 2007), an English account; Theodore Roosevelt, *The Naval War of 1812* (New York: Modern Library, 1999); Richard V. Barbuto, *Niagara 1814: America Invades Canada* (Lawrence: University of Kansas Press, 2000); Robert Malcolmson, *Lords of the Lake: The Naval War on Lake Ontario, 1812–1814* (Annapolis, MD: Naval Institute Press, 1998); Robert Gardiner, ed., *The Naval War of 1812* (London: Chatham, 1998); and for a crisp summary, Gordon Wood, *Empire of Liberty: A History of the Early Republic* (New York: Oxford University Press, 2009), Chapter 18. The Naval Historical Center also published a splendid documentary history of the naval war, William S. Dudley, ed., *The Naval War of 1812: A Documentary History*, 2 vols. (Washington, DC: Naval Historical Center, 1985), and Michael J. Crawford, ed., *The Naval War of 1812: A Documentary History*, vol. 3 (Washington, DC: Naval Historical Center, 2002). Henry Adams's classic history of the era, now back in print in two unabridged volumes, devotes nearly a fourth of its length to the war. Although Adams's history is a splendid read, it cannot be taken as a reliable account. Details are often incorrect, and it has, not unfairly, been criticized as Federalist history. See, e.g., Irving Brant, "Madison and the War of 1812," *Virginia Magazine of History and Biography* 74, no. 1 (January 1966): 51–67.

3. Latimer, *1812*, 32, 17, 407 (for 1835 invasion plan).

4. Dumas Malone, *Jefferson the President: Second Term, 1805–1809* (Boston: Little, Brown, 1974), 415–416; Adams, *History*, 2:1051 (*Times* quote); Wood, *Empire of Liberty*, 697–699, makes the case for the war as a confirmation of American sovereignty.

5. *Niles Weekly Register*, September 5, 1812, 5 (Connecticut); October 24, 1812, 116 (Massachusetts).

6. Geoffrey M. Footner, *Tidewater Triumph: The Development and Worldwide Success of the Chesapeake Bay Pilot Schooner* (Mystic, CT: Mystic Seaport Museum, 1998) 101–109.

7. Latimer, *1812*, 111.

8. Sinclair to Jones, September 3, 1814, in Crawford, ed., *The Naval War of 1812*, 3:574.

9. Hamilton to Chauncey, August 31, 1812, in Dudley, ed., *The Naval War of 1812*, 1:297; emphasis in original.

10. The most thorough account of the Chambers gun is William Gilkerson, *Boarders Away II: Firearms in the Age of Fighting Sail* (Woonsocket, RI: Andrew Mowbray, 1993), 123–139. Owen to Yeo, July 17, 1814, in Crawford, ed., *Naval War of 1812*, 3:536. Gilkerson presents the evidence, which he calls circumstantial, for the presence of Chambers guns on Lake Ontario, but the Naval Institute (Crawford, ed., *Naval War of 1812*, 3:537) takes it as settled. The rapid firing was transmitted from barrel to barrel by a cloth "roman-candle" fuse, ignited by the initial firing with the single lock.

11. Stoddard to Wadsworth, January 14, 1813, in Office of the Commander of Ordnance, *Correspondence*, National Archives, Washington, DC (hereafter OCO).

12. Barclay to Yeo, September 1, 1813, in Dudley, ed., *Naval War of 1812*, 2:551; emphasis in original.

13. For the ships on Ontario, I use the data assembled in the Appendices in Malcolmson, *Lords of the Lake*, 327–342. For Huron and Erie, I rely primarily on Roosevelt, *Naval War of 1812*.

14. Malcolmson, *Lords of the Lake*, 54.

15. Stoddard to Wadsworth, January 23, 1813, OCO.

16. Lavery, *Nelson's Navy*, 172.

17. Roosevelt, *Naval War of 1812*, 126.

18. Malcolmson, *Lords of the Lake*, 174.

19. Ibid., 169–170.

20. Roosevelt, *Naval War of 1812*, 136.

21. Malcolmson, *Lords of the Lake*, 194.

22. Ibid., 203.

23. Roosevelt, *Naval War of 1812*, 138. Roosevelt, however, faults Chauncey for not following all the way into Burlington Bay, because he "was afraid that the wind would come up to blow a gale" (139). But as Malcolmson makes clear, the gale was already raging during the chase, which is why it was so fast. Chauncey properly feared getting driven onto a lee shore where a large British army detachment was in camp. His squadron had an exhausting passage beating out of the bay against the storm and several times had to rescue one or the other of the lakers.

24. Latimer, *1812*, 194.

25. Barclay to Yeo, September 12, 1813, in Dudley, ed., *Naval War of 1812*, 2:556; Inglis to Barclay, September 10, 1813, in Dudley, ed., *Naval War of 1812*, 2: 554–555.

26. Latimer, *1812*, 184.

27. See, for instance, Ralph J. Roske and Richard W. Donley, "The Perry-Elliot Controversy: A Bitter Footnote to the Battle of Lake Erie," *Northwest Ohio Quarterly* 34, no. 3 (Summer 1962): 111–123, and Lawrence J. Friedman and David Curtis Skaggs, "Jesse Duncan Elliott and the Battle of Lake Erie: The Issue of Mental Stability," *Journal of the Early Republic* 10, no. 4 (Winter 1990): 493–516. An older source that presents Elliott's side of the story is Charles J. Peterson, *American Navy: Being an Authentic History of the United States Navy and Biographical Sketches of American Naval Heroes* (Philadelphia: James B. Smith, 1860), 401–417. Roosevelt, *Naval War of 1812*, 147.

28. Adams, 2:1186.

29. Jones to Chauncey, January 15, 1814, in Crawford, ed., *Naval War of 1812*, 3:386.

30. Robinson to Prevost, April 6, 1814, in Crawford, ed., *Naval War of 1812*, 3:413–415; Yeo to Prevost, April 22, 1814, in Crawford, ed., *Naval War of 1812*, 3:416–417; Yeo to Cochrane, May 26, 1814, in Crawford, ed., *Naval War of 1812*, 3:492.

31. Malcolmson, *Lords of the Lake*, 243.

32. Crawford, *Naval War of 1812*, 3:468–469.

33. For more information about the first footnote on page 28, see Malcolmson, *Lords of the Lake, 259.*

34. For more information about the second footnote on page 28, see Latimer, *1812*, 179.

35. Brown to Chauncey, August 10, 1814, in Crawford, ed., *Naval War of 1812*, 3:584–585; Chauncey to Brown, September 14, 1814, in Crawford, ed., *Naval War of 1812*, 3:587–588; Prevost to Drummond, September 16, 1814, in Crawford, ed., *Naval War of 1812*, 3:614; Prevost to Bathurst, October 18, 1814, in Crawford, ed., *Naval War of 1812*, 3:628.

36. Wellington, quoted in Adams, *History*, 2:988.

37. Report of Lt. Robinson RN, September 12, 1814, in Crawford, ed., *Naval War of 1812*, 3:613.

38. Latimer, *1812*, 232.

39. MacDonell to Beckwith, February 4, 1815, in Crawford, ed., *Naval War of 1812*, 3:688–689.

40. O'Conor to Melville, December 19, 1814, in Crawford, ed., *Naval War of 1812*, 3:672.

41. Prevost to Bathurst, October 18, 1814, in Crawford, ed., *Naval War of 1812*, 3:628.

42. Jones to Madison, October 26, 1814, in Crawford, ed., *Naval War of 1812*, 3:631–632.

43. Chauncey to Jones, October 12, 1814, in Crawford, ed., *Naval War of 1812*, 3:622.

44. Eckford and Browns to Chauncey, February 10, 1815, in Crawford, ed., *Naval War of 1812*, 3:690.

CHAPTER TWO

1. Rory Muir, *Britain and the Defeat of Napoleon, 1807–1815* (New Haven, CT: Yale University Press, 1996), 365; Niall Ferguson, *The House of Rothschild*, vol. 1: *Money's Prophets, 1798–1848* (New York: Viking Penguin, 1998), 96–98.

2. Cited in Ferguson, *House of Rothschild*, 111.

3. Joel Mokyr, *The Enlightened Economy: An Economic History of Great Britain, 1700–1850* (New Haven, CT: Yale University Press, 2009), 257–260, has a good discussion of the issues; the quote is on 258.

4. Adam Smith, *Wealth of Nations* (Amherst, NY: Prometheus Books, 1991), 9–10.

5. Robert C. Allen, *The British Industrial Revolution in Global Perspective* (New York: Cambridge University Press, 2009), 146–147. The factor-price theory (high wages, cheap energy) as the spur to the British industrial revolution is from Allen.

6. See ibid., 14–22.

7. The brief summary here follows ibid., 182–212.

8. The classic account is H. W. Dickinson, *A Short History of the Steam Engine* (Cambridge, UK: The University Press, 1939), 29–51, 66–89.

9. Allen, *British Industrial Revolution*, 217–293; H. R. Schubert, "Iron and Steel," in *A History of Technology*, vol. 4: *The Industrial Revolution, c.1750–c.1850*, Charles Singer et al., eds. (Oxford: Clarendon Press, 1958), 99–118, quote at 102.

10. K. C. Barraclough, *Steelmaking Before Bessemer*, vol. 2: *Crucible Steel* (London: The Metals Society, 1984), 102.

11. David S. Landes, *The Wealth and Poverty of Nations* (New York: Norton, 1998), 215–220.

12. N. A. M. Rodger, *Command of the Sea: A Naval History of Britain, 1649–1815* (New York: W. W. Norton, 2005), 172.

13. Dava Sobel, *Longitude: The True Story of a Lone Genius Who Solved the Greatest Scientific Mystery of His Time* (New York: Penguin Books, 1995); David S. Landes, *Revolution in Time* (Cambridge, MA: Harvard University Press, 1983), 145–170.

14. K. R. Gilbert, "Machine-Tools," in Singer, ed., *The Industrial Revolution*, 417–441; K. R. Gilbert, *Henry Maudslay: Machine Builder* (London: Science Museum, 1971); Joseph Wickham Roe, *English and American Tool Builders* (New Haven, CT: Yale University Press, 1916), 33–49.

15. Maurice Damaus, "Precision Mechanics," in Singer, ed., *The Industrial Revolution*, 379–416, quote at 414.

16. Gilbert, *Henry Maudslay*, 4.

17. James Nasmyth, *An Autobiography*, Samuel Smiles, ed. (London: John Murray, 1883), 148–149.

18. T. M. Goodeve and C. P. B. Shelley, *The Whitworth Measuring Machine* (London: Longman, Green, 1877), 16, 18.

19. Nasmyth, *Autobiography*, 270.

20. Sir Joseph Whitworth, *Miscellaneous Papers on Mechanical Subjects: Guns and Steel* (London: Longmans, Green, Readers & Dyer, 1873), 24. The military similarly rejected his fluid compressed steel, a very compact, nearly flawless steel (it was compressed under high pressure for some hours after it flowed from the converter) that was later adopted by Bethlehem Steel, the largest American heavy ordnance maker. (William Kent, *The Mechanical Engineers' Pocket-Book*, 6th ed. [New York: John Wiley & Sons, 1903], 410.) The Whitworth rifle was much favored by Confederate snipers during the Civil War. (Union sniper rifles were as accurate but weighed twenty to thirty pounds, compared to the nine-pound Whitworth rifle.) Although the British did eventually adopt the Whitworth bore size, some features of the original design that made it so accurate—like the hexagonal barrel with a larger number of rifling twists—made it prone to fouling with black powder ammunition. Accuracy was in any case not a great advantage with standard volley-firing infantry tactics. A British Civil War buffs' organization (www.americancivilwar.org.uk/index.php) has many details on the sales and use of the Whitworth rifle during the Civil War.

21. The account here including the Whitworth solution is drawn primarily from Goodeve and Shelley, *The Whitworth Measuring Machine*.

22. *Monthly Notices of the Royal Astronomical Society* 13, no. 1 (1852): 123–125, quote at 124.

23. Ibid., 124.

24. Doron Swade, *The Difference Engine: Charles Babbage and the Quest to Build the First Computer* (New York: Viking, 2001), is the best modern account of Babbage and his calculating engines.

25. Charles Babbage, *Passages from the Life of a Philosopher* (London: Longman, Green, Longman, Roberts & Green, 1864), 68–96, is his own account of the struggle over funding. Not all the dates agree with Swade's, which I take to be the definitive account.

26. Roe, *English and American Tool Builders*, chapter titled "Inventors of the Planer," quotes from 52, 59.

27. Babbage, *Passages*. The disputed phrase quoted in the footnote is on 71.

28. The description of number two and the rejection note are from Swade, *Difference Engine*, 173–176.

29. Ibid., 117–119.

30. Ibid., 121.

31. Charles Babbage, "On the Method of Expressing by Signs the Action of Machinery," *Philosophic Transactions of the Royal Society*, vol. 2, 1826, reprinted in *Charles Babbage and His Calculating Machines*, Philip Morrison and Emily Morrison, eds. (New York: Dover, 1961), 346–354, quote at 351, plates at 380–384.

32. Swade, personal communication.

33. Babbage, *Passages*, 452.

34. The account here is from Swade, "A Modern Sequel," Part 3 in *Difference Engine*.

35. Swade, *Difference Engine*, 292.

36. Ibid., 305. Note that Swade and his team did not attempt to make Babbage's printer, which was of the same size and complexity of the DE2 itself.

37. Ibid., 201.

38. Charles Babbage, *On the Economy of Machinery and Manufacturing* (London: John Murray, 1846).

39. Joseph Bizup, *Manufacturing Culture: Vindications of Early Victorian Industry* (Charlottesville: University of Virginia Press, 2003), 8.

40. Ibid., 150.

41. The most detailed available history and analyses are Carolyn C. Cooper, "The Portsmouth System of Manufacture," *Technology and Culture* 25, no. 2 (April 1984): 182–225, and Carolyn C. Cooper, "The Production Line at Portsmouth Block Mill," *Industrial Archaeology Review* 6, no. 1 (Winter 1981–1982): 28–44. See also Richard Beamish, *Memoir of the Life of Marc Isambard Brunel* (London: Longman, Green, Longman, Roberts & Green, 1862); Roe, *English and American Tool Masters*, esp. the chapter "Bentham and Brunel," 22–31; Simon Sebag Montefiore, "The Bentham Brothers: Their Adventure in Russia," *History Today* (July 2003), a UK-based web-based journal; and Gilbert, *Henry Maudslay*.

42. Gilbert, *Henry Maudslay*, 18.

43. Cooper, "Portsmouth System," 198.

44. Ibid., 206.

45. See, for example, Alfred Chandler, *Strategy and Structure: Chapters in the History of Industrial Enterprise* (Cambridge, MA: MIT Press, 1962), 284, where Chandler dismisses the importance of manufacturing issues, on the grounds that managers "had plenty of information to go on" from the "scientific management" movement of the 1920s. For a withering indictment, see Robert H. Hayes and William J. Abernathy, "Managing Our Way to Economic Decline," *Harvard Business Review* (July–August 1980): 67–77. Nevertheless, Hayes and Abernathy, both Harvard Business School professors, assiduously avoid mentioning the leading contribution of their own institution, or of their own previous writings, to the debacle they deplore.

CHAPTER THREE

1. *Niles Weekly Register*, October 29, 1825, 128; November 12, 1825, 173–174.

2. *Sydney Smith, The Works of the Rev. Sydney Smith*, vol. 1 (London: Longman, Brown, Green, Longman, Roberts & Green, 1859), "America," 281–292, at 291.

3. Michael R. Haines, "The Population of the United States, 1790–1920," in *The Cambridge Economic History of the United States*, vol. 2: *The Long Nineteenth Century*, Stanley L. Engerman and Robert E. Gallman, eds. (New York: Cambridge University Press, 2000), 156 (Table 4.2).

4. Gordon S. Wood, *Empire of Liberty: A History of the Early Republic, 1789–1815* (New York: Oxford University Press, 2009), 706; Jack Larkin, *The Reshaping of Everyday Life, 1790–1840* (New York: HarperPerennial, 1989), 8.

5. Rothenberg's work first appeared in a magisterial series of articles in the *Journal of Economic History*, beginning in 1981. They are collected and updated in Winifred Barr Rothenberg, *From Market-Places to a Market Economy: The Transformation of Rural Massachusetts, 1750–1850* (Chicago: University of Chicago Press, 1992).

6. Naomi R. Lamoureaux, "Rethinking the Transition to Capitalism in the Early American Northeast," *Journal of American History* 90, no. 2 (September 2003): 456–457.

7. Robert B. Gordon, *A Landscape Transformed: The Ironworking District of Salisbury, Connecticut* (New York: Oxford University Press, 2001), 29–30.

8. Ibid., 35–38, for a sketch of the Holley iron venture. The family tree and the personal details of the Holley family are all from Holley Family Correspondence, Connecticut Historical Society, and "Fragments of the Diary of Alexander H. Holley," Town Archive, Scoville Memorial Library, Salisbury, Connecticut. Both of the archives have a great deal of information on family and social matters, but business references are usually sketchy.

9. Daniel Walker Howe, *What God Hath Wrought: The Transformation of America, 1815–1848* (New York: Oxford University Press, 2007), 555–556.

10. Thomas M. Doerflinger, "Rural Capitalism in Iron Country: Staffing a Forest Factory, 1808–1815," *William and Mary Quarterly* 59, no. 1 (January 2002): 3–38; furnace data output from Tench Coxe, *A Statement of the Arts and Manufacturers of the United States of America for the Year 1810* (Philadelphia, PA: A. Cornman, 1814), Tables by States, Territories, and Districts (Table 10).

11. Donald R. Hoke, *Ingenious Yankees: The Rise of the American System of Manufactures in the Private Sector* (New York: Columbia University Press, 1990), 43–99, is the essential essay on Terry and his manufacturing innovations. The primary source for Eli's career and early Connecticut clockmaking is Henry Terry (one of Eli's sons), "A Review of Dr. Alcotts History of Clock-Making," *Waterbury American*, June 10, 1853. It is reprinted, along with much other primary material, in Kenneth D. Roberts, *Eli Terry and the Connecticut Shelf Clock* (Bristol, CT: Kenneth D. Roberts, 1994), 30–39, 45–61, 170–175.

12. Roberts, *Eli Terry*, 61.

13. Joseph T. Rainier, "The 'Sharper' Image: Yankee Peddlers, Southern Consumers, and the Market Revolution," *Business and Economic History* 26, no. 1 (Fall 1997): 27–44.

14. David S. Landes, *Revolution in Time* (Cambridge, MA: Harvard University Press, 1983), 311–313.

15. David J. Jeremy, *Transatlantic Industrial Revolution: The Diffusion of Textile Technologies Between Britain and America, 1790–1830s* (Cambridge, MA: MIT Press, 1981), is invaluable, with considerable detail on both the industry and specific machines and technologies; James Montgomery, *A Practical Detail of the Cotton Manufacture of the United States of America* (Glasgow: John Niven, 1840), has clear descriptions and drawings of contemporary spinning machines in both England and America.

16. For Slater, Barbara M. Tucker, *Samuel Slater and the Origins of the American Textile Industry, 1790–1860* (Ithaca, NY: Cornell University Press, 1984), and the traditional source, George S. White, *Memoir of Samuel Slater*, 2nd ed. (Philadelphia, 1836).

17. The partnership agreement is in White, *Memoir*, 74–75.

18. David R. Meyer, *Networked Machinists: High-Technology Industries in Antebellum America* (Baltimore: Johns Hopkins University Press, 2006), 59. Wilkinson's lathe was designed for cutting large industrial screws for fine manipulation of heavy industrial machinery.

19. Robert F. Dalzell Jr., *Enterprising Elite: The Boston Associates and the World They Made* (Cambridge, MA: Harvard University Press, 1987); Robert Sobel, *The Entrepreneurs: An American Adventure* (1986; rept., Washington, DC: Beard Books, 2000), 1–41; George S.

Gibb, *The Saco-Lowell Shops: Textile Machinery Building in New England, 1813–1949* (Cambridge, MA: Harvard University Press, 1950).

20. Charles Dickens, *American Notes* (New York: St. Martin's Press, 1985), 60–63.

21. A. Stowers, "Watermills," in *A History of Technology*, vol. 4: *The Industrial Revolution, c. 1750-c.1850*, Charles Singer, et al., ed. (Oxford: Clarendon Press, 1958), 199–213.

22. Patrick M. Malone, *Waterpower in Lowell: Engineering and Industry in Nineteenth-Century America* (Baltimore, MD: Johns Hopkins University Press, 2009) is the definitive work on the Locks & Canals Co.

23. Gibb, *Saco-Lowell Shops*, 179.

24. Louis C. Hunter, *A History of Industrial Power in the United States*, vol. 1: *Waterpower in the Century of the Steam Engine* (Charlottesville: University Press of Virginia, 1985), 322–342, 569–574.

25. Constance McLaughlin Green, *Holyoke, Massachusetts: A Case Study of the Industrial Revolution in America* (New Haven, CT: Yale University Press, 1939), 19–63, and Vera Shlakman, *Economic History of a Factory Town: Chicopee, Massachusetts*, Smith College Studies in History 20 (Northampton, MA: Department of History, Smith College, 1935), 24–80.

26. Dalzell, *Enterprising Elite*, 95–108.

27. Harriet H. Robinson, "Early Factory Labor in New England," in Massachusetts Bureau of Statistics of Labor, *Fourteenth Annual Report* (Boston: Wright & Potter, 1883).

28. Paul G. E. Clemens, "The Consumer Culture of the Middle Atlantic, 1760–1820," *William and Mary Quarterly* 62, no. 4 (October 2005): 577–624.

29. David R. Meyer, *The Roots of American Industrialization* (Baltimore: Johns Hopkins University Press, 2003), 69–71, 227, 228.

30. Howell J. Harris, "Inventing the U.S. Stove Industry, c.1815-1875: Making and Selling the First Universal Consumer Durable," *Business History Review* 82 (Winter 2008), 701–733.

31. H. W. Dickinson, *A Short History of the Steam Engine* (Cambridge, UK: The University Press, 1935), 94–95; Harley I. Halsey, "The Choice Between High-Pressure and Low-Pressure Steam Power in America in the Nineteenth Century," *Journal of Economic History* 16, no. 4 (December 1981): 723–744. Halsey concludes that economics alone drove the choice of the Evans-style engine; safety considerations were not a major issue.

32. Hunter, *Steam Power*, vol. 2, *History of Industrial Power*, 353.

33. T. J. Stiles, *The First Tycoon: The Epic Life of Cornelius Vanderbilt* (New York: Alfred A. Knopf, 2009), 84.

34. Hunter, *History of Industrial Power*, vol. 2, *Steam Power*, 371.

CHAPTER FOUR

1. Library of Congress, Statutes at Large, 5th Congress, Session 2, chapters 33 and 47; and Session 3, chapters 31 and 76. The Congress authorized a "provisional army" of 10,000 men in addition to the current force level, which I take to include a previous authorization for a regiment of artillerists and engineers. (A full-strength regiment was about 1,000 troops and officers.) The pre-existing national force was about 3,500 men, so I round the "authorized" total to 15,000. The additional power for an emergency troop raise was for twenty-seven regiments of infantry and cavalry, plus some additional riflemen and artillery. Some sources carry the emergency authorization at "50,000," but I can't find grounds for that in the statutes. The authorizations were mostly repealed once the "Quasi-war" with France ended in 1800. For background, see Stanley Elkins and Eric McKitrick, *The Age of Federalism: The Early American Republic, 1788-1800* (New York: Oxford University Press, 1993), 561–599.

2. Michael S. Raber, Patrick M. Malone, Robert B. Gordon, and Carolyn C. Cooper, *Conservative Innovators and Military Small Arms: An Industrial History of the Springfield Armory, 1794-1968* (Boston, MA: National Park Service, 1989), 54–55, 173–181. For Harpers Ferry, Merritt Roe Smith, *Harpers Ferry Armory and the New Technology: The Challenge of Change* (Ithaca, NY: Cornell University Press, 1977), 52–53.

3. William Avis, "Drilling, Reaming and Straightening Rifle Barrels," *Machinery* 22 (October 1915): 671–680, lays out the dozens of separate steps in producing a barrel at early-twentieth-century armories.

4. The discussion here follows Robert B. Gordon, "Who Turned the Mechanical Ideal into Mechanical Reality?" *Technology and Culture* 29, no. 14 (October 1988): 774–778.

5. The *locus classicus* for the anti-Whitney argument is Robert S. Woodbury, "The Legend of Eli Whitney and Interchangeable Parts," *Technology and Culture* 1, no. 3 (Summer 1960): 235–253. The traditional accounts are Jeannette Mirsky and Allan Nevins, *The World of Eli Whitney* (New York: Macmillan, 1954), and Constance McLaughlin Green, *Eli Whitney and the Birth of American Technology* (Boston: Little, Brown, 1956). The best assessment of Whitney's current standing among historians is Carolyn C. Cooper, "Myth, Rumor, and History: The Yankee Whittling Boy as Hero and Villain," *Technology and Culture* 44, no. 1 (January 2003): 82–96.

6. Cooper, "Myth," 44.

7. Whitney to Stebbins, November 27, 1798, in Whitney Correspondence, Yale University (hereafter WC).

8. Whitney to Wolcott, May 15, 1798, in WC.

9. Wolcott to Whitney, May 16, 1798, in WC; Whitney to Wolcott, June 2, 1798, in WC; Woodbury, "Legend," 240.

10. Wolcott to Whitney, May 16, 1798, in WC; Francis to Wolcott, June 7, 1798, in WC.

11. Whitney to Stebbins, November 27, 1798, in WC.

12. Whitney to Wolcott, July 30, 1799, in WC.

13. Mirsky and Nevins, *World of Eli Whitney*, 209.

14. Cooper, "Myth," 90.

15. Denison Olmsted, *Memoir of Eli Whitney* (New Haven, CT: Durrie & Peck, 1846), 50. This is a reprint of an 1832 article from the *American Journal of Science*. Also see Blake, *History of the Town of Hamden*, 125, and Joseph Wickham Roe, *English and American Toolmakers* (New Haven, CT: Yale University Press, 1916), 133. Cooper, "Myth," 87–93, is very good on all of this. I mildly disagree with her to the degree that she implies it is inconsistent to see Whitney as both a charlatan and a highly competent manufacturer.

16. Wadsworth to Wolcott, December 24, 1800, in WC.

17. Mirsky and Nevins, *World of Eli Whitney*, 214.

18. Whitney to Wolcott, May 31, 1799, in WC.

19. Mirsky and Nevins, *World of Eli Whitney*, 154–55, Green, *Eli Whitney*, 133.

20. Carl P. Russell, *Guns on the Early Frontiers: A History of Firearms from Colonial Times Through the Years of the Western Fur Trade* (Lincoln: University of Nebraska Press, 1957), 158–159.

21. Author's email correspondence with Richard Barbuto, June 2010.

22. In 1808, Whitney contracted to provide the New York militia with 2,000 muskets, probably delivered in late 1810. Another 2,000 were contracted for in 1812 (Mirsky and Nevins, *World of Eli Whitney*, 236, 246). Whitney's correspondence states that all of the second tranche had been delivered by 1813 (Whitney to Irvine, November 18, 1813, in WC). The final 1,000 were delivered in September 1814, after Tompkins's intervention

33. Felicia Johnson Deyrup, *Arms Makers of the Connecticut Valley*, Smith College Studies in History, vol. 33 (Northampton, MA: Department of History, Smith College, 1948), 62.

34. Robert B. Gordon, "Simeon North, John Hall, and Mechanized Manufacturing," Letters to the Editor, *Technology and Culture* 30, no. 1 (1989): 179–188, at 182.

35. Gary Boyd Roberts, *Genealogies of Connecticut Families* (Baltimore: Genealogical Publishing, 1983); Nancy Simons Peterson, "Guarded Pasts: The Lives and Offspring of Colonel George and Clara (Baldwin) Bomford," *National Genealogical Society Quarterly* 86 (December 1998): 283–305; "Joseph Gardner Swift," West Point Association of Graduates, www.westpointaog.org.

36. Cummings to Superintendent of all Stores, March 11, 1812, in "Letters Received," US War Department, Office of the Chief of the Ordnance Department, Library of Congress (hereafter OCO); Eustis to Wadsworth, August 30 and 31, 1812, in OCO; Arthur to Wadsworth, June 14, 1813, in OCO; Bomford to Wadsworth, August 4, 1813, in OCO; Freeman to Wadsworth, March 4, 1813, in OCO; Bealle to Wadsworth, August 11, 1812, and January 2, 1813, in OCO.

37. Bomford to Wadsworth, August 8, 1812, in OCO.

38. Bomford to Wadsworth, March 6, June 6, and June 11, 1813; March 15, 1814; April 14, 1813; April 28, 1813; June 10, 1813; July 6, 1813, in OCO.

39. Bomford to Wadsworth, June 22 and August 22, 1814, in OCO.

40. Bealle to Wadsworth, August 11, 1812; January 2, 1813, in OCO.

41. The role of Ordnance and the Springfield Armory in driving American manufacturing technology has been a favorite topic of industrial historians. Raber et al., *Conservative Innovators*, is the most complete and judicious analysis by senior scholars in the field. The report is available but difficult to track down; it should be published and sold through the Government Printing Office. Other important studies include Merritt Roe Smith, *Harpers Ferry Armory and the New Technology: The Challenge of Change* (Ithaca, NY: Cornell University Press, 1977); and "Army Ordnance and the 'American System' of Manufacturing," in *Military Enterprise and Technological Change: Perspectives on the American Experience*, Merritt Roe Smith, ed. (Cambridge, MA: MIT Press, 1985), 39–86; Gene Silvero Cesari, "American Arms-Making Machine Tool Development 1798–1855" (PhD diss., University of Pennsylvania, 1970); and the seminal Deyrup, *Arms Makers*.

42. Lee to Wadsworth, March 7, 1813, and March 28, 1814, in OCO; William Lee, *John Leigh of Agawam [Ipswich] Massachusetts, 1634–1671 and His Descendants in the Name of Lee* (Albany, NY: J. Munsell Sons, 1893); Henry F. Waters, ed., *New England Historical and Genealogical Reporter*, vol. 30 (Boston: New England Historical and Genealogical Society, 1876).

43. Smith, *Harpers Ferry Armory*, 53–56.

44. For more information about the footnote on page 137, see "Contract Between the United States and Simeon North," April 16, 1813, in WC.

45. Raber et al., *Conservative Innovators*, 136, 147.

46. Dumas Malone, *Jefferson and His Time*, vol. 2: *Jefferson and the Rights of Man* (Boston: Little, Brown, 1951), 25–26; "Contract Between the United States and Simeon North," April 16, 1813, in WC.

47. Quoted in David A. Hounshell, *From the American System to Mass Production, 1800–1932* (Baltimore: The Johns Hopkins University Press, 1984), 35; and see, e.g., Smith, *Harpers Ferry Armory*, 192–195, 220.

48. David A. Hounshell, *From the American System to Mass Production, 1800–1932* (Baltimore: Johns Hopkins University Press, 1984), 35; and see, e.g., Smith, *Harpers Ferry Armory*, 192–195, 220; Deyrup, *Arms Makers*, 88.

(Tompkins to Lewis [a militia major general], September 3, 1814, in WC). Whitney al
referred to his New York muskets as his contract standard, e.g., Contract between E
and Whitney, July 18, 1812, in WC.

23. S. N. D. North and Ralph H. North, *Simeon North: First Official Pistol Maker* (C
cord, NH: Rumford Press, 1913); Robert D. Jeska, *Early Simeon North Pistol Correspond
with Comments by Robert Jeska* (privately published, 1993). Unless otherwise indicated, I
the North and North book for personal information and Jeska for the pistol contracts. Je
distributed several hundred copies of the book; I purchased one of the last available n
copies from his widow. The book is available in major research libraries. His pistol coll
tion was auctioned after his death at an auction house in San Francisco. He is describ
as a "noted collector," and the auctioned items included: "flintlock pistols, many l
Simeon North, William Evans and Henry Deringer."

24. Jeska, *North Pistol Correspondence*, 10–13. Jeska's original question was why the pi
tols are stamped "S. North & E. Cheney" even though Cheney's name doesn't appear o
any of the payment or surety documents. Elisha Cheney, married to North's sister, was a
clockmaker, the son of Benjamin Cheney, Eli Terry's first master. He did supply screws
and other small parts for some of North's guns, but that normally wouldn't warrant a
name stamp. The contract was first awarded to Voight, a clockmaker who had worked
with the inventor John Fitch on his famous steam engines. Fitch, also a clockmaker, had
apprenticed with Benjamin Cheney at the same time as Elisha, so they must have been
well acquainted. The mint had been slated to close in 1799, presumably prompting
Voight's bid for the pistol job, and he must have changed his mind when the mint received
a reprieve. (He worked at the mint until 1814.) His friend Fitch may have introduced him
to Cheney and North, or he may have already known Cheney. Near-clinching evidence
for a contract sale is that the payment to Voight was made by the government and the
amount expressly offset against North's contract award.

25. Jeska, *Early Simeon North*, 43.

26. Ibid., 59–62.

27. Ibid., 66.

28. Ibid., 86, 74.

29. The Irvine-Whitney dispute occupies a substantial portion of Whitney's 1813 and
1814 correspondence. The essence of it is in Irvine to Armstrong (the secretary of war),
April 5, 1813; Whitney to Irvine, November 4, 1813; Irvine to Whitney, November 7, 1813;
Whitney to Irvine, April 25, 1814; Irvine to Armstrong, May 9, 1814; Whitney to Armstrong, May 10(?), 1814, in WC.

30. Jeska, *Early Simeon North*, 146.

31. Ibid., 187; 159–160; 204–205. The letter to naval procurement, dated May 10, 1816,
is addressed to the Board of Naval Commissioners and states that "I have now on hand
about 14 hundred pistols of superior quality that I made for the War Department all of
the size and dimensions of the one I left at the Navy office in Jany. last. The barrels have
all been proved and inspected by an officer appointed on the part of the Government, and
the locks are all made so uniformly alike that each of the respective locks may be fitted to
the whole number." Recall that North's barrels were proved in large quantities as they
were made, but he had never had an inspection of the finished pistols.

32. Jeska speculates that North was under pressure by Hartford-Convention federalists not to support the war effort, for Connecticut was the heart of the pro-British party.
But Nathan Starr and other military contractors in the area were active at the same time,
and in any case, selling weapons to militias was about as anti-British as selling them to
regulars.

49. Major James Dalliba, "The Armory at Springfield," October 1819, *American State Papers, Military Affairs, II*, 541–553, at 543–544.

50. Carolyn C. Cooper, *Shaping Invention: Thomas Blanchard's Machinery and Patent Management in the Nineteenth Century* (New York: Columbia University Press, 1991), is the best single source on Blanchard. Except as noted below, the narrative in this section follows Cooper. The original source is Asa H. Waters, *Biographical Sketch of Thomas Blanchard and His Inventions* (Worcester, MA: L. P. Goddard, 1878). Waters knew Blanchard, and the pamphlet was written as a eulogy after Blanchard's death.

51. For more information about the footnote on page 139, see Deyrup, Arms Makers, 95.

52. Waters, *Thomas Blanchard*, 5–7.

53. Lee to Blanchard, November 18, 1818, in Correspondence, Springfield Armory Archive, Waltham, MA (hereafter SAA).

54. Blanchard to Lee, March 18, 1820, in SAA.

55. Waters, *Thomas Blanchard*, 6.

56. Ibid.

57. Blanchard to Lee, February 2, 1819, in SAA.

58. Blanchard to Lee, June 9, 1819, in SAA; Lee to Blanchard, June 14 and June 18, 1819, in SAA; Kenney to Lee, June 11, 1819, in SAA; Blanchard to Lee, July 3, 1819, in SAA; Lee to Thornton, August 17, 1819, in SAA.

59. Blanchard to Lee, June 9, 1819, in SAA.

60. Blanchard to Lee, September 28 and October 7, 1820, in SAA; Lee to Blanchard, October 2 and October 14, 1820, in SAA.

61. Foot to Lee, February 21, 1820, in SAA.

62. Pomeroy to Lee, October 15, 1819, January 10 and February 20, 1820, March 2 and April 5, 1821, in SAA; Evans to Lee, March 28 and April 7, 1821, in SAA; Lee to Decatur, August 20, 1819, in SAA.

63. Foot to Lee, February 21, 1820, in SAA; Pomeroy to Lee, October 15, 1819, January 10, 1820, February 20, 1820, March 2, 1821, April 5, 1821, in SAA; Evans to Lee, March 28, 1821, April 7, 1821, in SAA; Lee to Decatur, August 20, 1819, in SAA; Blanchard to Lee, April 29, 1820, May 34, 1820, in SAA.

64. Blanchard to Lee, February 19, 1821, in SAA.

65. Charles H. Fitch, *The Manufacture of Fire-Arms: Report on the Manufactures of the Interchangeable Mechanism, 1880* (1883; rept., Bradley, IL: Lindsay Publications, 1992), 35.

66. Quoted in Cooper, *Shaping Invention*, 91.

67. Ibid., 47.

68. Waters, *Thomas Blanchard*, 1.

69. The best sources on Hall are Smith, *Harpers Ferry Armory*, 184–251, and R. T. Huntington, *Hall's Breechloaders: John H. Hall's Invention and Development of a Breechloading Rifle with Precision-made Interchangeable Parts and Its Introduction into the United States Service* (York, PA: G. Shumway, 1972), which has extensive selections from Hall's correspondence and various official reports on his rifles.

70. John H. Hall, *Remarks upon the Patent Improved Rifles Made by John H. Hall of Portland, ME* (pamphlet) (Portland: F. Douglas, 1816) 1, 5 (in the collections of the New York Public Library).

71. "U.S. Rifle Model 1819 Breechloading Flintlock Hall .52," Catalog Entry, Springfield Armory National Historic Site, www.museum.gov/spar/vfpegi.exe?IDCFile=spar/ DETAIL.

72. Smith, *Harpers Ferry Armory*, 186–194.

73. James Thomas Flexner, *Steamboats Come True: American Inventors in Action* (Boston: Little, Brown, 1978), 177–184; Malone, *Jefferson and the Rights of Man*, 385–387; *American National Biographical Dictionary* online.

74. Huntington, *Hall's Breechloaders*, 3.

75. Smith, *Harpers Ferry Armory*, 188.

76. Fitch, *Manufacture of Fire-Arms*, 6–7; "U.S. Rifle Model 1819"; John Walter, *Rifles of the World* (Iola, WI: Krause Publications, 1998), 159.

77. Smith, *Harpers*, 196; Huntington, *Hall's Breechloaders*, 305.

78. Huntington, *Hall's Breechloaders*, 17.

79. The discussion of Hall's technology contribution draws on Smith, *Harpers Ferry Armory*, 224–241, and his "John H. Hall, Simon North, and the Milling Machine: The Nature of Innovation Among Antebellum Arms Makers," *Technology and Culture* 14, no. 4 (October 1973): 573–591; Fitch, *Manufacture of Fire-Arms*, 56–63.

80. Raber et al., *Conservative Innovators*, 139–141; Fitch, *Manufacture of Fire-Arms*, 7.

81. Smith, *Harpers Ferry Armory*, 240–241.

82. Ibid., 200, 201.

83. The 1827 military board and manufacturing reviews are reprinted in full in Huntington, *Hall's Breechloaders*, 306–323, quotes at 311, 319–320, 323.

84. Gordon, "Simeon North," 183; Doron Swade, *The Difference Engine: Charles Babbage and the Quest to Build the First Computer* (New York: Viking, 2001), 229.

85. Green, *Eli Whitney*, 139.

86. John K. Mahon, *History of the Second Seminole War, 1835–1842* (Gainesville: University Presses of Florida, 1991), 120–121.

87. Robert B. Gordon, "Who Turned the Mechanical Ideal Into Mechanical Reality?" *Technology and Culture* 29, no. 14 (October 1988): 744–778.

88. Deyrup, *Arms Makers*, 182; Charles T. Haven and Frank A. Belden, *A History of the Colt Revolver and Other Arms Made by Colt's Patent Fire Arms Manufacturing Company from 1836 to 1940* (New York: William Morrow & Co., 1940), 389.

89. Raber et al., *Conservative Innovators*, 98–101.

CHAPTER FIVE

1. Frances Trollope, *Domestic Manners of the Americans, Edited, with a History of Mrs. Trollope's Adventures in America, by Donald Smalley* (New York: Alfred A. Knopf, 1949). The biographical note follows Smalley's. In her book, Trollope makes only the barest allusion to her entrepreneurial activities in Cincinnati.

2. Barbara M. Tucker and Kenneth H. Tucker, *Industrializing Antebellum America: The Rise of Manufacturing Entrepreneurs in the Early Republic* (New York: Palgrave Macmillan, 2008), 47.

3. Trollope, *Domestic Manners*, 6.

4. Robert E. Lipsey, "U.S. Foreign Trade and the Balance of Payments, 1800-1913, in *The Cambridge Economic History of the United States*, vol. 2: *The Long Nineteenth Century*, Stanley L. Engerman and Robert E. Gallman, eds. (New York: Cambridge University Press, 2000), 685–732 (Table 15.9).

5. Trade data from the Bureau of the Census, *Historical Statistics of the United States, Millennial Edition Online*, Table Ee7.

6. Namsuk Kim and John Joseph Wallis, "The Market for American State Government Bonds in Britain and the United States, 1830 to 1843," Working Paper 10108, National Bureau of Economic Research, November 2003.

7. Bray Hammond, *Banks and Politics in America: From the Revolution to the Civil War* (Princeton, NJ: Princeton University Press, 1991), 268–325. Thomas Payne Govan, *Nicholas Biddle: Nationalist and Public Banker* (Chicago: University of Chicago Press, 1959), is a detailed biography.

8. Hammond, *Banks and Politics*, 324, quoting Jacob Viner.

9. Govan, *Nicholas Biddle*, 92–95, 95–97, 205–206.

10. For criticism of Biddle, see William M. Gouge, *A Short History of Paper Money and Banking in the United States* (Philadelphia: T. W. Ustick, 1833), 183–184.

11. Hammond, *Banks and Politics*, 600–601.

12. Douglass C. North, *The Economic Growth of the United States, 1790–1860* (Englewood Cliffs, NJ: Prentice-Hall, 1961), 66–74.

13. Jeremy Atack and Peter Passell, *A New Economic View of American History*, 2nd ed. (New York: W.W. Norton & Co., 1994), 155.

14. Paul Bairoch, "International Industrialization Levels from 1750 to 1980," *Journal of European Economic History* 11, no. 2 (Fall 1982): 269–333.

15. Alexis de Tocqueville, *Democracy in America* (New York: Alfred A. Knopf, 1945), 1:53.

16. Quoted in Leo Damrosch, *Tocqueville's Discovery of America* (New York: Farrar, Straus and Giroux, 2010), 136.

17. Harriet Martineau, *Society in America* (New York: Sanders and Otley, 1837), 2:26.

18. Trollope, *Domestic Manners*, 43.

19. Ibid., 120–121.

20. Ibid., 52–53.

21. Ibid., 44–45.

22. Charles Dickens, *American Notes* (New York: St. Martin's Press, 1985), 180.

23. Martineau, *Society in America*, 2:211.

24. Damrosch has a fine discussion of Tocqueville's development of his doctrine of interest, which I follow here. All of the quotes in this section are drawn from his book, *Tocqueville's Discovery*, 47, 136–142.

25. Martineau, *Society in America*, 2:1–2, 21.

26. T. J. Stiles, *The First Tycoon: The Epic Life of Cornelius Vanderbilt* (New York: Alfred A. Knopf, 2009), 24, 31–32.

27. *Niles Weekly Register*, June 8, 1816, 234.

28. Louis C. Hunter, *Steamboats on the Western Rivers: An Economic and Technological History* (Cambridge, MA: Harvard University Press, 1949), is the basic source. Except as noted, this section is drawn from Hunter.

29. Hunter, *Steamboats*, 33, calculates that there were 187 operating steamboats on western rivers in 1830, representing about half of total American tonnage. Since eastern boats tended to be considerably bigger, there would have been correspondingly fewer of them.

30. Ibid., 63.

31. Ibid., 38.

32. Trollope, *Domestic Manners*, 49.

33. Hunter, *Steamboats*, 31–32; Joseph T. Rainier, "The 'Sharper' Image: Yankee Peddlers, Southern Consumers, and the Market Revolution," in *Cultural Change and the Market Revolution in America, 1790–1860*, ed. Scott C. Martin (Lanham, MD: Rowman & Littlefield, 2005), 89–110; David R. Meyer, *The Roots of American Industrialization* (Baltimore: Johns Hopkins University Press, 2003), 271–277.

34. Cincinnati population from Wikipedia (http://en.wikipedia.org/wiki/Cincinnati#Demographics); Michael R. Haines, "The Population of the United States, 1790–1920, in Engerman and Gallman, eds., *The Long Nineteenth Century*, Table 4.4.

35. Dickens, *American Notes*, 147.

36. Sean Wilentz, ed., *Major Problems in the Early Republic, 1789–1848: Documents and Essays* (Lexington, MA: D.C. Heath, 1992), 175–177.

37. Trollope, *Domestic Manners*, 49.

38. Ibid., 177.

39. Ibid., 177, 294.

40. Sean Wilentz, *Chants Democratic: New York City and the Rise of the American Working Class, 1785–1850* (1984; rept., New York: Oxford University Press, 2004), 211–275.

41. Rodney Finke and Roger Stark, *The Churching of America, 1776–1990: Winners and Losers in Our Religious Economy* (New Brunswick, NJ: Rutgers University Press, 1992), 89–95.

42. The account herein, and the quotations, are from Trollope, *Domestic Manners*, 167–175.

43. Sara R. Danger, "The Bonnet's Brim: The Politics of Vision of Frances Trollope's *Domestic Manners of the Americans,*" *Philological Quarterly* (Summer 2009), www.find articles.com/p/articles/mi_hb3362/is_3_88/ai_n57776663/?tag=content;col1.

44. For more information about the footnote on page 186, see Robert W. Fogel, *Railroads and American Economic Growth: Essays in Econometric History* (Baltimore, MD: Johns Hopkins University Press, 1964). The basic argument is laid out in the first chapter. Note that Fogel's argument is organized around agricultural commodities as the primary railroad freight, which permits him much greater flexibility in discounting the value of speed. Later in the century, railroad speed, in my view, was an essential precondition to the mass consumption economy.

45. J. Parker Lamb, *Perfecting the American Steam Locomotive* (Bloomington: Indiana University Press, 2003), 7–9.

46. John F. Stover, *American Railroads* (Chicago: University of Chicago Press, 1961), 21–25; Christian Wolmar, *Blood, Iron, and Gold: How the Railroads Transformed the World* (New York: PublicAffairs, 2009), 70–75; John H. White, Jr., *American Locomotives: An Engineering History* (Baltimore, MD: Johns Hopkins University Press, 1968), 8–10.

47. Harriet Martineau, *Society in America* (New York: Sanders and Otley, 1837), 2:10–11.

48. British data are from Grace's Guide (www.gracesguide.co.uk), which accumulates the data from *Bradshaw's Manual*, the equivalent of Henry Poor's compilations for the United States. The American data is from Old Railroad History (www.oldrailhistory.com), which accumulates the data from Poor's and several other manuals and reconciles them with those of the Census Bureau. The manuals give slightly higher numbers in earlier years and converge about 1850.

49. Robert V. Remini, *Andrew Jackson and the Course of American Empire, 1767–1821* (New York: Harper & Row, 1977), 252–255.

50. Trollope, *Domestic Manners*, 227, 235.

51. William B. Sipes, *The Pennsylvania Railroad: Its Origins, Construction, Condition, and Connections* (Philadelphia: Passenger Department of the Pennsylvania Railroad, 1875), 7–8.

52. Dickens, *American Notes*, 139–140.

53. William Bender Wilson, "Altoona to Pittsburgh," in *History of the Pennsylvania Railroad Co.* (Philadelphia: Henry T. Coates, 1899), 1:94–164.

54. Edward Harold Mott, *Between the Ocean and the Lakes: The Story of Erie* (New York: John S. Collins, 1899), 356.

55. Mott, *Between the Ocean and the Lakes*, 350, 352.

56. Ibid., 92–93; Frederick Lyman Hitchcock, *History of Scranton and Its People* (New York: Lewis Historical Pub., 1914), 1:23–26.

57. The account of the excursion follows Mott, *Between the Ocean and the Lakes*, 90–101.

58. Ibid., 52–56, 45.

59. Ibid., 91–92; Stover, *American Railroads*, 41.

60. Mott, *Between the Ocean and the Lakes*, 104.

61. Herzog zu Sachsen-Weimar-Eisenach Bernhard, *"Reise Sr. Hoheit des Herzogs Bernard zu Sachsen-Weimar-Eisenach durch Nord Amerika, in den Jahren 1825 und 1826,"* (Weimar: W. Hoffman, 1828); Captain Basil Hall, *Travels in North America in the Years 1827 and 1828*, Royal Navy, 3 vols. 12 mo. Edin., *Quarterly Review* 41, no. 82 (1829): 417–447, at 427, 420–421, 445. An English language version of the duke's book is William Jeroninus, trans., *Travels by His Highness Duke Bernhard of Saxe-Weimer-Eisenach Through North America in the Years 1825 and 1826* (Lanham, MD: University Press of America, 2001). Although an interesting travelogue, it is much blander than Trollope or Dickens and lacks the insight of a Tocqueville.

CHAPTER SIX

1. Robert A. Margo, "The Labor Force in the Nineteenth Century," in Engerman and Gallman, eds., *The Long Nineteenth Century*, 213.

2. Robert A. Gallman, "Growth and Change in the Long Nineteenth Century," in Engerman and Gallman, eds., *The Long Nineteenth Century*, 52 (Table 1.15).

3. Stuart M. Blumin, *The Emergence of the Middle Class: Social Experience in the American City* (New York: Cambridge University Press, 1989), 112–117; Brian P. Luskey, *Clerks and the Quest for Capital in Nineteenth Century America* (New York: New York University Press, 2010), 42–45, 89–91, 219.

4. Robert W. Fogel, *The Escape from Hunger and Premature Death, 1700–2100* (New York: Cambridge University Press, 2004), 11.

5. Jim Downs, *Sick from Freedom: African-American Illness and Suffering During the Civil War and Reconstruction* (New York: Oxford University Press, 2012), 4, 21–30, 170–180; Fogel, *Escape*, 16–18.

6. Albert Fishlow, "The American Common School Revival: Fact or Fantasy?" in *Industrialization in Two Systems: Essays in Honor of Alexander Gerschenkron*, Henry Rosovsky, ed. (New York: John Wiley and Sons, 1966), 40–67.

7. "Special Report of Joseph Whitworth, 1854," in Nathan Rosenberg, ed., *The American System of Manufactures: Report of the Committee on the Machinery of the United States, 1855* (Edinburgh: Edinburgh University Press, 1969), 388–389.

8. Stephen N. Broadberry and Douglas A. Irwin, "Labor productivity in the United States and the United Kingdom During the Nineteenth Century," Working Paper 10364, National Bureau of Economic Research, March 2004, 22 (Table 3).

9. There is no biography of Bird; the information here is from Wikipedia, which cites a biographical note from an introduction to one of her travel books, which I was not able to find.

10. Isabella L. Bird, *The Englishwoman in America* (London: John Murray, Albemarle Street, 1856), 141.

11. Isabella L. Bird, *A Lady's Life in the Rocky Mountains* (New York: G. P. Putnam's Sons, 1879–1880), 91.

12. Ibid., 294.

13. Ibid., 295–296; "Historical Background for the Rocky Mountain National Park" (www.cr.nps.gov/history/online_books/berkeley/rensch3/rensch3f.htm). The details of Nugent's death, such as they are, and the "cowardly" comment are from the National Park Service literature on Estes Park, where Bird lived. Given the backgrounds of Evans

and Nugent, it seems unlikely that Evans, who was usually drunk, could have killed Nugent in a fair fight. Estes Park was also the area where Alfred Bierstadt executed his famous Illuminist-school Rocky Mountain paintings.

14. Bird, *Englishwoman*, 114.

15. Ibid., 117–118.

16. Ibid., 118.

17. Ibid.

18. Ibid., 121–122.

19. Ibid., 125.

20. Rudolf A. Clemen, "Waterways in Livestock and Meat Trade," *American Economic Review* 16, no. 4 (December 1926): 640–652, 646.

21. Bird, *Englishwoman*, 125.

22. Steve C. Gordon, "From Slaughterhouse to Soap-Boiler: Cincinnati's Meat Packing Industry, Changing Technologies, and the Rise of Mass Production, 1825–1870," *Journal for the Society of Industrial Archaeology* 16, no. 1 (1990): 55–67; Charles T. Levitt, "Aspects of the Western Meat-Packing Industry, 1830–1860," *Journal of Business of the University of Chicago* 4, no. 1 (January 1931): 68–90.

23. Levitt, "Western Meat-Packing," 76–80. For more information about the footnote on page 205, on plant decentralization, see Robert Adudel and Louis P. Cain, "Location and Collusion in the Meatpacking Industry," in *Business Enterprise and Economic Change: Essays in Honor of Harold F. Williamson*, Louis P. Cain and Paul Uselding, eds. (Kent, OH: Kent State University Press, 1973), 85–117.

24. Gordon, "From Slaughterhouse to Soap-Boiler," 56.

25. David Hounshell, *From the American System to Mass Production* (Baltimore: Johns Hopkins University Press, 1984), 241.

26. "People & Events: Philip Danforth Armour (1832–1901)," PBS, n.d., www.pbs .org/wgbh/amex/chicago/peopleevents/p_armour.html.

27. See, e.g., Lynn Siprelle, "Make Your Own Lard," The New Homemaker, 2007, www.thenewhomemaker.com/makeyourownlard.

28. Except as indicated, the detailed descriptions of lard processing are from Gordon, "From Slaughterhouse to Soap-Boiler."

29. Procter and Gamble, "Our History—How It Began," n.d., www.pg.com/en_US/ downloads/media/Fact_Sheets_CompanyHistory.pdf.

30. Richard L. Bushman and Claudia L. Bushman, "The Early History of Cleanliness in America," *Journal of American History* 74, no. 4 (March 1988): 1213–1238.

31. Thomas L. Ilgen, "'Better Living Through Chemistry': The Chemical Industry in the World Economy," *International Organization* 37, no. 4 (Autumn 1983): 647–680, 650.

32. Chemistry was the first of the natural sciences to take root in American academia. See I. Bernard Cohen, "The Beginning of Chemical Instruction in America: A Brief Account of the Teaching of Chemistry at Harvard Prior to 1800," *Chymia* 3 (1950): 17–44; Glenn Sonnedecker, "The Scientific Background of Chemistry Teachers in Representative Pharmacy Schools of the United States During the 19th Century," *Chymia* 4 (1953): 171–200; and Daniel J. Kevles et al., "The Sciences in America, Circa 1880," *Science* n.s. 209, no. 4452 (July 1980): 26–32.

33. Bird, *Englishwoman*, 122.

34. Vincent S. Clark, *History of Manufacturing in the United States, 1607–1860* (Washington, DC: Carnegie Institution of Washington, 1916), 467–472. This is an older source, but it was the outcome of a decade-long project by the Carnegie Endowment to assemble the available contemporary sources. The sources for the study are primarily the census, *Niles Weekly Register*, and other sources that are still the starting point for the field.

35. J. Richards, *A Treatise of the Construction and Operation of Wood-Working Machines, Including a History of the Origin and Progress of the Manufacture of Wood-Working Machinery* (London: E. & F. N. Spon, 1872), 132–133.

36. Ibid., 121.

37. Joseph Whitworth, "Special Report," in Rosenberg, *American System*, 346.

38. Except as indicated, information on Mitchell and Rammelsberg are from Donald C. Peirce, "Mitchell and Rammelsberg, Cincinnati Furniture Manufacturing 1847–1881," in *American Furniture and Its Makers*, Winterthur Portfolio 13, Ian M. G. Quimby, ed. (Chicago: Published for the Henry Francis du Pont Winterthur Museum by the University of Chicago Press, 1979), 209–229.

39. Michael J. Ettema, "Technological Innovation and Design Economics in Furniture Manufacture," in *American Furniture and Its Makers*, Winterthur Portfolio 16, no. 2/3 (Summer/Autumn 1981) (Chicago: Published for the Henry Francis du Pont Winterthur Museum by the University of Chicago Press, 1981), 197–223. Richards, *Treatise*, includes detailed descriptions and engravings of specimens of all the machines mentioned here.

40. Richards, *Treatise*, iii–v, 30–35.

41. Quoted in Peirce, "Mitchell and Rammelsberg," 217.

42. Rosenberg, *American System*, 7n.

43. David R. Meyer, "Midwestern American Manufacturing and the American Manufacturing Belt in the Nineteenth Century," *Journal of Economic History* 49, no. 4 (December 1989): 921–937.

44. T. J. Stiles, *The First Tycoon: The Epic Life of Cornelius Vanderbilt* (New York: Alfred A. Knopf, 2009), 99–103, 123–127.

45. John H. Morrison, *History of the New York Ship Yards* (New York: Sametz, 1909), 95–96, 102.

46. David Budlong Tyler, *Steam Conquers the Atlantic* (New York: D. Appleton-Century, 1939), 164–169.

47. Cedric Ridgely-Nevitt, *American Steamships on the Atlantic,* (Newark Del.: University of Delaware Press, 1981) 149–177; Tyler, *Steam Conquers*, 181–183.

48. Stiles, *First Tycoon*, 194–212.

49. Ibid., 199–200.

50. Ibid., 227–233; Ridgely-Nevitt, *American Steamships*, 222–248.

51. Tyler, *Steam Conquers*, 336–337; Morrison, *New York Ship Yards*, 155–156.

52. Tyler, *Steam Conquers*, 352–353; Charles R. Morris, *The Tycoons* (New York: Henry Holt & Co., 2005), 277–281.

53. Except as indicated, this account is drawn from John K. Brown, *The Baldwin Locomotive Works, 1831–1915* (Baltimore: Johns Hopkins University Press, 1995).

54. Malcolm C. Clark, "The Birth of an Enterprise: Baldwin Locomotive, 1831–1842," *Pennsylvania Magazine of History and Biography* 90, no. 4 (October 1966): 423–444, 426.

55. Clark, "Birth of an Enterprise," has a detailed account of Baldwin's financial scramblings. For company rankings, see Brown, *Baldwin Locomotive*, Appendix B.

56. Brown, *Baldwin Locomotive*, 95.

57. Except as indicated, this section is drawn from Louis C. Hunter's splendid *A History of Industrial Power in the United States, 1780–1930*, vol. 2: *Steam Power* (Charlottesville: University Press of Virginia, 1985). Chapter 5 is devoted entirely to the Corliss engine; the quote is at 264. I have also reviewed the patent descriptions, the most important one of which is the first, United States Patent Office: Geo. H. Corliss of Providence, Rhode Island, Cut-Off and Working the Valves of Steam Engines, No. 6, 162, dated March 10, 1849.

58. John S. Ritenour, "Master Minds of Type and Press," *Inland Printer* 57, no. 2 (May 1916): 205–207.

59. The material on printers is all drawn from Robert Hoe, *A Short History of the Printing Press and of the Improvements in Printing Machinery from the Time of Gutenberg up to the Present Day* (New York: privately published, 1902). This Robert Hoe was the nephew of Robert Hoe III, the grandson of the founder who was still running the firm at the time of publication.

60. Luther D. Burlingame, "How We Came to Have the Micrometer Caliper," *Machinery* 22 (September 1916): 58–59.

61. Phillip Scranton, *Endless Novelty: Specialty Production and American Industrialization, 1865–1925* (Princeton, NJ: Princeton University Press, 1997), 363n62.

CHAPTER SEVEN

1. "Specification of the Patent Granted to James Hartley, of Sunderland, Glass Manufacturer, for Improvements in the Manufacture of Glass," enrolled April 7, 1848, *The Repertory of Patent Inventions*, enl. series 11 (London: Alexander MacIntosh, 1848), 297–298.

2. David W. Shaw, *America's Victory: The Heroic Triumph of a Gang of Ordinary Americans—and How They Won the Greatest Yacht Race Ever* (New York: Free Press, 2002), 155–156.

3. Except as indicated, the account here is drawn from Shaw, *America's Victory*; for the Baltimore Clippers, Geoffrey M. Footner, *Tidewater Triumph: The Development and Worldwide Success of the Chesapeake Bay Pilot Schooner* (Mystic, CT: Mystic Seaport Museum, 1998), 101–109.

4. Shaw, *America's Victory*, 184.

5. Ibid., 213.

6. Ibid., 213.

7. Ibid., 217, 218.

8. Nathan Rosenberg, Introduction to *The American System of Manufactures: The Report of the Committee on the Machinery of the United States 1855*, Nathan Rosenberg, ed. (Edinburgh: Edinburgh University Press, 1969), 1–53, at 7–8. The events of the exhibition and the *Punch* doggerel are drawn from Rosenberg's account.

9. Except as noted, the Collinsville account is drawn from Donald R. Hoke, *The Rise of the American System of Manufactures in the Private Sector* (New York: Columbia University Press, 1990), 102–130. Paul Uselding, "Elisha K. Root, Forging and the 'American System,'" *Technology and Culture* 15, no. 4 (October 1974): 543–568, is still useful, but his technical discussion has been superseded by Hoke.

10. Robert B. Gordon, "Material Evidence of the Development of Metalworking Technology at the Collins Axe Factory," *Journal of the Society for Industrial Archaeology* 9, no. 1 (1983): 19–28.

11. E. K. Root, Punching Mach., Patent No. 1027, December 10, 1838.

12. For Colt, beside the Colt correspondence at the library of the Connecticut Historical Society (hereafter Colt Correspondence, CHS), I use Barbara M. Tucker and Kenneth H. Tucker Jr., *Industrializing Antebellum America: The Rise of Manufacturing Entrepreneurs in the Early Republic* (New York: Palgrave Macmillan, 2008), 13–71 (for family and background); Herbert G. Houze, Carolyn C. Cooper, and Elizabeth Mankin Kornhouser, *Samuel Colt: Arms, Art, and Invention*, (New Haven, CT: Wadsworth Atheneum Museum of Art, 2006); Charles T. Haven and Frank A. Belden, *A History of the Colt Revolver and Other Arms Made by Colt's Patent Fire Arms Manufacturing Company from 1836 to 1940* (New York: William Morrow & Co., 1940).

13. Tucker and Tucker, *Industrializing*, 30; Houze, *Samuel Colt*, 66.

14. Houze, *Samuel Colt*, 66–67.

15. The dispute is captured in Christopher Colt to Samuel Colt, April 10, 1837; Dudley Selden to Samuel Colt, July 1 and 3, 1837, in Box 1, Colt Correspondence, CHS.

16. S. Colt, Impt. in Fire Arms. Patent No. 1304, August 29, 1839. There would be many more improvements, but this patent moves the appearance and the mechanisms of the pistol much closer to those of the 1850s and 1860s. A number of the improvements Colt cites in his 1855 lecture (discussed later in this chapter) are first seen in this patent.

17. Lawton to Colt, August 3, 1837, in Box 1, Colt Correspondence, CHS.

18. Haven and Belden, *History*, 389.

19. Colonel Samuel Colt, "On the Application of Machinery to the Manufacture of Rotating Chambered-Breech Fire-Arms," *Excerpt Minutes of the Proceedings of the Institution of Civil Engineers*, vol. 11, November 25, 1851 (London: William Clowes and Sons, 1855), 12.

20. Rosenberg, *American System*, 32–39.

21. *Report from the Select Committee on Small Arms: Together with the Proceedings of the Committee, Minutes of Evidence, and Appendix*, 1854 (236), Testimony of Mr. J. Nasmyth, 123, Qs. 1662 and 1663.

22. *Report of the Committee on the Machinery of the United States of America*, reprinted in Rosenberg, ed., *American System*, 87–197, at 89.

23. "Colonel Colt's Small Arms Manufactory," *Newton's London Journal of Arts and Sciences* n.s. 13, vol. 3 (1856): 1–11, 65–75.

24. Some details of the building are from Howard L. Blackmore, "Colt's London Armory," in *Technological Change: The United States and Britain in the 19th Century*, S. B. Saul, ed. (Suffolk, UK: Methuen & Co., 1970), 171–195.

25. "Colonel Colt's Small Arms," 4.

26. Nasmyth Testimony, Q. 1441.

27. Quoted in Rosenberg, *American System*, 45–46.

28. Charles Dickens, "Description of Colonel Colt's Fire-Arm Manufactory," *Household Words*, May 27, 1854, reprinted in Appendix to Colt, "On the Application."

29. *Report on Machinery*, 128.

30. "1908, Cadillac Precision Stuns Europe," *Generations of GM*, http://history.gmheritagecenter.com/wiki/index.php/1908,_Cadillac_Precision_Stuns_Europe.

31. My judgment, from the James-Sam correspondence.

32. Haven and Belden, *Samuel Colt*, 62–63.

33. Colt, "Application of Machinery," 13; David Hounshell, *From the American System to Mass Production* (Baltimore: Johns Hopkins University Press, 1984), 23, 21.

34. Hounshell, *From the American System*, 67–89, supplemented by multiple Willcox & Gibbs collectors' websites.

35. Hoke, *Rise of the American System*, 133.

36. Ibid., 132–178.

37. Ibid., 180–253.

38. See tables in Allen H. Fenichel, "Growth and Diffusion of Power in Manufacturing," in *Studies in Income and Wealth*, vol. 30: *Output, Employment, and Productivity in the United States After 1800*, ed. Dorothy S. Brady (New York: National Bureau of Economic Research, 1966), 443–478.

39. Duncan M. McDougall, "Machine Tool Output, 1861–1910," Brady, ed., *Output, Employment*, 502.

40. Robert A. Margo, "The Labor Force in the Nineteenth Century," in *The Cambridge Economic History of the United States*, vol. 2: *The Long Nineteenth Century*, Stanley L. Engerman and Robert E. Gallman, eds. (New York: Cambridge University Press, 2000), 214.

41. Eric Foner, *Free Soil, Free Labor, Free Men: The Ideology of the Republican Party Before the Civil War* (New York: Oxford University Press, 1970), 301–307; Roy E. Basler, ed., *The Collected Works of Abraham Lincoln*, 9 vols. (New Brunswick, NJ: Rutgers University Press, 1953–1955), 3:361–363; Wilma A. Dunaway, *The First American Frontier: The Transition to Capitalism in Southern Appalachia, 1760–1860* (Chapel Hill: University of North Carolina Press), 268–272.

42. Commodity and physical output data are from Robert S. Manthy, *Natural Resource Commodities—A Century of Statistics: Prices, Output, Consumption, Foreign Trade, and Employment in the United States, 1870–1913* (Baltimore: Johns Hopkins University Press, 1978), Tables N-1, 2, 4, and 5; MC-11, 20, and MO-3; for food, Tables AC-11, 12, 9, and 10. There are no comprehensive data on railroad loadings for this period, so I took a sample of large roads from the relevant *Poor's Manual of Railroads* (Henry V. Poor, *Poor's Manual of Railroads* [New York: Poor's Publishing, 1869]). For the Chicago, Burlington and Quincy; Lake Shore and Michigan and Southern; New York Central; Pennsylvania; and Union Pacific from 1871 (1872 for Union Pacific) to 1877, freight tonnage rose, respectively, 135 percent, 46 percent, 40 percent, 47 percent, and 89 percent, which is roughly consistent with the increases in commodity output. The 6.2 percent annual real growth rate is from the *Historical Statistics of the United States, Millennial Edition*, Tables Ca9-19, for the years 1870–1880. The phenomenon is even sharper if measured from 1869–1879. Nominal annual growth was only 1.2 percent, but real growth, at 4.4 percent, was 3.7 times as high.

43. Robert E. Gallman, "Economic Growth and Structural Change in the Long Nineteenth Century," in Engerman and Gallman, eds., *The Long Nineteenth Century*, 1–56; Rajabrata Banerjee, "The US-UK Productivity Gap Since 1870: Contributions from Technology and Population," Working Paper 2011–03, Centre for Regulation and Market Analysis, University of South Australia, Adelaide, Australia.

CHAPTER EIGHT

1. The story summarized in this chapter was the primary subject of my book *The Tycoons: How Andrew Carnegie, John D. Rockefeller, Jay Gould, and J. P. Morgan Invented the American Supereconomy* (New York: Henry Holt, 2005).

2. Henrietta M. Larson, *Jay Cooke, Private Banker* (Cambridge, MA: Harvard University Press, 1936).

3. Hiram A. Drache, "The Day of the Bonanza: A History of Bonanza Farming in the Red River Valley of the North," (Fargo, ND: North Dakota Institute for Regional Studies, 1964).

4. Jimmy M. Skaggs, *Prime Cut: Livestock Raising and Meatpacking in the United States, 1607–1983* (College Station, TX: Texas A&M University Press, 1983), 50–89 (ranching) and 90–129 (meatpacking); and Robert Adudell and Louis Cain, "Location and Collusion in the Meatpacking Industry," in Louis P. Cain and Paul J. Uselding, eds., *Business Enterprise and Economic Change: Essays in Honor of Harold F. Williamson* (Kent, OH: Kent State University Press, 1973), 85–117.

5. A. L. Holley and Lenox Smith, "American Iron and Steel Works, No. XXI, the works of the Edgar Thomson Steel Works (Limited)," *Engineer* (London), April 19, 1878, 295–301; April 26, 1878, 313–317; May 17, 1878, 381–384.

6. Jeanne McHugh, *Alexander Holley and the Masters of Steel* (Baltimore: Johns Hopkins University Press, 1980), 253.

7. Peter Temin, *Iron and Steel in Nineteenth-Century America: An Economic Inquiry* (Cambridge, MA: The MIT Press, 1964), "Appendix C: Statistics of Iron and Steel," 264–285 (for American prices); D. L. Burn, *The Economic History of Steelmaking, 1867–1939: A Study*

in Competition (Cambridge, UK: University Press, 1940), 103 (for British fob rail export prices.) Elbert Gary testimony in *Hearings before the Committee on Investigation of United States Steel Corporation*, 8 vols. (Washington, DC: U.S. Government Printing Office, 1912), I:220.

8. Allan Nevins, *John D. Rockefeller: The Heroic Age of American Enterprise* (New York: Charles Scribner's Sons, 1940), 1:486.

9. Harold F. Williamson and Arnold R. Daum, *The American Petroleum Industry*, vol. 1: *The Age of Illumination, 1859–1899* (Evanston, IL: Northwestern University Press, 1959), 6.

10. This section closely follows my treatment in *The Tycoons*.

11. Paul Bairoch, "International Industrialization Levels from 1750 to 1980," *Journal of European Economic History* 11, no. 2 (Fall 1982): 269–333; Stephen N. Broadberry and Douglas Irwin, "Labor Productivity in the United States and the United Kingdom During the Nineteenth Century," NBER Working Paper 10364, March 2004; W. Arthur Lewis, *Growth and Fluctuation, 1870–1913* (London: George Allen & Unwin, 1978), 17–18.

12. J. Stephen Jeans, ed., *American Industrial Conditions and Competition: Reports of the Commissioners Appointed by the British Iron Trade Association to Enquire into the Iron, Steel, and Allied Industries of the United States* (London, 1902), and Frank Popplewell, *Some Modern Conditions and Recent Developments in Iron and Steel Production in America* (Manchester, UK: University Press, 1906).

13. Jeans, *American Industrial Conditions*, 306–307.

14. Popplewell, *Some Modern Conditions*, 103.

15. Jeans, *American Industrial Conditions*, 121.

16. D. L. Burn, *The Economic History of Steelmaking, 1867–1939: A Study in Competition* (Cambridge, UK: University Press, 1940), 208, 106.

17. A conversation with the author.

18. Jagdish Bhagwati and Douglas A. Irwin, "The Return of the Reciprocitarians: U.S. Trade Policy Today," *World Economy* 10, no. 2 (June 1987): 113.

19. Burn, *Economic History of Steelmaking*, 312.

20. Jeremiah Whipple Jenks, *The Trust Problem* (Garden City, NY: Doubleday, Page and Co., 1914), 44.

21. American rail prices from Peter Temin, "Appendix C: Statistics of Iron and Steel," in *Iron and Steel in Nineteenth-Century America: An Economic Inquiry* (Cambridge, MA: MIT Press, 1964), 264–285; British fob rail export prices from Burn, *Economic History of Steelmaking*, 103.

22. Niall Ferguson, *The House of Rothschild*, vol. 2: *The World's Banker, 1849–1999* (New York: Viking Penguin, 1999), background at 360–368, quote 367.

23. *Historical Statistics of the United States, Millennial Edition*, Table Ee7.

24. Lance E. Davis and Robert C. Cull, "International Capital Movements, Domestic Capital Markets, and American Economic Growth, 1820–1914," in *The Cambridge Economic History of the United States*, vol. 2: *The Long Nineteenth Century*, Stanley L. Engerman and Robert E. Gallman, eds. (New York: Cambridge University Press, 2000), 733–812.

CHAPTER NINE

1. My understanding of Chinese issues was greatly advanced by a series of roundtable discussions at the Council on Foreign Relations, coordinated by Jerome Cohen of New York University and Elizabeth Economy at the Council. Speakers included, among others, Nicholas Lardy of the Peterson Institute; Kerry Brown, University of Sydney; and Patrick Chovanec of Tsing Hua University. I also benefited from discussions with Dr. Economy and Matt Pottinger, a Council fellow.

2. Michael Spence, *The Next Convergence: The Future of Economic Growth in a Multispeed World* (New York: Farrar, Straus and Giroux, 2012), Chapter 16: "The Middle-Income Transition."

3. Ann Woolner et al., "The Great Brain Robbery," *Businessweek*, March 15, 2012.

4. Siobhan Norman, "Chinese Hackers Suspected in Long-Term Nortel Breach," *Wall Street Journal*, February 14, 2012.

5. U.S.-China Economic and Security Review Commission, "2011 Report to Congress of the United States," November 2011, 174–175; Art Coviello, Executive Chairman of RSA, "Open Letter to RSA Customers" (undated), www.rsa.com/node.aspx?id=3872.

6. John Bussey, "China Venture Is Good for GE but Is It Good for the United States?" *Wall Street Journal*, September 30, 2011; Audrey Cohen, "GE to Develop Avionics with Chinese Firm," *Seattle Post-Intelligencer*, January 19, 2011.

7. David Caploe, "China High-End Value Added—The German Connection," *Economy Watch*, September 14, 2010.

8. James McGregor, "China's Drive for 'Indigenous Innovation': A Web of Industrial Policies," *U.S. Chamber of Commerce* (2011): 4.

9. Ibid., 27–29.

10. Elizabeth C. Economy, *The River Runs Black: The Environmental Challenge to China's Future*, 2nd ed. (Ithaca, NY: Cornell University Press, 2010); "China's Growing Water Crisis," *World Politics Review*, August 9, 2011; "China's Global Quest for Resources and Implications for the United States," testimony Prepared for the U.S.-China Economic and Security Review Commission, January 26, 2012; Edward Wong, "Plan for China's Water Crisis Spurs Concern," *New York Times*, June 1, 2001.

11. "A Comparison with America Reveals a Deep Flaw in China's Model of Growth," *Economist*, April 21, 2012; "The Consequences of an Aging Population," *Economist*, June 23, 2011.

12. "Table A.33: World Population Prospects: The 2010 Revision," Population Division, Department of Economic and Social Affairs, United Nations; Nicholas R. Lardy, *Sustaining China's Economic Growth After the Financial Crisis* (Washington, DC: Peterson Institute of International Economics, 2012), 126.

13. Lardy, *Sustaining China's Economic Growth*, 1–2.

14. Ibid., 43–65, quote at 51.

15. Patrick Chovanec, "Should China Be Bracing Itself for a Hard Landing?" March 24, 2012; "Bloomberg: Inflated Notions," April 21, 2012; "Roubini/Chovanec," February 9, 2012; "WSJ: Chinese Banks Are Worse Off Than You Think," July 22, 2011; and "Chinese Banks' Illusory Earnings," April 1, 2011, *Patrick Chovanec: An American Perspective from China* (blog), chovanec.wordpress.com.

16. Jing Wu et al., "Evaluating Conditions in China's Major Housing Markets," NBER Working Paper 16189, July 2010.

17. David Barboza and Sharon LaFraniere, "'Princelings' in China Use Family Ties to Gain Riches," *New York Times*, May 17, 2012; Catherine Tai, "The 'Princelings' and China's Corruption Woes," *CIPE Development Blog*, August 5, 2009, www.cipe.org/blog.

APPENDIX

1. Angela Lakwete, *Inventing the Cotton Gin: Machine and Myth in Antebellum America* (Baltimore: Johns Hopkins University Press, 2003), 45.

2. Whitney and Greene corresponded regularly the rest of her life, and his regular trips to the South were usually built around visiting with Greene. In Whitney's youthful correspondence with Yale friends, he affected a kind of pre-Raphaelite sensibility,

which he maintains throughout the Greene correspondence. The letters seem mawkish today, but it's hard to believe that they were not motivated by genuine feeling. Whitney did not marry until he was fifty-one, nearly a decade after Greene's death.

3. Ibid., 55.

4. Ibid., 51, 56.

5. Ibid., private communication.

6. Ibid., 56.

7. Ibid., 55.

8. Ibid., 69, 70.

9. Constance McLaughlin Green, *Eli Whitney and the Birth of American Technology* (Boston: Little, Brown, 1956), 48.

10. Eli Whitney, "Description of a New Invented Cotton Gin," US Patent (X)72, copy of patent filed June 20, 1793, certified correct by James Madison, Secretary of State, November 25, 1903.

11. P. J. Federico, "Records of Eli Whitney's Cotton Gin Patent," *Technology and Culture* 1, no. 2 (Spring 1960): 168–176. (Quotes in the footnote are on 173.) Federico was examiner in chief of the United States Patent Office.

12. Whitney, "Description."

13. Miller to Whitney, April 19, 1797; Whitney to Stebbins, November 27, 1798; Miller to Whitney, June 6, 1800, in Eli Whitney Correspondence, Yale University.

INDEX

Andrew Popper

CHARLES R. MORRIS has written twelve books, including *The Cost of Good Intentions*, a *New York Times* Best Book of 1980; *The Coming Global Boom*, a *New York Times* Notable Book of 1990; *The Tycoons*, a *Barrons'* Best Book of 2005; and *The Trillion-Dollar Meltdown*, winner of the Gerald Loeb Award and a *New York Times* Bestseller. A lawyer and former banker, Mr. Morris's articles and reviews have appeared in many publications including the *Atlantic Monthly*, the *New York Times*, and the *Wall Street Journal*. He is a fellow of the Century Foundation and a member of the Council on Foreign Relations.

PublicAffairs is a publishing house founded in 1997. It is a tribute to the standards, values, and flair of three persons who have served as mentors to countless reporters, writers, editors, and book people of all kinds, including me.

I. F. STONE, proprietor of *I. F. Stone's Weekly*, combined a commitment to the First Amendment with entrepreneurial zeal and reporting skill and became one of the great independent journalists in American history. At the age of eighty, Izzy published *The Trial of Socrates*, which was a national bestseller. He wrote the book after he taught himself ancient Greek.

BENJAMIN C. BRADLEE was for nearly thirty years the charismatic editorial leader of *The Washington Post*. It was Ben who gave the *Post* the range and courage to pursue such historic issues as Watergate. He supported his reporters with a tenacity that made them fearless and it is no accident that so many became authors of influential, best-selling books.

ROBERT L. BERNSTEIN, the chief executive of Random House for more than a quarter century, guided one of the nation's premier publishing houses. Bob was personally responsible for many books of political dissent and argument that challenged tyranny around the globe. He is also the founder and longtime chair of Human Rights Watch, one of the most respected human rights organizations in the world.

•   •   •

For fifty years, the banner of Public Affairs Press was carried by its owner Morris B. Schnapper, who published Gandhi, Nasser, Toynbee, Truman, and about 1,500 other authors. In 1983, Schnapper was described by *The Washington Post* as "a redoubtable gadfly." His legacy will endure in the books to come.

Peter Osnos, *Founder and Editor-at-Large*